GREG LeMOND'S
COMPLETE
BOOK
OF
BICYCLING

GREG LeMOND'S
COMPLETE
BOOK
OF
BICYCLING

GREG LeMOND
AND KENT GORDIS

G. P. PUTNAM'S SONS
NEW YORK

G. P. Putnam's Sons
Publishers Since 1838
200 Madison Avenue
New York, NY 10016

Library of Congress Cataloging-in-Publication Data

LeMond, Greg.
   Greg LeMond's complete book of bicycling.

   1. Cycling.   I. Gordis, Kent.   II. Title.
GV1041.L44   1987   796.6   87-2273

ISBN 0-399-13229-5

Book design by The Sarabande Press

Typeset by Fisher Composition, Inc.

   The photographs on the following pages are courtesy of Graham Watson:
6, 8, 25, 31, 33, 35, 38, 39, 40, 55, 58, 62, 63, 64, 66, 68, 108, 120, 129, 136, 141, 143,
150, 159, 168, 174, 177, 178, 180, 182, 183, 185, 186, 189, 191, 193, 195, 199, 243.

   The photographs on the following pages are courtesy of David Epperson/WILDPIC:
88, 92, 96, 98, 101, 103, 106, 112, 133, 134–35, 138, 148, 151, 162, 163, 167, 171,
172–73, 176, 208, 222, 247, 253, 278, 281–86, 288, 290–91, 294, 296, 301, 303–7,
312, 313.
   The photograph on page 24 is from the author's collection.

   The artwork on page 74 is courtesy of Lisa Amoroso.

Printed in the United States of America
1   2   3   4   5   6   7   8   9   10

DEDICATION

This book is dedicated to my mother and father, who supported me all the way, and especially to my wife Kathy, without whom I honestly couldn't have achieved half of what I've done.

—Greg LeMond

Acknowledgments

Many thanks to the following people who helped make this book a reality: Liz Barrett, whose imagination and enthusiasm were the impetus; Basil Kane, whose business brain provided a publisher in record time; Linda Allen, whose marathon typing exploits must constitute some kind of record; Roger Scholl, whose adroit editing trimmed the manuscript into a real book; Catherine Gordis, whose computer printing and cross-country mailing exploits were appreciated; Cyrille Guimard and Paul Koechli, whose training wisdom rubbed off and shaped my knowledge of cycling.

CONTENTS

1

The

Greg LeMond

Story

I was beginning to wonder if I would ever win the 1986 Tour de France. The eleventh day of this twenty-four-day, 2500-mile race had just ended with my French teammate Bernard Hinault in the yellow jersey as the overall leader. He had broken away from my group midway through the tough mountain stage without warning. At the finish line he had established what seemed an insurmountable five-minute lead in a race that is usually won by seconds. What had happened to his promise that he would help me win this Tour, as I had helped him the year before? I was confused, angry, frustrated and depressed.

I felt suspicious of Hinault's motives in making this attack. Although he had discussed his plan with another teammate, fellow Frenchman Jean-François Bernard, he had not informed me or my teammate Andy Hampsten, the other American on La Vie Claire. I felt misled. I had been forced on the defensive, unable to make my own moves. In the unwritten code of cycling ethics, all I could do was follow the wheels of the other main challengers and force them to try to catch the breakaway. Was Hinault my teammate or my rival?

That night in the Hôtel des Pyrénées near Pau in southern France, there was tension in the air. I felt there was going to be a war between Hinault and myself during the twelve days that remained before the finish of the Tour in Paris. We looked at each other across the dinner table coldly. I said to him, "Pretty strong stage . . ." He replied, *"Merci . . ."* Nothing more.

Hinault later exploded when told by a race official that I had counterattacked in the last few kilometers of the stage to regain a minute on him. But he seemed to forget that I had been forced to sit back in frustration, riding for him, for most of the day. I didn't want to sacrifice my hopes of winning the Tour de France for the second year in a row.

In 1985, shackled by team tactics, I had finished second to Hinault by less than two minutes, sacrificing my chances of winning to help Hinault. At the finish, Hinault promised to work for me in the 1986 Tour. But as the Tour approached, his tune changed. First, he said that he would work for me only if I was clearly stronger than him. Then, at a press conference on the eve of the opening stage, he said the leader of our La Vie Claire team would be the one who was the strongest when we began the key stages in the mountains.

The next stage climbed four mountain passes, including the incredibly hard Tourmalet pass, finishing at the summit of the road to the ski resort called Superbagnères. Logically, Hinault could control the race, ride conservatively and hold on to his lead. With a five-minute lead his victory was nearly assured, barring any mishap.

But Hinault is unpredictable. Common sense dictated he would follow the leaders the day after he had gained five minutes over me. But he broke away once again. I have known Hinault and raced with him for six years, and I have seen him race like this only twice in his career—when he was racing scared.

The first time was in the 1984 Tour de France, when he was coming off a one-year layoff after knee surgery. The second time was now. Both times Hinault knew he would have trouble winning the Tour. In his heyday Hinault usually would gain his lead in the time trials and then race conservatively. Now, he was attacking either to secure his victory in the Tour de France or to set himself up to be the hero if I won the race. And the French press was eating it up.

On the road to Superbagnères, Hinault was nearly three minutes up on me. Team strategy dictated that I should only block and not pursue Hinault. I was eight minutes down on him—everything seemed lost.

But Hinault began to falter. As soon as I heard that Hinault was weakening, I knew team strategy would allow me to play my own card. Hinault was eventually caught by the group of riders I was in. We then dropped him, that is, left him behind.

On the climb to Superbagnères teammate Andy Hampsten attacked and I followed him. Then I broke away alone, climbing harder than I ever had before. At the summit, I had taken back all but forty seconds of Hinault's lead.

Suddenly I was in the running again.

Then the war erupted. Hinault refused to give up his chances of winning what would be a sixth Tour de France victory (an outright record—Hinault already shared the record for Tour wins at five with Eddy Merckx and Jacques Anquetil). And I didn't blame him. But he had to realize he might only have been going for his *fifth* Tour victory if it hadn't been for my support the year before.

I was under tremendous pressure. Most potential Tour winners have a team to back them up. I had a few teammates loyal to me (Steve Bauer, Andy Hampsten, Guido Winterberg, Niki Rüttimann). But I had to fight my *own* team most of the way. Hinault kept telling the press the best man would win. Team owner Bernard Tapie told French television that a victory by Hinault would better serve his interests because Hinault was better known in the United States than Greg LeMond.

I was angry, isolated. Yet few people realized how determined I felt inside. As I watched Hinault talk it up with the press, I knew that the hardest part of the Tour de France was yet to come. And from my experience in the last three years, I knew I was a much better finisher in the mountains than Hinault. The Alps were still to come, with some of the hardest mountain climbs in the world.

In the low country between the Pyrenees and the Alps, the conflict between Hinault and me got worse. In a hard stage to the city of Gap, Hinault broke away with Urs Zimmermann, at that time the third-place man after Hinault and me—he was certainly the most dangerous opponent for the whole La Vie Claire team.

There was no good reason for Hinault to ride in a breakaway with Zimmermann, thereby bringing Zimmermann closer to me. Our teammate Niki Rüttimann told Hinault that he owed it to the team to draft on Zimmermann's wheel and not ride aggressively. But Hinault continued to push the pace and forced Niki to ride aggressively as well.

Hinault was caught but his intention was clear: to attempt to win at all costs over Greg LeMond, even at the risk of letting Zimmermann win.

The following day the stage finished at the summit of the Col de Granon—considered the hardest mountaintop finish of the 1986 Tour de France. I knew this was the stage in which I could make up minutes on Hinault—and possibly take over the lead. I was in a delicate position at that time because Hinault was still in the yellow jersey (of the overall leader of the Tour de France) and had I done to him what he had done to me in Gap the French press would have blasted me.

Once Hinault was dropped on the Col d'Izoard, the second climb of the day, I felt it was now up to me to isolate our biggest common opponents, the climbers. So I attacked at the top of the Izoard. I got away by myself, but Zimmermann caught me. At the bottom of the descent of the Izoard, I had

1:05 over Hinault. My coach, Paul Koechli, came up to me and asked me not to lead the pace for Zimmermann.

We had only the final, hard climb to the summit of the Col de Granon left to ride. I knew this was the time, if I was indeed the strongest in the Tour, to prove it.

I still had to play the team game. Hinault was technically still the leader. And even though I couldn't lead the pace, I managed to take two-and-a-half minutes out of Hinault.

I already knew at the bottom of the final climb that I would take the yellow jersey. At the finish when I did get it, I didn't feel the sense of elation that I thought I should have. It's a funny thing but when I got the yellow jersey I started thinking about what could go wrong. The struggle was far from over. We still had a week to go and I knew I would have to contend with Hinault.

That night at the hotel I felt a lot of the pressure had been released. My mood had changed because I was in the yellow jersey—and I felt I was the strongest rider in the race. From that point on I only had to worry about two riders: Hinault and Zimmermann.

The following stage was one of the hardest in the Tour de France, because it included the Col du Galibier, the Col de la Croix de Fer, and the mountaintop finish at the Alpe d'Huez. I felt that whoever had the yellow jersey at the finish at Alpe d'Huez would win the Tour de France.

That morning Hinault explained that he wanted to attack Zimmermann to gain time over him to secure first and second places. In the descent of the Galibier, Hinault broke away, presumably to secure our positions from Zimmermann. Even though I was in the yellow jersey, it would have been awkward for me to attack and bring Zimmermann along. Hinault was riding away on his own. Zimmermann wasn't chasing. Nobody was chasing. My lead was slipping away.

Left with no choice, I attacked a napping Zimmermann. I was lucky that I could attack on a slight uphill, because it's nearly impossible to break away from somebody on a descent.

After joining Hinault I didn't need to explain how I had dropped Zimmermann. But I could tell Hinault was surprised. When Hinault and I were alone on the Croix de Fer, Hinault said his knee was starting to hurt him. He wanted to set his own pace, as is usual for Hinault. By that time we had built a three- to four-minute lead over Zimmermann and I felt that all I had to do was ride to the finish line and the race would be over.

While we were riding in the valley Hinault again asked me to let him set the pace and to let him win the stage. To bury the hatchet I decided to cooperate with him. After all, why win the Alpe d'Huez stage when I could still win the Tour de France and perhaps mend a long and friendly relationship?

We crossed the finish holding hands. This was the first time during the

Tour that I felt genuine elation about winning this race. I felt that today it was over. We had eliminated all the competition. My relationship with Hinault seemed to be reestablished. And my victory seemed certain.

Thirty minutes later these impressions were shattered. Hinault and I appeared on a live show on French television. We sat right next to each other.

French television commentator Jacques Chancel asked Hinault whether the Tour was now indeed over.

Hinault answered that no race was over until the finish and that the best man would be in the yellow jersey after the time trial. This vague statement kept the challenge alive.

That evening I told coach Paul Koechli that the race between Hinault and me *had* to be over. I told him that if we kept fighting the whole team would lose. Ethically, it didn't seem right to me that Hinault should still challenge me. After all, when *he* was in the yellow jersey there was absolutely no question that I would challenge him.

For two-and-a-half weeks I had struggled with the race and my opponents. But I also had to contend with the challenge from Hinault. I didn't need that kind of extra pressure at that point in the Tour. The race was hard enough as it was.

The following day was a rest day. The entire La Vie Claire team was ragged from this conflict. Morale was at a low point and team owner Bernard Tapie knew something had to be done. He told us that whoever was still wearing the yellow jersey after the time trial two days later would be given full support.

Before the time trial in the city of Saint-Étienne, I felt confident that Hinault couldn't take two-and-a-half minutes out of me.

That day I was very nervous because I knew I had to beat Hinault. The challenge had been made and the press predicted only how much time I would lose—no one dared to say that I could win. The night before the time trial, Jacques Goddet, one of the race organizers, came to me and told me he thought it was a wonderful thing that an American should win the Tour. Goddet also warned me about Hinault and assured me that the Tour organization would see to it that the race was run fairly.

Once I was on my way the jitters were gone and all I could think about was winning—to show that I was really the best rider and that I deserved to be wearing the yellow jersey. I had never felt more total concentration than during this ride. Perhaps it was the adrenaline—I never felt any pain.

When I heard that I was gaining time on Hinault on the downhill section—for which Hinault was better equipped that day with an aerodynamic bike—I knew I was going to win. The last half of the race was uphill and I was conserving my energy. What's more, I was better equipped for the uphill with a lighter graphite bike.

Just before the course turned uphill, there was a narrow, sharp right turn.

Going into the turn, I felt that I had slowed to the proper speed. I couldn't believe it when—all of a sudden—my wheels slipped out from under me and I fell. As I was getting up, all I could think about was that I had to get back on my bike as quickly as possible.

In my haste to get back on the road, I didn't notice that the front brake was broken and rubbing on the wheel. Normally when I crash I don't think twice about taking a bike change. Because that way I can be sure there's nothing wrong with the bike. But I didn't want to change to a heavier bike, which was all I had as a spare.

I rode for two or three kilometers more. I tried to adjust my brake with my hand, completely breaking my concentration and rhythm. Then I asked my team car for a wrench but my coach told me that was against the rules.

I was forced to make a bike change. I had lost about twenty seconds in the crash. I lost about another ten seconds trying to readjust my brake. Then I lost fifteen more seconds in the bike change. I had lost my lead and a lot of my concentration.

I couldn't believe everything was going wrong—I had been riding on air that day. From that point on all I could do was ride as hard as possible. I didn't know exactly how much time I had lost—all I could think about was minimizing my losses.

When I finished, I asked Kathy, my wife, how much I had lost by. When she told me twenty-five seconds, I couldn't believe it. With the crash, the fiddling, and the bike change I had expected to lose by over a minute. I was frustrated. When I got up on the podium Hinault came up to me and said, "Greg, it's over. You won the Tour."

Later on that evening, I was able to reflect on the day's racing. Despite the crash and the bike change I had finished only twenty-five seconds behind Hinault. That was something of a personal victory. Team owner Bernard Tapie had said that whoever was in the lead after this time trial would be assured of team support. I still had some doubts, but because Tapie had made it clear that he would not tolerate any more feuding, I felt reassured.

In the last three days of the Tour, Hinault finally accepted the situation. He tried to make up for the week and a half of dueling by riding next to me, by offering his bike if I crashed—by being a true teammate. I felt this was late in coming but I appreciated the gesture.

The night before the final stage into Paris we had a team celebration. We drank champagne, and the mood was quite good for the first time since Pau.

The final stage. And that afternoon I would win the Tour de France. Yet because the Tour is never won in a flash, but over many days, I didn't feel a rush of excitement. In a sense the Tour had been over in Saint-Étienne, four days before the finish. But the risk of riding was still there, and I had to remain vigilant at all times. Up until the end anything can happen—

you can never relax. In fact, during the final stage I crashed when a spectator came out of the crowd and knocked down another rider, who knocked me down.

The funny thing is that when you are in the yellow jersey and you come into Paris, you realize you're very close and yet very far from the finish. You still have to ride fifty to sixty kilometers (six ten-kilometer laps) on the slippery cobblestones of the Champs Élysées and you still have to worry about not crashing.

The whole Tour had been so intense and so powerful that at the finish all my emotions had become blurred.

In December of 1968, the LeMond family moved to Lake Tahoe, California. Until then I had lived in Lakewood, California, not far from Long Beach. I had grown up in the Los Angeles area and my family was from the city, but it seemed that we were better suited to live in the mountains. In the city, all we saw were houses and beaches. The only thing we knew of the outdoors was the beach and we wanted more.

When we moved to Lake Tahoe it really opened our eyes to the outdoors. I was impressed by the mountains and the snow and the sense of freedom. Although I had never felt restricted as a young kid in Lakewood, living in the mountains would introduce me to a whole new way of living.

Oddly enough, bicycling wasn't my first serious sport. A few weeks after moving to Lake Tahoe, at the age of seven and a half, I discovered skiing, my first real introduction to the world of sports.

Two-and-a-half years later, we moved again, this time about fifty miles across one mountain range to the Washoe Valley, halfway between Carson City and Reno, Nevada. To my parents Nevada was mostly a virgin wilderness, a perfect place to bring up a family. To my father it was also a perfect place to start a real estate business, as Nevada's economy was growing quickly.

The following winter, in 1970–1971, I began to take skiing seriously. Skiing became an important part of my life. My dad and I drove all around the Sierra Nevada to find the best slopes. As I became better at the mechanics of skiing, I inevitably wanted something more challenging than just riding up a ski lift and whizzing right back down again. Although I liked racing, I was more impressed at the time with freestyle skiing. That kind of acrobatic skiing was really big back then and still very new. To me acrobatic skiing was the best brand of the sport, a mix of competition and incredible skill, of showmanship and derring-do.

Skiing appealed to me because it was an outdoor sport. I also enjoyed backpacking, fly fishing, hunting, and anything that had to do with the outdoors. I could never stand to be cooped up indoors in a smoky arena. I always needed the sense of freedom, the rush of being "out there" that I got from skiing, and that I get now from bicycle racing—although sometimes when it's thirty-five degrees and raining hailstones in a European road race I wonder. Perhaps most important to me, skiing was not a team sport, but an individual sport.

I wasn't the only athletic member of my family. Not only was my father an active skier but my younger sister Karen was an excellent gymnast. In fact, she was probably the best athlete in the family and she won the Amateur Athletic Union National Championship in 1977. She was also a member of the elite national gymnastics team. But in 1978, in a terrible accident on the balance beam, she hurt her back. She continued competing for two more years but eventually had to give it up.

The summer of 1974, I had made up my mind that I wanted to get a bike. Although I had seen some cycling on television during the 1972 Olympics, I didn't really know much about it. I just wanted a bike as a way of getting around town. To earn enough money for a bike, I found a job cutting lawns at a real estate development about two miles from our house.

At the end of the summer I bought myself my first ten-speed. If you think this sounds like the beginning of a made-for-Hollywood sports story, you're wrong. Certainly my first encounter with a bike was nothing like the stories they tell in Europe of great champions who as young boys see the Tour de France competitors ride by their house, work eighteen months shoveling coal to buy a bike, and win a world championship twelve months later.

At age fourteen, in the summer of 1975, I was still faithful to my first love, freestyle skiing. In fact, I hoped I had what it took to become a champion hot-dog skier. I watched the sport on television and yearned for an opportunity to learn the flips and tricks that distinguished the real champions from the good amateurs. So I enrolled in Wayne Wong's training camp at Whistler Mountain outside Vancouver, Canada. Wayne Wong was the top freestyle skier at the time. Unfortunately, when I finally made it to the camp, I hurt my back and wasn't able to do any of the flips I desperately wanted to learn.

But Wayne Wong taught me a lot about skiing. One thing he especially recommended as an ideal off-season exercise was cycling. As a result, I started paying attention to my bike for a change. It was the first time I had thought about my bike as anything other than a form of transportation.

It was an odd coincidence that a few days before I left for ski camp the Nevada state cycling championships had taken place on the road right in front of our house. My dad and I watched the race, and I was intrigued with the tremendous effort, action, and speed of the races—these guys had to be tremendously fit.

I came back from Vancouver with a half-hearted resolution to start cycling. At first, cycling seemed like hard work to me. But I was dedicated to freestyle skiing and if cycling was going to make me a better skier, I thought a little drudgery couldn't hurt.

My dad and I started looking for cycling anywhere we could find it. We discovered that the United States cycling team had its Pan American Games training camp in Squaw Valley and decided to go watch them. We followed an incredible road race up Spooner Pass and Mount Rose, down through the Washoe Valley and into Carson City. Although I didn't fully realize it at the time, this was vintage road racing at its best: difficult climbs, dangerous descents, and close to eighty miles of riding.

We followed the whole race in my dad's van, and saw America's top racers of the time, John Howard and George Mount, break away on the first climb. I was truly in awe of the tremendous physical effort it took to ride those mountain passes aggressively with still sixty miles of hilly road left to go.

After I became a cyclist, one of my first top performances was finishing second—at the age of sixteen—to John Howard in the 1977 Tour of Fresno. I couldn't even imagine coming close to him on that day in the Sierra Nevada in 1975.

After we got home from that race, my dad and I were sold. My dad had bought a couple of bikes a few weeks before we saw the Pan American trials race. He originally wanted the bike to lose a little weight he had gained over the years—about twenty to twenty-five pounds. He lost the excess weight quickly through cycling and has never put it on again.

In September of 1975, my dad and I started riding our bikes about twenty miles a day. And I was riding with much more conviciton. Of course, I was still a rank novice. I rode with running shoes (with my toe straps loosened), running shorts, and a tank top. In fact, I clearly recall thinking the tank top, with its mesh fabric, would keep me cooler, because more air would pass through all the air holes. (In fact, a cycling jersey is better because it's designed to absorb the sweat—something which a tank top can't do.)

Slowly my dad and I built up our cycling program. At first we tried some short rides, with a few point-to-point (location-to-location) outings. Soon our riding became serious, and we rode farther and faster, trying out some of the mountain passes around the Washoe Valley.

One day in October of 1975 I was talked into going deer hunting. I walked around the mountains from 4:00 A.M. to 11:00 A.M. When I got home my dad was returning from work and he asked me if I wanted to ride my bike with him up Spooner Pass to Incline Village. I don't know why but I agreed. I didn't really know how to gauge my efforts, so I didn't realize how difficult it would be to ride forty-five miles after what I had done that morning.

For most of the climb I felt OK. Toward the end, after about two-and-a-half hours of riding, I completely ran out of gas. And I was only about a mile from our destination. This is when I learned what it's like to be completely exhausted. I was so tired I could barely walk my bike—I was close to tears.

I soon became aware of the amount of effort it takes to ride a bike, of how difficult it was to ride hills that seemed effortless riding in my dad's van. I discovered the bikehandling skills that are needed and the danger involved in cornering and going downhill at high speeds. I was amazed at how fit you had to be. More than anything else, I think the fitness required is what really attracted me to cycling. I realized you had to be very fit to ride twenty-five or thirty miles a day, let alone sixty-five or seventy.

One of my first long, hard rides was a sixty-five-mile outing that my dad and I did later in 1975. Afterward, I was totally drained, but I felt I had accomplished something exciting. I was getting hooked.

Perhaps the most powerful impression those first months of riding made on me was how quickly you could get in shape by cycling. My dad lost his fat in a matter of weeks. And this was a healthy way to lose weight, toning his muscles and increasing his oxygen capacity.

I slowly became strong and flexible for a kid my age. I couldn't have gained the same kind of fitness in school sports, where being in shape meant doing situps and benchpresses. Instead, I was effortlessly climbing hills that had, months before, seemed insurmountable.

Skiing somehow became secondary. As the winter of 1975–1976 arrived, there was little snow, and I became more and more intrigued with bicycle racing. I bought a couple of cycling magazines, reading advice on cycling technique, training, and nutrition. And I followed a lot of that advice, not realizing that many of those "tips" were wrong. Back in those days there weren't any comprehensive books written in English to teach the rudiments of cycling. So I read what I could.

I also learned about the great European races and the legendary European cycling stars. I saw pictures of thousands of frenzied fans cheering cyclists on mountain passes that weren't so different from the ones I rode on around the Washoe Valley.

I started going to bike shops, thumbing through magazines, hoping to soak up a little of the world of bike racing. One day, I was looking through some racing magazines in a bike shop when a guy came up to me and asked me if I was interested in bike racing. "Yeah, I'm interested, but I don't know anything about it," I answered. He told me that I could come to a meeting of the Reno Wheelmen the following week, where I could learn about the sport. He told me the club held rides and training races. It sounded like fun.

By this time I was riding just about every day of the week. With the winter drought in full force, any hopes of spending my winter freestyle skiing had vanished. Yet I didn't miss the snow or the slopes; I was happy to be riding. I wanted to learn about this exotic, mysterious sport of bicycle racing.

When I showed up for my first club race, I saw how sophisticated the sport could be. Many of the riders had European cycling clothing and black, cleated cycling shoes, and a professional bike, with top-of-the-line Italian components.

Although I had a pair of cycling shoes, I still rode a middle-of-the-line ten-speed. I'm sure I must have looked a little out of place.

On the other hand, I finished second in that club race. These guys were tested racers and they could scarcely believe that a fourteen-year-old kid could keep up with them. One of the riders came up to me that afternoon to congratulate me. "You got a lot of talent, guy," he said, "but you should get a real racing bike." The rider, Roland Della Santa—a local racer, mechanic, and cycling aficionado—turned out to be one of the people who helped me the most in the early years of my career.

My dad and I realized I had outgrown my old ten-speed. My dad had also outgrown his ten-speed and was quickly becoming one of Reno's best cyclists, even though he was thirty-five years old. Together, we decided to go to Rick's Bike Shop in Reno to buy new racing bikes and an entire wardrobe of "professional" cycling clothes.

When we told the salesman what we wanted, he did his best to convince us to stay away from racing. "No way, no. Never get a racing bike, kid, you'll never want to race, it's just too hard, you'll never stay in it," he told us. He had probably seen dozens of other novices come into the store, buy a thousand-dollar Italian bike, and lose interest a few weeks later. Maybe that had given the bike shop a bad name. In any case, I think he was genuinely trying to be helpful.

But the LeMonds prevailed, and I came home with a canary-yellow professional racing bike, a new wardrobe of woollen cycling clothing, and a pair of top-of-the-line black, cleated cycling shoes. I felt as if I had suddenly become an honest-to-goodness bike racer.

All this gear was a big investment. Obviously there was no way that a fourteen-year-old kid could afford this expensive cycling equipment. I was lucky that my dad was so involved and loved the sport so much that he actually *encouraged* me to get the bike. As I soon learned, this was very unusual.

I won the first official race that I entered. This was a criterium—a short circuit race—in Sacramento over about ten miles, with a field of ten or so thirteen-to fifteen-year-old kids.

The next day, my family drove to Dublin, California, about fifty miles east of San Francisco, for the Tassajara road race. My dad was racing the Senior, category IV race. I was entered again in the intermediate age group of thirteen-to fifteen-year-olds. Tassajara was a point-to-point road race, one of the few held in California for our age group. I was excited, because I knew it was the same type of event as European professional races, although this race, of course, was a lot shorter and easier.

I broke away right from the start with another rider and pulled away quickly from the pack. At the finish, I won the sprint by ten or eleven lengths for my second consecutive victory. The rider I beat is the writer with whom I'm doing this book: Kent Gordis. What really surprised me was that the third man was left about ten minutes down. That was an unbelievable gap for an eighteen-mile race.

I didn't lose very often that season with the intermediates. My first defeat came in a 2.6-mile short ciruit (four laps of a circuit just over half a mile long) that caught me a little off guard. But for the most part, the intermediate competition was not much of a challenge.

Soon I petitioned for and received permission to ride with the juniors, the sixteen-to nineteen-year-old age group. This was much more of a challenge. For one thing, I raced mostly in Northern California, where the juniors were some of the most competitive in America at the time. The races were also much longer and there were much larger packs than among the intermediates.

I was now racing with riders who were much more physically mature and stronger than me. This meant that I had to work twice as hard to be competitive. Because of the rules, I also had to ride with my intermediate gears, which limited me to a smaller gear ratio than the juniors. In the high-speed junior events, I often spun out (turned the pedals at a very high rate), while the other riders were churning their junior gears more slowly. There were times when I could have used the bigger gears, but I think the experience of racing with the small gear that year probably improved my pedaling fluidity.

Since my first race, my parents had been as hooked on bicycle racing as I was. They were always very supportive. My dad and I usually raced the same races. My family drove down every weekend, my mom prepared special meals. Even my sisters showed up to watch my dad and me race. We couldn't get enough of bike racing.

Looking back I now realize that my parents were always encouraging because they participated with as much conviction as I did. I think that's one reason my sister became such a great gymnast and that I was able to do well in bike racing. A lot of parents who are supportive also push their children to excel at sports. I was lucky because my dad wasn't a coach, he was also racing. We were more like teammates than your traditional father and son.

The turning point of the 1976 season was my second-place finish with the juniors in the Nevada City classic. This was a famous race in the foothills of the Sierra Nevada, about twenty-five miles northeast of Sacramento. Here the short-loop consisted of a steep, uneven half-mile hill, followed by a short section of a slight rise and wrapped up by a dangerous descent. To make matters even more difficult, at the end of the downhill a sharp 170-degree turn squelched any momentum one could hope to take into the climb. And because the Nevada City race was held in the summer, the weather was absolutely unbearable—temperatures sometimes hit the hundreds.

Nevada City had a large crowd of spectators—about ten thousand. No other race in Northern California was as popular. After discovering what bike racing in Europe was like by reading magazines, this is what I imagined big-time bike racing was like. I wanted to win that race.

The race was hard and fast, and it was so hot it felt like riding in a blazing oven. On the downhills, I spun out my small intermediate gear while the other riders turned their pedals more slowly. But in the uphill—where the race was really decided—the gearing made no difference, and I stayed close to the front as the pack slowly began to disintegrate from the back.

In the end, I lost in my attempt to become the first intermediate winner at Nevada City, but not by much. I was beaten by Clark Natwick, a third-year junior who was much bigger and more experienced than me. But my second place was a good showing for a fourteen-year-old kid.

That second-place finish was a milestone in my career. It was then that I realized I could compete with some of the best American riders. But the problem was that American cycling was not very well developed. What I yearned for was to compare myself to the best competition I could find—a desire that eventually took me to the European professional circuit.

Roland Della Santa was a master frame builder. He soon became one of my sponsors and built my first custom bikes. Once or twice a week, I made it a habit to go to his shop and hang out while he worked. As he worked, he often told me stories of the great European stars, the thousands of screaming fans and the legendary races such as the Tour de France and the Giro d'Italia. Although it was as popular there as football and baseball in the United States, on this side of the Atlantic bicycling as a sport was almost unknown.

By the time I turned sixteen, I had read all about the legendary Belgian star Eddy Merckx and his awesome exploits in the Tour de France. Sometimes I imagined what it would be like to ride at the same level as Eddy Merckx, climbing up the narrow goat paths they called mountain passes, with millions of frenetic fans cheering, tugging at my sides. Although I probably didn't yet admit it to myself, somewhere in the back of my mind I somehow believed that I could do it, too.

In 1977, I was fifteen years old and in my first season as a full-fledged junior. I was made eligible, in certain events, to move up one notch and race with the seniors. My first major senior race was the three-day Tour of Fresno in central California. The race included some heavyweights from the then-powerful Exxon team.

The leader of the Exxon team was John Howard, the same rider I had seen on that day in Squaw Valley back in 1975, when my dad and I followed the Pan Am trials race in our van, and first got hooked on bicycle racing. Howard was generally considered America's top road cyclist in the seventies. By 1977, he had won five American national titles, had raced in three Olympics, and had won the road race in the 1971 Pan American Games in Cali, Colombia. Howard had also won the first two Red Zingers (the race that has since become the Coors Classic) in 1975 and 1976.

To most people's amazement, I finished second to John Howard in the Tour of Fresno, only ten seconds behind him after three stages. This was a feat that suddenly turned a lot of heads in the world of bicycle racing. Nobody had ever heard of any junior beating John Howard, let alone a fifteen-year-old high-school sophomore who wasn't shaving yet. For the first time in my career, I was being heralded as "that phenom from Nevada."

One night, I sat down alone and drew up a serious, carefully conceived plan of how I would approach my career as a cyclist.

I wrote out three sheets of goals for myself. First of all, I wanted to be national champion that year—in 1977. The year before in the nationals I had only finished fourth. My goal for 1978 was to place well in the junior *world* championship, which was being held in Washington, D.C. I could have set myself the goal of winning the junior worlds in 1978, but as a second-year junior, I didn't think my body would be quite developed enough. In 1979 my goal was nothing short of winning the junior world championship. In 1980, I wanted to be Olympic cycling champion, and by 1981 I was going to turn professional.

When I look back on that period, it seems that nothing was impossible. I just kept riding and winning and riding and winning. Amazingly enough, I met all my goals, except one: I never won the Olympics, because President Carter's boycott kept the United States out of the Moscow Games. But I did win the 1977 junior national championship. I also placed highly in the 1978 junior world championships, where I finished ninth despite a flattish course that never broke up the bunch.

In 1979, at the junior world championships in Buenos Aires, Argentina, I won not only the road race gold medal but also a silver in the individual pursuit and a bronze in the team time trial. This was actually the first time any rider had ever won three medals in any world championship competition, junior, amateur, professional, or anything else.

But I almost didn't win the road racing title. A young Belgian, Kenny De Marteleire, tried to box me in during the final sprint. The finish was on a large car track and De Marteleire tried to push me into the infield, where a series of old tires were set up. Faced with the prospect of crashing into the tires, I zigzagged frantically and came back onto the track. I started to come back on De Marteleire and it looked as if I was going to beat him. But he wasn't satisfied with boxing me in once and pushed me over into the tires once more. Again, I threaded the needle through the tires but ran out of road before he beat me to the line.

But De Marteleire's actions had been flagrant. Before I could even lodge a protest with the international officials, he was taken down to second place and I was junior world champion.

My ultimate goal was to become a pro in Europe. Ever since I had read about the great races at Roland Della Santa's house, I knew this would be the greatest test a cyclist—and maybe any athlete—could ever face. As a pro—I had written on those three sheets of paper—I wanted to win the world championship and the Tour de France by the time I was twenty-five. I made these goals because I knew that bike racing could easily take its toll on me, and I wanted to be focused. I wanted to be able to gauge my progress to know if I could ever become a top professional rider.

When I look back at my first years in the sport, the one thing that jumps to mind is how little support a young rider in America got in those days. Sure, there were sideline coaches everywhere, guys who gave you advice that was more often wrong than right. And you could always find somebody willing to hang on to you if it looked as if you were a potential winner.

But there was a real lack of knowledgeable coaching. America had been a minor cycling nation for decades. Few of the top coaches had ever raced much themselves and often repeated hearsay advice they had picked up in Europe or from the old school. I remember high-ups in the cycling federation telling me I would burn out because I was racing senior races as a junior. When I turned professional, the national committee of the United States Cycling Federation said I would burn out because I was making the leap to the pro ranks too young. They never realized that the senior racing program in the United States wasn't even as hard as the *junior* program in Belgium. The Belgian races for juniors were fifty or sixty miles, three or four times a week. You couldn't get that even in the best senior races in America.

Luckily, things are very different today, and one of the principal reasons is Eddie Borysewicz, or Eddie B. as he is called. He was a Polish cycling coach who decided to settle in the United States after the Montreal Olympics. In 1977, Eddie B. was hired as the national coach of the United States Cycling Federation. He started to turn things around overnight. Eddie B. brought an entirely new style to American cycling, an attention to detail and an Eastern European kind of rigor. In a few months, Eddie B. was able to take a lot of the raw talent and turn it into palpable results.

*Winning my first Belgian race at
age sixteen.*

Eddie B. played an important role for a lot of American riders. And he played an important role for me too. He was the first real coach I ever had. He provided me with the first systematic training program I ever knew. Using his connections, he also opened up an opportunity for me to race in a junior stage race in Poland in 1978 after a summer of racing in Switzerland and Belgium. Eddie B. counseled all the juniors on how to manage their careers, how much racing and training they should do, how far they could realistically push themselves.

This kind of counseling was probably less important for me than for the other riders on the national team. I had set my sights on a European pro career and I knew exactly how far I would have to push myself to reach that goal. I was probably doing more than Eddie B. wanted me to do. After all, he had been a top coach in Poland, a country that had no professional cycling, in which the ultimate was to be a top amateur. When the 1980 Olympics were boycotted, Eddie B. tried to convince me to stay in the amateur program, possibly till the 1984 Olympics.

There was no way I was going to do that. By 1980 I had learned the ropes of amateur cycling, and there would have been little or no challenge for me if I had stayed in that category. I have never been happy with sitting on my laurels—I knew I could do better, and the only way to do that, I thought, was to race against the best competition in the world. To me it was always

I first turned pro with the Renault team because I was impressed with team coach Cyrille Guimard and his record of turning rookies into stars.

clear that the best competition was in professional cycling in Europe.

I got my big break into professional cycling in 1980. Although I was the reigning junior world champion, I was a first-year senior and still relatively unknown in the elite circles of European racing. Certainly, no pro team had approached me, and if I thought that my junior world championship would somehow be a ticket to a pro contract, I was wrong: There had been many junior world champions before me who had turned out to be duds.

I knew I had to prove myself. In the spring of 1980, the United States national team went to Europe for a six-week trip. One of the races on the program was the Circuit de la Sarthe, one of the few European events that is open to both professionals and amateurs. Just as it had been unlikely for a fifteen-year-old to beat John Howard in the 1977 Tour of Fresno, so was it now unlikely that an eighteen-year-old American could win the Circuit de la Sarthe. After all, despite the influence of Eddie B., the United States was still very weak on the international circuit. No American had ever won a major stage race, professional or amateur, in the history of the sport.

As it turned out, I did win. Suddenly, I began to receive big press all around Europe. The European cycling writers were apparently very impressed with the fact that I was the first American (and the youngest rider of any nationality) in the history of the sport to win a major pro-am cycling event.

Thanks in part to that press, French cycling coach Cyrille Guimard, who had been following my career since the previous year, decided he would pay me a visit at the next event we were going to ride, the Ruban Granitier Breton, a stage race in the French province of Brittany. I didn't know anything about his visit, though, and when Guimard showed up the morning of the final stage, I wasn't quite sure why he was there. Although I knew he was the coach of cycling's top professional, Bernard Hinault, and he was probably coming to recruit fresh talent, I didn't know if he was coming to look at me or at French star Marc Madiot.

As it turned out I had one of the worst days of my career. I was in a good position to win this race and in a break with the top Soviet riders, four minutes ahead of the main pack. But I had a flat and waited something like three minutes before my team car finally made it to me. There, the mechanic fumbled with the wheel, costing me more precious time. After making me wait more than three minutes, the mechanic told me I should ride by myself and that I could get at least fifth or sixth place. He must not have realized that the main pack was only thirty seconds behind. I knew I would be caught and lose everything. I was so upset that I took the bike and flung it at the car and quit the race.

Surprisingly, despite what happened that day, Cyrille Guimard came up to me and said he was impressed with my spirit. "You have the fire to be a great champion," he told me. And he offered me a spot on his Renault team for the following season, 1981.

That summer I went through a series of negotiations with the brass at the Renault company. I also received offers from other teams, but never took them very seriously. A lot of people told me that Guimard would be the best choice for a young racer, that he would create a systematic program for my career. I looked at what Guimard had accomplished: He had turned Bernard Hinault, a little-known amateur in his youth, into the world's best cyclist. Before that, Guimard had taken Lucien Van Impe, always really talented but never ambitious, and coached him to a Tour de France victory. Guimard was the man for me.

I signed my contract with the Renault team the day the Tour de France finished in Paris. That afternoon, I was invited to the posh Renault Club on the Champs Élysées to meet with Cyrille Guimard and a representative from Renault. While most of the guests were enjoying a celebration in the Renault Club, I was in a small, cramped room upstairs, discussing the clauses of my contract with Guimard.

I looked over the contract carefully, going over every point in detail with Guimard. I was about to take a huge leap in my career and I wanted to make sure everything was done right. I was really nervous and the sweltering heat in that little room made me even more so. I remember calling my dad two or three times in Reno to get his advice. After about six hours and nearly as many phone calls, the deal was in the bag and I inked my first pro contract.

My first year as a professional was not an easy one. I had just gotten married to my beautiful wife, Kathy Morris, the previous winter. I had gained fifteen pounds because I hadn't trained enough. While living in my wife's hometown of Lacrosse, Wisconsin, I had actually been to the Heileman's brewery a few times. When I arrived in Europe, Guimard had decided to put me up in his hometown of Nantes, on the Loire River in northern France.

Kathy and I had trouble adjusting to Nantes and grew homesick very quickly. I arrived about a month before the first races to get settled into my house, receive my car, get to know my team, and show up for the team presentation. But when I arrived in Nantes there was neither a house nor a car. We were temporarily put up in a tiny hotel room for six weeks before we were finally told we could move into the house. Even then there was no furniture, no heat, and no hot water. And, believe it or not, there wasn't even a kitchen. It was only ten weeks later that poor Kathy was able to get settled in.

I figured a month of training in Europe with my new teammates would be better than a month of training in California since, after all, I was going to be a *European* pro.

But the weather turned out to be despicable (as usual—as I would later find out) that January, much worse than what I had left in California. The net result was that I ended up riding about four times a week, usually no more than sixty miles a day (as opposed to my ordinary regimen of seventy to ninety miles a day). The longer I stayed in France the more out of shape I became.

A few days before my first race, the Étoile de Bessèges in southern France, I was told I could take the team bus down to Bessèges, to save me the trouble of driving down there on my own. It was only about a three-hundred-mile drive and I figured it would be more convenient to take the team bus.

It left at four o'clock in the afternoon, two days before the race. According to our schedule we were supposed to arrive at our destination the following morning. But in France the pace of life is much slower than in America and we were on the road barely three-and-a-half hours when it was time to break for dinner. That dinner was a French meal in all its splendor and lasted a good two hours. By ten-thirty we were stopped again, this time in a motel for the night. The following day we got a late start and I arrived in Bessèges totally exhausted, carsick, and without having trained for two days.

The race was eighty-three miles long and had three pretty good-sized hills.

Right from the start I was off the back, dying. I just couldn't believe how fast they were going. I was in shock. Finally, after a long descent, I got back in the pack again. Guimard drove up to me and told me: "Boy, you've got to train. You've got to lose some of that weight, you're just too heavy." After that race I was pretty disgruntled and demoralized and I went out to train for another thirty miles before dinner.

The following day I raced again and got dropped two times. I did finish in the group, though, and then went out and trained for another forty miles.

It was certainly an inauspicious start for a young champion. When I look back at that period I tell myself I made a huge jump at the age of nineteen. I think one reason it was so hard for me physically was that I was in awe of the racers there. I was in awe riding with Bernard Hinault, with the European pros. One of the things I would recommend to any young racer is to make sure you capitalize on all your opportunities—there are many races I could have won that first season if I had attacked at the right times. But I was never sure if I could stay away or if I would get dropped once I got caught. And, on the other hand, I probably worked much too hard in some cases where I really didn't have to.

My first pro victory came about three months after my debut, in the first stage of the Tour de l'Oise, a relatively small French race. The race came down to a six-man sprint, and I barely inched out my friend Phil Anderson, an Australian who is now one of the world's finest pros. That first victory really boosted my confidence and helped me relax a little. After that, I raced with more aggressiveness and daring. I realized the great cycling heroes were human. I knew I could compete with any of them.

The major victory of my 1981 season came a few weeks later, not in Europe, but back in America, in the Coors Classic. Although the Coors Classic wasn't really a professional race, but an amateur race with professionals, this victory in Colorado was sweet. I beat the Olympic champion, Soviet star Sergei Soukhorouchenkov, the man I would have had to beat in Moscow for the Olympic gold, had there been no boycott.

Although the Coors Classic was the first major victory, the major stepping-stone was a major French stage race called the Dauphiné Libéré, run in May. The Dauphiné Libéré is a week-long race that covers some of the same mountain passes in the Alps as the Tour de France. That year Hinault was at the peak of his career and I was able to stay with all the great climbers, including Hinault, on the hardest Alpine climbs. I finished third overall and found my confidence really boosted. It showed me that I had the kind of climbing ability that you need to win the top European stage races.

Although I had my ups and downs that first season, it was a tremendous learning experience. I came back to Europe in 1982 armed with a better knowledge of the turf and the players, and of the inside game of bike racing.

That year, I finished second in the world championship, in Goodwood, England. It was a surprising performance because a week and a half before I had had a stomach virus that had left me completely exhausted. Two days before the world championship I wasn't even sure if I should go to England to race. But I went with an outside hope that my body would turn around and that I would have a good race.

Despite all the celebration, my silver medal at Goodwood did not come unchallenged. In the last mile of the race, the pack was still big and bunched together. The only other American left in contention, Jonathan Boyer, broke away looking for a victory. About five hundred yards from the finish line I could see Boyer was fading quickly and was about to be engulfed by the pack. Seeing that he had no hope of winning, I accelerated and sped past him, with the Italian Giuseppe Saronni on my wheel. At the line, Saronni beat me for the gold medal while Boyer had crumbled to tenth place.

Boyer later claimed that I had hunted him down, that I had cost him the once-in-a-lifetime opportunity to win the world championship. When I heard how Jonathan reacted, I felt terrible. I knew he was terribly disappointed. But in the heat of competition, things can get distorted, especially if a major victory is at stake, and I think Boyer misjudged how quickly he was going to get gobbled up by the pack behind. But I became angry at Boyer's insistence that he would surely have been world champion if it hadn't been for me.

In 1982 I won the Tour de l'Avenir—the pro-am version of the Tour de France—with a record ten-minute margin. This was the highlight of the 1982 season, and of my career up to that point. It was the first time that I totally dominated a major race as a professional. This victory gave me a great deal of confidence for the coming season.

I was improving quickly, thanks in large part of my coach, Cyrille Guimard. When I first came to Europe, Guimard and Bernard Hinault had stated that I could succeed Hinault as the next super champion of cycling. But what they didn't say was that it would take a lot of work to make it to the top. And that hard work could easily have come to nothing if it hadn't been for Guimard and his systematic approach. He did many things for me. Mostly he understood the importance of details.

To me, Guimard is one of the best coaches in cycling. For a guy who never graduated from high school, he is remarkably intelligent. It's not that he knows so much about theory as that he knows how to apply his knowledge to actual cycling. When it comes to race tactics, nobody does a better job than Guimard as *directeur sportif* (as the French call cycling coaches). For a green American kid like me, Guimard was the best possible influence. When I first came to race as a pro, I really didn't know much about tactics. In America I had always won by riding the hardest and the fastest. The United

States national team had never really been so much a team as a collection of individuals. But when it came to pro racing, tactics and teamwork became indispensable. Guimard was also an excellent leader of men, a coach who could mesmerize and rally his troops around a common goal.

If I had raced instead with another French or Italian team, I would never have gotten the same level of coaching. Most likely, I would have ridden the Tour de France in my first year as a pro, and I probably would have been totally burned out by now. What Guimard understood—and this was unique in 1981—was that a top champion was a commodity that needed a little nurturing. Unlike most of the other coaches, Guimard was willing to invest his time, energy, and money to see me develop. I am grateful to him for that.

My wife and I had never been comfortable in Nantes, and in the winter of 1982–1983 we decided to move. We wanted to live someplace where we could find a lot of good training and races and where Kathy could speak English with the neighbors and watch English-language television.

We settled on Belgium, where our friends Richard and Noël De-Jonckheere—two brothers who had helped me when I first came to Belgium in 1978—gave us a lot of help in finding a house for rent.

We chose to move to the city of Kortrijk, a beautiful town of forty-five thousand people about ten miles north of the French border. Kortrijk provided me with a lot of varied training, from the wind-swept coast of the North Sea to the steep hills of the Flemish countryside. Also, Belgium had minor races for training almost daily, a big plus for my cycling career.

According to the timetable set up for me by Guimard, my third season, in 1983, promised big things. And, faithful to his schedule, big things started happening. One of my first major victories came in May of 1983, when I won the Dauphiné Libéré stage race in southeastern France. This race is probably one of the most intense in Europe—all mountains. It's also the first warm-up of the year for the Tour de France and has always been used as a race to gauge riders for the big stage races of the summer months.

A few weeks before that victory in the Dauphiné, I had gone through one of the lowest periods of my career. In late April, Guimard had picked me to race the three-week Tour of Spain with Bernard Hinault and the top riders of the Renault team. I was hoping the Tour of Spain—my first major three-week stage race—would set me on the right track after a terrible spring. I also hoped the weather in Spain would be milder, allowing me to get in shape in a hurry.

But the rain in Spain was relentless and when it wasn't raining, it was cold. My riding continued to deteriorate. To make matters worse, Bernard Hinault, our team leader, was suffering terribly from a bad knee. That injury turned out to be so bad that he eventually forfeited riding the Tour de France in favor of surgery.

Life as a professional cyclist can be very difficult. In the 1983 Tour of Spain I almost threw in the towel because I was sick and riding poorly. But coach Guimard convinced me to stick with it. A few weeks later I won a major race: The Dauphiné Libéré.

I lost confidence in my riding and was dropped on climbs by burly sprinters. I was riding with the stragglers. Fortunately, Guimard was there to save the day. Calm, collected, and professional, he could see that this was only a passing crisis. He told me I ought to quit the Tour of Spain—that it was doing me no apparent good. Instead, he suggested that I go home and recuperate and, if I could, train intently for the Dauphiné Libéré by riding in the Alps for ten days.

For three weeks I trained around my home in Kortrijk. But I could hardly get out of my own way. I completely lost my morale. Four days before the Dauphiné I felt that there was nothing I could do, I stopped worrying about it. I was nearly ready to quit cycling for two months and take a break. I relaxed and forgot about cycling, and I went out and won the Dauphiné Libéré.

My victory didn't come without a little controversy, however. I had been inthe lead for a couple of days when the race hit the steep slopes of the Mont Ventoux, one of the most difficult climbs in France, a mountain that is nicknamed in France the "Bald Giant of Provence." On that day I broke away with French rider Pascal Simon, who was having his best season ever at that point. We rode strongly away from the pack until, about four kilometers from the top of the Ventoux, I cracked. I couldn't believe how fast Simon was riding and I simply couldn't keep up anymore. Simon kept riding away and won the stage, taking over as leader that day.

Needless to say, I was disappointed. Simon went on to win the Dauphiné Libéré while I finished in second place. A few days later, however, the tables were turned when it was announced Simon had been caught using a substance called Micorene. He was disqualified and I was declared the winner. And so I became the first American to win a major all-professional stage race.

The summer of 1983 was quiet for me. Guimard had decided not to start me in the Tour that year because he felt that at twenty-two I was still too young. Instead I trained and raced in smaller races. I watched my French teammate Laurent Fignon win the Tour in his rookie ride. I felt happy for him although I didn't fully realize how much of a problem he would be for me in my first Tour de France the following year.

I capped the 1983 season by fulfilling one of my boyhood dreams: winning the world championship. I had been riding very well since my debacle in Spain and had trained hard all summer for the worlds. When I arrived in Switzerland, where the world championships were being held in 1983, I knew deep inside that I had a very good chance of winning.

This world championship didn't go as unnoticed in the United States as had those in previous years. By 1983 American cycling was growing by leaps and bounds and there was much more interest focused on the sport.

The American professional federation, U.S. PRO, brought a full contingent of American pros to Switzerland. This team was funded in large part by Fred Mengoni, an Italian-American real estate developer from New York City who has poured considerable money into pro cycling for a number of years. Mengoni, one of my staunchest supporters and a close friend, follows my career and he came to watch me race. I think he must have sensed that something special would happen on that day.

When I made it to the starting line I was petrified that a night of little sleep—my nervousness had kept me awake—and a small breakfast would handicap me in the 175-mile title race I was about to ride. Again, it was Guimard who reassured me: "Great exploits are achieved on a night of restless sleep," he told me that morning. It put my mind to rest.

Winning the world championship catapulted me to the top. Not only did I make headlines but I was even mentioned in the United States in a growing number of cycling publications and in a number of the big dailies. More important to me at the time, I was suddenly in contention for the Super Prestige Pernod Trophy, cycling's version of the Formula One's driver's cup—the world championship of the entire cycling season.

Guimard and I looked over the Pernod Trophy standings. If I did well in the remaining races of 1983, I could have the trophy sewn up, and my victory in the one-day world championship would be enhanced. I could be a double world champion. In the following races, I raced hard, despite being

One of the highlights of my career. I won the world championship at the age of twenty-two in Altenrhein, Switzerland.

unfamiliar with some of the courses and despite a touch of mental fatigue. But I did well. I finished second in the fifty-five-mile Grand Prix des Nations individual time trial, fourth in the French classic Blois-Chaville, and second to Sean Kelly by about a quarter of an inch in the Italian "race of the fallen leaves," the Tour of Lombardy.

With that, the Super Prestige Pernod Trophy was mine and I was off to the United States for a few weeks of rest and a winter of training in Northern California. Life was definitely good that winter; I had done the best that I possibly could and was reaping the rewards while, at the same time, I prepared for another successful season in 1984.

On February 15, 1984, my life was further brightened with the birth of a beautiful 7.8-pound baby boy. My wife and I named him Geoffrey James.

But all the joy and happiness that Geoffrey brought to my heart also slowed my preparation for the 1984 season. This was going to be a very big season for me, the year when I was to do more than equal the performances of the previous year. In 1984, I was expected to win the Tour de France, as Bernard Hinault and Eddy Merckx had done before me.

The season started slowly for me, as usual. I suffered a little bit in the cold weather of the early season races where I still had a few pounds of extra weight to burn off. In the April classics I rode well but without any convincing performances. In the hilly Liège-Bastogne-Liège race I rode with a seven-man breakaway to the finish before sprinting to third place behind Sean Kelly and Phil Anderson.

Still, this was not different from my pattern of the previous few years. I knew I had a tendency to gain a little weight in the off-season; that weight took a long time to burn off completely. I felt strong and fit although I was perhaps a bit more nervous than in previous seasons. After all, I had the added pressure on my shoulders of wearing the world champion's rainbow jersey and being a top favorite for the Tour de France. That was a lot of pressure all at once.

When I showed up for the Tour de France I was nervous, almost jittery. Those jitters went away after the first week, but I soon came down with bronchitis. I also had a terribly inflamed foot that made it very difficult for me to ride. I fell to eighth place with one week to go while my teammate Laurent Fignon was on his way to racking up an impressive victory with five stage wins along the way.

Finally, in the last week of this disappointing 1984 Tour de France I recovered partially, enough to shoot up five places in the standings and finish third overall. Although it was disappointing to finish third while Fignon reaped all the glory, I had, nevertheless, won the white jersey rewarding the best rookie. I became the first non-European to crack the top three in the Tour de France.

I also learned some very important lessons. I had never completed a three-week stage race before and I had no idea how intense the Tour could be. Little did I know that I had to be vigilant every single stage, day in and day out. Finally, I realized that my preparation had been somewhat too casual and resolved that the following year I would make sure to ride a lot more— perhaps the Tour of Italy.

Although Guimard continued to provide me with a lot of coaching and moral support, he also had to worry about nursing his new superstar, Fignon. I realized that Fignon might be a roadblock for the rest of my career if we continued to jostle for top-dog honors on the same team. During the Tour that year I felt somewhat isolated at times. My team, understandably, rallied around Fignon and his dazzling success.

One of the people who had believed in me most during my career, Bernard Hinault, had split with the Renault team in 1983. In 1984, he was racing the Tour with a new team, La Vie Claire, sponsored by a maverick French businessman. This entrepreneur, Bernard Tapie, was a man who owned nearly forty companies and wanted to bring a new style to the old-fashioned world of European bicycle racing.

In that 1984 Tour, Hinault's experiment appeared to be somewhat of a

The first major crossroads in my career came when I was forced to shadow Laurent Fignon in the 1984 Tour de France. He won the Tour and I switched to La Vie Claire.

bust. He had had a lot of trouble putting the team together the previous winter; he was unable to challenge Fignon for the Tour win, after coming off knee surgery and a forced six-month layoff. But Hinault was still trying to build his team and one of the first people he looked at to improve his roster was me. Realizing that things weren't going my way with the Renault team and that Fignon appeared the leader over there, Hinault asked me, during the Tour de France, if I would be willing to join the La Vie Claire team in 1985.

I told him I would think about it. This was one of the biggest decisions I had to make in my life. One of the most important things I had to consider was how much freedom I could have within the team. Hinault assured me that we would both be leaders with La Vie Claire and that he would retire on the day of his thirty-second birthday, November 14, 1986. After that he would, in effect, be leaving team La Vie Claire to me. Hinault also told me La Vie Claire wouldn't be a French team principally filled with French talent, but an international squad. Renault, on the other hand, seemed firmly in Fignon's grip. The all-French makeup of Renault seemed to guarantee that Fignon would have an easier time relating to the other riders than I would.

I also worried about the future, and my family's security. When Bernard Tapie announced he would offer me a million-dollar contract spread over three years with an option on a fourth, there was no way I could disregard that. Cycling, after all, is a dangerous and haphazard way to make a living and, in the best case, a career lasts about ten years. And I felt that I owed it to my wife and baby son to provide them with the most financial security that I could manage.

The only drawback was that I would have to leave Cyrille Guimard. He had shaped my pro career, developed me. He had encouraged me when I was close to throwing in the towel and going back to Nevada. He had impressed me with his profound knowledge of training and diet and his acute sense of race tactics.

In return, La Vie Claire promised me Paul Koechli, the man who had helped trained Guimard at the Sports Physiology Institute in Mâcolin, Switzerland. Koechli was a brilliant theoretician, a scholar who had developed complex computer software for the training of cyclists—yet I didn't know anything about his tactical sense.

I asked Renault if it would be willing to increase my present contract, and when Renault refused to budge one franc, I knew my mind was made up. After the world championships, I announced that I would be leaving Renault for Hinault, La Vie Claire, and a new lease on life.

I approached my training the following winter with a lot of determination. I looked forward to riding in 1985 with Bernard Hinault and my friend Steve Bauer. Bauer had been more or less unknown in Europe until he won the Olympic silver medal a few weeks before turning professional and immediatleiy took the bronze medal at the professional world championships.

I put in some good performances in the early part of 1985, including a fourth place in the muddiest Paris-Roubaix of recent memory. It was the first time I had ever finished this cobblestoned, acrobatic race. Later, in June, I played a key role in helping Bernard Hinault to win the Tour of Italy, finishing third myself. But the Tour of Italy was more than just a good performance, it also struck me as the best way to prepare the Tour de France. In the Tour of Italy we raced distances similar to those of the Tour de France, for the same number of days. But, unlike the Tour de France, the Italian tour was far more laid back and could provide some easy training days without the added mental stress of trying to train alone, away from racing.

Perhaps the most important aspect of that Tour of Italy was that it thrust Bernard Hinault and the entire La Vie Claire squad to the top. The previous year, La Vie Claire had been a stumbling, new team, but now we were considered state-of-the-art, ready to confront the Tour de France as real favorites.

Strangely enough, the situation I had partially hoped to avoid by jumping to La Vie Claire—racing on the same squad with another top star—had reared its head on La Vie Claire. Hinault looked in good shape and was hungry for a fifth Tour de France win. Strangely enough, Laurent Fignon, my big rival on the Renault team, had a knee injury and was sitting out the 1985 Tour de France. Guimard was quoted in the press as saying that if I had stayed with him, I could have won the Tour de France.

Hinault and I agreed that La Vie Claire wouldn't ride with a preordained leader. We agreed that whoever was stronger would take the lead. The team would work to defend that man—whoever he would be—for the benefit of the team as a whole.

The Tour started off with Hinault taking the lead, predictably. After all, he was better in the time trials and there were a lot of time trials in the first part of the Tour. When the Tour hit the first serious mountains, on the road to Morzine/Avoriaz, Hinault broke away with Luis Herrera. Hinault and I had agreed he would attack in the early going of that stage just to test the opposition. But when it turned out that nobody reacted, he stayed away for good, catapulting himself into a solid lead. He never intended that break to last till the finish.

Behind, I attacked strongly on the last climb to the ski resort of Avoriaz. But Hinault and Herrera had gained too much of a lead, and I fell four minutes behind Hinault on the overall standings. Then it looked as if Hinault's bid for victory might be shattered a few days later when he crashed in a routine stage finish in the southern French city of Saint-Étienne. His fall looked gruesome, with blood gushing from his nose. When he was taken to the hospital, the doctors found that Hinault only had a bad cut and a bruise. Tough as he is, Hinault recovered quickly and spent the next two transition days riding at the front of the pack as a sign that he wasn't dead yet.

The big controversy in the 1985 Tour arose on stage seventeen, one of the hardest mountain stages of the race. The road took us, that day, up the very difficult Aspin and Tourmalet passes before finishing at the summit of the Luz Ardiden roadway. Hinault had been pushing himself very hard the past two days and looked a bit tired as we started off this stage.

The stage started with a slow, easy ride for the first fifty kilometers. We rode slowly and everything was calm. But the storm was about to erupt. The real race got its start a few kilometers before the Aspin pass, where Spaniard Jose Del Ramo broke away.

Ahead, we still had to climb the longer and more difficult Tourmalet, one of the hardest and steepest climbs in the world. As we climbed into a thick mist, Hinault visibly began to weaken. Suddenly, about a mile and a half from the top, Hinault cracked and the race broke wide open. I kept riding strongly, eventually crossing the summit with Irishman Stephen Roche and Colombian Fabio Parra. While Hinault continued to falter, I rode the best I could, matching a fast pace with Roche and Parra.

A few minutes after I crossed the summit, I heard that Hinault was over three minutes behind. I couldn't believe it. Suddenly, Hinault and his yellow jersey had cracked. I was just about in the lead of the Tour de France. In the final climb to Luz Ardiden, I wanted to push ahead as strongly as possible, to make sure that, as Hinault fell behind (and I was hearing that he was getting dropped some more on that final climb), I could take over the yellow jersey—to make sure the yellow jersey would stay on our team.

As soon as I started to pull the pace, Maurice Le Guilloux, the assistant coach of the La Vie Claire team, drove to my side to tell me that I could ride alongside Stephen Roche—the only other serious rival for first place—but I couldn't pull the pace.

I was confused, because with Hinault losing minutes on me and me riding so well it seemed strange to coast up the last climb, but this was what I had to do. With Hinault probably about four minutes down, I thought, why wouldn't Le Guilloux want me to take the yellow jersey and safeguard first place within La Vie Claire?

Well, as it turned out, I had been misinformed. Actually, Hinault was over three minutes down on the stage leader Pello Ruiz-Cabestany at the top of the Tourmalet. He was only 1:16 down on me at that point. In any case, if I had been able to ride my own race up the final climb to Luz Ardiden, I felt I could have had the yellow jersey.

Unwillingly, I pulled back to Stephen Roche's level; the pace slowed considerably. I rode in complete frustration, because I knew that I was in the best shape of my life. I had a golden opportunity and I was throwing it away. Every once in a while I would turn back to look at the approaching pack. About halfway up the climb to Luz Ardiden a group of eight riders caught us and stayed with us all the way to the top.

At the finish I was in tears. When I heard that Hinault came in 1:13 behind me, I was convinced I had thrown away a once-in-a-lifetime opportunity to win the greatest cycling race in the world. I sat behind a scaffolding and cried while my coach, Paul Koechli, tried to explain what had happened. He told me that he would have let me ride away only if I could have attacked Roche and dropped him. Roche, he told me, was the only rider who could spoil La Vie Claire's one-two showing.

I felt that I could have gained an extra minute, maybe two, from Hinault that day. Those feelings were partially confirmed when Hinault fell back some more the next day. When I won the final time trial, I realized that an

Have I just given up my chance to win the 1985 Tour de France? Here I am riding the climb to the Aubisque pass. The previous day I had held back while Bernard Hinault consolidated his victory in the Tour de France.

extra minute or two at Luz Ardiden could have made the difference, that it could have been the catalyst for a victory in the Tour de France.

The 1985 Tour de France ended in frustration for me. Although I might not have won the Tour, Hinault wouldn't have won without my help either. When Hinault needed help in the mountains, I was always there. And after he crashed in Saint-Étienne, I didn't leave his side for two stages. There were several stages in which I could have made up time, like the ride to Morzine/Avoriaz where I let Hinault and Herrera walk away with it.

Hinault was definitely superior in two time trials, especially in the very long forty-six-mile effort in stage eight. But I think that if I had been allowed to play my hand fully on the terrain that best suited me—the mountains—I could have shown myself to be the equal of Hinault.

The next year would prove my case.

Following the Tour, I returned to California to ride my first race in America since 1981. The La Vie Claire team had accepted an invitation to ride in the Coors Classic. Hinault agreed to race so he could see what American racing was all about. In the end, La Vie Claire had an easy time winning at the Coors classic. My teammate Steve Bauer won three stages, Hinault won one stage. I won the overall prize.

I'm riding the race of my life. In a few minutes I'll be the first American ever to win a stage in the Tour de France (stage twenty, Lac de Vassivière time trial, 1985).

Throughout my career I have always agreed to struggle to achieve excellence. In the 1986 Tour, I struggled with the course, the competition, Bernard Hinault, and myself. But one thing that cycling has taught me is that if you can achieve something without a struggle it's not going to be satisfying.

And perhaps the greatest satisfaction in cycling has been to discover that there are few things you can't do as long as you're willing to apply yourself. There are many times I wish I was playing eighteen holes of golf instead of training in miserable cold weather. But in the final analysis, I'd rather win the Tour de France than play eighteen holes of golf. That's why I do it.

2

The World

of

Cycling

*M*any people want a bike just to ride on the weekends. Others use their bikes as a healthy form of transportation to and from work. Most people who cycle start out riding recreationally. Later, some slowly graduate to medium- and long-distance touring. Others eventually take their interest in cycling to racing. That was the case with me—I got my first bike because I enjoyed the outdoors; after a few months I was ready to start racing.

Everyone's goal in cycling is different. I know riders who have no interest in road cycling at all and have dedicated themselves to off-road, or mountain, bike riding. Even mountain biking has its own categories: Some enjoy riding quietly along trails in wildlife terrain, while others have a decidedly competitive bent—a number of off-road races have popped up, mainly in the West.

Some people are interested only in long-distance touring. This branch of the sport is completely separate from either road racing or mountain bike racing. Touring cyclists (or simply tourists) ride on specialized bikes with racks mounted on the back and front wheels. They usually carry a good deal of equipment and have a very wide range of gears.

Touring is probably the most common type of cycling. Although the term seems to imply riding across vast distances, touring actually includes any kind of recreational cycling that doesn't involve the practical applications of commuting or delivering groceries or the competitive intensity of racing.

Touring is cycling's equivalent to jogging, a recreational form of exercise that millions of people enjoy. Unlike jogging, touring also allows one to see a bit of country. Some tourists ride their bikes ten or fifteen miles a day, while others ride vast distances for days or weeks at a time, carrying supplies and a tent packed on their bike.

Touring can be competitive, too. Century rides have been an American tradition for over one hundred years. A century is a ride of one hundred miles; the object is simply to finish, rather than to win—though the front runners always ride a little more aggressively to finish at the top.

What really differentiates competitive touring from racing is the intensity. Tourists rarely ride beyond a certain intensity. Instead they emphasize endurance, sometimes riding extremely long distances.

Whatever kind of cycling you begin with, it's easy to branch into other cycling pursuits. If you commute to work, you can easily graduate to touring and eventually racing. If you've been road racing and you want a change, try track racing. Or stay on the road, drop the intensity a notch or two, and enjoy the countryside with a day-long or overnight ride.

The beauty of cycling is that there are no closed niches. Any branch of the sport is open to you as long as you're willing to pursue it. The only constraints are your level of fitness, which must be improved gradually before you increase your intensity, and any equipment you may need. There are no set body types and, for the most part, no specialized experience required to begin. And it's easy to achieve a high level of fitness in cycling, because the sport is much easier on the body than most other sports.

RECREATIONAL CYCLING

Millions of people in the United States own a bicycle—for most, it is a source of recreation, and little more. Although recreational cyclists don't really have to worry as much as tourists or racers do about the kind of bike they're buying, I strongly recommend buying the best bike you can afford. Any extremely inexpensive model will only be worth as much as it costs— although there are better values and worse values. Once you decide that you want to buy a bicycle in a price range above $250, I would recommend always buying a bike in a professional bike shop.

Some recreational cyclists are only interested in three-speed bikes with a wide saddle and upright bars. That's fine as long as you don't have to climb any significant hills or ride for long distances. If you do, you'll find the three-speed bike very uncomfortable, heavy, and sluggish. The more varied the terrain the more important it is to have a bike that can comfortably handle the variations in topography.

Whatever bike you buy, always be sure to fit your bike correctly, as described in Chapter Four. Even if you only ride two or three miles at a time, there's no reason to have a bike that doesn't fit properly.

Remember, when you are riding recreationally, like any moving vehicle you have to respect all the rules of the road. Always ride to the right of the road and signal any time you want to turn. On a bicycle, a left turn is signaled by holding the left arm fully extended to the left. A right turn is signaled with the left arm bent upward in a ninety-degree angle at the elbow.

You must stop at all stop signs and put one foot on the ground. Likewise, you must obey all stoplights, just like a car. If you come to a weight-activated right-turn light, ride on the edge of the sensor at the right side of the road— that will activate the light. An adult should never ride on the sidewalk—it's dangerous and illegal. A young child may ride on the sidewalk to avoid a very congested street, but only on a very small bike that doesn't qualify as a moving vehicle, and only at very low speeds. (An adult must ride on the road to respect the safety of pedestrians walking on the sidewalk.)

Never ride against the flow of traffic. A lot of recreational cyclists think they'll be safer because they can see cars coming their way. In fact, it's much more dangerous to ride against the flow because it's unexpected. It is also illegal. In the case of an accident, your body would suffer the impact of a full head-on collision. *Never* ride against traffic.

Although training isn't necessary for a recreational cyclist, it's still a good idea to be in good shape before you ride, especially if you're going to ride in hot weather. Get a complete medical examination to make sure your body is fit enough to withstand the physical demands of riding a bike in the heat.

Although bike riding is good, healthy exercise, the actual benefit derived from riding only a few miles a day at a purely recreational pace is only about equivalent to a slow, half-hour walk. This is because the bicycle is such an efficient machine. Riding at a moderate pace uses very little energy. This means that—unless you're really pushing yourself, riding a long distance— the health benefits can be relatively small.

If you are riding primarily for health reasons, I recommend graduating to touring. Light touring (twenty to twenty-five miles a day) is probably the best way—of any sport—to get into shape and lose weight. If you ride ninety minutes a day, before long you'll find yourself in much better shape and enjoying whatever kind of cycling you do a lot more.

COMMUTING

A bicycle can be a practical form of transportation for commuters. Among the most common bicycle commuters are college students and inner-city commuters. In most cases, such commutes are rarely more than a few miles.

Cyclists who live in New York City, Chicago, Boston, San Francisco, and other major cities have to be especially courageous to commute to work by bike. After all, the bicycle is at best an extremely vulnerable vehicle that provides little if any protection to the rider if there's an accident. In the worst of cases, a bike can even be a target for an angry driver.

That's why I heartily recommend buying a mountain bike to commute in a big city. For one thing, a mountain bike will be much better equipped to deal with the guerilla-like conditions of riding in the city. Mountain bikes have wide, gnarly tires with a very thick tread that's made to grip the road in the worst conditions. They are built for jarring, potholes, and bumps. Also, the mountain bike frame has a softer geometry and a more comfortable saddle than most racing bikes. The handlebars are cushioned and upright and are more comfortable over the short haul.

But most important, since you're upright, you're much more visible on a mountain bike.

Some people may choose to use a standard ten-speed but with wider tires that have thicker tread. Keep in mind, though, that a ten-speed cannot accommodate tires as wide as the ones used on a mountain bike.

Inner-city commuting *does* have some real drawbacks. Most commuters must transport materials to and from work—a briefcase, textbooks, and so forth. If that's the case, you will need either a backpack or paniers or wire baskets for your bike. Remember, however, that the size of your briefcase will be limited to what will fit in your pack or panier.

Another drawback to commuting is the difficulty of finding a place to leave the bike once you've arrived at work. Some companies will let employees keep bikes at the office, which is the best solution. If you can't keep your bike at the office, you'll need to find a reliable garage or storage place. If you leave it with another establishment—a local gas station, for example—you'll have to worry about the place closing if you have to work late.

But the biggest drawback of commuting to an office job is clothing. You may find yourself arriving with a rumpled or mud-splattered suit. This is especially true when commuting in the rain or snow.

One solution is to leave a set of office clothes at work and ride in a sweatsuit. Another solution is to carry a spare set of office clothes with you on the bike—your clothes may be slightly wrinkled, but at least they'll be clean.

Although it seems inconvenient, my dad commutes by bike the twenty-five miles to and from his office as a way of keeping in shape. He is lucky to run his own business. He doesn't have to worry about where he leaves the bike. He also has a shower and a spare set of clothes waiting for him when he gets there.

One further problem almost everybody commuting to work in the city encounters is darkness. This is especially true riding home from work in the winter. Riding in darkness is one of the most dangerous things you can do on your bicycle. Personally, I would suggest only commuting in the summer months on days when you know you won't be working late. But if you have to ride at night, be sure to outfit your bike with reflectors and lights. I recommend a battery light over the front wheel. (Friction lights that generate electrically by rubbing on the tire are not as useful—if you're going slowly, they don't provide much light at all.) I also recommend using a battery-operated leg light (the white light should be pointed ahead and the red light behind—it's important to have it pointing correctly in order not to confuse drivers). You should also get a battery-operated red light for the rear. White reflectors should be mounted on the spokes of the wheels. As the bike moves the reflectors spin with the wheels, warning drivers that you're on a moving bicycle. Unlike most other reflectors, wheel reflectors are light and easy to take off if you don't want them on your bike during the day.

Most important of all, wear reflective strips on your helmet, windbreaker, and shorts. These will make you more visible. They could save your life.

One final safety measure *all* commuters (and all cyclists) should take is to wear a hard-shell helmet. Many people seem to think that, with so many hazards, a helmet won't help much. While it is true that if you get run over by a cement mixer, a hard-shell helmet probably won't do you any good, it can be useful in many other accidents on crowded city streets. Too many cyclists have suffered unnecessary head injuries from falls because they weren't wearing a helmet. A strong protective helmet can be a lifesaver. Always wear one.

Despite all the inconveniences and dangers, some people enjoy commuting to work on their bikes. They find it a good source of exercise. It certainly teaches you to be an excellent bike handler. And there are other benefits too. You don't have to worry about finding a parking space. If you need to go crosstown during rush hour, it's often the fastest way to go, because you can ride between the lanes of traffic. And in most cases a commuting bicycle is inexpensive compared to the yearly cost of driving and parking a car in a city or riding public transportation every day.

Not all commuters are big-city commuters. Many people who live in the suburbs get good exercise from commuting to and from work. Pete Penseyres, the 1984 Race Across America winner, likes to ride his bike forty miles to and from work every day to stay in shape for his ultra-marathon rides. Penseyres, of course, is an extreme example—he rides four hundred miles on the weekends, for a total of eight hundred miles a week—much more than I ride. However, unless you ride *at least* ten or fifteen miles to and from work every day, don't expect commuting to be a real source of physical fitness. You'll probably be riding very defensively and in a lot of stop-and-go traffic.

TOURING

There was a time, as recently as the early 1960s, when touring was a very specific kind of cycling. Tourists were long-distance specialists whose bikes were fitted with baskets and paniers holding large amounts of equipment. These riders were very well trained, and they had considerable stamina and endurance. They often rode across continents and up and down mountain ranges.

In those days cycling wasn't nearly as accessible as it is today. To buy a good touring bike often meant commissioning a private frame maker to build an expensive frame with special braze-ons for baskets and paniers and with specific frame angles needed for touring.

Today all that has changed. Most tourists today are mainstream fitness enthusiasts who like to ride for exercise and enjoyment. With running having proven to be destructive to the body, people are increasingly turning to cycling as a way to get and stay in shape. Usually, they turn to what was once the specialized activity of touring.

Today a tourist is really anybody who uses cycling as a path to fitness or recreation or for just plain touring—of course, if you're doing it right, touring should result in a synthesis of all three. Unlike jogging, touring allows you to roam through miles of countryside and discover nature in an absolutely unique way: You're traveling fast enough to get a lot of variety and yet slow enough to enjoy it.

People who get started in cycling and find they like it inevitably gravitate to touring. I did. I enjoyed the sense of freedom that my bicycle gave me. Quickly enough, I was challenging myself to twenty-five-and thirty-mile rides. Later my dad and I rode over mountain passes in the Sierra Nevada near the Washoe Valley where we lived. I remember feeling a tremendous sense of exhilaration and achievement.

Of course, eventually my competitive drive took me into racing. But many people discover, as they get more serious about cycling, that touring is the perfect route for them because it's challenging and enjoyable without being as intense as racing.

Because it's easy to cover relatively large distances quickly and without too much effort, touring is the perfect activity/sport for anybody interested in the outdoors. Tourists range from part-time riders taking in a twenty-five-mile ride on the weekends to tourists who camp overnight and ride for hundreds of miles on end—some have even ridden all around the world.

Many tourists ride not specifically for fitness, but because touring is fun. Nonetheless, tourists who ride for hours on end develop a high degree of endurance fitness—usually their bodies are extremely low in fat content.

Touring for fun has become so popular in the United States that it has become a minor industry. In a number of cities, businesses offer cyclists packaged cycling tours all around the world. One tour organizer in New York has tours ranging from an afternoon up the Hudson River Valley to two weeks touring the Loire Valley châteaux in France to a tour of ancient Egypt's great monuments.

Although touring is not a competitive sport like racing it's organized almost as methodically. Touring has a very old tradition in America. Long before anybody thought of organizing bike races in the United States, tourists had banded together in a group known as the League of American Wheelmen. Formed in Providence, Rhode Island, in 1880, the LAW, known today as Bicycle USA, is the oldest American governing body of cycling. Today Bicycle USA has fifteen thousand members and is involved in promoting cycling through its magazine, safety clinics, and annual almanac.

The group also has an influential Washington lobby that has pushed hard for cyclists' rights. The group played a role in making it possible for cyclists to use bridges and is currently fighting for tougher bottle laws—broken glass is a common hazard for cyclists—and stricter drunk driving standards.

All around America and the world, there are bicycle clubs that specialize in touring. Often these clubs combine to organize the most common touring event in America: the century ride. The century, so named because it's a hundred-mile affair, is actually America's oldest cycling event, having first been held in the 1870s. In those days, the only bike around was the ordinary or high-wheeler, and finishing the century was quite a challenge. Cycling was a great new fad in those days and close to one hundred thousand people are said to have ridden centuries.

There are many variations on the century. The most common are the quarter-and half-centuries that clubs promote to encourage novices to get into bicycle touring. These rides have much the same appeal as the longer centuries, but they are more manageable for someone just starting out.

There are also longer rides. One of the most famous is the Tour of the Scioto River Valley, in central Ohio. This is a 210-mile, two-day event that attracts about thirty-five hundred people every year. The Tour of the Scioto River Valley—commonly called TOSRV—was founded in the 1950s by Charles Siple, a frustrated racer who tried to recreate a stage of the Tour de France with this event. The TOSRV, although not a race, was his way of developing cycling in his home region of central Ohio.

Another famous long-distance touring event is the Davis double-century, a two-hundred-mile ride in and around Davis, California. This event has become so popular in California that it often attracts tourists and racers alike. The Davis double is much more than just a friendly outing, though, and the competition for the top places—although they are not officially rewarded as they would be in a race—can be fierce. The biggest prize, though, is not necessarily finishing first, but breaking the course record, which has dipped slightly under ten hours in the past ten years.

Most centuries are really very similar to running marathons. They have a small group of highly trained athletes vying for the top prizes while behind most of the riders are trying to reach purely personal goals in finishing a grueling test of endurance. Just as in marathons, century finishers always receive a medal or a certificate when they finish (there's usually a twelve-hour limit for official finishers). Some veteran century riders like to ride with their various patches prominently visible.

I think these kinds of events are going to see a lot of growth in the coming years. The intense competitive races can scare a lot of people. But riding in organized centuries allows people to get that competitive feeling without the intensity and the risk. The century is really cycling's best participation event.

Touring has traditionally brought out the inventive and eccentric side of America. Unlike racers, for whom there are well-defined limits on the type of bicycle that can be used, tourists have always experimented with new technology.

Right before the turn of the century, tourists adopted an invention that promised to soften the ride of their bicycles over the bumpy roads of the time: the pneumatic tire. Although pneumatics turned out to be very successful by 1890, many racers refused to use them for another five years. They claimed that the pneumatics flatted too often and that, as racers, they had no need to be comfortable—just fast.

Well, it turned out that being more comfortable meant going faster—that useless bit of racing bravado was soon replaced by common sense.

More recently, the huge centuries and tourist rallies have attracted a large contingent of bicycles with aerodynamic shields, known by the vague-sounding name of Human-Powered Vehicles, or HPVs. Because there are no rules banning aerodynamic shields in touring, these have flourished and developed largely as a tourist phenomenon in America.

In an effort to reduce air friction to a minimum, for a number of years HVPs have been built on which the rider lies on his back in something known as the recumbent. Another alternative has been to place the rider on his stomach, on a prone bicycle. Both of these models have become staples of the American touring circuit. It isn't unusual to see a number of these machines—covered with plastic shields to reduce air friction—riding through the thousands of ordinary ten-speed bikes on a century ride.

If high-tech aerodynamics has been one unexpected offshoot of touring, another has been the rapid development of ultra-marathon riding. Although marathon riding has been a part of the American scene ever since somebody figured out you could ride a bike from coast to coast, ultra-marathon cycling boomed in the mid-1970s when John Marino, a former minor-league base-ball player, crushed the transcontinental record by crossing the country in an amazing ten-and-a-half days. In 1986, forty-three-year-old Pete Penseyres lowered that record to an awesome eight-and-a-half days.

Marino has taken his cross-country competition and turned it into the premier ultra-marathon event, the Race Across America—known as RAAM. People have asked me how the RAAM can be considered a touring event if it's a race. The reason is very simple: RAAM has always been a contest of endurance and not intensity. Over the years, the transcontinental record has been lowered as riders improved their endurance to such a point that they're getting by on thirty minutes of sleep every night. But the intensity of racing just isn't there, although the event can be fast in the first three hundred miles or so. Don't get me wrong. I think it takes incredible talent and fitness to ride at this level. Honestly, it's something I doubt I would want to attempt. But fitness doesn't mean you race with a high level of intensity—and that's what differentiates these riders from professional racing cyclists.

Since RAAM is a race, with an official winner, it tends to come close to racing. In fact when professional racer Jonathan Boyer became the first world-class professional racer to ride RAAM in 1985, he easily captured first prize.

While RAAM has been making big headlines with impressive records and an award-winning show on ABC's *Wide World of Sports,* Europe has had its own version of RAAM for close to a hundred years. That event, Paris-Brest-Paris, got its start in 1891 as a fully professional race. The event, eight hundred miles long, was organized as a dare by one of France's leading cycling publications. It was deemed so demanding that promoters agreed it would be held only once every ten years.

But eventually Paris-Brest-Paris became outdated. European racing be-came more intense and many more races began to crowd the calendar when in 1951, after only a handful of second-rate pros showed up to race Paris-Brest-Paris, the event was taken off the racing calendar. Since 1961, it's come back as a tourist event and has been held fairly consistently every four or five years. Many of America's top ultra-marathon tourists, like Lon Haldeman and his wife, Susan Notorangelo, got their start in the really long races in Paris-Brest-Paris.

Most fitness-oriented cyclists probably won't choose Human-Powered Ve-hicles or ultra-marathon riding. What most cyclists want to do is challenge themselves and get fit in a reasonable way. That goal is easy to achieve in touring as long as you keep in mind that you need to ride at least an hour a day to get any real benefit. Unless you live in the center of a big, sprawling city, you should be able to find a nice variety of rides in the twenty-to thirty-five-mile range. If you ride about an hour to ninety minutes a day, and then a little more on the weekends, you'll find that your fitness will improve quickly. And you won't suffer from any of the damage that's so common in running, because the bike carries your body weight, and the pedaling motion is very smooth.

But there are a few things to keep in mind. The first is that—just as in recreational jogging—you have to develop a fairly systematic approach to your riding. While many people realize they have to develop their running technique and weekly schedule, most cyclists tend to take a very casual approach to their training regimen.

Riding ten or fifteen miles a day and then going out and riding seventy-five miles on the weekend is not the best way to get in shape. At first it may seem like more fun, or just easier, to do it that way. But soon enough you'll discover that your cycling habits will become erratic. After one of your long rides, you'll probably come back exhausted and sore, because riding ten or fifteen miles a day won't prepare you to ride seventy-five miles on the weekends. You'll probably have to take a few days off—something that will undermine your fitness even more.

It's no different from jogging. If you jog only two or three miles a day, you can't expect to run a half-marathon on a weekend comfortably or safely. The only real difference is that because cycling is much easier on the body, the effects of suddenly increasing your distance won't be obvious quite as soon.

If, on the other hand, you ride twenty-five miles—or about ninety minutes (measuring riding in time instead of distance is much more meaningful)—every day, then you'll be much better prepared to go out on a sixty-to seventy-five-mile ride, or a three-to four-and-a-half-hour ride, on the weekend.

It's important to keep in mind that you must ride at a certain intensity for it to do you any appreciable good. This is the main difference between cycling and jogging. When you're jogging, the very fact that you're running forces your heartbeat to at least 65 percent of its maximum capacity. A number of studies have shown that this is the minimum intensity to achieve physical fitness. But when you're on a bike, you can easily just coast along with a heartbeat that's close to normal, about 45 percent of your maximum. (The maximum heartbeat can be measured approximately as 215 beats per minute minus your age. For a complete discussion of the importance of heartbeat, look at Chapter Six.)

To get around that problem, without constantly pushing yourself to ride too hard, you'll have to find varied, hilly courses. The hills will act as natural "intensifiers," forcing you to raise your heartbeat to 65 percent and more of your maximum heart rate. And unless you're riding in the Rockies or the Alps, you should be able to reach the summit within a reasonable time.

If you live in a very flat part of the country, chances are you're still going to be able to find short, steep hills that can challenge you on a bike. Many Midwestern states, for example, are not nearly as flat as people seem to believe. In a state such as North Dakota or Nebraska you can easily find many short hills.

If you happen to live in the flattest state in the Union—Florida—then there aren't many hills. On the other hand, there's always plenty of wind along both Florida coasts, and when there are no hills, wind is a good substitute. The only drawback to riding in a headwind is that it won't be nearly as easy to get a break from it. But at least you'll be able to get in good shape in a hurry. After all, many of the world's top racers have come from Belgium, a very flat country with a combination of short, choppy hills and a constant wind driving off the North Sea.

Even though touring as a way to get fit is in many ways more attractive than jogging, there are a few hazards too. Probably the major danger of cycling for exercise instead of running is the hazard of riding on the open road with careless drivers.

Unless you live in an extremely sparsely populated area, you're going to have to deal with traffic safely and effectively to protect yourself. The best way to do this is to avoid traffic as much as possible. Find small, country roads where there's much less truck traffic and congestion—you'll not only be safer, but you'll have a lot more fun too. The air will be cleaner and you won't have to worry constantly about the car coming up behind you.

Even in most uninhabited areas, though, you'll probably have to ride on at least one major road. Make yourself as visible as possible. Wear reflective strips. Ride safely to the right, while making sure the driver understands you have as much right to the road as he does. If there is any question of safety, however, get off to the side of the road.

Remember, cycling can be the perfect exercise for fitness. It has all the cardiovascular potential of running, provided you push yourself enough, and causes none of the connective tissue damage that ravages runners. It provides you with an efficient, light vehicle that's fast enough to let you see a lot of country. And best of all, cycling is something you can do into your eighties and beyond, because it's so easy on the body.

BICYCLE MOTOCROSS
(or BMX)

Probably the most typically American form of cycling is bicycle motocross. In the early 1950s, American bike manufacturers began coming out with bicycles that were marketed as the kids' equivalent of motocross motorcycles. Soon enough, though, the kids took to the trails and began to cross on their bicycles. BMX is especially popular in Southern California, where there are a number of tracks and many different competitions each year.

Although many kids like to ride BMX bikes around their neighborhood, BMX was first created as a form of motorcycle cross for those who were too young to ride a motorcycle.

Although young people of all ages are involved in BMX its primary appeal seems to be to adolescents. In most of the races the kids are between the ages of eight and sixteen.

One offshoot of BMX has been the popular BMX stunt riding that is often featured at major American bike races and cycling industry trade shows. Every year at the Coors Classic, a group of well-trained youngsters puts on a BMX show that dazzles audiences while they wait for the bike racers to come by.

In the 1970s, BMX grew in Europe, where it is popular among young kids, especially in France and West Germany.

OFF-ROAD (or MOUNTAIN) CYCLING

A few years ago, a new breed of bicycle was born in Marin County. Up to then serious cyclists had always looked down on anybody riding a heavy bicycle with fat tires. Those bikes looked dumpy and had balloon tires and upright bars.

But the "clunker" found its application in serious cycling when some inventive riders in Marin County decided they wanted to ride up and down the steep trails just north of San Francisco.

Up to then there had been only two types of off-road cycling: cyclo cross and bicycle motocross. Cyclo cross was always a European specialty. The light cyclo cross bikes with their drop handlebars and relatively thin tires required much skill and fitness to ride. They looked like racing bikes and basically had the same nervous feel.

Bicycle motocross bikes had low, shallow diamond frames with gnarly tires fashioned after those of motocross motorcycles. Although the BMX riders were low on their bikes, they could tackle most off-road challenges in a fun, challenging way.

The innovators in Marin County looked at the BMX bikes and realized that, by combining them with some racing technology, they could come up with a performance trail bike that would also be fun to ride. At first, they adopted the basic, laid back frame geometry of the BMX bike. Then they added cantilever brakes from the cyclo cross bikes. They took the derailleurs and top-of-the-line components from racing bikes. Finally, they added the wide, knobbly tires.

Next they changed the frame slightly. They added elements of the racing frame by incorporating lugs, and a tighter, more upright geometry. They added more gears—to go up the very steep trails—by using the fifteen-speed drivetrains common on tourist bikes. They lightened the wheels by incorporating the latest racing technology. They improved the tires by producing them from the toughest and lightest rubber compounds. And so the mountain bike was born. This new kind of cycling grew very quickly.

By the early 1980s, mountain bikes had become a big phenomenon. All around America, people were riding on trails, in parks, and through the wilderness: The mountain bike gave people an incredible sense of freedom. Inner-city commuters and messengers adopted mountain bikes because they were more practical in the urban jungle than the traditional ten-speed. Soon, mountain bikes spread all around the world. I've seen people riding them all around Europe and I hear they're becoming popular in Japan as well.

But the mountain bike hasn't lost its roots: Even the French call it a mountain bike—usually pronounced more like *moon-teyn bake*.

Mountain bike racing has become popular, especially in the West. The sport has spawned its own stars and teams and has become quite popular even though it is still very young. Mountain biking even has its own governing body, the National Off-Road Bicycle Association—NORBA.

But recently this Cinderella story of cycling has run into difficulties. Most of the early pioneers of mountain biking were nature lovers who wanted to use the bike as a nonpolluting way to get closer to nature. But the sport's tremendous popularity has led national and state parks to ban any type of cycling on their trails. The officials at NORBA have protested vigorously and some compromise may be reached in the near future.

The problem, of course, is that any time you have a large number of people going over the same trails, you're going to get a lot of erosion. Some parks have even closed remote locations to pedestrians because of that problem. And a mountain bike can cause a lot more erosion than a pedestrian. There's also the fact that many riders like to zip around at high speeds— often frightening horses and hikers.

Luckily, though, there are still a lot of wide-open spaces left to mountain bike. I use my mountain bike in the winter around my home in Rancho

Murietta, California. I think it's a thoroughly enjoyable and beneficial form of exercise—and fun, too.

In fact, mountain biking may just be the ideal kind of cycling for many people. Although I don't think you should ride *only* a mountain bike, it's a great way to break the routine of riding on the road all the time. For one thing, it's easy to get a good workout in only a short time because you're riding over dirt and mud trails that slow you down. You also get much closer to nature than you would riding the road. Also you're far away from the hazards of traffic. And because you can buy a decent mountain bike for as little as three hundred dollars it's not an expensive investment.

The greatest drawback of mountain cycling is that, unless you pick a very flat and easy trail, you'll have to have pretty good bike-handling skills. The most advanced mountain bikers like to challenge themselves by riding down steep gorges and up stiff hills. But if you try to follow an advanced rider on one of these trails you'll find yourself slipping and sliding (and possibly crashing) on the downhills. On the uphills, you'll need to be in excellent condition, or you could injure your knees or pull a leg muscle.

And unless you live in an area like Marin County, with many hilly trails, or Jackson Hole, Wyoming, with all the open spaces, you're going to find yourself riding the same trails over and over again. In fact, it's safe to say that the more urbanized your area, the harder it's going to be to find varied trail riding and the easier it's going to be to find a good selection of roads.

If you decide to buy a mountain bike and nothing else, you'll find you won't have much fun riding on roads; it's like owning cross-country skis and trying to ski downhill—you just won't be able to ride very effectively. A mountain bike is best suited to riding on the road in adverse conditions on the short haul.

If you want to go out and do some serious road riding, the mountain bike will be heavy and slow. The upright position that's comfortable on short rides will begin to pinch your back. Most of your weight will be over the rear wheel and you'll have to worry about oversteer. You won't have as much natural momentum.

That's why I think most people should consider a mountain bike as a second bike. If you can mix road riding and mountain bike riding, then you'll have the perfect mix of cycling.

Of course, even if you just ride a mountain bike for fun, you need to prepare yourself as you would on your road bike. You have to make sure your cycling position is set up correctly, with the same measurements as your road bike (although your bars will be upright, of course). You'll need to make sure your riding skills are good enough to get you out of any situation you might get yourself into. And you should ride in a systematic way, without attempting any major changes in distance or intensity that could hurt your body.

Cyclo cross was developed as a hybrid of cycling and cross-country running. It's a winter sport that allows cyclists to ride in cold weather because of the lower speeds. Here 1986 world cyclo cross champion Roland Liboton rides in a Swiss cyclo cross race. Note the thick tires, the cantilevered brakes, and the shift levers on the ends of the handlebars.

CYCLO CROSS

The original form of mountain bike riding is cyclo cross. Cyclo cross was first developed in Belgium and France in the late 1940s when riders were looking for an easy way to stay in shape during the winter, when road riding in most of Europe was impossible because of the cold weather. Track racing was an alternative for some, but required a track and special bike-handling skills.

Riding in the fields was a logical solution. Because speeds were so much lower in the mud and snow, there would be less wind chill—riders would have no trouble staying warm. The cyclo cross bike was adapted to ride off-road. It was designed with slightly wider tires, more brake clearance, and derailleur shifters on the handlebars so you'd never have to take your hands off the bars.

Because much of Europe is so wet and muddy in the winter, cyclo cross developed into a hybrid sport. Courses were fashioned in small forests, up steep hills, and down muddy ravines. On many courses, riders had to run as much as they had to ride. Because so much riding was done in sticky mud, cyclo cross became an excellent way to stay in shape in the winter and develop good cardiovascular fitness.

Today, cyclo cross is a staple of the European circuit. Many top road racers prefer cyclo cross to six-day track racing because it has far fewer pitfalls and dangers—how badly can you hurt yourself if you fall into a pile of mud? Some riders are cyclo cross specialists and only ride occasionally on the road to stay fit in the summer.

Most cyclo cross events last one hour plus the distance to the finish line on the final lap. Even though they're short, these races are extremely intense. When I first turned professional, my teammate Bernard Hinault did a lot of cyclo cross in the winter. I started riding off-road a few weeks each winter, and now I'm hooked on it as a good winter alternative to road riding. Even though I live in Northern California where I could ride on the road, cyclo cross gives me a good mental break from road training and racing.

Many people ask me if there's any difference between cyclo cross and mountain bike riding. Well, superficially there isn't. But the cyclo cross bike is different—it's more like a racing bike. It doesn't have the same range of gears as the mountain bike. It's a little harder to ride and it's not as comfortable. Because cyclo cross racers have to carry their bikes so much, the bikes are a lot lighter than fat-tired mountain bikes.

Cyclo cross bikes are designed for competition and performance—the races are muddy and physically demanding. Mountain bikes are better suited to zooming down very steep trails—they're designed for fun and convenience. The mountain bike is hard to carry on your shoulder because it weighs close to thirty pounds. It won't handle as well in the very muddy European races. Someday, however, I think we'll see a synthesis of the mountain and cyclo cross bikes as American and European cycling grow closer together.

If you're interested in riding off-road as a way to stay in shape for racing or touring, I would recommend a cyclo cross bike, which will provide you with a better workout—especially if you don't live in a mountainous area. But mountain biking is fine if you don't require that extra performance edge. And it could be more fun and easier to handle. Unless you plan on riding the cyclo cross world championships, you probably won't need the slight performance edge of the cyclo cross bike.

RACING

Although bike racing is growing fast in the United States, it's still a long way from being the major international sport that it is in Europe and certain countries in South America. Bike racing is one of the most popular sports in countries like France, Italy, and Colombia, something like football and baseball here. It's a major professional sport that has millions of fans and is covered extensively on television and in the papers.

ROAD RACING

Although racing is a convenient umbrella term, there are really dozens of different kinds of racing. Bikes are raced on trails, tracks, and roads in all different sizes, shapes, and weights.

The most common type of racing in modern times is road racing. As the name indicates, road racing is any kind of competition that takes place on a road. Road races are usually held on public roads, but can also be held on private roads. The 1977 Tour of Italy even constructed a special plankway to hold a short individual race over the canals of Venice. And the 1980 Moscow Olympic road race was held on a circuit built especially for that race.

Most road races consist of large packs of riders. The first man over the line is declared the winner, very much like a running marathon or an automobile race. Road racing is especially challenging tactically; for example a rider who drafts behind another rider's slipstream, by getting tucked in right behind another rider, can save up to 30 percent of his effort, leaving him fresher for the finish. Of course, if you never lead you also can't capitalize on any opportunities and you'll probably lose out to a more aggressive rider. That's why road racing requires experience and savvy.

Most road races in America are held on circuits. These circuits sometimes form a huge loop that covers the entire distance of the race. Sometimes the circuits are shorter, and the riders cover a number of laps to complete the race. Although distances do vary, most amateur circuit road races in America are about eighty miles long, while the women race about forty miles, the junior men about fifty miles, and the veterans about sixty-five miles.

Each different kind of road race has its own special tactics. If you're racing a course with a big loop, of, say forty to fifty miles, then you'll have to survey the course before you ride. Otherwise you might get surprised by a hard climb or a dangerous descent. Never rely on hearsay information from other riders. It could be wrong (remember these guys are your opponents) or it might be wrong for you.

If a circuit is much shorter, say ten to fifteen miles, then you'll have an easy time riding the course to check it out. And in a circuit road race on a course that has several laps, you should keep your eye open in the first few laps to see where key action might develop. You might notice, for example, that an innocuous straightaway has a gusty wind blowing from the side, slowing the pace. This is a good place to break things up. Or you might find a steep hill right after a sharp turn. Because the pack will be slow in riding around the turn, this is a good place to attack and stay away. In a sharp turn one rider is always more nimble than a large pack.

Circuit races are common in America because they're easier to organize than point-to-point races. In most states the highway patrol is unwilling to

Criterium racing: These short circuit races have courses rarely longer than a mile and a half. High speeds, frequent turns, and intermediate sprints make these exciting races for spectators. Here, a large crowd watches the 1986 London Kellog's criterium. Criterium racing requires skill: Note the riders pulling to the outside to maintain maximum speed through the turn.

close or restrict traffic on major roads for a bike race. But on a circuit, traffic is restricted for a smaller portion of road, and usually only for a few minutes at a time.

The shortest circuits are called criteriums. These races have courses no longer than a mile and a half or so. The races have numerous laps. Criteriums are mostly flat races raced at very high speeds. There is an element of danger in such races. Of all the different kinds of racing, this is the most common in America. It's even easier to organize than a longer circuit—all you have to do is shut off four corners of a city block. It's also the type of racing in which spectators can watch the most action. The riders come by every few minutes, keeping the audience alert, whereas in longer circuits there is much more dead time (times when the riders are not in view). Promoters often add sprints at the finish line during many of the laps in the race, known as primes (pronounced preems). This further enhances the excitement and speed of criteriums. Often the prizes are donated by spectators.

Some criteriums with flat, extremely short courses come close to track racing. Not surprisingly, some of the best criterium experts are also track specialists. Other criteriums, though, have hilly courses that favor extremely fit road-racing cyclists. Probably the best example of the hilly criterium in

America is the race in Nevada City, California, in the Mother Lode outside of Sacramento. This race has a half-mile course with a quarter-mile hill.

Some of the greatest races of the sport are point-to-point, or races that start in one city and finish in another. Often the biggest roads are closed to traffic for hours as the races go by—it is an inconvenience Europeans seem to live with. Point-to-point racing is common in Europe. Because cycling is an important professional sport with a long, rich tradition, European cycling doesn't run into the kinds of roadblocks that it does in America.

Point-to-point racing can be a very special challenge. Because it is hard to survey an entire course thoroughly before the start of a race—especially in the long international amateur (110–120 miles) and professional (150–190 miles) point-to-point road races, experienced riders often get an edge. I had trouble as a rookie professional in some of the great European classics—the sport's most prestigious point-to-point events—because I didn't know exactly how to measure my effort. Every hill, every descent, and every turn in the road was a new lesson to learn. Often that lesson was harsh.

The hardest point-to-point race in the world is probably Paris-Roubaix, a 265-kilometer (or 165-mile) race in northern France that goes over a forty-mile stretch of the most wretched and disjointed cobblestones ever seen. This unusual—some say sadistic—event is one of the top sporting and media events in Europe. It's so difficult that the first time I rode it I crashed five times—and I didn't finish.

It took me three more tries before I finished. The combination of trying to stay with the leaders, negotiating the cobblestones, and battling the fatigue make it very difficult for an inexperienced cyclist to do well in this race.

The important thing in the classics isn't so much being the strongest rider as knowing the race itself. Many of the classics, because their courses are so difficult, favor the local riders who are more familiar with the course. After I turned professional, it took me two to three years of racing to learn how to race the classics.

In the 1984 Paris-Roubaix, for example, I was not completely familiar with the difficult Arenberg Forest section of cobblestones. But I knew that I had to be ahead at that point to have any chance of doing well. I had crashed twenty or thirty miles before the Arenberg Forest and had to chase for quite some time. I just caught the pack as we entered the forest and its old, disjointed and wet cobbles.

All I remember is trying to make it to the front. But I wasn't sure exactly where the course suddenly changes from a modern, wide road to an unbelievable path of what looks like small tombstones sticking out from the ground. All of a sudden, I came onto the rough stones, and I felt mud flying all over my face. And the next thing I remember was lying on the cobblestones with mud all over my body. That section of cobbles is so bad that it's impossible to get back on your bike from a standing start because you can't find your balance.

As I got up I noticed that my whole team had crashed right behind me. I knew that this wasn't going to be my day.

I then had to run with my bike to the end of the Arenberg Forest section— one kilometer up the road. I rode for five more miles and after hearing that I had lost six or seven minutes, I packed it in.

I swore I would never come back. But, of course, the following year I did and placed fourth.

Point-to-point races in America are much shorter and not as dangerous. In a point-to-point race you can always use the unknown factor of a new hill or a blind turn to your advantage tactically if you want to break things up. Remember, though, that if you're not familiar with a course yourself, you should be cautious in whizzing down a hill.

Another common type of racing in Europe is stage racing. Most of the famous European stage races—like the Tour de France—are made up of any number of point-to-point races. When all the point-to-point races are added up, they make a big circle or tour—that's why many of the top European stage races are called tours.

In stage racing, the winner is the man with the overall lowest elapsed time. That means that every day, the entire pack is clocked and those times are added together as the race progresses. The man who completes the stage race in the shortest overall added time is the winner. The overall winner is usually the man who has covered the course and all its challenges—flats, time trials, mountains—the most consistently. He is considered the best overall athlete.

Many stage races, like the Tour de France and the Coors Classic, have othe sideline competitions. A common award is the best sprinter's jersey. Unlike the overall winner, the best sprinter is the cyclist who finishes with the highest number of accumulated points. The points are established for all the stage finishes in any way the promoters want. A lot of people wonder why the best sprinter should't be the overall winner. But what they don't realize is that the fastest rider in a sprint is rarely the fastest cyclist up a mountain. And you lose a lot more time in the mountains than you do on the flat stages, because it is easy to draft on the flats. In the mountains you're fighting against gravity and speeds are too low for drafting, so every rider is on his own. In the end, sprinting is a great skill but only one aspect of stage racing—the best sprinter is nothing more than a highly skilled specialist.

Another common award is the king-of-the-mountains jersey. The king of the mountains is similar to the best sprinter in that he competes for points. Unlike the best sprinter, the king of the mountains competes for points on mountain summits. The king-of-the-mountains points are usually awarded to the first rider who crosses a line painted at the summit of each significant hill. Like the best sprinter, he is a specialist.

Stage racing—especially the kind I do on the European pro circuit—takes a very special set of skills and tremendous fitness and stamina. The great national tours like the Tour de France last a little over three weeks and cover close to twenty-five hundred miles. The route takes the racers over mountains, on cobbles, sometimes in tremendous heat, wind, and cold. But this kind of racing also takes a tremendous amount of tactical savvy. You have to know how to pace yourself, when to attack, when to lay back (rarely). Finally, if you ride right, you'll find your fitness improving tremendously as the race progresses. If you don't learn when and how to take mental breaks you'll be shattered by the end of a stage race.

Stage racing is generally known to be very taxing. But I think you can only realize *how* taxing after you race the Tour de France. You can't say that professional bike racing is ever easy. But in the Tour de France, the level of intensity is so high that I honestly believe we're approaching some kind of human limit. What's unique about the Tour is that it requires the same level of endurance as the longest races *and* the same level of intensity as many shorter races. That's an awesome combination.

The first year I rode the Tour de France, 1984, I had raced practically every other major professional race. I had won the Tour de l'Avenir, which was supposedly the junior version of the Tour. *Supposedly*. In that first Tour, I couldn't believe there was never any letup. I could never recuperate. In the first Pyrenees stage, suffering from bronchitis, I was in so much pain that I could barely see! My legs felt as if they were no longer there. I kept pushing and getting dropped on the climbs. All I could think about was quitting.

Most of the stage racing in America is quite different. The longest American stage race is the Coors Classic, which is now a little over a thousand miles long and lasts two-and-a-half weeks. I had a nice chuckle a few years ago when I read somewhere that a panel of American cyclists rated the Coors Classic more difficult than the Tour de France. This made me smile because the Coors Classic is shorter, has less competition, and has climbs not nearly as steep. The funny thing was that the panel of experts had never ridden the Tour de France. But after American pro teams began to ride the Tour, Americans learned how hard the Tour is. Of course, the Coors may not be the Tour de France, but it's definitely one of the best races in the world.

There are few, if any, point-to-point races in American stage racing. Because all the events except the Coors Classic are amateur events, the distances are considerably shorter. Most of the stages are circuit road races or criterium stages, where it's much easier to stay with the pack. And with a little experience (or a lot of talent), you can use a little tactical know-how to break out near the finish. Although American racing has become much

The greatest cycling races are the national tours, the three-week stage races such as the famous Tour de France. Here, the pack climbs the Dolomites in the Tour of Italy, a race comparable to the Tour de France but not as competitive.

more intense over the past few years, it's still possible for a less-talented but savvy rider to win in America because the courses are less demanding than those in Europe.

Nevertheless, stage racing of any kind is a tremendous challenge. You have to play your card at just the right time, without using all your energy. It's something that only experience and tremendous fitness can teach you.

There are few variations on road racing. Australia and Switzerland are the two countries where handicap racing is common. Riders are given time handicaps according to their past performances, and a large part of the suspense here is watching the pack catch the leaders. Some stage races are so disconnected that they are actually accumulated results of otherwise unrelated events. That's the case, for example, with the Tour of Texas, a major early-season event.

TIME TRIALING

One of the most intense road-racing events is the individual time trial. This is not a pack race. Instead the riders set off alone at regularly spaced intervals (depending on the length of the event) and are clocked at the finish. The rider with the overall lowest time is the winner. Because there is no way to draft off a rival, and because the only judge is the clock, the individual time trial has been called the "race of truth."

Riding a time trial teaches you to maintain a steady pace. To do well in time trials one of the most important things to do is to relax your body. Any tension will rob you of energy and ultimately slow you down.

The most common kind of individual time trial in America is the twenty-five-mile distance. Most of these races have an out-and-back course that has the competitor ride twelve-and-a-half miles down a road, turn around, and return. These events tend to be held on flat courses and measure speed more than power.

In Europe, time trials are much more diverse and courses vary over all distances. The granddaddy of time trials events is the Grand Prix des Nations, a forty-five-mile French event that includes very steep hills in the area outside Nice and dangerous descents along the French Riviera. I've ridden both the American and European time trials, and I'm afraid the twenty-five-mile American event is scant preparation for what you'll find in Europe. But it's a lot better than nothing at all.

There's also a team trial event. The most common team time trial in the amateur branch of the sport is a four-man event that covers one hundred kilometers (or sixty-two miles). In the 1984 Olympics, the American team of Ron Kiefel, Roy Knickman, Davis Phinney, and Andy Weaver won the bronze medal in the team time trial. In 1987, the fifty-kilometer team trial for women was inaugurated.

I did quite well in the team time trial as an amateur. I got a bronze medal in the 1978 world championship and again in the 1979 title race. Team time

The most intense type of road racing is the individual time trial. Here, Swiss time trial specialist Daniel Gisiger is on his way to winning the 1983 Grand Prix des Nations, the most prestigious time trial victory for a professional. Note Gisiger's specialized time trial equipment: the radial-laced spokes on his front wheel, the one-piece skinsuit. Today's time trial bikes have evolved even further, with spokeless moon-disk wheels and in some cases a smaller front wheel.

The Paris-Roubaix classic is the most prestigious and feared of point-to-point races. The last portion of the course is covered with cobblestones. Here, I'm doing my best to stay balanced on the misshapen cobbles of the Arenberg Forest section of the 1986 Paris-Roubaix race (I'm the rider with the goggles).

trials at the amateur level can be grueling. It's two-and-a-half hours of all-out effort. It requires excellent technique, especially in drafting (riding in the slipstream of the rider in front of you to reduce wind resistance).

TRACK RACING

Although road racing is more popular today both in America and Europe, there was a time when track racing was the biggest ticket in cycling. In America, until the 1930s, professional track cycling—mostly concentrated around the Eastern seaboard—was one of the major professional sports. Track legend Bobby Walthour was so popular as a great cyclist that he was often compared to Babe Ruth. In Europe, track cycling has never died out, although it has gradually lost its popularity since the end of World War II.

As in road racing, there are many different types of track racing, each suited to different athletes. The shortest event, the two-hundred-meter match sprint, lasts about ten seconds. The longest event is the six-day race, a two-man event spread out over ten hours a day for six days.

Unlike road racing, track racing has a well-defined, closed forum: the bicycle track or velodrome. Because speeds can be very high, bike tracks all have banked turns. The very shortest tracks can have turns as steeply banked as fifty degrees and more. Although the standard length for an outdoor track is 333 meters (three laps to a kilometer), bike tracks come in all sizes. Many of the older outdoor tracks are as long as 500 meters. Most of the outdoor tracks have a cement-based surface that is smooth and can withstand bad weather. But some outdoor tracks, such as the Vigorelli stadium in Milan, Italy, and the Mexico City track, are built out of wood. These surfaces deteriorate quickly, though, and have been restored many times.

Most of the indoor tracks have to be much shorter to fit in a stadium. These tracks are removable tracks that can fit into a major sports arena like Madison Square Garden or the Forum in Los Angeles. The removable tracks are sometimes made out of an inexpensive wood, often little more than sheets of plywood nailed or screwed together. They are usually used for six-day races that hope to attract large crowds and are sometimes as short as 150 meters with extremely steep bankings.

There are also some permanent indoor tracks. The only one in North America was built for the 1976 Olympics in Montreal, Canada. This track has a beautiful 250-meter wood surface—it's considered one of the finest indoor tracks in the world. Unfortunately, the building is not often available to cyclists and is underused when it is. There are many permanent indoor tracks in Europe, where six-day bicycling racing is a major attraction. Ironically, there are only two indoor tracks in France, in Paris and Grenoble, although the Grenoble track was burned to the ground in 1985. There are half a dozen major cycling arenas in West Germany, where cycling is not nearly as popular as it is in France, but where six-day bike racing enjoys particular popularity. Most of the European indoor tracks are 150 to 250 meters long.

The one thing most people notice right away about track cycling is the different bike. Unlike road (or mountain) bikes, track bikes have only one gear on a track. Because clearances are very tight and there's no need to change gears, track bikes have a fixed sprocket and no hand brakes. When people first hear this, they simply can't believe that track racers don't fall like flies. Well, it's really not very dangerous, but it does take skill to ride a track bike.

With a fixed gear, you can't stop pedaling. In other words, there is no freewheel for coasting. That means that you can pretty much control your speed by applying reverse pressure to the pedals. In a track situation with steep turns and tight clearances, this back-and-forth pressure on the pedals is actually more fine-tuned than a hand brake. At the finish, you simply apply a lot of pressure on the pedals, and you'll be able to come rapidly to a stop.

If the fixed gear is so practical on the track why don't road racers use it? Well, simply put, the track doesn't have nearly the hazards of the road. There are no downhills, where the fixed gear would be dangerous. There's no traffic.

To ride a track bike takes a certain degree of bike-handling skill and

Soviet track star Sergei Kopylov demonstrates the kind of bike-handling skills track riders develop. Note the banking on the curve of the track behind Kopylov.

experience. Most track bikes are built much more stiffly than road bikes. They are usually more responsive and nervous. If you want to ride on the track, you should already have plenty of experience riding a bike on the road—track riding is not suited to someone just learning how to ride a bike.

A track racer must learn how to use the track. The first time you go to a track you'll probably be impressed with how steep the banking on the turn looks. Most tracks require that you ride at a minimum speed on the bankings, or you'll slip off and fall off. The steeper the banking, the faster you have to ride to stay on. One of the steepest tracks in history was the old Berlin track, which had fifty-seven-degree bankings—racers had to ride at least twenty-seven miles per hour not to crash. This track no longer exists—it was destroyed by the Allies in 1944.

The most spectacular of the track events is the match sprint. This is one of cycling's oldest and most prestigious races. It is a test of pure speed. The match sprints are run off in heats of two or three riders. Although match sprinting used to be run at variable distances, today the distance is standardized at a thousand meters. But only the last two hundred meters are clocked, leaving the riders free to slowly battle for position in the first eight hundred meters. In most races, the first eight hundred meters are a tactical game of cat-and-mouse.

Although there are no set tactics, match sprinters like to start the sprint—in the last two hundred meters—a few feet behind their opponent. This gives them a draft in the initial burst of acceleration. The opponent, open to the wind, has to work much harder to ride at the same speed. At the finish, the rider in second position often uses the energy saved by drafting to dash around to win at the finish.

A few sprinters, though, have such a powerful initial burst of acceleration that they can sprint in the lead in the last two hundred meters.

It's often said that the great match sprinters are born, not made. To a certain extent that's true. It's an event that requires a tremendous amount of brute power. It's this power that creates the speed of sprinters. It's an event for athletes who have a high percentage of fast-twitch muscles. The fast-twitch muscle fiber reacts more quickly to nervous impulses—in layman's term, it's speed muscle. Although extensive training can increase your fast-twitch content somewhat, it's often a small increment. But some match sprinters make up for their lack of physical ability with a cunning sense of tactics.

Personally, I've only ridden a few match sprints, in my early days in California. Since my body didn't match the specific requirements for a top mach sprinter, I concentrated on the kind of racing that is best suited to me—road racing.

An event that's very close to match sprinting is the thousand-meter (or kilometer) individual time trial. Unlike the match sprint this is an individual

American road-racing star Connie Carpenter riding to victory in the 1983 pursuit championship. Note the special "longhorn" handlebars, the lack of brakes, and the lightweight, aerodynamic track frame.

event, in which each rider is timed separately. At the end of the event, the rider with the lowest time wins. Because you are not riding against an opponent, there are no tactics to employ. The kilometer, known as the kilo, is an event of pure, brute power. It's an all-out effort that lasts a little over a minute. Because it is so short, it's an event that has many of the same requirements as match sprinting: brute power and fast-twitch muscle. Some match sprinters are good kilo men. But for the most part, each event has its own specific training schedule, and racers rarely mix the two events anymore.

One common misconception about the short-distance track events is that since they're short they require only short-distance, easy training. The truth is that the top sprinters and kilometer riders train close to 350 miles a week, with an emphasis on speed and intensity. It's not easy at all.

The middle-distance track event is the individual pursuit. Ranging in distance from three thousand meters for women and junior men to four thousand meters for amateur men and five thousand meters for professionals, the individual pursuit is cycling's version of running the mile. It's short enough to be intense and long enough to require real endurance. To me this is the event that requires the highest level of fitness of the track events.

Unlike the running mile, the pursuit, as the name indicates, is an event in which two riders chase each other around the track. The riders start out and finish at opposite ends of the track. Although the opponent can be used to pace and push yourself, the real race in pursuit is against the clock. After all the riders—set off in heats of two—have finished the event, the rider with the lowest overall time is the winner.

The pursuit is exciting to watch and exhilarating to ride. It's also a tremendous mental game, as riders often try to push each other beyond their limits to get ahead. Sometimes this works, leaving your opponent exhausted. But you can also exhaust yourself.

Because the pursuit is much longer than the match sprint or the kilometer, it's an event that's suited to road riders. In fact, I would say that training for road racing is often the best way to prepare for the pursuit. At the junior world championships in Argentina in 1979, I had never ridden a pursuit race in competition when I won the silver medal. The principal reason I did so well was that I had been training very intensely for the road race, which was held a few days later. Most of the top pursuit world champions are either road racers or riders who ride many road races to stay in shape. In fact, many pursuit world champions are also among the best world-class road riders. I feel that one reason American pursuiters have not been very successful at the international level is that many of them don't train themselves as road riders.

There's also a team pursuit race, which is ridden by amateur men only, over four thousand meters. This is a spectacular-looking event that combines high-tech machinery with clockwork precision and a lot of speed.

Many track programs include a points race, which is usually about an hour long. This is a race that has a pack, just like most road races. Every few laps or so, the pack sprints for points on a finish line. At the finish, the rider with the most points is declared the winner. One variation on the points race is the elimination race, in which the last man over the line every few laps or so is eliminated. Because these races often have big packs snaking along the tracks at high speeds, they can be spectacular—and dangerous.

MOTOR-PACING

One of the oldest forms of track racing is motor-pacing. Riders on special bikes wearing large crash helmets tuck behind motorcycles on the track. This is a specialized area of cycling that was the rage in the 1920s and 1930s, when there was no limit to the size or power of the motorcycle. In those days, speeds of eighty miles per hour were common in motor-paced races. But accidents and deaths were just as common too. Since then, strict limits have been placed on the power of the motorcycles. A minimum weight has also been imposed, to make sure they stay firmly attached to the track surface. As a result, speeds of fifty miles per hour are the norm today. But it's still a very dangerous sport. The motor-pacers—known as stayers—ride in packs behind their motorcycles, riding in the draft of the motor-pacers, circling the bike tracks at fifty miles per hour. It's quite a sight.

The riders have to wear special, old-fashioned crash helmets that have changed little since the 1930s. The bikes have a small front wheel with a very strong construction. Bars and tubing are reinforced. The forks are turned into the frame so the rider can be as close to the motorcycle as possible.

The motorcycles, too, are unique. They're custom-made machines— most of them very old. The driver sits on a special seat that makes him literally stand up to provide the rider behind with the best shield against the wind. The motorcycles have a roller behind the rear wheel so that if the cyclist grazes it he won't crash.

In motor-pacing, the drivers are often as important as the riders. For the most part they're former motor-pacers who are very familiar with the sport. They know when to accelerate, when to slow down; the best ones have a feather touch on the throttle.

But motor-pacing is a dying sport, almost a novelty today. Most of the riders (and drivers) are older men who are part-time riders, even if they're officially professionals. In 1983, for example, fifty-one-year-old Dutchman Mathé Pronk captured the silver medal at the world championships.

In America motor-pacing is basically nonexistent. In fact, when Colorado Springs hosted the 1986 cycling world championships, it was decided not to include any motor-pacing events there because the heavy motorcycle wheels would tear up what's considered one of the fastest tracks in the world.

KEIRIN RACING

One branch of cycling that's growing is the Japanese institution of keirin racing. A staple in Japan, keirin (literally translated as "competition wheels") is one of the four legalized forms of betting in that country. Although keirin has been popular in Japan since World War II, the sport became internationally recognized when Koichi Nakano, keirin's top rider, won a unique streak of world professional match sprint championships that stood at ten in 1986.

In 1980, keirin racing was added to the program of the world championships. Keirin is basically close to match sprinting. But instead of being run off in heats of two or three riders, keirin includes nine or ten riders. It's a setup very similar to horse racing. Ironically, Koichi Nakano didn't win the first keirin world championsip—the Japanese riders don't compete in this world championship event. Keirin riders in Japan win a percentage of the bets, and feel they cannot afford to go to the world championships where they are unpaid.

THE SIX-DAY RACE

The biggest show of track racing is the six-day race. Originally developed and promoted in Great Britain and the United States, six-day racing was one of the biggest tickets at places like Madison Square Garden and Chicago Stadium. But with the 1930s and the Depression, six-day bike racing died out in America. Although a few six-day races have been held since then—Madison Square Garden 1961, Los Angeles 1973, Detroit 1974, Montreal 1976—the sport has never become popular again in America.

In Europe, it's a major winter attraction. Stadiums fill up as many of the road racing stars take to track bikes and the "boards," as wooden tracks are known, to peddle their fame for fairly large contracts. European sixes are run according to the modern two-man formula. Although riders may be on the track as much as six hours a day each, there are only a few hours of intense racing each evening, usually about prime time, when tickets are most expensive.

The European stadiums are often lavishly decorated with banners and flags. In the infields, chic cafés serve dinners at hefty prices—getting a table in the infield of the Paris six-day is something like having a luxury box at Texas Stadium to watch the Dallas Cowboys.

Six-day racing is a combination of points racing, pursuits, sprinting, and eliminations. It's really a dazzling show of everything track racing has to offer—it's track racing's version of stage racing.

OTHER KINDS OF CYCLING

Although bicycles are generally used to get you from one point to another—whether it be commuting, touring, or racing—there are a few special kinds of cycling. One of those is the sport of acrobatic cycling, which is especially popular in Czechoslovakia. At first glance, acrobatic cycling looks like circus stunts on bikes. I'm sure that's how the sport got its start. But today acrobatic cycling is a serious, if minor sport that has strict rules and an international federation, and features world championships. An acrobatic cycling meet, in fact, is not unlike a gymnastics competition, in that it mixes sport and acrobatics.

Another cycling sport that's popular in Eastern Europe is cycle ball. This is basically soccer on bikes. The riders have special one-speed bicycles and rush around a court kicking what looks like a big volleyball. A netminder sits in front of the goal on a big bike, which he can move around to protect the goal mouth.

Bike racing has many variations. The only constant is that you must pedal on your own power. One important decision to make is what kind of cycling is right for you. You may feel that you want to do only some light touring. Perhaps you will be most comfortable with mountain biking.

If you want to race, you'll need to learn to test all the waters to learn what you like. I especially recommend that young riders get a taste of all of cycling's disciplines. A young rider who may feel uncomfortable with road racing might find he is better suited to match sprinting on the track. But if he never tries it, he won't know. What's more, all the different disciplines in cycling are complementary. You'll learn about the sport and improve at the same time.

Whatever kind of cycling you decide is right for you, you'll find that no other forms of exercise can give you as much speed without motors and as much physical fitness for so little pain and discomfort. The world of cycling can indeed offer you much.

3

How to

Pick

Your Bike

*P*icking your first bike is probably one of the most important things you'll ever do as a cyclist. If you get the wrong bike, it could discourage you from cycling. Things have changed quite a bit since I picked my first racing bike in 1976 at Rick's Bike Shop in Reno. Back then, the market was flooded with a few very expensive European bikes and a lot of cheaper but really very poor middle-to lower-range bikes. If I had listened to the salesman who tried to talk me out of buying an expensive racing bike, I probably would have gotten a bike that wasn't right and didn't fit properly. Trying to race on less than a top-quality bike would have been such a headache that I would have been discouraged and might have given up cycling.

Keep in mind that you want your bike to fit your needs. If you plan to ride your bike only around the block or to the store for milk and eggs, your requirements in a bike are far different than if you tour long distances over the weekend or race competitively.

For most serious cyclists, I recommend a racing bike. Racing bikes used to cost an arm and a leg—at least $1,000 if not considerably more. But today, thanks to the popularity of cycling and the proliferation of high-volume, high-tech manufacturers, you can find a complete bike for racing or touring

The Parts of a Bicycle

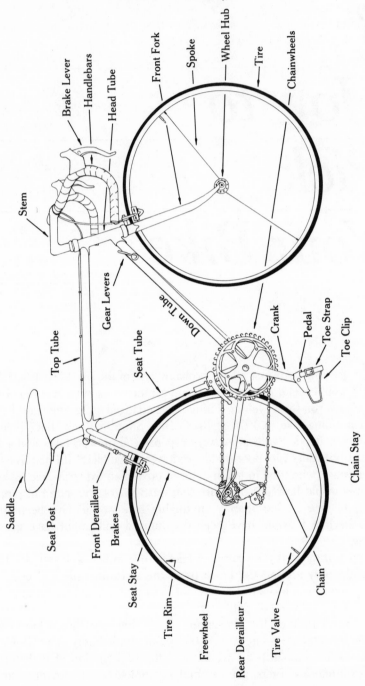

for as low as $500. A bike in this range will have all the features you would expect to find on practically any professional bike, except that most of the equipment will usually be Japanese instead of the more expensive Italian lines. But, believe me, that could almost be a blessing in disguise, as I'll explain later. You might even be able to find a good racing bike for as little as $400 (or even $300). I think $500 is a good watershed.

At that price you can buy what I call a "complete" bike, a bike that has all the features of any top-of-the-line machine, except in a slightly heavier or less-well-finished variant. In fact, a good bike in the $500 range today is 96 percent of the value of a bike priced at $1,000 or more.

Maybe you're wondering what's so great about a "complete" bicycle. Maybe you think only serious racers need this kind of bike. The fact is that a "complete" bike is just like the less expensive models, but better. For anybody. It's lighter and therefore easier to ride. It runs more smoothly, it's easier to fix. It'll make just about any kind of cycling more enjoyable.

Of course, you may not need a "complete" bike. You may not need alloy handlebars that are lighter and sturdier than their steel counterparts found on the cheaper bikes. You may not need strong double-butted tubes (tubing that is thicker at its ends) that is not only lighter and sturdier but also much longer-lived than straight gauge tubing found on the cheaper models. You may not be able to afford a "complete" bike. But in most cases if you settle for a bike for $150 to $300, you're getting about 50 percent of the value of the $500 bike. And that's a big price to pay for a savings of a $150 or so.

Whatever price you buy at, the important thing you have to remember— and many people make a mistake here—is that your bike has to fit perfectly. I don't care if you go out and buy an aerodynamic, gold-plated, limited-edition, $3,000 Italian monster machine; if it doesn't fit right it'll be just about as useless as a clunker with fox tails and an air horn.

I just can't emphasize too much how important the fit is—it's the single most crucial determining factor in purchasing a bicycle. A less expensive bike that fits right will increase your endurance, performance, and comfort much more than a sleek racing machine that doesn't fit. In fact fit is so important that I've devoted the entire next chapter to it.

MOST PEOPLE SHOULD PICK A RACING BIKE

The first step in picking a bike is to ask yourself what kind of cycling you intend to do. Some people want to get a bike to tour on the weekends. Others want to commute to work on their bike and then take it off-road on Saturdays and Sundays. Still others look to their bike as a source of serious, daily exercise. Some of those eventually turn to racing. There are tourists who enjoy hundred-mile century rides and the occasional overnight, long-distance tour.

I believe most people should look for what's generally called a racing bike. When I say racing bike I mean any bicycle that has pretty tight frame geometry, good alloy components, drop handlebars and at least ten gears. It should also weigh no more than twenty-three or twenty-four pounds, depending on your size. Don't let the term *racing bike* frighten you. You don't have to be a racer to own a racing bike any more than you have to be a champion marathoner to own a pair of running shoes.

A racing bike will do two things for you. First of all, it will provide you with a good, responsive machine that will transmit your effort in the most efficient way. And when you're huffing and puffing up a steep hill you'll be thankful for that. But also, you'll discover that the racing bike is an amazingly versatile machine. If all you need is a bike for general recreational cycling and short trips, it'll serve you fine. But if, on the other hand, you want to graduate to serious touring or racing, the racing bike is the perfect machine for the fastest, most enjoyable ride. If, initially, you buy something less than a racing bike and later find that your enthusiasm is growing, you might find yourself going back to your bike store every so often to upgrade to a better machine—hardly a good way to save money.

If you're genuinely interested in buying a bike to ride around the block or to have around as an occasional hobby, the question you have to ask yourself is how much you're willing to spend. I would still recommend a racing bike for around $400 or $500, what I call the "complete" bike. It's simply a better machine. And compared to what you're going to find for $150 to $300, it's twice the value.

If you want to stick with a lower-priced bike, I think the best values can be found in the $220 range. Here you have a bike that is considerably less expensive than the $500 "complete" bike but still has some of its features. At this price range, you want to look for features like double-butted tubing, quick-release hubs, alloy handlebars, an alloy cotterless crankset, a padded saddle, and high-pressure clincher or wired-on tires.

At about $170, you're going to find straight-gauge tubing, heavier and not as resistant; steel handlebars, heavy, subject to rust; heavy wheels with low-pressure clinchers; and an inferior crankset. At this range, the average bike weighs about thirty pounds, instead of the twenty-seven pounds that $250 bikes average. If you decide that you want to cycle more seriously, this bike will quickly become a handicap.

Many people dislike the low position forced on them by the drop handlebars when they first get on a racing bike. At first, it may be a little difficult to get used to. But you'll discover that for any serious riding, your body weight will be balanced much more equally with drop handlebars than with the traditional upright bars; with the drop bars most riders have about 55 percent of their body weight concentrated on the saddle and about 45 percent on the bars. In the long run the drop handlebars are much more comfortable because there is much less stress on your lower back because you can adopt several different hand positions. And, of course, the drop bars are also more aerodynamically efficient, resulting in a faster ride for less exertion—and that means less fatigue over the long run.

One model I don't recommend is the "mixte" or ladies' bike. This type of bike has two thin tubes extending down from the front of the frame instead of a top tube. The reason people buy mixte frames is that they are afraid they will have trouble standing above the top tube. The truth is, if the frame fits you should always clear the top tube easily. In addition the ladies' or mixte frame is considerably weaker and less stiff.

There are a couple of exceptions to the rule that cyclists are better off with a racing bike. The first is people who want to do a lot of off-road riding. For that purpose, a mountain bike is a much better choice than a conventional racing bike. This is also true if you commute in an inner city such as Manhattan or Chicago, in which case the mountain bike, with its wide, gnarly tires and upright position (which makes you more visible) will provide you with an element of comfort and safety that the lighter, leaner racing bike cannot. Most of the bicycle delivery people in Manhattan are using mountain bikes, with good reason: They are safer and more comfortable. I've ridden a mountain bike quite a few times in the winter, and I've found it to be tremendous fun and very practical in negotiating difficult terrain. But remember, any time you want to take a long road ride, the mountain bike will be a serious handicap. It is much heavier, the thick tires develop a great deal of resistance and friction—much more than a racing bike with narrow tires—and the upright handlebar position will pinch your lower back and cause a lot of strain.

Another off-road bicycle is the cyclo cross bike. This looks a lot more like the conventional racing bike, with drop handlebars and relatively thin tires. But the cyclo cross bike is even more specialized—it's intended primarily for serious cyclo cross racing. The cyclo cross bike is not really intended for extended road riding. Just as with the mountain bike, the cyclo cross bike has special gnarly tires. Unlike the mountain bike it most often has a specific set of gear ratios not suited to road racing. The pure cyclo cross bike also has an extended wheelbase that makes it less responsive on paved roads than a road bicycle. Also, you'll find that dealers carrying cyclo cross bikes and spare parts are hard to find.

The other exception is people who want to do a lot of very long touring and are looking for a very comfortable ride. In that case you'll want to get something that looks very much like a racing bike but has a longer wheelbase and gentler frame geometry for a slightly softer ride. The serious touring bike, which you can equip with paniers to carry a good amount of camping gear, should also provide you with fifteen gears for climbing steep inclines while carrying heavy loads, center pull brakes, and lights for night riding.

Serious tourists need to buy a bike that has good overall geometry, which, ironically, is not really any different from the geometry racers need (although racing bikes today are often built with head and seat tubes that are too steep). Of course, a tourist needs special brazed-on bosses for attaching racks that hold touring paniers. Don't look at a bike simply because it has the label "touring" bike. Top professional racers have the same needs as long-distance tourists, because their races are very long. What you want to look for—even as a tourist—is a seat tube angle of about seventy-two or seventy-three degrees for a fifty-six centimeter frame. (See chart for the relationship between angles and sizes.) Your head tube angle should be about seventy-three or seventy-four degrees for the same fifty-six-centimeter frame.

This provides you with the ideal general bike, not one that is suited only for "touring" or "racing," but one that is suited for riding.

Of course, tourists have specific needs. A classic touring bike also comes equipped with a triple-chainring crankset that provides the rider with fifteen, eighteen, or (occasionally) twenty-one gears, depending on freewheel sizes (five, six, or seven sprockets). Because long-distance tourists often tackle high mountain passes while loaded down with equipment, the specialized touring bike should have a wide-ratio derailleur capable of handling freewheel sprocket sizes ranging from fourteen to thirty-six.

A good touring bike comes equipped with aluminum racks, three water-bottle bosses, and fenders.

Touring bike prices can vary from $500 for a Japanese model to $860 for an American one to $2,000 and more for a custom-made touring bike from American and English manufacturers, who—more than the Italians who specialized in the racing bicycle market—have traditionally built beautiful touring bikes.

THE SECOND STEP:
CHOOSING THE RIGHT DEALER

It's tough, of course, to know exactly what kind of bike you want before you see what's available. That's why the second step in picking your bike—choosing the right dealer—is so important. Your dealer will be the person you'll have to trust to outfit you correctly.

There are occasionally people selling bikes who don't really know what they are doing. Like any salespeople, many bike shop dealers work on commission, which tends to bend their objectivity to a certain degree.

This is why it's so important to pick the right dealer. Most areas in the United States have a good selection of bike shops to choose from. It's still a very rustic industry and most bike shops tend to be small businesses run by cycling enthusiasts. Nevertheless, it's usually fairly easy to find a good shop and a good salesperson who will help you.

Pick a bike shop that carries the kind of bike you're looking for, has a large selection so you can make an educated choice, and has professional people who are willing to go out of their way to help you with your purchase.

A new concept in helping cyclists to equip themselves is the Team Le-Mond Center. I will be helping train some of the dealers, teaching them how to sell the customer the right kind of bike. Most of all, I will emphasize the importance of the right fit when buying a bike.

THE BIKE SHOP DILEMMA: SMALL OR BIG?

It can be difficult to tell a good bike shop from an average one. Sometimes the very biggest bike shops are run like chain-line assemblies and will carry only a wide variety of low-and middle-range bikes. But that's not always the case. There are some very big and very famous bike shops that have an excellent selection of all kinds of bikes in all the price ranges and a professional staff that knows exactly how to help you.

On the other hand, small bike shops can sometimes provide you with much more personal attention. Many smaller bike shops are run by dyed-in-the-wool cycling enthusiasts, who will bend over backward to steer you the right way even if it means they'll make less money. But this isn't always true either—some small shops tend to have a very limited selection. Often they will carry only one line, and you could have trouble finding exactly what's right for you within that brand. Other small shops are geared almost exclusively toward the serious racer; the salespeople there might try to convince you that anything but the top-of-the-line equipment is not worth owning, and that's simply not true.

My coauthor, Kent Gordis, took an informal survey of bike shops all around California and the Eastern seaboard. After visiting quite a few stores he found that there was, unfortunately, no easy way to distinguish among them. One shop in the San Francisco Bay Area looked very promising from the outside but turned out to carry mostly a single brand of bicycle that didn't provide the best value for the dollar. Another shop, in a nearby town, promised little from its drab, small storefront. But here the selection of brands was much more complete and, most important, the salesperson turned out to be a thoroughly knowledgeable and charming young man who directed Kent to the best value in every range.

Here are a few of the telltale signs of a good shop:

1) Look at what kinds of bikes the store carries. If you notice a predominance of children's bicycles or BMX bicycles you're probably in the wrong place. Unless you're buying a bicycle for a younger person, this shop won't be able to provide you with an adequate value for training, touring, or racing. The same is true for the big-volume, "supermarket" bike shops that often cater to young people who want a bike as simple transportation. This kind of shop is especially common in college towns. If you want a bike for anything more than short-distance commuting or riding around the block, look for another store.

2) Once you find a shop that carries good racing, touring, and mountain bikes, look at the brand names. If you notice a preponderance of one brand, you may not get the kind of selection you need, though you might find the best value for you with that brand. To find out, of course, you'll need to do some comparison shopping. If the shop also carries a variety of mountain bikes, it is probably the kind of shop that will cater to the needs of most serious enthusiasts without being exclusively racing-oriented.

3) Look at all-important details. Does the shop have a complete selection of cycling clothing and shoes? Does it carry a full line of accessories and cycling-related paraphernalia? Make sure the shop has a full service department so that if anything goes wrong with your new bike the dealer will be able to fix it for you. One shop we visited had a one-year shop warranty on all new bicycles. That's a real plus.

4) Trust your own judgment. If the surroundings and the salesperson give you a good feeling and you're satisfied with the selection, you've probably found the right store for you. If, on the other hand, you get an uncomfortable feeling about the salesperson or the store, look around some more.

WHY FIT
IS SO IMPORTANT

Why is fit so important? Because the bicycle is not an inert machine like a car or a refrigerator, but a synergetic element that has to meld perfectly with your body to function efficiently. Once you're on your bike it becomes a part of you, like a piece of clothing that molds to your contours. You wouldn't run a marathon with a pair of shoes two sizes too big. For the same reason, you must be absolutely sure to pick a bike that fits right.

The first step in sizing your bike is already taken care of: deciding what kind of bike you want. Next, you should examine the frame geometry of the bike. The frame geometry refers to the angles between all the tubes on the frame. If you examine a bicycle frame closely, you'll notice that that central "diamond" is composed of four tubes of varying length. The first is a long vertical tube in the back that extends from the crankset up to the saddle. This is the *seat tube*. Extending from the top of the seat tube forward is a long horizontal tube. This is the *top tube*. The short, vertical tube, extending about three to six inches down from the top tube, is known as the *head tube*. Finally, there's a long diagonal tube connecting the frame—the *down tube*.

When cyclists talk about frame geometry, they usually refer to the angles of the seat and head tubes. These are the crucial angles because they determine, to a certain extent, the length of the wheelbase; that is, the distance between the front and rear wheels. Because bicycles don't have any suspension, the frame geometry is the only thing that can cushion the ride. A bicycle with "tight" angles—very upright seat and head tubes—will have a short wheelbase. The short wheelbase, with less mass, is tighter, provides less cushion. A bike with looser angles has shallower seat and head tubes and a longer wheelbase. With longer tubes and more mass, there is more cushion. This is the bicycle's only suspension (along with whatever cushion your seat provides). But more important, the seat tube angle determines the rider's position on the bike. And that's what's really important. In my experience as a racer and in the training camps I have held in the past few years, I have found that many top-of-the-line racing bikes have a seat tube angle that's so steep—about seventy-four degrees or more—that you can't get the seat far enough back to set up the perfect pedaling position.

For years frame builders have been steepening the seat tube angle to make an aggressive-looking bike that was thought to be more responsive. But it's gotten to the point that some of the bikes are built with a seat tube angle that's simply too steep. You really don't need such a steep seat and head tube.

There is an important correlation between your body type or size and your frame geometry. If you have a long femur (thigh bone), you will need a shallower *seat* tube in order to set up the proper pedaling position. If you have a short femur, you could use a steep seat-tube angle to set the right pedaling position.

The bicycles that I rode to win the 1983 professional world championship and then the 1986 Tour de France were built with relatively shallow angles, 72.5 degrees for the seat tube and 73 for the head tube. That never affected the bike's performance, but it allowed me to set up the ideal position. And that's what really gave me the performance edge.

Luckily, if you're just starting out, you'll find many bikes starting at $350 with the right seat-tube angle. When you look at the bike, of course, it's hard to tell what the right angle is—I can't tell the difference between a seventy-two-and a seventy-four-degree bike on sight, although I do know if my position's wrong when I'm riding the bike. If you're looking seriously at a bike, ask your dealer for some literature on that model. If he doesn't have any literature on the model you're interested in, ask him for the manufacturer's manual, which should have all the design specs.

THE MOST IMPORTANT ELEMENT: THE FRAME

The frame is the most important element on your bike. You can always change the components or the wheels if you don't like them. If your derailleur isn't shifting right, you can fix it or replace it. If you think your wheels are too heavy, you can replace them. But the frame, the most expensive single item, is the bike's heart and soul. It must be stiff, light, strong and—as I described—built with the right geometry to accommodate both performance and position.

The material that forms the frame is the tubing. Most "supermarket" bikes have *straight-gauge tubing*, barely one step up from ordinary pipe tubing. This kind of tubing tends to be heavy and unresponsive. It's not a good choice for somebody who wants to do serious racing or touring. If you buy a bicycle under $200 you'll find that many models are built of straight-gauge tubing. As you move to the $220 range, you'll find that most of the bikes are built with *double-butted* (or in some cases triple-butted) *tubing*. Double-butted tubing is light and made from a highly resilient steel alloy composed of chromium molybdenum, known in cycling jargon as CroMoly. Double-butted tubing is called that because its wall thickness increases near the ends. In other words, double-butted tubing is thicker near both ends and thinner in the middle. Double-butted tubing is lighter than straight-gauge tubing. It's also much more responsive because its geometry is better suited to a dynamic kind of effort. It will provide you with an efficient and strong frame that can serve you in just about any situation. *Triple-butted tubing* is usually found on bikes in the $500 range. Triple-butted tubing is the invention of Japanese manufacturers who reinforce their tubes not only at both ends but in the middle of the tube as well. This allows them to "butt" a lesser grade of tubing.

Of course, there are many different grades and brands of tubing, double-butted or otherwise. The less expensive the tubing, the thicker the tubing wall is, the heavier the frame will be. The higher-priced grades are composed of a higher grade of chromium molybdenum that allows them to have remarkably thin walls. The thinnest production tubing has a wall seventenths-of-a-millimeter thick.

Perhaps the best-known manufacturer of bicycle tubing is Reynolds, a British company unrelated to its American namesake, which produces aluminum foil. Other top tubing companies are Italy's Columbus, France's Vitus and Japan's Tange. Although cyclists like to disagree about the relative merits of these three tubing manufacturers, all produce top-grade products.

A few bikes are made from aluminum or graphite or a combination of both. For the most part, these frames are very expensive and are only used by racers looking to gain a slight competitive edge. Remember, aluminum is far more flexible than steel and you'll lose efficiency as you gain lightness. Personally, I've almost always ridden on a double-butted steel chrome molybdenum frame. I think it's the best compromise of strength and lightness.

I have had a special bike made of aluminum and graphite wrapped in kevlar built for me, but it's only in the experimental stages at this point. This is going to be one of the few frames that's both light and rigid at the same time. I think it has a great future.

For the most part, aluminum frames are not as rigid as the steel chromium molybdenum frames. In some cases the manufacturers add steel to make the aluminum more rigid. But that, of course, makes them heavier too. I would use an aluminum frame in a highly specialized hilly race like a time trial, in which the effort of fighting gravity provides a weight advantage despite the whippier qualities of aluminum.

The tubes that make up the frame are connected by bindings known as *lugs*. If you see an inexpensive frame that doesn't have lugs, but instead has tubes welded directly together, it most likely will not be a good quality bike. Welding tubes directly together forms a weak link, and also weakens the tubes by putting them through a great deal of metal fatigue. Direct welds are usually an indication that the whole bike will be of inferior quality. In most cases these bikes can be found in large retail outlets and sell for $80 to $120. For as little as $150 you can buy a bike with a lugged frame.

Lugs are used to braze the tubes together at low heat with a silver or brass welding material—they make for strong connections with a minimum of metal fatigue. Some bikes have short lugs, others have long lugs. That really doesn't make any difference. What is important is to make sure that the lugwork is done cleanly. Of course, it's nearly impossible to measure whether the tubes were joined together at the correct angles, without any bending, just by looking at them. But if you see some gaps or bubbles in the welds, this is usually a sign that the bike wasn't put together with very much care.

Some of the very expensive, high-end bicycles have a lugless design.

Although this would seem to contradict what I've just said, this lugless construction bears little relationship to the cheap, welded frames. These top-end lugless bikes are usually built with space-age materials, such as the light alloy titanium or a graphite compound wrapped by kevlar, or with special, oversized tubes. And usually what looks like a lugless construction from the outside simply means that the lugs are set on the inside of the tubes. (Again, unless you really have your heart set on one of these machines—usually $2,000 or more a pop—I doubt the extra expense is worth it for any but the rider most concerned with weight as a factor of performance.)

STARTING OUT

If you're just starting out, I would recommend looking at bikes in all the ranges, so you can see what the differences between the bikes are. On the cheapest bikes, of course, you'll find straight-gauge tubing and lugless construction. You'll also find that most of the cheap bikes have heavy steel components with outdated designs. These bikes rarely weigh in at less than thirty pounds, and that can be a real handicap. The more expensive, lighter bikes will have steel chrome molybdenum tubing, alloy components, and lighter wheels.

THE BEST BIKE
FOR THE BEST VALUE

Unlike the old days when you had to spend close to $1,000 to get a halfway decent bicycle, you'll find that there is now an excellent selection of quality bikes starting at about $350. In this range you'll find bikes that are—for all intents and purposes—racing bikes similar to the fancy $2,000 racing machines that I ride. They have frames that could easily be raced on and components very similar to the ones professional racers use, and they usually weigh in at twenty-three or twenty-four pounds, tops.

There are a few differences, of course. The main difference is that the midrange bicycles are almost exclusively made in factories in the Far East while the expensive bikes are usually made by frame builders, most often in Europe. In the midrange, however, even most of the European brands— often the best value at this price—are actually made in Taiwan, Korea, or Japan. They usually have frames that are machine-made by robots, as opposed to the expensive, hand-welded Italian bikes. And though the Asian frames certainly lack the attention to detail of the European bikes, they are biult solidly and, in some cases, with far more precision than the human eye can achieve.

When you look at one of these midrange bikes, you may be told that the frame geometry is too shallow for racing. But remember, most of the top-of-the-line bikes are built with seat tube angles so steep that you can't find your ideal position. If your midrange bike has a seat tube angle of seventy-three degrees (see Appendix C; ask the dealer to check the manufacturer's specifications), you're probably in better shape than with a bike whose price and seat tube angle are both steeper.

The midrange bikes also don't have the top-of-the-line Italian Campagnolo components that most pros use. Many people would never use anything else. The Japanese components you'll find in the midrange bikes are as good and occasionally better. The Campagnolo components are like a Mercedes—reliable, tried, tested, and dependable. The Japanese, on the other hand, have improved their product every year. The Japanese have been proven leaders for values in the mid-range. The Italians, however, have made a strong comeback and now provide an excellent product as well.

If, on the other hand, you have the money to spend, Campagnolo is definitely an excellent product. I would recommend it for anybody who wants to do serious racing; you'll be riding on the same equipment as everybody else and you'll have an easier time finding spare parts in case something breaks down.

Often, though, salespeople will pressure you into buying a much more expensive bike equipped with Italian components when you don't need it. Most of the time they honestly believe it's better. But if you're not very serious about racing you don't need them. You may get a bike that all the racers are using, but remember, there will be a tremendous increase in cost.

If you do buy a midrange Japanese bike, the one thing you will have to change if you want to get into racing is the wheels (as I explain below). But wheels are easily interchangeable and you can always use a second set.

WHEELS

Wheels are a key feature on any bike. Because they turn, the wheels exert a tremendous amount of centrifugal force on the bicycle. The heavier they are, the higyer this centrifugal force will be. And that centrifugal force makes each ounce on the wheels feel like two ounces. That's why switching to lighter wheels can be beneficial. But occasionally, centrifugal force in the wheels can be an advantage. This is especially true in a flat race where you can maintain a constant pace. Italian champion Francesco Moser understood this better than anybody else in his attempt to break the one-hour world record. Before him, riders had always equipped themselves with the lightest possible wheels. But Moser knew that once he got up to speed, he would maintain a constant pace during his record attempt. So Moser outfitted himself with heavy wheels that had rotating weights, to increase his centrifugal force and therefore his momentum. As with anything else on the bicycle, if you get something that's too light, you'll lose a great deal of rigidity and thus efficiency.

The axis of the wheel is the *hub*. Most cycling hubs have hard-forged steel bodies. There are two types of hubs: low-and high-flange. The *low-flange hub* is more common on the better bikes and consists only of a steel body and a very low flange, or circle, where the spoke heads are threaded through. The *high-flange hub*, on the other hand, has the same body but a larger circle extending at the ends into which the spokes are threaded.

Although high-flange hubs are slightly stiffer than the low-flange models and allow the use of shorter spokes, either hub is a good choice. Most racers prefer to use a low-flange hub on their road racing machines because this allows for a slightly softer ride. But if you find a good bike that happens to have a pair of high-flange hubs, don't worry about it. If you find later you want to get low-flange hubs, that'll be a good excuse to get a second set of wheels.

Most hubs have a steel axle that extends through the body of the hub and sticks out about half an inch, where it is attached to the frame. You'll discover that some very expensive models have titanium axles. Although this space-age metal is quite strong and very light, the overall weight saving is not great and this kind of axle is much more expensive. And if it ever breaks you'll have to spend a lot of money to replace it.

On many low-priced bikes the wheels are simply attached to the frame with massive *steel nuts*. This is not a good solution. Having two nuts means you'll have to carry two heavy wrenches whenever you need to take off the wheels (one wrench to hold the first nut steady while you loosen or tighten the other one). Any time you get a flat you'll really be in trouble if you don't have those wrenches. If you want to put your bike in the trunk of a car or take it on a plane, which means taking off the wheels in most cases, you're in for a lot of hard work.

Wheels can also be attached to the frame by *wingnuts*. Wingnuts have two inch-long "wings" that look like the rotors on a propeller. These wingnuts are a tremendous improvement on plain nuts. You'll be able to take your wheels off and put them back fairly quickly and without any wrenches. And there will be plenty of times when you'll want to do that.

But wingnuts also have their disadvantages. First, you still have to fasten them very tightly—otherwise the wheel can slip off, a dangerous situation. And with constant use, tightening and untightening wingnuts can damage the threads on the hub axle and warp the metal on your fork-and chainstays. Not good news.

The best bindings for wheels are *quick release levers*. This is the binding that's used by all bike racers or tourists, and any serious cyclist should have them. Originally invented in Italy in the 1930s, the quick release lever has an elliptical lock inside its main body that tightens the wheel firmly to the frame when the lever is turned inward.

The quick release lever actually forms a second axle within the axle, although it isn't "structural." At first, when people see a quick release skewer, they're afraid that the wheel's somehow going to pop off more easily than with a nut or wingnut attachment. But if your quick release lever is well tightened and directed to the back of the hub, there will be practically no danger of this. In fact, in my ten years of experience as a cyclist I have never seen a quick release lever come undone.

I read in a popular book on bicycle maintenance that unless you want to race seriously you shouldn't use quick release hubs. Instead, the book advised the traditional nut attachment. The argument the author used was that the quick release hub weighs a couple of ounces more than the traditional hub. I don't think that's a viable argument, especially if you count the weight of the two wrenches you'll need to carry. Although you probably won't need to make wheel changes in ten seconds or so as pro racers do, the convenience of the quick release hub is a benefit to any cyclist.

Connecting the hub to the rim are the *spokes*. Most lower-price bikes have heavy, spongy, straight-gauge spokes. Unless you're exceptionally heavy or do a lot of heavy-duty sprinting you'll never need the extra strength of straight-gauge spokes. All the better mid-and high-range bikes should have double-butted (or occasionally triple-butted) spokes. As with the tubing on the frame, double-butted spokes are lighter and are designed to absorb your pedaling force more efficiently.

Standard spokes have a circular cross-section (they feel round all the way around like a string of spaghetti). These are the kind most often used by racers. But some bikes will have aerodynamic spokes that have an elliptical cross-section. Looked at from the front, they are "flat" and therefore more aerodynamically efficient. These tend to be a little bit weaker than the traditional spokes and can be hard to replace when they break. They should be used only in special situations, such as time trials or triathlons, in which aerodynamics play an important role. And they're not necessary in a non-competitive situation.

Most stock bikes will be equipped with wheels that have thirty-six spokes, while top-of-the-line racing bikes have thirty-two-spoke wheels. I would recommend thirty-two spokes for racing and thirty-six for training (you want a training wheel to be very sturdy). Sometimes you may find a rear wheel that has forty spokes—this is quite common on tandems and bikes that have to take a heavy load. If you start looking around, though, you'll notice that many high-performance wheels have *fewer* than thirty-two spokes, usually twenty-eight, or twenty-four. Most of these wheels are used for very specialized races, such as flat time trials or track pursuit races. Unless you're

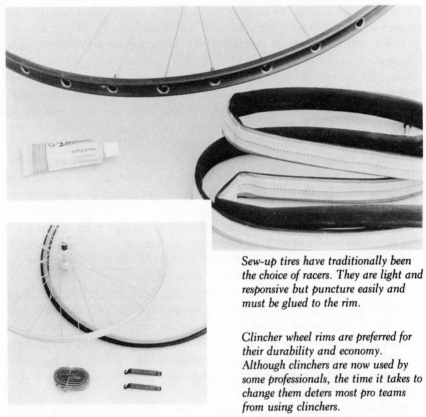

Sew-up tires have traditionally been the choice of racers. They are light and responsive but puncture easily and must be glued to the rim.

Clincher wheel rims are preferred for their durability and economy. Although clinchers are now used by some professionals, the time it takes to change them deters most pro teams from using clinchers.

competing in that kind of event, I would recommend you stick with the thirty-two-or thirty-six-spoke wheels. You'll have a stronger wheel (and a much easier time finding spare spokes if one ever breaks), because the spoke length varies according to the number of spokes fitted on each wheel. The fewer the spokes, the shorter each spoke is.

If you look closely at your wheel, you'll notice that the spokes don't simply extend straight up from the hub to the rim: They cross over. Most wheels that have thirty-two or thirty-six spokes cross over three or four times. That means that each spoke crosses three or four other spokes from hub to rim. Crossing over is a way of significantly increasing the strength of a wheel. Some wheelmakers even solder the spokes where they cross to further strengthen the wheel. Remember, if you have wheels with soldered spokes like this, you'll have a tough time fixing a broken spoke. (Note: Some very exceptional wheels have radial spoke patterns. On these wheels, the spokes don't cross over at all. These are usually used on twenty-four-spoke wheels for extremely specialized track events. I would never recommend them for anything else.)

The large metal circle that forms the circumference of the wheel is the *rim.* Bicycle rims are usually quite thin and sleek. All low-range bikes and some midrange bikes have steel rims. All the better bikes have lighter aluminum rims. But the important distinction among rims is whether they're clincher rims or sew-up rims.

The *clincher rim* is far more common than the sew-up rim. Clinchers can be found on a range of bikes, from children's tricycles all the way up to serious touring bikes, competition mountain bikes, and now even racing bikes. It's a rim that has a lip all around the edge that holds the tire—known as the clincher tire—securely in place. The inner tube is separate from the tire; it is held securely between tire and rim by the pressure of the beaded tire walls against the rim.

In the old days no racer or serious cyclist rode on clinchers. The tires were heavy, wider, rode poorly, and were difficult to change when they flattened. But in the past ten years clincher technology has developed tremendously. Nowadays, you can find a clincher that is remarkably light and quite responsive. They can still be a hassle to change but on the other hand they tend to puncture much less frequently than other kinds. Clinchers have become so much lighter and perform so much better that they recently made their debut in the Tour de France. In 1986, the Italian Malvor team decided to use clinchers instead of sew-ups. And although it was slightly more work for the mechanics to change the clinchers when they flatted, they had fewer flats to fix. And the clinchers are far less expensive than sew-ups.

There are two distinct kinds of clinchers. The first kind is the wider, thicker model that is pumped up to about 75 pounds per square inch. This kind of tire is heavy and sluggish. Because it is so much wider it creates much more friction and can slow you down. The new clinchers are similar to racing sew-ups. They are light and thin and are inflated to 100 or 120 pounds per square inch. They have the same kind of "presta" valve as sew-ups and can be inflated with an ordinary hand pump. The heavier clincher requires inner tubes with larger "schraeder" valves that can befound on car tires. These have to be inflated by going to a service station and using its air pump.

That alternative is the *sew-up rim.* Unlike the clincher rim, the sew-up rim is only slightly cupped and has no lip to hold the tire in place. Instead sew-ups are secured to the rim by means of a very sticky, and often messy, special tire glue. Unlike clinchers, sew-ups are one-piece units in which the tire, as the name suggests, is sewn around the inner tube. While clinchers are made of a rubber compound, sew-ups are actually strands of finely woven cotton or silk with a strip of rubber tread glued all around the top.

Sew-ups have always been the choice of racers because they are extremely responsive, light, and easy to change in a hurry. But sew-ups have a number of drawbacks. They're expensive to buy (anywhere from fifteen to forty dollars) and they tend to puncture quite easily. While you can simply replace the inner tube whenever a clincher punctures (a relatively inexpensive prop-osition), you need to buy an entire sew-up every time you have a flat with a sew-up. And while it's relatively easy to patch a clincher inner tube, fixing a sew-up is a long, drawn-out process that is hardly worth the time and effort.

Most of all, sew-ups need to be very well secured to the rim. If you don't put enough glue on the rim, or if there's a buildup of glue, you can roll a sew-up off your rim in a sharp turn. The same thing holds true if you brake constantly on a long downhill and the glue begins to melt due to the heat that builds up from the braking action. And rolling a tire in a turn can be a very painful way to crash.

Don't get me wrong. For any kind of serious racing, I would recommend riding on sew-ups. But even if you are a serious racer, there's no reason not to train on clinchers. They used to say that you needed to train on fast wheels, but the fact is, your body doesn't know how fast your wheels are. Clinchers are a good choice for younger racers and many serious riders who don't race.

Sew-ups, however, are still much more responsive. They can be inflated to very high pressure—120 pounds per square inch in some cases. They're also light and easy to replace. But you'll have to be prepared to spend more money on spare tires. And you'll always have to make sure to secure your sew-ups properly to the rims.

With the new technology, however, I think clinchers can be a good alternative. For anything other than racing, I think they're a better alter-native. You'll spend a lot less money buying new inner tubes, and if you want, you can patch them up (though inner tubes are so inexpensive that it's not worth the trouble most of the time). Flats are less common with clincher tires, and there are now clinchers that are as narrow as the top-of-the-line sew-ups. Most of all, you'll never have to worry about rolling a tire. Still, you'll have to remember to bring along a set of tire irons on each ride, to change the inner tube if you have a flat.

THE DRIVETRAIN

Once you've determined what wheels are right for you (remember, if you have clincher rims, you can always get a spare set of wheels later) you should examine the drivetrain—all those components that are connected with the chain that powers the bike.

The largest item in the drivetrain is the *crankset*. The crankset is composed of a large spindle on the chain side and usually has three or five arms extending outward. Connected to the spindle arms are the chainrings, those large circular metal plates around which the chain runs. Most models have two chainrings, although some specialized time trial and track bikes have only one, and touring bikes may have three chainrings (three chainrings allow you to have a fifteen-, eighteen-, or twenty-one-speed bike, depending on the number of cogs you have on your freewheel). Extending from the center of the spindle is the crankarm, which extends about six-and-a-half inches to the pedal. Connected by the bottom bracket axle is a mirror image of the crankarm on the side opposite the chain, but without the spindle.

The crankset is the primary point of contact between rider and machine. For this reason it's important to get a good-quality crankset that will combine lightness and rigidity. You want to avoid the steel cranksets found on lower-priced models. These cranksets tend to be overly heavy and have an outdated design. Most steel cranksets have separate crankarms that are attached to the spindle by a huge metal cotter. Others attach the crankarm to the spindle without a cotter, but they're still built of two separate parts. This is not a good solution, as the cotter can loosen and damage the entire assembly. In the best of cases a "cottered" crankset cannot transmit your pedaling power nearly as efficiently, because the spindle and the crankarm are two separate pieces that will tend to flex and move under a great deal of strain—exactly when you need a crankset to be solid.

Most two-piece cranksets are found on bikes below $220. If you're considering a bike in that range, look for an alloy crankset instead of a steel one. If you can find a one-piece crankset, you will have a bargain for a bike selling for $220 or less.

If you find a two-piece crankset—alloy or steel—on a bike more expensive than that, you're not getting good value. There are plenty of bikes starting at about $220 that have alloy, one-piece, cotterless cranksets.

Luckily, most midrange bikes have good alloy, unitized-construction cranksets. The best models are one-piece and cold-forged for minimum metal fatigue and maximum life. You'll notice that some crankset spindles have only three arms. Personally, I've always used the five-arm cranksets, and I think they are sturdier and far more rigid.

Although a number of manufacturers produce cranksets, most top-of-the-line cranksets have a similar design. They are usually made out of alloy, cold-forged for reinforcement. The standard was set by Campagnolo with its Nuovo Record and Super Record cranksets in the late 1960s and 1970s. Now most of the competition has caught up. The Japanese make some high-quality cranksets. Shimano makes an excellent crankset in its Dura Ace line of components as does rival SunTour in its Superbe Pro line of components. Lower-priced but relatively good-quality cranks are made by Japan's Sugino.

Among European manufacturers, Spain's Zeus makes a very light crankset with chainrings "drilled out" for weight saving. I wouldn't recommend this model for a powerful or heavy rider. You could break it. Italy's Ofmega makes what is called in cycling jargon a "campagnolo-clone," while France's

The freewheel. This is a six-speed model.

Stronglight and Mavic make good solid cranksets used by some French professional teams.

With the recent emphasis on aerodynamics, crankset design has been honed to slice the wind more efficiently. Campagnolo came out with a new line of components in 1984 dubbed simply Record. The crankset is smoother than the traditional design. The crankarm smoothly blends into the five spindles instead of being rounded off as in the traditional models. There are also Japanese versions of the aerodynamic crankset.

Over the years, a recurring invention in cycling has been the elliptical chainring. At times an uneven ellipse shaped something like an egg, the elliptical chainring has been marketed extensively by the Japanese manufacturer Shimano in what it calls its biospace line. Although Shimano claims the elliptical chainring is easier to ride for a less advanced cyclist, I don't recommend using it. First, the uneven diameter of the elliptical chainring adds strain to your pedaling motion and encourages you to develop an uneven pedaling style. This will be an impediment if you're trying to learn correct pedaling technique, and pedaling is the key motion of cycling.

The *freewheel* is the rear counterpart to the crankset. This is the collection of five or more small sprockets that is wrapped by the chain at the rear hub. You'll notice right away that the freewheel sprockets are much smaller than the chainrings up front. That's just the way the bicycle was originally designed, because there was more free space around the crankset than around the rear hub.

Although some high-end bikes have aluminum freewheels and lightweight sprockets, these tend to be very pricey and fragile. I wouldn't recommend them if you have to buy your own equipment—you'll find that you have to replace freewheel sprockets (and therefore the chain and the chainrings) every few months.

Although my team provides me with an alloy freewheel, I rarely use it.

Most of the season, I'm outfitted with a steel freewheel because it's sturdier and more dependable in the grueling European races I ride.

One of the big questions you need to address regarding the freewheel is whether you should have five, six, or seven speeds. Certainly, it seems logical that the more gears you have the better off you'll be. That's true. The greater the number of gears, the easier it is to fit your bike for such widely varied terrain, as steep hills, long downhills, and flat sections. But as with anything else in life, the extra speeds don't come without a price tag.

The seven-speed freewheel is a highly specialized component that requires a special chain. And because there are so many sprockets, your rear wheel has to be dished away from the chain so the whole thing can fit in your frame stays. Dishing the wheel that much weakens it and it will require constant retruing (tightening the spokes to keep the wheel round). Although the seven-speed freewheel has become the standard among professional racers, it isn't the standard on most stock bikes. It does require a little more attention and, if you're not familiar with the mechanics, could be more of a problem.

Unless you live in an area with a lot of grueling climbing, or you're a top-level racer, I don't think the seven-speed freewheel is necessary. Tourists who travel in very hilly terrain rarely even consider the seven-speed freewheel because they already have a triple chainset, providing them with fifteen or eighteen gears. Racers don't use the triple chainset because of its weight and poor aerodynamic characteristics.

The best compromise, and a common choice, is the six-speed unit. Although you still have to dish the wheel a bit more than with the traditional five-speed freewheel, you can still use a conventional chain. With the combination of the six-speed freewheel and the two chainrings you can get up to twelve gears, a very large selection for any rider.

The components that actually shift the chain from one gear to another are the derailleurs. Above the chainrings, you'll find the *front derailleur*, a simple mechanism that encloses the chain and directs it from one chainring to the other when you activate the levers you are pedalling. The derailleur literally pushes the chain onto the next chainring. The word derailleur comes from the French; it literally means "the machine that derails." The front derailleur is a very basic design that has changed little since it was first introduced over 50 years ago.

There are a couple of things to look for in a front derailleur. On many better bikes, you'll notice that the front derailleur is attached to the seat tube above the chainrings by a brazed-on mount. This makes the whole thing a lot easier to install and looks a lot neater.

Make sure your front derailleur is properly adjusted so that it doesn't rub on the chain when the gears are highly crossed over. (In other words, when you have the chain on the big chainring, on the outside, you should be able to ride on the biggest freewheel sprocket, all the way on the inside, without rubbing the chain against the front derailleur.) Although crossing over the chain this far is never recommended in normal riding, your bike should be properly adjusted to handle it. If the chain rubs when crossed over like this, ask your dealer to make sure the front derailleur is properly installed. If it still rubs, you might have a front derailleur that is not suited to your needs.

The *rear derailleur* is a far more delicate gadget. The rear derailleur sits on the dropout—the point at which the back of the frame comes to an end—linking the seat-and chainstays (these are the much thinner tubes that compose the rear triangle of the frame along with the seat tube). The derailleur, originally designed in the 1930s in Italy, consists of a spring-loaded parallelogram body that changes angle when you activate the derailleur lever (The lever is connected to the derailleur by a cable that stretches or releases the spring in the derailleur). As the body moves, the rollers below the body that zigzag to enclose the chain sweep over and the chain skips from sprocket to sprocket. Although basically simple, most derailleurs have about twenty-five pieces, including ball bearings, springs, and adjusting screws.

Unlike the front derailleur, the rear derailleur never needs to have its position on the frame adjusted. Most bikes have an integral brazed "ear" on the dropout onto which the derailleur is mounted. Most midrange bikes have this "ear." If the bike doesn't, the derailleur has to be held by a flimsy clamp that's screwed onto the dropout. It will eventually loosen and destroy the dropout, and perhaps even the derailleur. Not worth it.

When you buy a middle to higher-range bike you should get an excellent derailleur combination. Most derailleurs on the market today have good shifting action and are easy to use. I'm especially impressed with how smooth many of the Japanese models are. One interesting innovation is the ratchet shifter now produced by Shimano, Suntour, and Campagnolo. This is an entirely new technology in the derailleur. While most derailleurs simply push the chain over when you pull the derailleur lever, the ratchet shifter has a special ratchet that positions the lever at the exact point where the derailleur shifts to the next cog. Instead of estimating where the derailleur will shift, you just pull back to the first ratchet. If you want to shift two cogs over, simply pull the lever through two clicks of the ratchet. Racers are somewhat wary of using the ratchet, however, because they fear their opponents will hear them shifting gears.

There are a couple of drawbacks with the ratchet system, though. First, you need a special freewheel and chain that are slightly more expensive than the traditional top-of-the-line accessories. Second, the ratchets can and do fall out of adjustment.

The most common derailleur used by professional cyclists is the Campagnolo Super Record model (and its close cousin, the Nuovo Record, the same basic design minus two titanium bolts). This is the derailleur I have used since I first got into cycling. It's reliable and doesn't break down very much, and spare parts are readily available. It's not on the cutting edge of technology. But it's about as tested as any racing technology can be: It's been around in the same basic form since 1933 and close to three-quarters of all professionals use it—it's an extremely dependable form of technology.

Campagnolo has recently come out with a new design, dubbed simply the Record. I rode with the Record in 1986. It's an excellent component, more aerodynamically efficient than the Super Record. The shifting action feels to me perhaps a little spongier than the older model. But it isn't significantly different from the Super Record in a structural sense, although some of the design is somewhat different.

Just remember that both front and rear derailleurs have a maximum range and that most competition rear derailleurs have a limited range of thirteen to twenty-eight teeth (in some cases even thirteen to twenty-four teeth). If you're interested in getting much larger freewheel sprockets for mountain touring, you can get special derailleurs. Campagnolo, SunTour, and Shimano all produce a model that can accommodate a freewheel arrangement of fourteen to thirty-two and in some cases fourteen to thirty-six. French manufacturer Huret also makes a light, wide-action derailleur that is a favorite of tourists.

One way to make sure your dealer is doing a good job is to inspect the rear derailleur tension. Since most bikes are shipped disassembled to bike dealers, the shop mechanics put the bikes together before wheeling them out to the showroom. When the dealers install the chain, they should leave enough links in the chain so that the rear derailleur rollers are never fully extended, even when placed in the combination of the biggest chainring and biggest freewheel sprocket (complete crossover). Your chain should be as long as possible, which means that you should maintain the minimum tension on the rollers where the chain is placed on the small chainring and small sprocket (opposite crossover). The only exception to this rule is a touring bike with a tremendous differential in gear ratios, which may well stretch the rear derailleur rollers to their limit.

One final note about derailleurs. A good bike will always have brazed-on cable guides and derailleur lever mounts. What that means is that the cable extending from the derailleurs to the levers on the down tube should be guided by small, integral loops or guides in the frame. If you find that your cables are guided by metal clamps that are screwed on, you'll risk having loose cables if the clamps slip, and eventually you'll have rust under the clamps. The same holds true for the derailleur levers on the down tube. All good bikes have mounts that are brazed on. If your derailleur levers are clamped on they could slip or rust, which is not good news. Your bike should

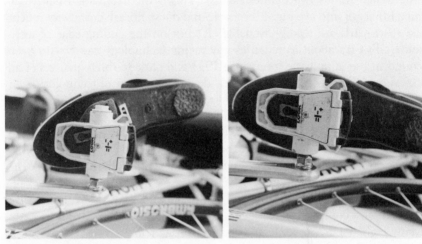

The new Look pedal system. This strapless system holds your feet tighter in the pedals without constricting the blood flow through your feet. These two photographs show how a cyclist slips into the binding.

not have the derailleur levers clamped on the handlebar stem. That's an awkward, unsafe setup.

The final element of the drivetrain is the most important one: the *pedals*. This is where your body will come into constant contact with the bicycle: This is the synergetic link between man and machine. You want to make sure this point of contact will be efficient and comfortable.

Many people picking their first bike are afraid of toe clips. And I don't blame them. I don't think there's any top racer who can say he's never fallen over when he couldn't unfasten his toe straps at a red light—it's happened to me a number of times.

Of course, falling over is not a major catastrophe. Falling is part of cycling and keeling over while stopped at a red light is one of the least painful ways to hit the tarmac. In any case, I would never recommend buying a racing bicycle without toe clips or toe straps. Toe clips and toe straps insure that your feet (the primary point at which man meets machine) are firmly attached to the pedals. What's more, any serious riding without toe clips or toe straps leaves you open to an accident caused by your feet inadvertently falling off the pedals. If you're not used to riding in toe clips and toe straps, you can leave the toe straps unfastened for the first few weeks. Remember, without any form of binding, your feet will slip and slide. It'll be difficult, even dangerous, to get out of the saddle in climbs. You simply can't ride a bike seriously without some way to hold your feet on the pedals. It would be like skiing in a pair of sandals.

But toe straps and toe clips may very well be a thing of the past. For decades, inventors have searched for a way to replace them. Finally, I think they've found the answer with the Look pedals that my teammate Bernard Hinault began riding in 1984. At first I was very skeptical about this new pedal system. But I've always had foot problems with my flat feet and I tried the new pedals in 1985. At first, they took a little getting used to. I had always ridden with the toe clips to enclose my feet. The Look pedals, by contrast, only held me in with a ski binding–like cleat on the bottom. It felt kind of naked.

Now I'm convinced that this type of pedal is the answer for the future. For one thing it does away with all the hardware and, most of all, eliminates the toe strap that you constantly have to tighten, which eventually cuts off the circulation to your feet. It's also far more efficient; your feet are securely attached to the pedals during the entire pedal rotation. Best of all, it's much safer—just like a ski binding. If you have to take your feet out in a hurry, you click them out like ski boots (the pressure at which you release is variable).

There are a number of other brands similar to the Look system now out on the market. The only drawback to this binding system comes for people who don't want to get cycling shoes with cleats. The new pedal systems require special cleats, like any cycling shoes, they're not very easy to walk in. But when you go skiing, you don't expect to ski in Birkenstocks. Or when you run, you wouldn't wear a pair of Earth shoes. I would not recommend tackling cycling as a serious pastime without cycling shoes. For those of you who want to ride in tennis shoes or touring shoes (a hybrid between cycling and running shoes), however, Look does make a pedal with a flat side for noncleated shoes.

BRAKES: SIDE-PULL OR CENTER-PULL?

Most bikes today have *side-pull brakes*, with the brake cable directed into one side before the braking action is equalized by a spring inside the brake itself. The top Italian brand, Campagnolo, makes the most widely applauded side-pull brakes, and most of the other makers have copied them. Top Japanese brands Shimano and SunTour both make top-of-the-line side-pulls that are excellent brakes.

Chances are most of the middle-and top-range bikes you're looking at will have side-pull brakes. For the most part the common Japanese and European brands will make brakes that have about equal stopping power. Some of the brands might have a more "positive" feel or a more "gradual" action. But, quite honestly, I have never really been able to tell them apart. For me the choice of a good brake pad (the rubber pad that actually touches the rim) has

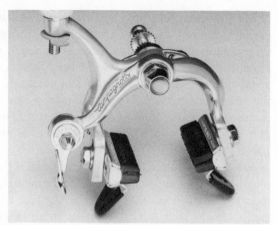

*Campagnolo side-pull brakes:
the state of the art.*

as much to do with a brake's stopping power as with its construction. In my experience the consistently best brake pad has been the Campagnolo replacement pad. But the other major manufacturers also make good pads, with Shimano and SunTour again leading the bunch. A couple of very small companies in the United States specialize in making brake pads that are touted for their extra stopping power. But I have never used them. Remember, the key to stopping power in a brake pad is the rubber. The harder the rubber, the more gradually the brake pad is going to stop your bike (a good feature), but also the harder it will be to slow down. The softer the rubber, the more abruptly you will come to a stop but the easier it will be to stop your bike. (Note: I do not recommend Modolo brake pads, because the brakes stop too solidly.)

There is another kind of brake: the *center-pull brake*. Although you probably won't find it on any of the better bikes, the center-pull brake, with the brake cable centered between the two calipers, is actually the better brake. It's

Center-pull brakes. This variant has cantilevers (the arms that extend the cable away from the brake) for extra stopping power. Although center-pulls probably have more stopping power, they are more difficult to maintain.

just plain physics: The side-pull applies all the force to one side, forcing the spring inside the brake to adjust so that braking force is applied equally. When that happens, some braking force is lost. The center-pull, on the other hand, applies force, directly from above, cleanly, simply.

Why, then, aren't more bikes equipped with center-pulls? For one thing they're messy and hard to install. A center-pull requires a special washer placed inside the headset. It's also hard to adjust and sometimes requires two people to hold all the cables and wrenches.

The side-pull became popular among racers because it stops the bike almost as well as the center-pull and is much easier for mechanics to install. But it's also probably a matter of fashion. Back in the 1960s, center-pull brakes were the rage. Then Campagnolo came out with high-quality side-pulls, and soon everybody else followed. I'm convinced that if somebody sat down and worked at it, an improved center-pull brake could be designed.

When stopping power is really crucial, as in cyclo cross or mountain bike riding, all the brakes are center-pulls, and they're cantilevered for extra leverage. A cantilevered brake is bolted to the frame. Each caliper is tilted down and attached to the cable bridge by a long section of cable. This leverage provides extra stopping power.

If your middle to high-range bike has a pair of reputable side-pulls, you'll be fine. Just make sure that the reach on the brake calipers conforms with the point where the rim touches the brake pad. Many expensive Italian bikes are built so tight that the wheels are scrunched all the way into the brakes and often the brake calipers are too long to make contact with the rim of the wheel. If that's the case with your bike, ask your dealer for a pair of a short-reach side-pull brakes, available in most brands.

As with the derailleurs, make sure the rear brake cable is routed along the top tube by integral, brazed-on loops. If your brake cable is attached by three metal clamps on the top tube, not only will you risk rust, but you can scrape yourself hitting your leg against the screws. Fortunately, most middle-to high-range bikes have braze-ons nowadays. Some bikes even have two holes drilled into the top tube where the brake cable, in a special lubricated housing, is routed inside the top tube and back out at the other end. This is usually an acceptable solution, but it will make servicing your rear brake cable a little bit more difficult.

Also, make sure you have *hooded* brake levers attached to the handlebars. If your brake levers are unhooded—just denuded steel—your riding position will be very uncomfortable. The brake levers are not just for stopping, they're also a key anatomical feature. Riders often rest their hands on the brake levers. If the levers are denuded steel, they are hard, uncomfortable, and slippery when you sweat.

By the same token, never buy bicycle brakes with those lever extenders or "safety" brakes. Because they are attached loosely to the top of the brake lever, they provide you with very little leverage. They require a tremendous amount of travel to brake adequately. As soon as your brake cables begin to extend, the lever requires more travel to stop and the extenders quickly run out of travel: They lose nearly all their breaking power.

The irony of "safety" brakes is that although manufacturers are well aware of how ineffectual they are, they continue to supply them on their inexpensive bikes because the public considers them a safety feature. Many people believe that they will be able to stop more safely if they have these extenders, rather than having to reach down to the brake levers. Beside the fact that extenders don't provide adequate stopping power in an emergency, using them develops bad habits. When you encounter a situation in which you have to stop in a flash, the extenders could prove to be hazardous. I recommend taking off lever extenders if your bike has them and relying only on the brake levers.

HANDLEBARS AND STEM

The *handlebars* are an important component for the fit and comfort of your bicycle. A good bicycle should always have a set of alloy handlebars. If you're looking at a bike with heavy steel bars you're probably not looking at a good bike. The one exception is a specialized track sprinting bike: On these bikes, the bars are always made of steel.

The handlebars should be about the width of your shoulders. Most stock bikes come with standard forty-centimeter bars. This should fit most people; if you have exceptionally wide or narrow shoulders, ask your dealer for bars that will fit your shoulder width (bars usually come in a thirty-eight-to forty-four-centimeter range).

The handlebars should be designed so that the portion extending out from the stem is not curved for about six inches or so. That flat section of "tops" (as the top of the handlebars is called) will be a natural spot to position your hands. If you find bars that curve immediately away from the stem, you'll have a hard time being comfortable. Such curving bars are used by most track sprinters (in a steel version especially designed for the track) and by some road racers. On the whole, I think most riders find curving bars less comfortable, especially for any kind of riding that involves a lot of hills, where you need to put your hands comfortably on the tops.

My favorite handlebars are the Cinelli Campionato del Mondo (model 66) bars, because they have the deepest drop (the distance from the top of the bars to the bottom when looking at the handlebars from the side). I like that because I can sit up and rest on the tops or ride on the brake levers comfortably. But when I want to get into an aerodynamic tuck, I can put my hands

The Campagnolo Record group of components. Note the aerodynamic brakes (top left).

on the deep "drops" (the bottom portion of the bar in the curve). With the deep drop I have a good aerodynamic position on the drops without sacrificing the comfort of riding more upright on the tops of the brake levers.

Most often a showroom bike will come packaged with a standard type of handlebars. The standard bars have a straight section on the tops, as I described above, and a standard drop of four to five inches. If you have exceptionally long hands or prefer the deeper drop for the same reasons I do, you can switch to a pair of Cinelli Campionato del Mondo (model 66) handlebars.

Make sure you have plugs in the handlebar ends when you buy your bike; without plugs the ends can become lethal weapons in an accident. The plug covers the exposed rough metal of the end of the handlebar tubing.

Connecting the handlebars to the frame is the *stem*. Like the bars, the stem should always be made of alloy. If you see a bike with a heavy, unwieldy steel stem, look at a different bike. You'll notice that some stems have a thinner body than others. This doesn't mean they're weaker, it's just a different design—the metal is very strong.

There are two major kinds of good-quality stems to consider. The first, and most common, stem has the bolt that holds down the handlebars directly under the bars. This is the traditional arrangement and remains the most economical and the strongest.

Certain models have a special bolt that tightens the handlebars from the rear, inside the stem. Instead of having a bolt underneath the bars, these stems will be flush. This setup was introduced in the 1970s and is slightly more aerodynamically efficient. Unless you're racing time trials or very fast road races, though, I think it's unnecessary. This kind of handlebar stem is more expensive, and if it's not properly installed it will tend to creak a little bit. I use one of these stems because that's what my team provides me with, but I'd be just as happy to use the conventional model.

THE SADDLE: NARROW IS BETTER

Finally, there are the seat and the seat post. The *seat* (or *saddle*), like the handlebars, is an important component in determining how comfortable and efficient you'll be on the bike. One of the most common misconceptions regarding the seat is that a wider seat is more comfortable than a narrow seat. At first, it may be like an easy chair, softer, more agreeable. But as you start riding, you'll feel a lot of chafing and, more important, you'll notice that the wide seat doesn't support your body anatomically. After a few long rides you might start to develop a rash between your legs. Your whole butt will be sore.

When you first look at a racing saddle it's hard to believe that it's really going to be comfortable. Most racing saddles have a very thin, sleek nose and only widen enough in the back to support part of your cheeks. But re-member, you want the saddle to be as unobtrusive, as thin as possible without being so thin that it doesn't support you. Although some saddles made for tourists are wider and softer than the racing models, tourists have the same requirements in a saddle as racers. They need good, firm support.

Whatever type of cyclist you are, the longer and more frequent your rides, the more you'll need a thin, firm saddle (with a layer of foam padding). A bicycle saddle is much like a car seat. When you first sit down in a big American car with a down-soft, plush seat, you feel comfortable. But be-cause there is no support, your muscles quickly get tired and you get aches. A firm car seat, however, is ergonomically developed to support your body.

When you first ride on a racing saddle you'll probably be sore for a couple of days. But as your body adapts to it, the racing seat will become so comfortable you won't notice it anymore.

Most of the racing saddles on the market today are well-designed. Al-though the leather saddle was once predominant, the vast majority of saddles today are made with a plastic shell covered with a dense pack of foam and wrapped with a thin skin of leather. You'll notice that some of these saddles have a suede covering. That won't make any difference and after about a week you'll notice that the constant friction will have worn the suede down to a shiny, leather surface.

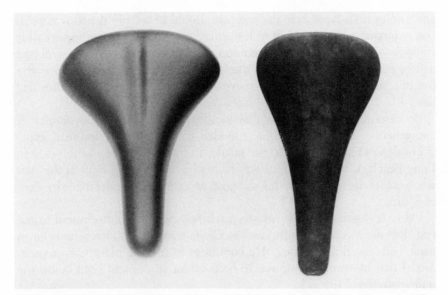

The women's saddle, on the left, is wider and slightly shorter than the saddle on the right to accommodate the female anatomy.

If you really want to get an old-fashioned leather saddle, you should be prepared to have a much heavier seat, and endure at least six months of constant riding to break it in. Until then it'll be rock-hard and extremely uncomfortable. With the high quality of the modern saddles, I don't think there's any need for a leather saddle anymore.

Personally, I have used a variety of different plastic, foam-covered saddles that my teams have provided me with and I found all of them to be fine. The only thing I would watch out for is saddles that are too thick in the nose: They'll cause chafing and make your pedaling awkward.

One word of caution. Avoid plastic saddles without any covering whatsoever, foam or leather. If you find a bike with this kind of saddle and the rest of the bike is generally good, I heartily recommend you spend an extra thirty dollars to buy a good saddle. It'll make all the difference in the world, believe me.

Most women will probably need a special saddle designed for their wider pelvic bones. There are a number of saddles on the market designed especially for women that work well. Not every woman needs a special saddle, but if your saddle seems to be causing you pain, by all means investigate the special saddles. Look for a saddle with a seat wider in the rear—the nose shouldn't be significantly wider than that on a men's model, although it should be shorter to better fit the female pelvic structure.

The *seat post* is the metallic tube that connects the seat to the frame. On any mid-or high-range bike the seat post should be a fairly standard item. If you're buying a bike for $350 or less, make sure that you're getting an alloy seat post—at this price it's still common to find steel seat posts. The steel post will be heavy and could rust out the inside of your frame, especially if you live in a rainy climate. More expensive bikes should always have an alloy seat post.

Be careful about seat posts that sacrifice strength for aerodynamics or convenience. Some of the lightest models have a tendency to break, especially along the attachment to the saddle. In the late 1970s, a junior race in Long Beach, California, that I was racing had a big crash right at the start when one of the riders broke his seat post, an extra-light model made by Zeus of Spain.

Other seat posts have an easy-to-reach bolt below the attachment to the seat. But the mechanic on the La Vie Claire team, Alain Descroix, believes these bolts are not as strong. He continues to use the older Campagnolo model that has two (hard-to-reach) bolts on an attachment right below the undercarriage of the saddle.

The seat post has to be sturdy because it helps to support about 55 percent of your body weight.

BE SMART:
LOOK AT DETAILS

Look at the details on the bike. Make sure your frame has brazed-on mounts on the down tube for a water bottle holder. Some models may even have them on the seat tube, above the front derailleur. Does the frame have chromed forks and chainstays? That's always a nice touch, especially on the chain-side chainstay where it'll be a lot easier to wipe off the grease that inevitably will drip from your chain.

Does the paint job look rich and consistent? Look at the bolt in the lug at the top of the seat tube that holds the seat post into the frame. If that bolt isn't flush with the seat-post lug, you'll have a lot of trouble tightening your saddle and ultimately you could risk injury and a broken seat-tube lug.

Look at the brake cables. Most bikes have brake cables that jut straight out of the brake levers in a big loop through the cable housing to the brakes themselves. But some "aerodynamic" bikes have brake cables that lead from the brake lever, actually *inside* the handlebars, and out a hole drilled in the bars to the brakes. There's nothing wrong with this system. But remember that it's going to be more difficult to replace and adjust your brakes and brake cables. The aerodynamic advantage gained is small but noticeable. In most cases, however, the extra hassle in maintenance and repair isn't worth the slight gain in aerodynamic efficiency. Also remember that the holes that are drilled in your handlebars will weaken the bars (in 1985, I remember French rider Martial Gayant had a terrible crash in the Tour de France when his bars broke this way).

Be careful not to confuse this kind of arrangement, in which the cable is fed *inside* the handlebars through a hole in the bars, with another common style, in which the brake cables are taped to the *outside* of the handlebars and then held in place by the handlebar tape.

CYCLING FASHION: PRAGMATIC COMFORT

Once you've decided what kind of bicycle to buy, you have to consider what kind of cycling clothes you'll need. Most novices feel foolish riding around in tight, black cycling shorts and a skin-fitting jersey. Some people also seem to feel uncomfortable about buying cycling shoes with cleats.

Cycling clothing is not a matter of fashion, although I think you can look very good in it. I've seen many people go out and buy a nice bike but continue to ride in tennis shoes, running shorts, and a tank top. That's what I did when I got my first bike. I thought I needed to wear the tank top because the mesh fabric would ventilate my body.

I discovered the hard way why cyclists wear cycling clothing. The tank top flopped around and gave me rashes where the stitches touched my skin. The running shorts I was wearing bunched up around my crotch and I got a terrible rash from the lining at the seams. Finally, my tennis shoes proved difficult to get into the toe clips and inefficient, because the sole was flexible. As I pedaled, some of my pedaling energy, instead of going into the bike, was lost in the flex of the soles of my shoes.

As I've already mentioned, no one should ever consider riding seriously without cycling shoes. Most important, never ride without toe clips. This is inefficient and dangerous. Without toe clips your feet aren't anchored and they deliver power much less efficiently, and only in the downstroke. If you get out of the saddle, you risk your foot falling off the pedal if you hit a rough spot or pothole in the road. And if your foot falls off, you probably will too.

Cycling shoes are designed with a light mesh or leather upper that conforms to your foot and allows it to "breathe." Remember, when you're cycling, your feet aren't carrying nearly as much weight as when you're walking or running. For this reason you don't need the extra bulk and support of running or tennis shoes.

Three models of cycling shoes made by Puma: above left, the all-leather racing shoe; above right, the leather and mesh racing shoe; left, the touring shoe, a compromise between the true cycling shoe and a running shoe.

Cycling shoes have a cleat underneath that attaches to the pedal. Most cycling cleats are fastened to the sole of the shoe by small screws or allenhead bolts and are adjustable. The cycling cleat, unlike cleats found on football or baseball shoes, consists of a plate placed below the ball of the foot. Inside that plate, there is a narrow groove or slit, where the pedal fits. When your foot is in the toe clip and tightened by the toe strap, the groove in the cleat is held tight to the pedal. Thus, you can ride without slipping, you can use your pedals in both portions of the stroke (upstroke, downstroke) and you can get out of the saddle safely without worrying about your feet slipping off the pedals.

As I mentioned earlier, there is a new pedal system in cycling that's based on ski binding technology. This kind of pedal looks more like a ski binding attached to the crankarm by an axle. To use this kind of pedal—pioneered by Look (a ski binding company) and now produced by Adidas, among others— you'll need a special cleat designed especially for the model of pedal you're using.

I have been using the Look pedal system since 1985. I prefer it to the traditional toe clips and toe straps method because I used to have foot problems caused by very tight toe straps. Now my feet are free of any binding and I feel they're even more securely attached to the pedals because they're now in a real binding, as opposed to being simply strapped in.

Cycling shoes also have a stiff sole that captures all the force of your pedaling motion. If you ride in just about any other type of shoes, you'll have a softer sole that may be more comfortable when you're walking or running, but will be too flexible and inefficient on the bike. In the long run, if you do any serious riding in a running or tennis shoe, you will actually get sore feet. Of course, if you have extremely sensitive feet, some hard-soled cycling shoes might be a bit too stiff. But you can always look for a model of cycling shoes with a softer sole: Ask your dealer what's available.

Many people say they can't walk comfortably on cycling shoes. That's true. In fact, after ten years of cycling I still find walking in cycling shoes awkward. But remember, when your primary activity is cycling, it's better to be a little awkward when you're walking than to be uncomfortable while you're on a long ride. After all, walking in ski boots is also awkward. But you wouldn't ski in sandals, would you?

The truth is you can walk a little bit on cycling shoes, but you don't ever want to go too far. The bottoms of cycling shoes are usually not made to walk on any hard surface. If you walk a lot on your cycling shoes you could destroy them.

If you really need to do a lot of walking and riding on the same trip, you could try a touring shoe. This is a hybrid, a cross between a racing cycling shoe and a running shoe. Touring shoes have uppers that look like running shoes but are usually a little bit stiffer. The soles have a semicleat, three or four incisions in the rubber where your foot can grip the pedal. Sort of. The soles are like those of running shoes, but they're harder so as to be more comfortable on the bike. If you like a touring shoe, get it. But I think touring shoes tend to be impossible compromises that end up making you feel uncomfortable both on the bike and on foot.

Personally, if I had to ride and walk, I would get a pair of top-of-the-line racing shoes and I would carry a pair of running shoes with me whenever I wanted to walk for extended periods of time. Not as convenient, but perhaps better for your feet in the long run.

When you shop for a pair of cycling shoes you'll notice that there's a wide selection. Some cycling shoes have a leather sole, others a plastic sole. Some even have extremely stiff wooden soles. Some shoes have a thin sole, which doesn't always mean it's going to be softer. Others have huge, thick soles. Always choose what feels most comfortable. Wear a pair of thin cotton socks when you wear your shoes. Anything thicker will compromise the snug fit of the shoe.

*Clothes for cold-weather
riding. Note the "booties"
to cover the shoes, and the
gloves, caps, and tights.*

Always buy a shoe that fits snugly without being tight or constricting. You never want the shoe to cut off circulation to your feet: You want your feet to be able to "breathe." If you decide to buy an all-leather shoe, though, you'll have to get it just a bit tighter, as the leather stretches.

One of the most important steps in fitting your cycling shoes is positioning the cleat. This is an extremely important and precise process. I describe how to fit the cleat in Chapter Four, "How to Fit Your Bicycle." If your cleat is incorrectly adjusted, it could result in the long run in serious knee, ligament, and muscular problems.

Many people wonder why cyclists wear skin-tight black shorts. Well, the reason they're black is that the Union Cycliste Internationale, the governing body of bicycle racing all around the world, has a rule that states that all shorts have to be primarily black, because black hides the dirt more easily— unless you live in Southern California and never have to ride in rain.

But there's a very good reason why the shorts are designed the way they are. Good cycling shorts should always mold to your body. They should fit snugly without ever constricting your circulation or body movements—they should be like a second skin.

When I first started riding, the only kind of shorts you could find were wool shorts. They were heavy and after a long ride they tended to stretch and ride up your leg. Whenever it rained, the wool shorts would get soaked, and sometimes the black dye would run all the way down your leg.

Luckily, we now have shorts in a variety of modern materials, including Lycra. Most shorts you'll find at a reputable bike shop will be well-made and should serve you well. You'll notice that the higher-quality shorts usually have a shiny, almost slimy surface. The material should stretch but also bounce back after being stretched.

You'll notice that the seat of the shorts is padded with light brown chamois. Look for shorts with this chamois: It is an essential feature that will save your behind from becoming sore on practically any ride. Some lower-priced shorts have synthetic chamois. These can actually last longer than the real thing, but they will usually provide you with less padding.

One of the most important things to look for in a good pair of cycling shorts is the stitching. Turn the shorts inside out. Look carefully at all the stitching. Run your fingers all along the stitches. Are they smooth and recessed? Good cycling shorts should have stitches that are smooth and barely noticeable when you run your fingers along them. If the stitches feel rough, this is not a good pair of shorts and you'll end up getting a rash, as I did when I wore running shorts as a kid. You may have to spend a little more money for good shorts, but it's really worth it. This is one case where you really don't want to sacrifice your body (remember, this isn't football).

When you first put on the cycling shorts you'll probably be amazed at how long they are. Cycling shorts that fit right should run all the way down your thighs to about two inches from the top of your knee. There's a good reason why cycling shorts are so long: They're meant to protect your body and keep you warm without being obtrusive.

One model of cycling shorts that I particularly recommend is the integral bib. When you put these shorts on, you simply slip the bib over your shoulders and you never have to worry about the shorts slipping down your legs. If you don't get the shorts with the bib, you'll probably have to get suspenders, which are slightly less convenient.

If you're in a good bike shop you'll probably see an incredible selection of jerseys. When I first started riding, everybody insisted on heavy wool jerseys with floppy pockets on the front. Things have changed a lot, and now you can find excellent jerseys ranging from wool to cotton, from natural–manmade blends to pure man-made fabrics. Personally, I prefer a jersey that's made of material called Swiss Tex. This is an acrylic that absorbs perspiration but is also really easy to maintain. I like to wear something that's reliable, doesn't shrink, and is tough, durable, and comfortable. Of course, the new technology is evolving rapidly, and new materials are introduced all the time.

An important item of clothing many people overlook is cycling gloves. Many people seem to think that cycling gloves are optional and, of course, you *can* get away with not using them. But I would recommend always riding in gloves. First of all, a good pair of cycling gloves will cushion the vibrations your hands receive from the handlebars. Without that cushion, you could get sore wrists. Cycling gloves also play an important safety role. Whenever you fall, it's a human instinct to throw out your hand to protect your body. Without gloves you could scrape or cut your hands very badly, and that's simply not worth it.

There are many different kinds of cycling gloves. All gloves should have some kind of leather or chamois padding in the palm. Some gloves are made of a heavy fabric mesh—they can be used in mild or cool weather. Other gloves, made of Lycra or light cotton, should be used in hot weather. Just remember, though, that the lighter your gloves the more quickly they'll wear out.

I also recommend wearing some kind of eyewear. Until recently, wearing sunglasses or goggles was impractical and dangerous. If you crashed wearing sunglasses you could cut yourself or break your nose. In fact, that's what happened to Bernard Hinault in the 1985 Tour de France. He was wearing a pair of aviator sunglasses when he crashed at the finish of the stage in Saint-Étienne. If he hadn't been wearing those glasses he probably wouldn't have injured himself. As it was, his nose was bleeding profusely and he had to be rushed off to the hospital for stitches.

For a few years I've worn plastic cycling eyewear made of an extremely flexible plastic. This eyewear has protected my eyes from the sun and the dust and all the bugs. The kind I wear is made by Oakley, but there are a number of other brands you can consider. This kind of "eyewear" (they're really not glasses or goggles) is very light and practical. You can pop in and pop out different color lenses depending on the weather. And they're made of a very soft plastic rubber—they're very safe.

You don't have to wear cycling eyewear, but in the long run it'll be easier on your eyes if you do. Of course, if you already wear prescription glasses, you won't be able to wear this cycling eyewear. Also, if you have trouble focusing through any kind of lenses, I wouldn't recommend it.

When you've decided what kind of cycling clothes you want to buy, be sure to buy more than one of each item. You should always have at least four pairs of cycling shorts and at least two jerseys. You can probably get away with two pairs of gloves—one for hot weather, one for cold—but you will have to replace them eventually. You'll only need one set of eyewear frames but you should get all the lenses.

The next piece of equipment to consider is a helmet. Unfortunately the matter of head protection is a very controversial one in the cycling world. Most racers are opposed to the idea of wearing helmets, except when they have to. That attitude has changed somewhat, though, since 1986 when the United States Cycling Federation (USCF) imposed the rule that hard-shell helmets must be worn by all riders competing in official races sanctioned by the USCF.

What's a hard-shell helmet? It's any hard helmet built of hard plastic or polyutherane that has a shell surrounding the cranium. It's what anybody else would call a helmet. But in cycling we also have the hair net, which most racers use in Europe. The hair net is a flimsy contraption made of three strips of foam wrapped in leather. It does provide minimal protection but I would never recommend it to anybody who doesn't want to take a risk.

You'll find that most racers, myself included, still train without a helmet. Whenever people ask me about helmets, I always say they should wear one. Then they realize that I don't most of the time and they ask me why.

The reason is very simple: I'm a professional cyclist and I depend on the sport for my living. Helmets can be very constraining and hot, especially hard-shell helmets. In many of the long, hot stage races like the Tour de France, wearing a hard-shell helmet would be unrealistic. The helmets are heavy and they're venilated only to a certain point. On a seven-or eight-hour road race the helmet would be a significant fatigue factor. I simply can't afford to lose any time because of a helmet.

Unlike most European professionals, though, I do wear a helmet in some cases in which it's not required. I was one of the first to wear a helmet on the cobblestones of Paris-Roubaix. And I was the first professional to wear a hard-shell helmet in certain stages of the Tour de France.

But most people aren't professional cyclists. In fact there are only about fifty professional cyclists in America today. Most likely, you won't be riding 175 miles a day to earn your bread. Most likely you'll also be riding a lot on the open road with traffic of all kinds. And traffic is by far the single most dangerous hazard cyclists face. At the same time, you'll probably find yourself riding with some riders who may not be very experienced. I've seen many good riders get into accidents in Senior III and IV races (the bottom two of the four categories in American amateur racing) in America because some of the other riders around them didn't have any idea how to ride in a pack. For all these reasons, I think wearing a helmet is just common sense.

There's a lot of bravado involved in not wearing a helmet. Some riders think they'll look foolish in a big, bowl-shaped hard shell. Others think they'll be able to outsmart any hazards.

What is true is that some hard-shell helmets are extremely heavy. They might give you a sore neck or they might distract you and could force you into a crash.

But there have been many new developments in helmet technology. Some new hard-shell helmets weigh a little more than seven ounces. That's less than most cycling jerseys. I've worn this kinds of helmet in a number of races, including the Tour de France, and although it is definitely light and

A floor pump can be very useful at home.

comfortable, it doesn't offer the same kind of impact protection from a piercing object.

In the end, the decision to wear a helmet is personal. I think the USCF is right in requiring riders to wear hard-shell helmets. Cycling can be a dangerous sport and there's no good reason to increase your risk. I think that if you make an intelligent purchase, you can buy a hard shell that meets all the safety requirements and that's also light and will look good. As far as the hair net is concerned, I don't think you should wear a hair net and expect it to provide any real protection. Racers wear hair nets because they can get away with it—but it won't protect you when you need it the most.

I understand the USCF's decision, but I wonder if the elite racers really need the same safety precautions in such events as hilly races.

ACCESSORIES

Make sure you equip yourself with all the accessories you'll need for your bike. Your bike will probably already have a water bottle holder. If it doesn't, buy one. Make sure to buy plenty of water bottles—they're inexpensive and they can get stale and old pretty quickly. Buy spare tires (or innertubes if you have clinchers) and make sure to always carry a spare with you when you ride. Get a good pump that can fit on your bike without a clamp—make sure the nozzle fits the kind of tire nipples you have. You should also get a sturdy floor pump you can use at home before the start of each ride—it'll be much faster and easier to use than the hand model that fits on your bike.

Make sure to get a few extra rolls of handlebar tape—there's a big selection to choose from, get what you like best. If your bike has leather handlebar coverings, though, you won't need to change it, just wash it in warm, soapy water. (If you crash, leather handlebar covering can be a headache to replace.)

Once in a while you'll have to go back to your bike shop to get something fixed or replaced. In the meantime you should get a set of tools so you never get stuck (see Chapter Eight, "Bicycle Maintenance").

Unless you live in Southern California or Hawaii you will need a good set of winter training clothes. These are just as important as the cycling shorts are in the summer. Because cyclists move so fast on the bike, they develop a lot of wind chill. And as soon as the temperature dips below sixty-five degrees and the sky turns gray, you want to wear long cycling tights and long sleeves. If it gets below fifty degrees, you have to wear the same tights, a special cycling jacket made for winter riding, a cap, gloves, and polyurethane "booties" to cover your feet.

Cold is the cyclist's number-one enemy in the winter and early spring. If you decide to brave the elements without the proper clothing, you'll find that as you develop speed, your body will become very cold, especially on downhills. Your body will have secreted a lot of perspiration on the flats and in the climbs and you'll be ripe for coming down with a bad cold or something worse.

Toes and fingers can easily suffer from mild frostbite in cold-weather riding. But if you arm yourself with some special winter clothing, riding in the cold shouldn't be much of a challenge—it can even be a lot of fun, because the air's so crisp and clean.

When I first started riding, winter clothing was a very tenuous proposition. I remember going out to a camping store and buying a huge pair of wool hiking gloves—and still my fingers froze. The worst thing back then was freezing my toes. I remember people used to do a lot of zany things like take a pair of thick hiking socks, cut out a hole in the bottom and slip them over their cycling shoes. The socks would never fit in the toe straps—instead, they cut off your circulation and made your toes even colder. Other riders used to take ziplock plastic bags and cut out a hole on the bottom. That didn't work either. When I return to Europe for the early-season races in February and March it's often very cold. In the old days, the Europeans used to endure tremendous pain and often frostbite because there was simply no way to protect yourself. With all the new winter clothing that's no longer the case.

Now there's a whole range of winter accessories that make winter riding much more pleasurable. The big breakthrough was the use of high-tech man-made fabrics that truly insulate the body. Now when you buy a pair of winter gloves especially designed for cycling, they really keep you warm. The synthetic boot covers—known as "booties"—that cover your cycling shoes are an absolute requirement if you're going to train in any temperature below fifty degrees. They are light, for the most part well-designed, and will keep your feet warm. The same holds true for the winter caps that are available now.

Even if you never ride in the winter, I would recommend getting at least one good pair of cycling tights. Like the shorts, these should be made of a thin stretchy material that will mold to your body but also flex when you bend. Unlike the shorts, the tights usually don't have any chamois padding—you can just wear your shorts underneath.

I would recommend riding in leg warmers. These are something like the ballet leg warmers some women like to wear at their aerobics classes, except that cycling leg warmers are made of a woolen acrylic material that keeps your legs warmer than the pure acrylic of tights. Leg warmers can be practical because if there's a sudden shift in weather you can take them off easily, stuff them into your jersey pocket, and still have your shorts.

When I ride in cold weather I sometimes like to wear a one-piece rubberlike skin suit that keeps me warm. This suit is very good in cold weather becaue it insulates me from the cold and rain. Because it's one piece, I don't get any drafts where my tights and jersey would meet. Remember, cold is your number-one enemy in the winter or the early spring.

Well, that's it. You should be all set to fit your bike. Remember, sizing your bike is definitely the most important stage in buying a bike. If your bike doesn't fit properly, it won't work properly and it won't feel right, and this might result in injuries.

Before getting to that, though, let's review the steps of selecting a bicycle:

1. *Decide what kind of bike you want.* A racing bike? A mountain bike? A touring bike? Remember, even if you don't want to race, the answer is usually a racing bike.
2. *Find a reputable dealer.* Does he carry a full selection of racing and mountain bikes? Does he have what you're looking for? Is he helpful and knowledgeable? Does the store have a full service department? Finally, do you get a good feeling from the place?
3. *Consider the frame.* This is the most important element on your bike. Does it have double-butted tubing? Most important, does it have the right seat-tube angle to set up the right pedaling position? More important than how much it weighs is how *stiff* a frame is.

4. *Decide how much you want to spend.* Can you afford a high-priced Italian racing bike?
5. *Decide whether you want low-or high-flange hubs* (a matter of personal preference) *and whether you want clincher wheels or sew-up wheels.* Clinchers will be a bit cheaper in the long run and are less susceptible to flats, but you'll need tire irons to change tires. Sew-ups, on the other hand, need to be very carefully secured on the rim. They're more expensive but also more responsive and easier to change. Overall, I would suggest sew-ups for any competitive racing and high-quality, high-pressure clinchers for touring.
6. *Examine the components on your bike.*

Cranksets: These should be alloy, unitized (one-piece) construction with a five-arm spindle.

Freewheels: Stay away from fancy, expensive alloy freewheels except where you know you need it (in a competitive situation requiring a light bike, such as a championship time trial). For most riders a good compromise between five-and seven-speed models is the six-speed freewheel. Make sure sprockets on your bike are suited to any hill riding you do.

Front derailleur: Make sure the front derailleur shifts smoothly. The chain should not rub on total crossover (big chainring, big freewheel sprocket). Remember, if you have a brazed-on mount for the front derailleur you'll have limited flexibility in changing chainring sizes.

Rear derailleur: Make sure you have a brazed-on "ear" to attach the rear derailleur to the frame. Make sure that the shifting action is smooth. Check roller tension. Make sure you know what the range of your rear derailleur is (some models only accommodate thirteen to twenty-four, others as much as fourteen to thirty-six). Make sure cable guides and shift lever mounts are brazed to the frame.

Pedals: Decide whether you want strapless pedals (like the Look pedal) or a traditional model. Remember that you need to ride with some sort of binding, either toe strap or strapless.

Brakes: If your bike has alloy side-pull brakes you're probably in good shape. Center-pull brakes actually have better stopping action than side-pulls but are more difficult to install and maintain. Make sure brake levers have cushioned hoods.

Handlebars: Make sure you get good alloy handlebars. Width of bars should approximate width of shoulders. Unless you have a special preference, get bars with straight, flat tops and a big drop. Plug the ends of the bars.

Handlebar stem: This should be alloy. You can consider two models: the traditional style with the bolt tightening the bars underneath and the aerodynamic model with the bolt inside the stem behind the bars. The aerodynamic stem cuts down wind resistance slightly but tends to creak and is more expensive.

Seat: The seat should not be wide, but narrow enough to be unobtrusive yet wide enough to provide support. Although the all-leather saddle was once popular, I recommend the plastic saddle covered in dense foam and wrapped in leather. This is a nearly ubiquitous saddle among pros today.

Seat post: The seat post should always be alloy. A steel seat post is heavy and could rust the inside of your seat tube. The seat post should be examined for strength and the bolt attaching seat post to saddle should be convenient to reach.

7. *Look for details.* Make sure you have brazed-on mounts for a water bottle holder. Inspect the paint job: Make sure it's consistent and rich. Inspect the quality of the bolt attaching the seat post to the seat tube. If it isn't flush, you could have trouble down the line.

8. *Pick the right cycling clothes.*

Shoes: Anybody who wants to ride a bike should have cycling shoes with cleats. If you absolutely need to walk and ride you could choose touring shoes, but they're at best a compromise.

Cycling shorts: You should pick shorts that are made of a high-quality fabric that stretches but molds to your body. Shorts don't have to be black but should come to about two inches above the top of your knee. Make sure you have high-quality chamois padding on the seat of your shorts. I prefer the bib-style shorts that eliminate the need for suspenders.

Jerseys: Pick a number of jerseys in short-and long-sleeved models. Buy extra jerseys so you'll always have a fresh one. Make sure the stitches don't stick out.

Cycling gloves: You don't need to ride in cycling gloves but they can save your hands in a fall, and they help to absorb road vibration. Gloves should be padded in the palms. Ride in lighter gloves when the weather warms up.

Eyewear: In the old days wearing sunglasses was dangerous. But the new cycling eyewear can protect your eyes from sun, dust, and debris. And it's safe.

Helmet: Even though many riders don't like to wear one, you should consider a hard-shell helmet for your safety. Always buy a hard-shell that meets recognized requirements. You can find models that are light and comfortable.

Accessories: You'll need to have water bottles, spare tires, and a pump. You should also get a foot pump for use in your house.

Winter clothing: Unless you live in certain parts of Southern California or Hawaii, you'll need winter clothing. An excellent selection of tights, gloves, booties, and long-sleeved parkas can be found in a reputable bike store.

4

How to Fit
Your Bicycle

*T*here once was a time when fitting your bike was a casual, haphazard operation. You would go to your bike shop and if you could straddle the top tube without too much trouble, the bike fit you. Then you'd hop on the saddle and you'd put your feet on the back side of the pedals and start pedaling backward. When your leg was pretty much extended at the bottom of the stroke, the bike shop mechanic would give the seat post bolt a swift turn of the wrench and you'd be in business. With that and a pat on the back you had yourself a bike. It didn't matter that the back side of the pedals was considerably different from the top side. It didn't matter that you might have been wearing thick sneakers or a pair of thin running shorts, throwing this measurement completely off.

Luckily, cycling has evolved quite a bit since then. Bicycle manufacturers have developed sophisticated bikes at much lower prices. And, on the whole, bike shops have become much more knowledgeable about the sport of cycling.

Unfortunately, though, correctly fitting your bike remains an exacting science that has few well-informed practitioners. As soon as you start asking people how to fit a bicycle correctly, you'll discover that there are usually as many opinions as there are people; everybody has his own theory. For the most part these theories are based on completely unproven, untested information. It's not uncommon to hear a rider advise others to ride with the saddle pointing down because that's how he's been riding for ten years and he's won a couple of century rides after setting the "record" for a local hill climb. The rider never understood that he might have ridden even faster and more comfortably if the seat had been positioned correctly.

Although it is true that your body can adapt to virtually any position, you will not get the full benefit out of your riding if you don't set up the correct position. I rode with my saddle position too low for six years and won a lot of races. Had the information been available to me at the time about the correct position, I might have done even better.

YOU MIGHT GET ONLY HALF THE STORY

Even at the better bike shops you may get only half the information you need. Many bike shops still sell bicycles that are *too big*, because that has been the American tradition. Parents often buy a bike that's a couple of sizes too big for their children because they think their kids will grow into it. They don't realize that the bike may be so uncomfortable that it may discourage their child from enjoying the bike.

Even some best-selling books on cycling print unproven, personal experiences as gospel. Although tests have shown for some time that a higher saddle allows the rider to ride more efficiently, one popular book explains that the saddle height should be positioned in the old-fashioned way, by placing your heel on the back of the pedal. The writer backs up his claim with some examples of American amateurs he's coached in the past. Ironically, most of the successful riders have increased their saddle height since that book was written.

Most American cyclists tend to set up incorrectly on their bicycle. The traditional approach of placing your heel on the back of the pedals results in a low seat; other riders are too high on their saddle because they have not carefully established their saddle height. This is unfortunate, because position is by far the most important single factor in determining how your bicycle will perform. I always laugh when I see people riding two-thousand-dollar high-performance Italian bikes that are way too big. They seem to think that all the light equipment and the tight angles will give them better performance; the truth is that the best machine in the world is not going to do them one bit of good if it doesn't fit correctly.

Remember, the bicycle is not just an inert machine, but a synergetic link that must meld perfectly to your body to work well. It's like a pair of ice skates or running shoes. If it's too big or if it's too small it just won't perform

When I first turned pro, French coach Cyrille Guimard raised my saddle an inch and a half.

optimally. If you forget everything else I tell you, always remember to size yourself correctly on your new bike. It's important.

THE FRENCH FORMULA FOR PEFECT FIT

The formula that I have used to size my bike and that I have taught at my cycling clinics was developed by French coach Cyrille Guimard. He managed the Renault team with which I turned professional in 1980. In 1978 and 1979 Guimard undertook an extensive series of tests to determine the most efficient cycling position. Guimard, a former pro himself, had become frustrated with all the hearsay advice that permeated cycling. Very few studies had ever been done to test cycling position and most of the top pros simply followed the hand-me-down advice of their coaches.

Guimard was convinced that there was a more scientific approach. He enlisted the help of Dr. Ginet, one of France's top physiologists. Guimard's system was confirmed a few years ago by Swiss engineer Wilfried Hüggi—a friend of mine—who did an independent study with all the top champions in cycling. He found that Guimard's formula for position was within millimeters of being ideal. Using the massive wind tunnel at the Renault automobile plant, he tested fifteen riders of his Renault team.

What Guimard discovered is that the traditional approach of establishing position resulted in a low saddle height. He discovered that when the saddle was raised, the muscles delivered power to the pedals much more efficiently. He also discovered that the higher position was more aerodynamically efficient—resulting in less fatigue over the long run.

When Guimard first saw me racing as an amateur in France, he couldn't believe the power I had with such a low saddle position and overly high handlebar-stem position. He told me that if I had had a better position for the 1979 junior world championships in Buenos Aires, Argentina, I could have lowered my time in the pursuit—possibly getting a gold medal instead of the silver that I did get.

When I first turned professional, Guimard raised my position an inch and a half. That is like increasing your shoe size three sizes. He measured my inseam and told me I had to raise my saddle an inch and a half. I was shocked. Although he told me to raise it slowly, I increased my position by the entire inch and a half just for one day to see how it was. It felt as if I could barely touch the pedals. Yet Guimard was right—now the saddle height seems perfectly normal. If I went back to the old saddle position, I would feel as if I were squatting. People back in America were shocked that I was raising my saddle so much—some even thought I would damage my knees.

Well, it did take a little getting used to, like any major change. But once I got used to it, I realized how much difference the right position makes. Not only did I ride better, but all the muscles in my body loosened up. I never had lower back pain anymore, my arms were never sore. Most of all, I was using the muscular force delivered by my legs much more efficiently. This meant that my entire body was better rested at the end of a long race. Because I was higher on the saddle and somewhat lower on my bars, I also had a much more aerodynamically efficient position, which meant that I needed to use less energy to slice the air. I always chuckle when I see people riding the new aerodynamic bikes when their position is so bad that all the aerodynamics on the bike are for naught.

One common misconception about cycling position is that the *only* important element is saddle height. That is not true. Your cycling position should actually be set by a series of different measurements. The *first* measurement to establish is the saddle height. Next, you must make sure that the cleat on your cycling shoe is perfectly positioned. This can be an exacting process, but if you don't position your cleats correctly, you risk pain and injury. After that, you need to determine the fore-aft position of your saddle to get the right pedaling position. Next, determine the length and height of your stem (and thus the height of the handlebars) to get the right extension for your upper body. Finally, you must make sure that the handlebars are set at the right angle and that brake levers are installed in the most comfortable position on the bars. I'll cover all of these steps in detail in the pages that follow.

THE FIRST STEP: THE RIGHT FRAME SIZE

Before buying a bike, you have to determine what frame size you'll need. Unless you have the right frame size, it may be practically impossible to achieve the right cycling position. Some people mistakenly feel that frame size isn't all that important. The most common argument I've heard is that you can adjust the seat to make up for a frame that's too small or too big.

The truth is that a big frame is heavier, less responsive, and not as stiff as a correctly sized frame. You might also have trouble setting up your correct front-and-back position, because a bigger frame is also a longer frame.

If, on the other hand, you get a frame that's too small, you'll run out of seat post to raise your saddle and you'll have a dangerously long—and breakable—handlebar stem. A very small frame will be harder to control than a frame that's correctly fitted to you.

The key is to find a bike that is as small as possible vertically, while being long enough horizontally that it doesn't bunch you up. The smaller frame is preferable because it's stiffer and lighter. It'll be easy to handle without being overly nervous. It will be responsive but also flexible enough to cushion you.

The right frame gives a balance between height and length, between responsiveness and comfort.

To determine the right frame for you the first thing to do is to take an exact measurement of your inseam. This is something you should do at home before shopping for your bike. To take your inseam measurement, put on the kind of cycling clothes you will ordinarily ride in. If you don't have any cycling clothes, I recommend you go out and buy a pair of high-quality cycling shorts with a chamois lining in the crotch before you do anything else. This is important because the thickness of the material and the chamois will affect your inseam measurement. Remember, you want to measure your inseam exactly as it will be on the bike. If buying a pair of cycling shorts before you measure your inseam is too much trouble (for example, if you live far away from any bike shop), you *can* make a first, preliminary measurement to determine the frame size you need and come home later with your bike and clothes to determine the exact measurement to fit the seat and handlebar posts correctly.

Wear only a pair of thin riding socks. Don't put on your cycling shoes. Next, you'll need a large, hardcover book about an inch-and-a-half thick and about five inches long. Go to an *uncarpeted* area where you can make a small mark on the wall (the garage is a good place for this). You want to make sure to stand on a hard, uncarpeted surface so that your measurement will be exact.

For this measurement, the book will act as your saddle. Face the wall, place the book between your legs, and apply enough pressure to simulate riding—without pushing too hard. The front and back covers should be perpendicular to the ground. Once you're satisfied with the position, mark the line along the top edge of the book on the wall. Take a ruler and measure the line from the mark to the floor. This is your inseam. My inseam is exactly 84.3 centimeters (I prefer to work in centimeters because it's easier to get more accurate measurements). If you don't have any way of measuring in centimeters, see the metric conversion table in Appendix A.

To determine your correct frame size, take your inseam measurements and relate it to the chart in Appendix B. In my case, that gives me a frame size of 54.8 centimeters (or 21.5 inches). If you're measuring yourself in centimeters but need a frame size in inches, refer to the metric conversion table in Appendix A.

How was this formula arrived at? This is a figure that was determined by Wilfried Hüggi, a Swiss engineer. Hüggi tested a large number of cyclists to determine a formula that would achieve the minimum possible frame height and length for a cyclist without bunching up the body or leaving the rider dangerously perched on an overextended seat post. After testing various mathematical formulas, he concluded that the optimal formula for frame size was inseam measurement multiplied by .65. Although you should take all measurements exactly, this formula isn't designed to give you a precise figure down to a third decimal point. However, frame sizes don't vary by thousandths or hundredths of an inch either, and the formula fulfills its function very well.

If you have a very unusually proportioned body, the formula will provide you with the right frame size, but you'll need to have a disproportional handlebar stem to make up for your body shape. If you have very short legs and a very long torso, you'll need a special bike with a long top tube. If you have very long legs and a very short torso, you'll need a short top tube. If you fit either of these descriptions, you probably won't be able to find the right fit on any stock bicycle. In that case you will need to get a longer or shorter handlebar stem. But remember, stock bikes can fit the vast majority of people, even most of those with somewhat disproportional bodies.

A helpful rule of thumb is that the amount of seat tube showing should be approximately the same as the inside length of the head tube. The head tube is the shortest of tubes. It's the one that extends from the bottom of the handlebar stem to the top of the forks. If you have a very small bike, the head tube could be as short as an inch and a half. If you have a big bike, it could be as much as seven or eight inches.

When I say "inside length of the head tube," what I mean is the portion of the head tube extending between the bottom of the joint with the top tube and the top of the joint with the down tube. If your bicycle is small, you don't want seven inches of seat post showing. Conversely, if your bike is big, you want a lot more than an inch or two of seat post showing. That's why the length of the head tube provides a good rule of thumb, because it gets bigger as the bike gets bigger. Of course, it's only a rough measure, as some bikes may have smaller head tubes than others in the same frame size, depending on the design. And if you have a very large frame, you don't want as much seat post showing as with a very long head tube. But this rule of thumb should help you get the right bike if you have an unusually proportioned body and you decide not to get a custom bike.

Once you've taken your inseam and calculated what size frame you need, you are ready to go to a dealer. However, even if you know your frame size, you won't know how far back your saddle or how long your stem will need to be. That's why, when you're buying a new bike, I recommend setting up your ideal position on a friend's bike that has the same frame size as you will need. Of course, that's not always possible. In that event I would take a tape measure and a calculator to the bike shop to size yourself as you go along.

If you already own a bicycle, taking exact measurements of your saddle position is all the more important. You *may* already have a perfect position, but chances are you are too low on the saddle and bunched up by a short stem. If you discover, using the formula described here, that your frame size is incorrect to begin with, you'll likely have more trouble fitting your bike correctly. But even if your frame is off, you can still find the ideal position by changing your saddle height and switching (if necessary) to a different handlebar stem. What you won't have with a wrong frame size is the ideal combination of responsiveness and comfort that Hüggi's formula provides.

THE FIRST OBSTACLE: STANDARD SIZES

When you start sizing your bike, the first obstacle you'll encounter will be standard sizes. Many manufacturers make bikes in two-inch increments. Some have only four-inch increments, making it hard sometimes to find a frame between nineteen and twenty-three inches. Usually though, the two-inch increments, however rough, should fit most people fairly well.

One thing you should ask your dealer when looking at frame size is whether the frame is measured from the center of the bottom bracket to the top of the seat tube, or from the center of the bottom bracket to the *center* of the seat-post lug. All the frame sizes that I'm giving you measure the frame to the *center* of the seat tube. Both methods are fairly common and have their advantages. The advantage of measuring the frame only to the *center* of the seat tube is that you get a consistent measurement of the frame size even if the design of the lug is different from the standard model.

If you buy a top-of-the-line European bike, you should find a much larger selection in centimeter increments. Since centimeters are smaller units than inches, you'll be able to fine-tune your frame size much better than with a bicycle made in inch increments. This continues to be a strong selling point for the European (and American) craftsmen who hand make bikes. Although these bikes will definitely be more expensive, you should seriously consider one if you can't find your frame size with a production Japanese bike.

One thing to be careful of is companies that make bikes in inch increments but market them in centimeters. Some manufacturers market their inexpensive bikes in inches up to the $400 range. Then the bikes start appearing in their catalog in centimeters. But if you look carefully, the units might be centimeters, but the *increments* are still inches. In other words, frame sizes jump from 55.0 centimeters to 57.5 centimeters to 60.0 centimeters. Each increment is 2.5 centimeters, or the rough equivalent of an American inch.

If you are looking at a bike whose frame is a standard size all is not lost. In most cases, manufacturers build standard frame sizes in two-inch increments. If that's the case with the bike you're looking at, then you need to try the *closest* frame size to the ideal number you got with the sizing formula. If you split the difference between two standard frame sizes, then you should try the *smaller* frame first. In other words, if you found that you need a fifty-four-centimeter frame, but that frame sizes for the model you're considering come only in fifty-three and fifty-five centimeters, then you should try the fifty-three-centimeter frame first. This is true because the general rule states that you always want to fit the smallest frame possible. But if you have too much seat post showing on this smaller frame, then you won't be able to ride that bike. You'll have to consider the larger frame instead.

If you're in that situation, it is very important to see if the smaller frame can fit you before buying it. You definitely don't want to go home to discover that you need to extend the seat post eight inches while seven inches is the maximum.

There are some exceptions. If you have a long upper body, then a smaller frame could easily bunch you. You'll have a hard time finding a long enough stem to allow you to set up the correct upper body position. In the case of a youngster who is growing quickly, you probably should go for the larger frame if the frame size formula determines that your ideal frame is right in the middle of two standard frame sizes.

The larger frame size will definitely be safe, but most likely only an imperfect compromise. You probably won't have to extend the seat post very much, and you'll most likely need a short stem. You'll have a rideable bike but you'll have to settle for a heavier, more unwieldy machine. It will be much like a pair of standard-size jeans that are a little too big at the waist and bunch up around the ankles.

If this is an unacceptable compromise to you, then look at another model that has something closer to your ideal frame size.

Luckily, frame size can vary. Because the final measurement is overall saddle height, your frame can be a little bigger or smaller than the ideal number in Hüggi's formula. I have a custom made bike, and despite that, I think the frame size I'm used to riding is about half a centimeter too big. That's a very small amount. But in most cases, a bike with a standard-size frame, even in two-inch increments, will fit well enough so you can set up your overall saddle height and upper body extension correctly.

It is always preferable to ride the perfectly sized frame. But we live in an imperfect world. If you can't find the right frame size for you in two-inch increments, your next step is to look for a bike in one-inch increments. Bridgestone is a Japanese manufacturer that makes bikes in one-inch increments. The variation from the perfectly sized frame becomes much smaller with one-inch increments. Although you may not find the ideal frame size for you, the variation will be quite small (at most half an inch) and won't hurt your performance.

If you're a real perfectionist, you may want to look for a bike in centimeter increments or a custom-made model. In most cases, you'll pay much more for this kind of frame, especially a custom model. In most cases, the increase in value to your cycling won't justify the increase in cost.

THE SECOND STEP: OVERALL HEIGHT

Now that you've determined your frame size, you have to determine what your overall height on the bike will be. Overall height is probably the single most important measurement in determining your cycling position. While you can get away with a frame that's a little too big by riding with a slightly short stem, if your overall height measurement is off you will seriously reduce your effectiveness as a cyclist and even risk injury.

Why is that? Simply put, cycling is an exercise that is centered on the legs. The arms play a secondary role, supporting your body weight, pumping some extra power into the stroke only when you get out of the saddle. The lower back is important but it's usefulness is linked with how well your position allows you to use your legs.

If you're too low on the bike, your legs will be bunched up and you won't be able to use their full muscular force. In addition, you'll be straining the legs because they will have to work harder to achieve the same speed; you will tire out much more quickly. In addition, the strain from the muscles will act as a source of stress for all your connective tissue—ligaments, cartilage, and tendons.

If, on the other hand, you're riding too high, you will stretch out too much and you won't be able to achieve full power in the crucial downstroke of your pedaling motion. In addition, you'll be constantly overstretching the muscle and connective tissue of the legs—a ripe situation for muscle pulls and connective tissue injury.

(If all this sounds terribly serious, to put it in perspective you could probably hurt yourself much more easily by running in the wrong shoes, because running is much harder on the body than cycling.)

Finding the right position, in fact, should be quite easy. To measure your overall height, you begin with the same inseam measurement you used to determine your *frame* size. Next, take that number and multiply it by .883 or refer to the sizing chart in Appendix B. This figure was developed by French coach Cyrille Guimard. It's the result of numerous tests and years of experience with professional riders. My inseam is 84.3 centimeters; multiplying it by .883, I get an overall height of 74.4 centimeters, or 29.3 inches. That is the overall distance, in a straight line, from the center of the bottom bracket to the top of the saddle. Remember, though, that what's meant by the top of the saddle is the cupped part where you actually sit, not the lip that rises to the back of the saddle.

To determine your overall height, adjust the seatpost and saddle so that the total distance from the center of the bottom bracket axle to the top of the cupped part of the saddle is your overall height measurement. In my case, if I adjust my saddle correctly, that distance is 74.4 centimeters or 29.3 inches.

Remember that this overall height formula was determined with the standard Campagnolo racing pedals and standard, medium-thickness cycling shoes such as Brancale, or Sidi nylon mesh shoes.

You should always measure any distance in a line parallel with your seat tube. Since your crankset sticks out farther than your saddle you'll need to add two or three millimeters to your measurement when using the tape measure, or you'll get a shorter overall height measurement.

Use the overall height formula for frame size and for overall height. With a 21.5-inch frame I have a bike that fits up-and-down but also front-and-back. I also have the smallest frame practical for my size, which means my bike is stiffer and lighter than a bike with a bigger frame. With my overall height at its optimal level, I use all my muscles efficiently and I benefit from an aerodynamic position.

There are a couple of additional, but important, things to keep in mind. The overall height formula assumes that you ride in cycling shoes with an average sole thickness. Even though you measure yourself only in socks, the formula is calculated to include the thickness of your cycling shoes (presumably you never ride in bare feet). But if you have a pair of those Italian cycling shoes with the thick, wooden soles, you'll have to add the difference between the average sole (like Brancale) and your soles to your frame height. In other words, Adidas shoes—to take Hüggi's model—have a sole thickness of about twelve millimeters (including the thickness of the slot on your cleat). If your model has a sole that measures, for example, twenty-two millimeters, you'll have to measure the difference between the twelve-millimeter standard used by Hüggi and your shoe. Then *subtract* the difference from the overall height measurement. If your soles are thinner than the Adidas models, you need to *add* the difference in thickness to the overall height.

The best way to measure the soles of your shoes is to take a pair of calipers and measure your soles at the center of the ball of the foot. Be sure to put the calipers through the slot in your cleat—remember you want to measure everything as it would be on the bike. If you can't do that, take a piece of string, estimate the thickness of the sole at the center of the ball of your foot (including the slot in the cleat). You can then measure that string with a ruler.

If you are extremely concerned about exactness, measure the thickness of your cycling shoe soles. But really, it's not going to make a big difference. Remember, when you're within a centimeter of your correct overall height measurement, you'll be fine. Also, external factors like shifting your position on the saddle and riding in wet cycling shorts will change your position a little anyway. Don't get overly hung up on the minor details of setting up your position—if you do it could become a psychological crutch.

The overall height formula also assumes that you're going to ride with the standard-length 170 millimeter cranks. Of course, you may ride with different cranks, depending on your needs and personal preference. The reason for changing crankarm lengths is to get more leverage (with longer cranks) or more speed (with shorter cranks). If you change your overall height to accommodate the difference in crankarm lengths, you'll reduce the added leverage or speed you could get with a different length of crankarm.

The formula for overall height that I describe here is calculated for 170-millimeter crankarms. But I ordinarily ride in 175-millimeter cranks and still use the same measurement. Bernard Hinault likes to change crankarm lengths when he rides in time trial races. But he doesn't change his overall saddle height. When Hinault changes from his ordinary 172.5-millimeter cranks to 175-millimeter cranks, he would lower his overall position by 5 millimeters at the top of the stroke (adding the lowered saddle to the length-

Sean Kelly rides low on his saddle and very bunched up on his upper body.

ened crankarm) if he tried to compensate for the longer cranks. And this is something no one should do because it provides less efficiency at the top of the pedaling stroke.

If you ride with the new strapless pedal systems (like the Look pedal), the value for overall height will be three millimeters less.

Of course, some pedals may place the bottom of your shoe a few millimeters higher over the pedal axle. In that case you need to, first of all, place your cycling shoe into your strapless pedal system. Next, take a tape measure and measure the *vertical* distance between the top of the cleat slot and the center of the pedal axle. Next, take the vertical distance of the cleat plate on a conventional pedal, which is approximately fifteen millimeters, and *subtract* it from the value for your strapless pedal system. Then, take that difference and *subtract* it from the overall height value.

SADDLE HEIGHT CONTROVERSY

Controversy has surrounded the matter of saddle height. You'll still find many people, both in America and in Europe, who stand by the old-fashioned method of placing your heel on the back side of the pedal. The choice of saddle position is, of course, in part personal and in part psychological. Some top racers ride too low on their bikes, like Irish superstar Sean Kelly. He probably determined his position a long time ago, before anybody knew better, and simply got used to it. Now he would probably have a lot of trouble changing. Personally, I'm convinced that if Kelly improved his position he could do even better than he has the past few years. Actually, I'm not sure his inefficient position is so bad, for my sake.

To make matters worse, there are many conflicting scientific methods out there. In his excellent book *Bicycle Road Racing*, United States Cycling Federation national coaching director Eddie Borysewicz recommends that your saddle be positioned at 96 percent of your leg length, with the leg measured all the way up to the center of rotation of the greater trochanter of the femur (the bump that sticks out from the outside of your hip).

Since Borysewicz uses an entirely different method, you need to make a few calculations to compare the method developed by Guimard—which I recommend here—and Borysewicz's method. Borysewicz's method comes out with a lower saddle position than the Guimard method.

Why? Because Borysewicz quotes the results of a test conducted in 1982 by exercise physiologist Mark Hodges. Those results show that optimal oxygen consumption results at 96 percent of leg length (with the leg measured to the bump on the outside of the hip). Seven of ten of the riders who took part in the test—including some of America's top amateurs of the time—found that they had been riding too low on their bikes. But the new position, higher than the traditional heels-on-the-pedal method, wasn't significantly higher in most cases.

Although the test results show that a higher position can produce even greater power, Borysewicz feels that since oxygen consumption falls off at any position higher than 96 percent of leg length, the extra power can't be used efficiently.

Unfortunately, the results of the Hodges test contradict the results of the test conducted by Dr. Ginet, and supervised by Cyrille Guimard, in Nantes in 1978 and 1979. But there is a reason why. The one factor that the carefully orchestrated Hodges test didn't take into account was "muscle memory." Hodges tested the riders only for ninety minutes a day and for a limited period of time. In between tests, riders continued riding with their original positions. As Borysewicz points out in his book, the muscles can become adapted to riding in an incorrect position—soon that position provides optimal oxygen consumption, as the body adapts to its circumstances.

The French test, on the other hand, was conducted over a longer period, and Guimard's riders gradually raised their saddles—to "reeducate" their muscles—over a period of five months. Meticulous records were kept in an effort to log the effect of muscle memory and the changing positions.

Even the Hodges study found that optimal power comes at a point higher than 96 percent of leg length. In fact, optimal power comes at a point closer to 99 percent of leg length (with the leg measured to the bump on the hip). Significantly, this figure is backed up by a British test undertaken in the 1960s and is also the figure of Dr. Ginet's test when measuring the leg all the way up to the rotation of the greater trochanter of the femur.

The conclusion that can be drawn from comparing these two tests is that it'll take some time to adapt to the best position if you have been riding at a much lower position—for instance, with the traditional heels-on-the-pedal method. You'll have to increase your saddle height gradually to "reeducate" your muscles. In fact, you should never raise your saddle more than a quarter of an inch every two weeks. But what Dr. Ginet's study shows is that, as your body familiarizes itself with a slightly higher position, oxygen consumption becomes more efficient. If you have been riding with a traditional position, it could take up to six weeks before the optimal position I recommend will become your point of optimal oxygen consumption. But the wait will be worth it. Because then you'll have a combination of optimal oxygen use and optimal power.

I believe that the tremendous success of teams coached by Guimard is proof that his theory of saddle position is right. The first of Guimard's pupils to excel was Bernard Hinault. After Guimard changed my position, I felt more powerful in my stroke after a period of time.

It is true that if you have been riding with a lower position, you will need to stretch to adapt to a gradually higher position. At first you'll feel as if you're bouncing on the saddle, but that is purely a matter of coordination and adaptation.

On the other hand, you shouldn't think for a minute that a lower position is a safeguard against knee problems. Connie Carpenter almost quit cycling in 1982 when she suffered terrible knee problems. Her solution was to raise her saddle. Until her retirement at the end of 1984, when she won an Olympic gold medal, she never suffered from knee trouble again.

In the end, habit is a hard beast to slay. Sean Kelly wouldn't change his position for the world. In fact, many of the top pros also have incorrect positions—I think their success should not be attributed to their position but to their talent. Many of these riders have not had the proper coaching.

Some people find they are more comfortable on a lower saddle, all bunched up with a low stem. Most of the top American riders have an incorrect position—some are too low, others are way too high. But that's their style, and they seem to think it works pretty well for them.

If you are used to a more "comfortable," lower saddle position, it's going to take a little effort at first to raise your saddle position. You can start by raising your saddle about an eighth of an inch (or a half centimeter). This will definitely give you a comfortable ride that won't feel as if it's stretching out your legs. When you get used to that position—usually after about two weeks—raise it about another eighth of an inch. Do the same thing two weeks later. Before you know it you'll be riding at the optimal position without any pain or anxiety.

You should always change your position in the winter months when your body doesn't have the added strain of racing. If you want to change your overall saddle height during racing season, you're going to have to do it in even smaller increments.

BE WARY OF
STEEP SEAT TUBES

Once you have found the right frame size and overall height, the next step is to ask your dealer what the angle of the seat tube is. As I explained in the previous chapter, many top-of-the-line racing bikes are built with very aggressive seat tube angles. I have found in my cycling clinics that these very aggressive seat tube angles—seventy-four degrees—often make it impossible to move the saddle back far enough to achieve the right pedaling position.

If you find a bike with a seat-tube angle of approximately seventy-two or seventy-three degrees you should be fine. If your bike has a seventy-four-degree seat-tube angle, though, it will be very difficult to achieve the right pedaling position unless you have extremely short thighs.

Why the steep seat tubes? Well, a steep seat tube does contribute (in part) to a shorter wheelbase. To understand why this is so, visualize a seat tube that is perpendicular to the ground (no bike is every built like this, but let's assume it is for this example). Because the seat tube is steep, the rear wheel can be fitted very tightly behind the seat tube. Similarly, if the head tube and fork are perpendicular to the ground, then the front wheel is very tight. This short wheelbase makes a bike that is nippy around corners and very (almost overly) responsive. More important, the angle of the seat and head tubes is the frame's only suspension, cushioning blows from the road's surface. With a ninety-degree frame geometry, there is no suspension, no give, and therefore no loss of power. There is also no comfort, though. The bike is so tight that the body is quickly worn out by all the vibrations. In the end, most serious cyclists discover that an aggressive bike does not perform better, because it tires out the body.

In the old days when road surfaces were much worse, most ordinary bikes had much shallower seat tubes, while racing bikes had seventy-one-or seventy-two-degree seat-tube angles. But then roads improved and racing became faster. Slowly, bikes became more aggressive.

Now seat-tube angles have gotten to the point where more isn't better. If you can't set up the correct position on the bike, it won't be right for you. I don't care if all you do is race in criteriums and flat time trials—poor position will hurt your performance more than the aggressive angles will help it. Of course, you could find a seat whose railings can move back far enough to compensate for a steep seat-tube angle. But even there there is a limit.

When I first raced as a professional in Europe, I rode bikes with seventy-three-degree seat-tube angles. But because I've got such long thighs, I con-

Here I'm using a guide to measure the position of my cleats.

stantly had to keep forcing the saddle back as far as it could go to set up the right pedaling position.

A year later, Guimard changed my bike to a seventy-two-degree seat-tube angle, allowing me to center my saddle more securely. The bike I rode to win the 1983 world championships and the one I rode to win the 1986 Tour de France both had seventy-two-degree seat-tube angles. I didn't have the aggressive angles, but I had the right position.

The only time you will need a very tight bike is if you're a track sprinter or kilometer time trial racer. But these are extremely specialized applications.

If you already have a bike and you're trying to determine what the seat-tube angle is, it will be hard to tell just by sight. A good way to find out is to set up your saddle to measure your pedaling position.

THE THIRD STEP:
SET UP YOUR CLEATS

To find your ideal pedaling position, you adjust the cleats on your shoes. If you forget to do this before you determine the fore-aft position of your seat, you'll probably have to go through the whole process of finding the best fore-aft saddle position all over again. Don't waste your time. Do it right the first time.

Unfortunately, there are no simple formulas for finding the best cleat position. The basic rule of thumb, though, is that you want the cleat to sit squarely on the center of the ball of the foot. You want to have the ball of your foot over the pedals because this is the point on your foot with the maximum surface area—the ball of the foot provides the greatest contact and therefore the most efficient transmission of power to the pedals.

Some riders, though, like their cleats to be a little bit behind the center of the ball of the foot. This, they feel, gives them a little more leverage. The only danger with placing the cleat behind the center of the ball of the foot is

Tightening my cleats after placing them.

that your arch begins to rise very quickly behind the ball. Because the arch provides so little surface area, and therefore contact with the pedals, you can end up having a much less efficient transmission of power and sore feet.

Other riders, mostly track sprinters, like to move their cleat slightly forward on the shoe. This gives them less leverage but more immediate power—it's an advantage only in the highly specialized field of track sprinting they're involved with. I would never recommend placing the cleat forward on your shoe if you're riding on the road.

The best place to start out is in the "zero" position, squarely over the center of the ball of the foot. When you set up your cleat, make sure that your shoes are pointing directly ahead. Never adjust the cleat so that your toes are sticking in or out—this could cause knee trouble. If your feet are slightly off-center, then you might need to adjust the direction of the cleat, something you can do as you go along.

You always want to adjust the cleats to what feels comfortable for you. But you want to stay within certain boundaries, never moving the cleat very far from the center of the ball of the foot. If you are terribly pigeon-toed, or the

Cleats in the "zero" position, facing straight ahead.

opposite, you might need some special orthopedic assistance in setting up your cleats.

The Fit Kit (see Glossary) is a special process for finding your position on the bike. The riders I have seen who have determined their cleat position with the Fit Kit have always had a very good cleat position.

When I get a new shoe, I play with the cleats for about ten days before I'm really satisfied with their position. Often, I'll even take a wrench with me when I ride so that I can stop and adjust my cleats en route. After I decide what the best position is, though, I don't change anything until I get a new pair of shoes.

If you're buying a new pair of shoes, make sure to avoid cleats that are nailed into the shoe. Fortunately, these aren't very common anymore. But if you do get a set of these cleats, you won't really be able to change anything after you nail them into the shoe without a lot of effort and damage to the shoe.

THE FOURTH STEP: PEDALING POSITION

Once you've established exactly what your overall height and cleat position should be, you can proceed to determine your pedaling position. First, put on the cycling shorts you'll be wearing when you ride. Next, put on your cycling shoes with the cleat position adjusted. Before you make any measurement you should loosen the bolt on the seat post underneath the saddle and slide the saddle as far back as it will go. When you do this, you'll notice that

Measuring the saddle height and level.

the railing that attaches the saddle to the seat post continues all the way up to the nose. You can probably force the saddle back beyond its maximum, where the railing starts to narrow. But if you do this you can weaken or break your saddle railing.

After you've gotten the saddle as far back as it'll go (without forcing it), tighten the bolt on the seat post.

Next, prepare a plumb line. Since you're probably not a professional mason, most likely you don't have a plumb line lying around the house. But you can easily make one out of any piece of string or a long shoelace. Simply tie a key to one end of the string or shoelace and you'll have a plumb line.

Lean your bicycle against the wall. Get on the bike and turn the crank-arms so that they're exactly parallel with the ground, in the three-o'clock–nine-o'clock position. You should be on a flat surface while doing this—any incline will make this test useless, as the plumb line always falls according to the direction of the force of gravity, which is straight down.

While you're sitting on the bike, your cranks in the three-o'clock–nine-o'clock position, take the plumb line and hold the top of the line to the front of your kneecap.

If you're in the correct pedaling position, the plumb line should bisect exactly the center of the pedal axle or fall as much as one or two centimeters behind. If you're primarily going to ride criterium races and road races, then a position slightly farther forward, with the plumb line bisecting the pedal axle, will be better. This is a good yardstick position. But most top road riders find they like to have their saddle farther *back*, because that provides them more of the power from the back of their legs. My saddle, for example, is positioned so that the plumb line falls a little more than a centimeter behind the pedal axle.

Americans tend to ride too far forward on their saddle. In this position you're far less efficient when pedaling, both in the down stroke and when pulling back. I would recommend that all cyclists set up the correct pedaling position, because it's more efficient and more comfortable.

Since you're on the bike, it's going to be a little hard to hold the plumb line and see if it bisects the pedal axle all at once. Ideally, you should have somebody help you with this operation. If nobody's around, measure yourself in front of a full-length mirror. One important note: As you measure your pedaling position with the plumb line, be sure to keep the sole of your shoe in your normal pedaling position while applying force to the bike.

If the plumb line bisects the *center* of the pedal axle exactly you have the steepest possible seat-tube angle that can provide a correct pedaling position—remember, your seat is as far back as it goes. If the plumb line falls *in front of* the pedal axle, then the frame geometry of your bicycle is so tight that you can't set up a correct position. The only recourse here is to see if your dealer has a saddle that will slide farther back than your current model. (Remember, never force the saddle railing, even if the plumb line falls only slightly in front of the pedal axle—you risk damaging and eventually breaking the saddle railing. And that could mean a serious and very painful injury if the seat breaks.) If this doesn't work, I would seriously consider buying a new frame with a seat-tube angle that will allow you to find the right pedaling position.

Chances are, however, that the plumb line will be *behind* the pedal axle. If this is the case, which it should be if your bike has a seventy-three-degree seat-tube angle, then all you need to do is move the seat forward on the seat post by half the amount that your plumb line is behind the pedal axle. In other words, if the plumb line falls about one centimeter behind the center of the pedal axle, then get off the bike, loosen your seat bolt, and move the saddle forward half a centimeter. Now the plumb line should exactly bisect the center of the pedal axle. Once you've done this, of course, tighten the seat again and check to see if you made the correct adjustment. Don't be impatient, it might take you four of five tries to get it just right. But since proper pedaling position is so important, setting up the right pedaling position should be done with a great deal of care.

If you've had to move the seat considerably since you measured the overall seat height, then you might have to take another measurement for overall

Upper-body extension. With your pedals in the one-o'clock–seven-o'clock position, your elbow should be about an inch and a half from your knee.

height. This is especially true for bikes with shallow angles that force you to move the seat very far forward. If you have moved your seat forward very far, then what you've done effectively is lowered your overall height. In that case you need to raise your saddle slightly and take another measurement of overall height. Remember to always measure overall height from the center of the bottom bracket axle to the top of the part of the saddle you sit on. If your saddle is far forward then chances are your tape measure won't be exactly parallel with the seat tube—don't worry about that, it doesn't matter.

Once you've changed your overall height, though, you'll have to re-measure your pedaling position position as well, since the two are connected. With a few tries, you'll be able to fine-tune this very closely. And for the vast majority of people, the original overall height measurement will remain correct.

THE FIFTH STEP: UPPER-BODY EXTENSION

The next step in finding your ideal position is also the most subjective: upper-body extension. Unlike frame size and overall height, there are no easy answers here. But like frame size, your upper-body extension should be a perfect balance between aerodynamics and comfort.

The first step in determining your upper-body extension was taken care of when you calculated frame size. Because the frame determines how you will sit on your bike, it plays a big role in upper-body extension. If you had gotten a bigger frame than you need, for example, you would have to ride with a shorter stem to achieve the same overall upper-body extension. But you wouldn't have as much of your body weight over the front wheel, and that means you'd have a bike that handles less well. You'd also be less able to benefit from the momentum created by the motion of your bike.

The first consideration in upper-body extension is to determine how long your handlebar stem should be. The best way to find this out is to get on the bike. You should place your pedals so that your kneecap comes closest to touching your elbow—this usually comes with your legs in the one-o'clock–seven-o'clock position. Next, put your hands on the drops of the handlebars, right inside the curve (don't place your hands on the flat part behind the drops). Try to simulate a comfortable, aerodynamically efficient position, with your arms at about a 65 or 70-percent bend.

Your elbow should be within an inch or two of touching your kneecap. If you're considerably more stretched out, you're going to need a shorter stem. But chances are—if you followed Hüggi's formula for frame sizing—you should be a little bunched up. Most stock bikes sold in America come with a stem that's too short for a correctly fitted bike. In that case I recommend that you consider spending the extra money for a longer stem.

This is not, unfortunately, a very precise rule. If you're tall, or you have short arms, you might feel more comfortable with your elbow more than an inch from the kneecap. Similarly, if you're short or have long arms, you might be better off with your elbow closer to your kneecap.

There's a subjective element here. If you feel uncomfortable about a certain upper-body extension, then you're probably going to strain your back and risk fatigue and muscle pulls. Keep in mind that the first time you get into what is actually a good, aerodynamically efficient position you will feel extremely stretched out. Give yourself several weeks to get used to the position. However, if any upper-body extension gives a great deal of discomfort, then readjust it.

The only thing to remember is to avoid being bunched up on the bike. At first, the bunched-up position may feel a little more comfortable. After you start riding, however, you'll find that what was comfortable for a few instants on the showroom floor may not be comfortable on the open road. For one thing, if you're bunched up, you'll most likely experience lower back pain because your lumbar vertebrae won't be stretched out enough. You'll also find that your arms will have to strain to hold your body bunched together (something like a spring holding down a mouse trap). Your hands could get numb from pushing up against the handlebars.

If you used Hüggi's formula to determine your frame, you should find that you end up with a fairly long stem for your size. Stem length measures the stem from the bolt over the steering tube to the center point where the stem wraps around the bars. I ride an average size bike—21.5-inch frame—but I use a twelve-centimeter stem (the longest is fourteen centimeters). The long stem allows me to ride on a smaller frame, which, as I explained earlier, is stiffer and more responsive. At the same time my body weight is distributed better, with a greater percentage over the front wheel.

With more body weight over the front wheel I can benefit better from the momentum my bike creates. With a bigger bike, on the other hand, most of a rider's body weight is concentrated over the rear wheel, which creates oversteer and a harder-to-manage front wheel.

If you find you need to, install a longer stem on your bike and test the upper-body extension as you did above. Remember, if you are very tall you will need a very long stem. If you are very short, you'll need a shorter stem. You never want to disrupt the basic geometry of the bike.

HOW HIGH SHOULD YOUR STEM BE?

The next step is to determine how high the stem should be positioned. Stem height measures how much stem sticks up from the top of the head tube. It is an entirely vertical measure. This is an entirely subjective evaluation. Again, you have to contend with a trade-off between aerodynamics and comfort. If you want an aerodynamic position—usually because you're racing seriously—then you should consider a lower stem position. If, on the other hand, you're not overly concerned with aerodynamics, then you can raise it.

At the median point, the top of your stem should be about five to eight centimeters (or two to three inches) below the top of your seat. This number is variable with your height. If you're a tall rider, then your saddle will be high above the seat tube, and your stem will have to be—relatively—a bit lower. For a short rider, the saddle is never very high above the seat tube and thus can only be so high above the top of the stem.

But use five to eight centimeters (two to three inches) as a general yardstick. Most of all, find the right stem height by testing it on the road and making your own adjustments. Just remember that if the stem is too low, you probably won't ever feel comfortable, even with your hands on the tops of the handlebars. By the same token, if you raise the bars too far, you risk snapping the stem from the head tube. Practically every quality stem on the market has a mark on the side that indicates the minimum amount of stem which can safely be in the steering tube. If your stem doesn't have this mark then you shouldn't have less than two inches of stem in your steering tube. Anything in between is strictly up to you. Although a more aerodynamically efficient

Different handlebar styles. Note Marino Lejarreta's narrow bars (left), compared to mine (behind in white jersey) or those of Claude Criquielion (right).

position will feel less comfortable at first, it will help you use less energy while riding and could make you a better cyclist.

HOW TO DETERMINE HANDLEBAR SIZE

While it might take a couple of weeks to find your best stem height, handlebars can be adjusted very quickly. Before you do anything else, make sure that the handlebars on your bike are the right width. To do this, take a tape measure and measure your shoulders from the outside edge of the protruding rotator of your shoulder blade. That's the bone that sticks out beyond your collar bone. That measurement should correspond, within a few millimeters, to the width of your handlebars. If you find that you have forty-two-centimeter shoulders but only thirty-eight-centimeter bars, you're going to need a wider set of bars.

Like anything else that doesn't fit on your bike, narrow bars will constrict you and make you feel uncomfortable. They will result in fatigue and muscle strain. Most professionals agree that wider bars are better than narrow bars, because the wider bars (usually forty-two centimeters) allow you to relax your chest while riding. Some people think narrower bars have less aero-dynamic drag. But if your bars are narrow they will force your elbows to stick out and create much more drag.

Handlebars come in stock sizes of thirty-eight to forty-two centimeters. Occasionally, a set of forty-four-centimeter bars can be found. These sizes should fit the vast majority of people. If you happen to be outside this range, but only by a centimeter, then use the closest size that fits you. If you're way out of the range you should consider having a pair of custom bars made—ask your dealer how that can be arranged.

Handlebars need to be well-positioned. For one thing, they should be comfortable: You're going to have to rest your hands on the bars while you're riding for perhaps hours at a time. Many people, when they first get a bike, think that they'll be more comfortable if their bars are tilted upward. But just as with the bunched-up position, upward-tilted bars only seem better for an instant in the showroom. You'll find, as you ride, that you'll have to fight to keep your hands from slipping on the drops.

Handlebars should always be adjusted so that the bottom of the bars (known as the drops) is *parallel* with the ground, or nearly so. If your bars are tremendously tilted upward when you first get your bike, make sure you readjust the bars when you get your bike home so they're parallel to the ground. You can have a slight tilt, but no more than the tilt on the fork crown (the top of the fork tube)—this is no more than a rule of thumb.

One of the most important adjustments to make on your handlebars (or simply bars) is the position of the brake levers. Poorly placed brake levers will make it harder to stop. More important, you'll need to use the brake levers whenever you want to get out of the saddle, or simply if you want an alternative to riding on the drops.

Brake levers should be placed in the middle of the bend on your handle-bars. On most bars, this means that the bottom tip of the levers should be at about the same level as the bottom of the drops. With your brake levers placed this way, you'll be able to grip the levers firmly and also benefit from the leverage of the bars when you get out of your saddle to sway the bike back and forth, which all cyclists do to loosen the muscles and get a rhythm going.

If you place your levers any lower, you'll get sore hands trying to grip the lever hoods, and you'll have trouble controlling the bike when you get out of the saddle. You'll also have trouble braking effectively, because by lowering the lever you decrease the travel of the lever.

If your levers are higher, you won't have nearly as much leverage or control over the bike. If you put your hands on the bars over the lever hoods—a common position—you won't have anywhere to anchor your palms and the first pothole in the road could throw you off the bike.

With the handlebars and the brake levers in place, your bike is fitted. As I

The key to enjoying cycling is good position. Note the extension of my legs and arms. As you can see, Martin Earley's legs are not as fully extended.

explained earlier, if you have been riding in a much lower or higher position don't radically change your position all at once. Instead, adjust your seat height by an eighth of an inch every two weeks until you reach your optimal level. Never change your cleat position to something that feels painful: If it's painful, your body is telling you this isn't right. Similarly, don't radically lower your stem height if it's going to give you back pain. You should never be happy with the wrong position, but any change should be gradual.

Most important, don't change your position without a good reason. Don't lower or raise your saddle because of some hand-me-down advice and don't experiment with a different position just to see what it's like. Remember, common sense should always prevail. But you must arm your common sense with the important and effective guidelines that I've given you here. If you follow these guidelines in a rational, systematic way I can guarantee you'll go a long way to reaching your potential as a cyclist. Without the right position all of your other efforts will be in vain.

Here is a review of some of the major steps in fitting your bike:

Although American cycling has come a very long way in the past decade, many people still follow some very old-fashioned ideas about cycling position. Don't listen to just anybody—fit is the most important aspect of your bike.

Cyrille Guimard developed a new formula to determine saddle position because he was fed up with all the hand-me-down advice and old wives' tales that permeated cycling until the 1970s. He commissioned one of France's top exercise physiologists and the Renault wind tunnel to determine what the ideal saddle position should be. His findings have been largely confirmed with actual racing results.

Frame size: Before you do anything else, you need to get the right frame—the heart and soul of your bicycle. The trick is to get a frame small enough to be responsive and tight, big enough to cushion the ride and accommodate your upper body.

Standard sizes: You might be very disappointed after working hard to determine your frame position to discover there are no standard frames in your size. If that's the case, then try a bike made in centimeter increments—these should fit just about anybody.

Overall height and the saddle height controversy: You'll find a lot of conflicting information. But don't believe anything until you have a convincing argument to back up any claims. Remember that Eddie Borysewicz's method will give a lower position than my method. You'll have to adapt slowly to any change in position. If there's anything you can learn from all the controversy surrounding saddle position it's that you'll have to change your position slowly. If you're off by a lot, you should never change more than an eighth of an inch every two weeks.

Steep seat tubes: Be wary of these. Many top-of-the-line racing bikes are made so aggressively today that you can't move the seat back far enough to establish your ideal pedaling position. If your bike has a seat-tube angle of about seventy-three degrees you should be fine. But the best way to find out if your seat tube is too steep is by setting your pedaling position.

Set up your cleats: This is the first step in setting up your pedaling position. Start out with the "zero" position, with the cleat squarely placed over the center of the ball of the foot. Move it around *slightly* until it is comfortable. But never vary too much from that "zero" position: You could injure yourself.

Set up your pedaling position: To set up your pedaling position, move the saddle as far back as it'll go. Get on the saddle and drop a plumb line from the front of your kneecap. If the plumb line bisects the center of the pedal or falls about a centimeter or so behind, you've got the right pedaling position. Anything else is wrong.

Upper-body extension: This is probably the most subjective measurement in determining your position. Basically with your legs in the one-o'clock–seven-o'clock pedaling position, you want your elbow to be touching your kneecap, or within an inch of it, when your hands are on the drops and your elbows are bent at a sixty-five-to seventy-degree angle.

Stem height: How high should the stem be? As a general rule, the top of the stem should be about five centimeters from the top of the saddle. You can adjust your own stem height. Keep in mind that a higher stem will be more comfortable but a lower stem will be more aerodynamically efficient. Don't pull the stem too far out or you risk snapping it out of the head tube. Don't go beyond the mark on the side of the stem. If there isn't a mark, leave at least two inches in the steering tube.

Sizing your handlebars: Remember, your handlebars should be just about the same width as your shoulders. Adjust them so the drops are parallel to the ground. Make sure the brake levers are adjusted halfway down the bend on the bars.

5

Cycling

Techniques

and Tactics

*C*ycling is like anything else: If you don't do it right, you won't become very accomplished and probably won't have much fun. Since the basic act of riding a bike comes easily to most people, too often riders never really learn the proper cycling techniques. As a result, millions of people don't get nearly as much out of cycling as they could. These same people may spend a small fortune learning how to swing a tennis racket or drive a golf ball. It makes sense to spend a short time learning how to properly ride a bike.

Luckily, you won't have to spend a fortune to learn the correct cycling techniques—I'll go over what you need to know in the following pages. Later, you'll be able to use this information to determine the most comfortable and efficient riding position for you. A good riding position comes only with experience. But first, you have to know how to begin.

First, let me caution you again: Make sure you have a bike that fits. You might want to review Chapter Four, "How to Fit Your Bicycle." While a perfectly fitted bike is crucial to advanced cyclists, it's also important for novices. If you get a bike that's too big or too small, or that has incorrect seat height or handlebar position, your bike will be uncomfortable and inefficient. It'll be unwieldy and more difficult to manage.

HOW TO BEGIN

Your first few rides should take place in an area as free from traffic as possible. If you live in the country, try the back roads. If you live in the city, you might want to go to a park or drive out to the suburbs to ride. Avoid roads with gravel or dirt—they'll be more difficult to ride on. Be sure to wear a helmet.

If you are a complete novice and can't simply straddle the top tube and start riding, you need to anchor yourself. To get onto the bike, place yourself near a wall or a telephone pole you can lean against. Get on the saddle. Put one foot on the pedal. If you're right-footed, put your left foot on the pedal (you're right-footed if you kick a soccer ball with your right foot). If you have toe clips—and you should have toe clips right from the start—put your foot in the toe clips, leaving the toe strap very loose. (Note: If you have toe clips and you attempt to ride on the back side of the pedals the toe clips will probably rub against the ground. You could fall if your balance is tenuous.)

With one foot in the toe clips, the point of your other foot should just barely touch the ground. This'll be your safety valve in case you lose balance whenever you're at a stop. Some people think it's better to have both feet in the pedals before you start moving. To my mind, for somebody who's never ridden a bike before this is the best way to keel over, because you'll still be stationary and won't have any momentum.

Once you feel comfortable on the saddle, experiment with different handlebar positions. The lowest position is the one on the "drops" of the handlebars, in which your hands are tucked into the curve of the bars, with easy access to the brake levers. But that position is usually pretty low and doesn't allow you to use your upper body to help you ride.

You can drape your hands over the brake hoods. This position is less crouched over and allows you to get out of the saddle more easily. This position also gets you close to the brakes.

You can place your hands on the bars, right above the brake hoods, with the edges of your palms resting on the hoods. This is one of the most comfortable positions and it is my favorite handlebar position, because it allows me to be higher when I'm training and also close enough to the brakes so I can react quickly if I need to. But it doesn't allow you to get out of the saddle, because you can't grip the bars as well. To brake with your hands like this, you need to move them to reach the brake levers.

You can also put your hands on the "tops" (the top portion of the handlebars, the straight section of the bars that extend away from the stem). This is the most upright position. Because your body isn't as crouched over as in the other positions, your breathing is more natural (the rib cage doesn't impede the flow of air through your lungs). This is a position I like to use when I'm

Riding in traffic. I am riding slightly to my right of the white line to stay out of traffic. But I don't ride too far into the breakdown lane because there is often a lot of debris there.

climbing and the speed is slow enough that aerodynamics aren't important. I also need to breathe efficiently when I climb; this is the most comfortable position when climbing. Also your body is cooled down.

The most important thing to remember about bike handling is that your bicycle is a vehicle. And because it's a vulnerable vehicle, you've got to be an alert rider. Stay out of the way of traffic by riding as far to the right as possible. On many roads you'll notice that the gutter or the paved shoulder has debris, such as dirt and broken glass. Even though you want to avoid as much glass as possible, I prefer to ride in a little dirt—or occasionally glass—to reduce the risk of riding too far out in the lane of traffic.

When you're riding on a straightaway, keep to the right and act as predictably as possible. Never swerve out into an active traffic lane, even if you're trying to avoid a big pothole.

As you're riding, keep your head up, your eyes on the road. Many people who like to tour often take their eyes off the road to look at the scenery around them. If you're riding on a road with little or no traffic and you're an experienced rider, fine. But be careful in heavier traffic.

Personally, I like to keep an eye on the road and dart around from side to side once in a while to take in the scenery. This is good not just for aesthetic reasons; it also breaks up the monotony of looking at the road all the time.

Since you're riding with the flow of traffic, you must use your sense of hearing to alert you to any vehicles coming behind you. Because of this, never impair your hearing by riding with a portable stereo like a Walkman— it's illegal, and you risk getting into an accident.

If you hear a loud, deep diesel roar coming up fast behind you, this'll most likely be a fast-movng truck or bus. Move over as far to the right as possible and brace yourself for a gust of wind as the truck passes by.

Sharing the road with cars, buses, and trucks is like playing a game of cat and mouse. The vast majority of drivers are very courteous. But you can't rely on the good nature of drivers. Most riders will never have any problems with unfit drivers. But because a cyclist will always lose a fight with a car, you should know how to handle this situation.

Cyclists who ride in groups often like to ride side by side. If the road you're riding on is virtually free of traffic and has good visibility ahead, then you might be able to ride side by side without any danger. But always use your ears—if you hear any kind of motor approaching from behind you, you should quickly fall into single file on the far right of the road. It's not a good idea to ride three abreast or more on a two-lane road; I would avoid it.

In the winter when a group of elite riders comes to train with me around my home in Rancho Murieta, California, I always have trouble with riders taking up the whole lane of traffic. I find myself trying to tell them to get into single file. Some of the elite riders in the United States feel that they deserve half the road when they're training. But all this does is irritate drivers and cause problems—sometimes serious ones. One time a crazy pickup driver even came at us brandishing a loaded pistol. That's the kind of thing nobody needs to have happen to them. Better to get a flat than to get shot.

TURNS

Making turns is an important bike-handling skill. You'll need to know how and when to lean your bike in the turn. You'll also need to know how to keep your bike over to the far right as much as possible.

Because the bicycle is a two-wheeled vehicle, turns are taken by leaning the bike. The faster you go, or the sharper you turn, the more you'll have to lean the bike. Of course, the bike leans itself naturally as you maneuver around a curve.

When rounding a curve, always slow to a safe speed *before* entering the turn. If you come into a turn too fast, you'll have to brake in the middle of the turn, which can cause a loss of control. You risk sliding and crashing the bike if you brake too hard, especially if there's any gravel on the road.

When starting out, it's better to err on the side of safety. Approach a turn cautiously, and if you're on any kind of downgrade, let yourself speed up *in the turn* to get a better sense of how fast you can take a curve on a bicycle. Remember that accelerating in a turn is much safer than slowing down in a turn—even if your overall speed is higher as you leave the curve.

Unless you're making a long, sweeping turn, avoid pedaling in a turn,

Two examples of cornering in a sharp turn. On the left, Bernard Hinault cornering in the prologue of the 1983 Tour de France. Note that his inside pedal is held at the top of the stroke to avoid scuffing his pedal and to provide him with better balance. His right hand is about to change to the brake lever hood as he looks ahead to a steep hill. On the right, German rider Klaus-Peter Thaler (an excellent bike handler) is leaning deeply into a turn. Note, again, his inside leg and his concentration. In both cases, the riders are keeping a light touch on the brakes.

especially a sharp turn. Any turn with a sharp angle will force you to lean your bike quite a bit, and you can hit your inside pedal on the ground. Sometimes all that means is that you'll scuff your pedal and slide a few inches. But you can also crash, and if you're riding with other cyclists behind you, you can take them down too. A sharp turn is also a short turn, so pedaling in the curve won't make very much difference anyway.

Many racers think they should pedal in turns, especially in the high-speed criterium races, to keep their momentum high. To pedal through sharp turns you probably need short cranks and a high bottom bracket. That means you'll be sacrificing your position, which will negate any slight performance edge you could gain in the turns. I always feel a little uneasy when I come back to race in criteriums or in the Coors Classic, because I know many of the so-called criterium specialists will take unnecessary risks in the turns that could also endanger me. Not surprisingly, these specialists end up on the pavement half the time.

The universal arm signals. Here I'm indicating a left turn.

A right turn. Notice my arm is bent at the elbow.

If you're concerned with speed, a much better way to tackle a sharp turn is to *enter* the curve a little faster. Then you don't need to pedal through the curve. The momentum will easily take you through the turn and will also give you a little break.

When you ride through a tight turn, always raise the inside pedal to its highest position—twelve o'clock. This will give you a great deal of clearance, and you'll also be able to counterbalance your turn with the inside leg by moving your knee slightly outward.

In a race, you need to build up speed quickly after the curve. Get out of the saddle to "pump a few strokes of power" (by swaying the bike back and forth with your arms) into your bike as you leave the curve.

If you're riding on the open road and you need to change lanes in a turn—say, to get into a left-turn-only lane—signal your change of lanes as you would in any vehicle. Cyclists use the universal arm signals used by motorists when their turn-signals break down. To make a left turn, simply extend your left arm straight out. To make a right turn, don't extend your right arm, but bend your left arm at the elbow to make a right angle. If you're to the right of the rightmost lane, where you should always be in a straightaway, you should signal a left turn to switch over to the left-turn-only lane.

When you're riding in the left-turn-only lane or the center lane always ride in the rightmost portion of that lane. This will place you on the right-hand side of the road when you've completed your turn.

If you do any serious touring or training, chances are you'll venture far away from congested roads. When riding on a road with very little traffic, you can use the whole lane to make an efficient turn.

When using an entire lane to make a turn, ride out into the far side of the lane, close to the center dividing line. As soon as you begin to hit the curve, gently swoop into the inside of the turn. You should hit the right edge of your lane of traffic about halfway through the curve.

As you start to come out of the turn, let your momentum take you to the outside of the turn, near the center of the road. Then, when you're back on the straightaway, gradually move back to the righthand side of the road (unless, of course, you're making an S-turn, in which case you want to stay on the far side of your lane of traffic before making the second half of the S-turn).

This is the most efficient way to take a right curve. To take a left curve, you start out with the righthand side of the road. You have to be careful about swinging into the center of the road in the middle of your turn. As you come out of the turn, you're on the righthand side of the road again.

When there's no traffic this is the safest way to turn because it gives you the best visibility into the curve at the outset. But if you're on a road with a lot of traffic, you cannot afford to swing out into the middle of the road. Stay as close to the edge of the road as possible.

BRAKING

Although both your brakes look exactly the same, the front brake is the primary source of braking power. When you apply both brakes equally, the front brake will provide most of the braking force.

When people hear this they sometimes ask me why they need a rear brake at all. First, the rear brake does provide *some* baking power. Most of all, it balances the braking force of the front brake. That's why it's important to apply braking power evenly over the front and rear brakes. If you ever have to brake suddenly in a straightaway, applying only the front brake could lock the front wheel and send you flying over the handlebars. If you apply both brakes, on the other hand, you'll find that the extra braking power of the rear unit will reduce the pressure you need to apply to the front brake—and you'll be less likely to lock the wheels. Even if both brakes do momentarily lock, both wheels will skid together. You'll be much less likely to crash.

The key to effective braking is to learn to apply your brakes so that they don't lock. All brands of brakes are slightly different, and the amount of pressure you'll need to apply will depend on your weight, your speed, the road conditions, and the situation you're in. But as a rule the best way to brake, other than in emergencies, is to apply pressure on the brakes gradually. Even if you need to brake suddenly, bicycle brakes will respond better if you can *build up* the pressure, even if only for an instant. Pumping the brakes as race cars do won't really help you stop and it'll make your riding choppy and unpredictable for any riders behind you.

Nowhere is the balance between the front and rear brakes more important than when you're turning. In a curve, your direction—the vector of force— is constantly changing. Any braking action will be applied in the direction you are riding at the instant you're applying pressure. Most of the time, the tires grip the road well enough to absorb this vector of force. But if you brake suddenly in a curve, you can lose traction and slip. If there's any kind of gravel or dirt, the chances of slipping are even greater. The front brake is more likely to cause you to crash in a turn than the rear brake. Because the front wheel is directing the bike, any sudden lockup—especially if it's wet— is more likely to make you crash. The rear, on the other hand, is more likely to slide but without the same dire consequences.

Again, the best way to negotiate a sharp turn is to brake before a turn.

Many people think that as a professional racer I must ride the turns like a madman. People have seen me riding in the Tour de France on television and are impressed with how steep and dangerous the mountain descents look. The truth is that, over the years, I've actually become more cautious on the descents. Although it is true that compared to the average cyclist we ride the downhills at a very fast pace, the years of experience have taught us how to take turns safely, allowing us to ride very fast. But we still try to be cautious. We go very fast in the straight portions of the downhills, but we always slow to the proper speed so we don't take the corners dangerously. That's the key to proper descending: going fast in the straightaway and slowing just before a turn.

When I first started racing, going fast downhill was a thrill. But now I realize that taking unnecessary risks on a downhill could jeopardize the race—and my career. Riding more cautiously on the descents has rarely cost me any time, because it's so hard to pick up much time going downhill.

In mountain biking or cyclo cross, good braking technique is practically an art. Many top off-road riders are very adept at screaming down straightaways, braking quickly in a huff, and turning safely. Some know how to manage the oversteer created when the rear wheel slides out from under them. But these are advanced techniques that are a matter of experience. And remember, in mountain racing, the bikes have wide tires with gnarly tread that helps you to regain good control quickly.

If you have sew-up tires, you should be cautious about braking for a long time down a very long descent. Because sew-ups are held to the rim with glue, when you brake for an extended period of time the heat created by the brake shoe friction can melt the glue holding your tire to the rim and dislodge the tire. There are other consequences of applying a great deal of brake pressure on a steep downhill. In the 1986 Giro d'Italia (the Tour of Italy) we had a stage that started at the top of a descent but rode to the bottom as a neutralized race.

The hill was so steep and the lead car going so slowly that all the riders in the pack were forced to apply a great deal of brake pressure the whole way down a four-mile descent. When we got to the bottom, there were about fifty punctures in the pack within five hundred yards. What had happened was that the brake pressure had melted the glue and the tires started to slide on the rims, ripping off the valves.

The solution to this is to brake intermittently. Unless you're on a very steep downhill, you won't need to brake constantly. Take your hands off the brakes for a few moments. If you really can't afford to stop braking, try alternating brakes—though only as a last resort. If you do this, you'll find that when you're applying only the rear brake, you won't be slowing down very much at all. That'll force you to apply more pressure to the front brake—meaning more heat on the front rim.

The frequency with which sew-up tires come unglued in descents shouldn't be exaggerated. If your tires are well glued onto the rim and the tires are fully inflated, you should never roll a tire unless you take dire risks at high speeds.

SHIFTING GEARS

One of the most important cycling skills to master is using the gears correctly. Many people starting out refer to the different gears by numbers, such as "first gear" or "second gear." Unfortunately, that really doesn't mean very much in cycling. You could assign a number to the gear because you've numbered the cogs one, two, three, four, and five and the chainrings one and two. Then you could multiply the freewheel cog by the chainring. You could be riding in cog number five and chainring number two. Five times two equals ten. That's tenth gear.

But you haven't learned anything about the gear. You don't know how big each gear is or what the relationship between the gears is. It's very possible that your so-called sixth gear could be much smaller than your fifth.

You should learn to describe your gears as "gear ratios" from the start. If you use the gear ratio, you'll have a way of identifying the gears and learning what they are. If you start hanging around cyclists you'll hear a lot of people talking about their "52 × 14" or their "42 × 18." These are gear ratios (although they are written as a multiplication, gears are simply referred to as "fifty-two-fourteen" or "forty-two-eighteen" in conversation). The larger number refers to the number of teeth on the chainring while the second, invariably smaller number refers to the teeth on the freewheel.

Most chainrings have the number of teeth stamped into the metal, right along the rim of the ring. The standard setup on stock bikes is a large chainring of 52 and a smaller one of 42 teeth. Most road bikes stay close to this standard. On my bike, for example, I ordinarily use a 53 and a 42 (although sometimes I use 53 and 44).

To find out how many teeth each sprocket on your freewheel has, consult the manufacturer's brochure for your bike. If you don't have the brochure or your freewheel is different from the one listed in the literature, you'll need to count the teeth for each sprocket one by one. Remember to mark the first tooth as you count so you don't forget where you started.

Once you've established how many teeth you have on the chainrings and on each cog of the freewheel you can determine your gear ratio. An easy way to estimate which gear is bigger and which is smaller is to look at which chainring you're using. Using the big chainring results in a bigger gear than using the small chainring (for each cog on the freewheel). In other words, a 52 × 14 is *bigger* than a 42 × 14.

With the freewheel, a *smaller* cog results in a larger gear than a bigger cog. A 52 × 14 is a *bigger* gear, for example, than a 52 × 18.

Confusion may arise, however, when you start crossing over chainrings and freewheel cogs. Which is bigger, a 52 × 18 or a 42 × 14? Offhand it's hard to say. That's why you need to look at the gear ratio chart on the next page to determine the relative sizes of the gears.

Logically, the measurement of a gear should be by the distance traveled in one revolution of the crankarms. Although this measurement, known as a *development*, is used outside the United States, we continue to use an older and more arcane measurement that is steeped in the rich lore of cycling. Back when bicycles had no gears, only direct drive, the only way to increase "gear" size was to make the wheel big. The bigger the wheel, the bigger the "gear." The smaller the wheel, the smaller the "gear." That's when bikes evolved into the famous high-wheelers, or penny-farthings, as they were known.

When the chain-driven bicycle—then known as the "safety," for obvious reasons—was introduced, the cycling community felt the need to relate the gear size on the safety to the size of the old high-wheelers. Thus, Americans began to talk in gear ratios, a measurement that calculates the gear in terms of the equivalent diameter of a direct-drive high-wheeler. For some strange reason, nearly one hundred years after the demise of the penny farthing, we still use this system.

To measure a gear ratio, take the number of teeth on the chainring and divide by the number of teeth on the freewheel cog. Then multiply by the diameter of the wheel (usually 27 inches on adult bikes). Take 52 × 14 as an

Gear Ratios Chart

Number of Teeth in Freewheel Sprocket	Number of Teeth in Chainwheel									
	38	39	40	41	42	43	44	45	46	47
12	85.5	87.8	90	92.2	94.5	96.7	99	101.3	103.5	105.7
13	78.9	81	83.1	85.2	87.2	89.3	91.4	93.5	95.5	97.6
14	73.3	75.2	77.1	79.1	81	82.9	84.9	86.8	88.7	90.6
15	68.4	70.2	72	73.8	75.6	77.4	79.2	81	82.8	84.6
16	64.1	65.8	67.5	69.2	70.9	72.6	74.3	75.9	77.6	79.3
17	60.4	61.9	63.5	65.1	66.7	68.3	69.9	71.5	73.1	74.6
18	57	58.5	60	61.5	63	64.5	66.0	67.5	69	70.5
19	54	55.4	56.8	58.3	59.7	61.1	62.5	63.9	65.4	66.8
20	51.3	52.7	54	55.4	56.7	58.1	59.4	60.8	62.1	63.5
21	48.9	50.1	51.4	52.7	54	55.3	56.6	57.9	59.1	60.4
22	46.6	47.9	49.1	50.3	51.5	52.8	54	55.2	56.5	57.7
23	44.6	45.8	47	48.1	49.3	50.5	51.7	52.8	54	55.2
24	42.8	43.9	45	46.1	47.3	48.4	49.5	50.6	51.8	52.9
25	41	42.1	43.2	44.3	45.4	46.4	47.5	48.6	49.7	50.8
26	39.5	40.5	41.5	42.6	43.6	44.7	45.7	46.7	47.8	48.8
27	38	39	40	41	42	43	44	45	46	47
28	36.6	37.6	38.6	39.5	40.5	41.5	42.4	43.4	44.4	45.3
29	35.4	36.3	37.2	38.2	39.1	40	41	41.9	42.8	43.8
30	34.2	35.1	36	36.9	37.8	38.7	39.6	40.5	41.4	42.3
31	33.1	34	34.8	35.7	36.6	37.5	39.3	39.2	40.1	40.9
32	32.1	32.9	33.8	34.6	35.4	36.3	37.1	38	38.8	39.7
33	31.1	31.9	32.7	33.5	34.4	35.2	36	36.8	37.6	38.5
34	30.2	31	31.8	32.6	33.4	34.1	34.9	35.7	36.5	37.3

example. Divide 52 by 14. That yields 3.714. Then multiply by 27. Your gear ratio for a 52 × 14 is 100.3 inches (always round off to the closest tenth).

Although relating your gear ratio to the diameter of a high-wheeler won't help you much, the American gear ratio system is still a good comparative measure. You know a 52 × 14 is a 100.3-inch gear. A 52 × 18 is only 78 inches while a 42 × 14 is 81 inches. And a 52 × 24 is only 58.5 inches while a 42 × 18 is 63 inches. Now you truly know which is your biggest gear, your second-biggest, your third-biggest and so on down to your smallest. But never say you're in "second" gear; remember the gear ratios.

Although I learned how to calculate gear ratios when I first started racing, I find it more practical and easier simply to refer to my gears as "52 × 14,"

Number of Teeth in Freewheel Sprocket	Number of Teeth in Chainwheel								
	48	49	50	51	52	53	54	55	56
12	108	110.2	112.5	114.8	117	119.2	121.5	123.7	126
13	99.7	101.8	103.8	105.9	108	110.1	112.2	114.2	116.3
14	92.6	94.5	96.4	98.4	100.3	102.2	104.1	106.1	108
15	86.4	88.2	90	91.8	93.6	95.4	97.2	99	100.8
16	81	82.7	84.4	86.1	87.8	89.4	91.1	92.8	94.5
17	76.2	77.8	79.4	81	82.6	84.2	85.8	87.4	88.9
18	72	73.5	75	76.5	78	79.5	81	82.5	84
19	68.2	69.6	71.1	72.5	73.9	75.3	76.7	78.2	79.6
20	64.8	66.2	67.5	68.9	70.2	71.6	72.9	74.3	75.6
21	61.7	63	64.3	65.6	66.9	68.1	69.4	70.7	72
22	58.9	60.1	61.4	62.6	63.8	65	66.3	67.5	68.7
23	56.3	57.5	58.7	59.9	61	62.2	63.4	64.6	65.7
24	54	55.1	56.3	57.4	58.5	59.6	60.8	61.9	63
25	51.8	52.9	54	55.1	56.2	57.2	58.3	59.4	60.5
26	49.8	50.9	51.9	53	54	55	56.1	57.1	58.2
27	48	49	50	51	52	53	54	55	56
28	46.3	47.3	48.2	49.2	50.1	51.1	52.1	53	54
29	44.7	45.6	46.6	47.5	48.4	49.3	50.3	51.2	52.1
30	43.2	44.1	45	45.9	46.8	47.7	48.6	49.5	50.4
31	41.8	42.7	43.5	44.4	45.3	46.2	47	47.9	48.8
32	40.5	41.3	42.2	43	43.9	44.7	45.6	46.4	47.3
33	39.3	40.1	40.9	41.7	42.5	43.4	44.2	45	45.8
34	38.1	38.9	39.7	40.5	41.3	42.1	42.9	43.7	44.5

"42 × 18," and so on. But it is nevertheless important to understand gear inches because they are good *relative* value for gears.

The smaller the cog on the freewheel, the bigger the gear is going to be. On most stock bikes the smallest cog ordinarily has 14 teeth. Although each model is different, a typical arrangement would be 14, 16, 18, 21, 24, and 28 teeth for a six-speed freewheel (which is the most common choice on new bikes). Almost all stock bikes come with 52 and 42-tooth chainrings.

The smallest gear with this arrangement would be the one with the biggest freewheel cog and the small chainring; 42 × 28. This is a small gear that is best suited to riding up steep hills. A 42 × 24 is somewhat bigger, best suited to a short hill or slow riding on the flats. A 42 × 18 is a good base gear, suitable for short hills, comfortable at a slow pace on the flats. The largest gear is a 52 × 14, suitable only for the fastest riding, usually downhill, or in a sprint.

Once you become familiar with the chart of gear-inches, you probably will find it more practical to describe your gears as "52 × 14." I remember learning gear inches when I first started racing. This was something I especially used as a junior because the restricted gear for that category is a 92.3-inch gear.

At the nationals in 1977, I remember hearing a rumor at the "rollout" (when the officials roll the bike one revolution of the cranks to see if the riders have the correct restricted gear). The rumor had it that a "53 × 15" would pass for the "52 × 15," which was our restricted gear. And it did pass! Everybody rushed out to get a fifty-three-tooth chainring. From that point on all the juniors in the United States started racing with fifty-three-tooth chainrings.

The fact is your choice of gears is entirely personal and will be based on personal experience. When I train, even in the winter months when I'm not emphasizing my training, I sometimes use a gear as big as a 52 × 15. But for most cyslists this would be too big in the same circumstances. After you've been riding for some time, you'll know which gear is right by measuring your heart rate and pedal cadence.

Just remember that if you buy a bicycle with a very closely spaced set of freewheels sprockets, say 14, 15, 16, 17, 18, and 19, you may not have a small enough gear to take you up any significant hills. Although most stock bikes tend to be packaged, the better bike shops will let you trade the original freewheel for one that suits you better. If not, then it's worth your while to ask the salesperson what the best freewheel size for you is and purchase some extra sprockets.

What the gear ratios can't tell you is when to use what gear. That's something that is determined by pedal cadence and heartbeat (which is discussed later). I might use a 52 × 17 during my winter training rides where a 42 × 17 might be more realistic for a more casual cyclist. Remember that the gears are a tool that you should pick and choose according to your physical needs. Never let the gear rule you (as in: "I *have* to use a 42 × 15 on this stretch of road"). If you're riding in a 52 × 17 and suddenly you feel yourself laboring, then switch to a smaller gear, perhaps a 52 × 19, if you want a gear that is only marginally smaller, or a 42 × 17 if you want a gear that is considerably smaller (as a rule changing chainrings changes the gear size more than changing one freewheel sprocket).

Changing or shifting gears if a skill that is easy to learn. As you move the derailleur shift levers the derailleur will skip the chain from one sprocket to another sprocket.

Here are a few things to keep in mind. Unless you have one of the new

Anticipating gear shifts. Italian rider Roberto Visentini has just seen the hill coming up ahead, and he's shifting gears. Note that Visentini is firmly gripping his left brake lever hood as he reaches down to the derailleur shift lever (especially because we're riding on cobbles).

ratchet shifting systems you won't be able to shift down (that is, shift to a lower freewheel sprocket to produce a *smaller* gear), or move the shift levers away from you, if you're going up a very steep hill or you're practically stationary. If you need to shift to a smaller gear when you're going uphill, or as you first get onto your bike, you'll have to be going fast enough so that you can *let up* on the pedals without stopping to pedal. (The chain needs to be moving to skip from one sprocket to another. But the two derailleurs don't work very well if there's a lot of force being applied to the chain.) To shift to a smaller freewheel sprocket or the smaller chainring, even if there's a fair amount of pressure on the chain, does not require the same let-up of pressure on the pedals.

Of course, one good way to avoid the trouble of changing gears while the chain is under tension is to anticipate gear changes. If you can see a steep hill coming up in the road, shift gears just as the gear you are in becomes difficult to turn easily. This should be just as you start climbing the hill, or about fifteen to fifty feet into it if you've just come off a long downhill.

Unless you have a ratchet derailleur system, you'll have to give yourself a little lead time in shifting gear, as it takes a moment for the derailleurs to switch the chain onto the next sprocket. This is especially important for racers who depend on accurate gear shifts to make the difference in a race. You'll learn by trial and error how far you have to move the derailleur shift lever to change to any given gear. You'll probably have to *overshift* just a bit to shift quickly. Then, as your chain skips to the sprocket you're looking for, you can bring the shift lever back a few millimeters. All of that will take place in about a second or less, but it's a fine touch that will help you ride more effectively.

Gear-shifting technique is very important in racing, especially in time trials, where a missed gear shift can cost you several seconds and make the difference between winning and losing.

Some situations require switching to a radically different gear. If you have been riding uphill and suddenly come to a fast downhill stretch, you're probably going to shift from the small chainring to the large and then from one of your large sprockets to a smaller sprocket (which results in a bigger gear).

If you're changing all the way to the smallest sprocket, the one that creates the largest gear, simply push the shift lever all the way forward. If you're shifting all the way to the largest sprocket to deliver the smallest gear, *pull* the lever all the way back toward you.

At times you may need to shift from the second-smallest cog to the smallest. With experience, you'll know just how far to move the shift lever.

More important than knowing what gear inches you have is getting to know what kind of gear you should ride in. The gears you pick will determine your pedal RPMs (revolutions per minute). Many novices get a feeling of power from riding in a big gear. Of course, in most cases, this is very inefficient. The beauty of having so many gears is that you can adapt your pedaling speed to any riding environment you may confront.

PEDALING TECHNIQUE

Anybody can get onto a bike and turn the crankarms, but that's as close to good pedaling technique as taking a tennis racket and swinging it wildly. Good pedaling technique is the heart of the cycling exercise, and is as important for the part-time fitness enthusiast as for a professional racer.

Many people don't like to think about their pedaling style. They are happy with the way they're riding—changing seems like a hassle. Some people never change. One good example is Belgian professional Michel Pollentier who had a choppy style after ten years on the European circuit—Pollentier, though, was blessed with tremendous power and talent, and that made him a winner.

But good pedaling technique can improve your performance and make cycling more enjoyable. Improving pedaling technique can substantially improve your comfort, performance, and effectiveness of cycling. That's especially true if you're not as talented as Michel Pollentier and don't have as much brute talent as he did.

The most important thing to understand about pedaling technique is that your rate of pedaling determines your heart rate and the effectiveness of your exercise. It also determines how efficiently you can use the power transmitted from your legs to the bicycle. It's that synergetic link between man and machine. If your body is in tremendous shape but your pedaling technique is inefficient, then you'll be wasting your fitness and talent. If you're out of shape, on the other hand, and you have good pedaling technique, you'll be able to get in better shape more quickly and with less pain.

The first thing to consider in pedaling technique is the shape of the stroke. Most people naturally get onto the bike and stamp on the pedals. They like to push down forcefully and rest on the upstroke. This seems effective because the thigh, one of the biggest muscles in the body, is doing most of the work, while you're getting a natural breather in the upstroke.

Unfortunately, these seeming truths are false. For one thing, simply pushing down on the pedals virtually eliminates all the power of the other muscle groups in your legs: the calves and the hamstrings. Since you're not using these muscles, you're delivering less power to the bike, thereby tiring the thighs more quickly.

Worse yet, pushing down on the pedals creates a very short, syncopated stroke. Because you only push once with your thigh, from the two-o'clock position through the eight-o'clock position, you're losing most of the stroke. The "dead spot" in the top of the stroke is indeed dead. As a result you seriously limit the momentum of your pedaling stroke with each revolution. Pedaling in this way would be like running with a five-inch stride and stopping for a second each time your feet hit the ground.

To minimize this dead spot in the stroke, many cycling coaches have taught their riders to "pull up" on the upstroke. Of course, to be able to pull-up, you must ride with toe clips, toe straps, and cycling shoes with cleats. With your feet well strapped to the pedals, you can pull them any way you want without slipping. I was taught to pedal by pulling up this way at first, and I remember consiously trying to pull up while I rode, using the cleats on my shoes to pull up on the pedals.

Although this is definitely a better solution than just pushing down on the pedals, it's really the wrong solution for the right problem. Studies undertaken by Cyrille Guimard have shown that the direction of force applied by a rider pulling up is primarily directed to the back. There's only a minute amount of force directed up, and this plays a small role in helping performance.

Pulling up limits the effective duration of the upstroke. Worse yet, it

Developing proper pedaling technique minimizes the dead points—points at which no power is exerted—in the stroke. The greatest force is exerted in the downstroke. To minimize the dead point at the bottom of the stroke, pull back on the pedals in the upstroke. Notice that my heel drops naturally on the downstroke and rises naturally on the upstroke.

doesn't eliminate the dead spot at the top of the stroke. And because of the shape of the pedaling action, it doesn't use all the leg muscles effectively.

What is the better pedaling stroke? Unfortunately, a good pedaling stroke is not as easy to acquire as a good running stride. Basically, you want to pull *back* as you ride through the upstroke. This is not like the motion of pulling up, as you want to pull back starting at the three-o'clock portion of the stroke—in other words, halfway through the downstroke. By pulling back, you get all your muscles into the motion. You'll also be able to apply power for a longer period in the upstroke. More important, once you get the knack of it, your stroke will create a smooth transition from up-to downstroke.

It's safe to say that pulling back doesn't come naturally to most riders. For about two years I rode by pulling *up* and then I realized it wasn't the most efficient method. It took me some time to adjust to the new method. But

once I adjusted, it became second nature and my riding improved. This pedaling technique allowed me to improve my cycling.

One of the most important aspects of correct pedaling technique is being correctly fitted on your bike. If you have incorrect overall height or pedaling position, it will be difficult to reach optimum efficiency in your pedaling technique. I found that my riding improved when I combined pulling back on the pedals with the new overall height and pedaling position Guimard provided me with.

To learn how to pedal back effectively, you should start at home, in a pair of running shoes. Go to a carpeted area where it won't matter if you rub on the carpet. Then get into a semicrouch close to your riding position and rub your feet along the ground. You'll feel all the muscles in your legs working: the thighs, the calves, the hamstrings. Next, try it on your bike. At first you'll find that it'll be easy to pull back when you're riding slowly and not concentrating too much on going hard. As soon as you pick up the pace, though, you'll find yourself going back to your old style. That's natural—don't worry about it.

But if you gradually adopt the new method, sooner or later it'll become second nature, and it will feel easy and natural. Your pedaling style will be much more fluid, and you'll be eliminating the dead spot to a great degree while using more of your leg muscles.

Even now, as a seasoned professional, I still concentrate on pulling back as I pedal. The downstroke is the natural part of the stroke. But learning how to pedal on the upstroke requires constant practice and work.

Of course, pedaling technique, like any technique, is partially a matter of individual preference. Some champion tennis players do not have the "book-perfect" swing, but they still manage to win. By the same token a lot of top cyclists have their own style—like Sean Kelly. But in cycling I think most riders pedal incorrectly more out of habit than out of choice. Because the sport has developed so quickly in the past few years, many of the older riders are using outdated techniques developed decades ago.

Whether you're a novice cyclist or a budding amateur or professional, I would recommend giving this pedaling technique a serious try. If you simply can't get the hang of it, fine. But in the vast majority of cases, pulling back on the pedals in the upstroke will be beneficial and although it will require constant attention, it shouldn't be very hard to learn.

USE YOUR GEARS
TO HELP YOU PEDAL

Mastering the right stroke is only half of successful pedaling, however. Because cycling is such a dynamic sport—carrying the rider over hills, through headwinds, down steep descents—you'll have to know exactly how to adapt your pedaling to best suit your body and road conditions.

Your greatest ally here is the gears. Because the terrain is constantly changing, you'll be able to shift gears accordingly, to always maintain your optimal rhythm. Think of your body as a motor and the gears on your bike as the gears on a car. You wouldn't drive uphill at thirty miles per hour in fifth gear—the car would labor and lug and barely make it up the hill. Nor would you zip down the freeway at fifty-five miles per hour in first—the engine would be turning over so fast that it would likely burn out.

Riding your bicycle in the wrong gear is no different except that it's not a motor that's "lugging" or "turning over"—it's your body.

To optimize your gas mileage in a car, you always try to find the right gear for the road conditions you're driving in. The same thing is true on a bike: You want to shift gears to achieve the optimal RPMs for your body. When you reach a hill, shift to a smaller gear (one that's easier to turn); when you ride with a strong tailwind on the flats, you should shift to a bigger gear.

The ability to shift gears and tailor your RPMs to any terrain makes cycling unique among the endurance sports. On a bike, you can ride up hills and into strong headwinds, shifting gears to adapt your rhythm perfectly to your riding environment.

Of course, this is something cyclists and coaches have known for decades. The problem was that optimal cycling performance was always measured in RPMs. When a young rider begins training, that rider is told to spin (that is, turn the pedals at high speed; to increase leg speed). A rider needs to be able to spin without bobbing up and down on the saddle at up to 120 RPMs. One of the most common ways to achieve this is to ride in a fixed-gear bike (a bike with no freewheel, on which you can't stop pedaling) like a track bike.

Although coaches for decades have taught that riding the fixed gear was the best way to develop a good, round pedal stroke, the fact is that it's an artificial way to create a round stroke, because the fixed gear does a lot of work of creating the round stroke for you. In the long run it then becomes difficult to take the round stroke you learned on a fixed gear and apply it to a normal road bicycle. Also, if you ride on hilly courses, you'll always be forced into the wrong cadence by the changing terrain. You'll be pedaling at low RPMs on the uphills and spinning out on the downhills. I hardly think that is the kind of riding that can teach you correct pedaling technique. Riding fixed gears in the winter is a strong myth that exists in cycling—but there is painfully little evidence to back it up.

I think it's far better to learn a good, round stroke on an ordinary bike by *concentrating* on your stroke. This will really teach you how to eliminate the dead spots. But, for the most part, I think coaches overemphasize the usefulness of spinning: Once you learn how to do it you should spin only a few weeks out of the year as you're getting in shape.

In most situations, you want to pedal at close to 90 RPMs. As a general rule, higher revolutions per minute emphasize leg speed and lower revolutions per minute emphasize leg power. Ideally, you want to blend the two (a point achieved at approximately 90 RPMs). But situations that require speed, such as sprinting, require higher RPMs (as high as 120 RPMs). Situations that require power, such as hill climbing, require lower RPMs (as low as 75–80 RPMs). On fast downhills, you'll spin out—you really don't need to pedal at all on the very fast descents. For most riding situations 90 RPMs is a good standard to maintain.

To determine how fast you're pedaling, look at your wrist watch; if you make 15 revolutions every ten seconds, you're pedaling at 90 RPMs. If you make 20 revolutions every ten seconds, you're pedaling at 120 RPMs. After some time, you will know instinctively how fast you are turning over the pedals.

But RPMs alone don't tell you enough about your motor—your body. You need to know how your body is reacting to any given gear and pedaling speed.

That's why optimal pedaling speed—which is just another way of saying RPMs—has to be measured along with your heart rate. This is your body's version of miles per gallon. Your heart rate will tell you how much good a certain type of exercise is doing you. The more intense the exercise, the higher your heart rate (and the less time you'll be able to maintain an aerobic state). The less intense the exercise, the lower your heart rate (and the longer you'll be in aerobic state).

If all you ever do is try to maintain a certain RPM level, you might be missing the point entirely. Riding at 90 RPMs might be ideal on the flats, but then it would be too fast on a steep hill, forcing you into an anaerobic state that would drain you quickly. Pedaling at 90 RPMs could also be too slow in a heated sprint—keeping your heart rate at a low, ineffective rate that won't allow you to be competitive.

I've always believed that a rider shouldn't just know how to do something, he should know *why*. If you measure your pedaling speed simply by RPMs, you'll never be sure if you're doing yourself any good, some bad, or nothing. If you measure your heart rate, on the other hand, you will have an exact measure of how your body is reacting to your training.

I'll discuss heart rate in more depth in the chapter on training. But you'll need to know something about heart rate now to establish your correct pedaling technique.

The first thing to do is to find out what your normal resting heart rate is. This should always be measured in the morning right after you get up. Take

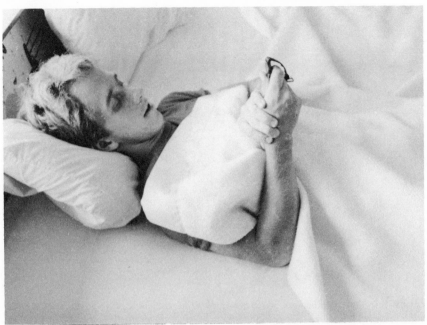

Take your pulse first in bed: Count it for fifteen seconds and then multiply by four.

your pulse, either at your wrist or neck, for fifteen seconds. Then multiply the figure you get by four. This will give you your pulse rate per minute. To get an exact measurement, you should take resting pulse readings every morning and keep a diary.

Next, you need to compute your *maximum* heart rate. The generally accepted rule of thumb is that your maximum heart rate can be determined by subtracting your age from 215. In other words, if you're thirty-five, 215 − 35 = 180. If you can, I would encourage you to get an exact measurement of your maximum heart rate by taking an electrocardiogram or a stress test, which will take you through a full battery of heart tests.

Once you know your maximum heart rate, you can calibrate your riding according to your needs. To determine this fully, you'll need to read the chapter on training. But if you want to improve your riding, you'll need to train at a minimum of 65 percent of your *maximum* heart rate. For a thirty-five-year-old person that's going to be close to 115 beats per minute. Training at about 65 percent of your maximum heart rate is considered endurance training. It's the kind of training recreational and touring cyclists should concentrate on. If you want something more intense, including hills on your rides will fit the bill.

For serious racers, read the complete explanation on race training to

Taking your hands off the handlebars is important for stretching, eating, and taking your pulse while riding. Here, New Zealander Eric MacKenzie is adjusting his rear brake.

understand how to use your gears to best advantage. You'll find all of that in Chapter Six, on training.

Every training ride is different and requirements among riders vary. But if you're a casual tourist who's looking to cycling as a way to get in shape, you want to train at 65 to 80 percent of maximum heart rate (the endurance range). Even a world-class professional trains at this rate, but only as one facet of a more intense riding program.

The key, of course, to making this work is the ability to measure your heart rate while you ride. Offhand this might seem a little impractical. You probably can't visualize yourself clutching your neck every hundred yards or so to take your pulse. Luckily, you won't have to do this to get a good idea of how to calibrate your pedaling speed.

Even if you've been riding for quite some time, chances are you've never measured your riding pulse. If you're just starting out, taking your pulse will be an excellent way of measuring your progress. Of course, it *is* impractical to measure your pulse every few minutes. But you don't need to. You really only need to measure your pulse every time your riding environment changes.

Start out on the flats. Let yourself warm up and measure your pulse after about fifteen minutes. Take your hands off the handlebars (this is an important technique, which you'll need to master because it will help develop your balance: You'll also need to take your hands off the bars while eating and stretching), then measure your pulse in your wrist or your neck. Remember, though, that if you measured your resting pulse at your wrist, continue measuring it there for the greatest consistency. If you're far below the 65-percent minimum for endurance training—and you're riding at about 90 RPMs—then you're probably turning too low a gear. Shift up; tailor the gears to the requirements of your body.

Give yourself about another fifteen minutes and take your pulse again. If you're in the 65 to 80 percent range—again at about 90 RPMs—then you're riding at the right gear for you on that terrain.

If your pulse is too fast on your first measurement, say 95 percent of your maximum (presuming you want to ride at endurance pace) and you were keeping even, 90-RPM strokes, then you're probably riding a gear that's too big. Shift down and ride for about fifteen to twenty minutes before you take a second measurement. Keep in mind, though, that your first pulse measurement could also have been high because you were riding hard (irrespective of the gear). But if that's the case and you were in a very big gear, chances are you were riding way below the 90 RPMs standard you want to shoot for. The disadvantage of riding in a big gear is that you'll be using your muscular power very inefficiently. Ultimately you'll make your muscles sore and risk serious damage to the connective tissue.

The right gear on any given terrain is different for different people. The actual gear you choose will depend on your state of physical fitness, your age, and the kind of riding you do.

Many old-school cyclists like to say that racers in training should never ride a big gear in the winter. One time, I was riding along the coast near Long Beach, California, when I passed an Irish rider. Seeing that I was riding a big gear, he told me that Sean Kelly never rode anything bigger than a 42 × 17 in the winter. This is a common piece of advice among racers.

If that works for Sean Kelly, it's not because it's a good method, it's because he's a tremendous talent. Remember, the gear has nothing to do with your body. You could be riding a 42 × 17 and get no benefit out of it— if you're not riding at the proper heart rate.

It's your body that's getting the exercise, not the bike. If you're only starting out, or you've taken a long layoff from cycling, a 42 × 17 *might* be right. But it won't be right *because* it's a 42 × 17, it'll be right because it will be able to provide your body with the correct cardiac rhythm. Unlike the gears, your heart rate is always specific to you and your needs—it's the only exact measure of what you really need.

Really, the important thing about learning about your heart rate isn't to determine *exactly* how you're training. That's unrealistic. It's to understand why a certain gear works for you in a certain circumstance and not in another. After you learn what's right for you, you don't need to keep checking your pulse. But you *will* know what's right for you. You'll never blindly follow advice—for example, riding a 42 × in the winter because somebody says you should—if you understand why you're choosing gears.

If you don't check your heart rate, chances are, if you ride at a given RPMs or, possibly, in a given gear, you might get the right cardiac rhythm for a certain portion of your riding. But it's extremely hit and miss. Worse yet, if you entrust yourself just to RPMs and gear size, you'll be riding without knowing *why* you're doing it. You could be wasting a lot of your riding energy.

Finding your heart rate is something that becomes easier with time. The first few times you measure your pulse, you'll need to take it any time there's a significant change in riding rhythm. If you go up a hard hill and you start to breathe hard, take your pulse at the summit. If you run into a section with a strong wind and you start to push and tire, take your pulse. Don't take your pulse, though, on every rise in the road—your pulse won't react fast enough to tell you very much on a short hill. But you'll know how much to shift down on a short hill by listening to your body. If a gear becomes impossible to turn, you'll need to shift down one or two freewheel sprockets or more, depending on the steepness of the grade. Remember, though, that you will naturally use lower RPMs on hills because this is more of a power exercise, and lower RPMs emphasize power.

As you get a full range of pulse rate readings, you'll begin to know exactly what gear and what pedaling speed are right for you in most situations, and you probably won't need to keep taking heartbeat measurements.

As you become more fit you'll notice that it'll become easier for you to ride faster. You may need to reevaluate your optimal gears. Take a new set of pulse rate measurements and you'll be able to calibrate your gears just right.

It may sound complicated here, but it's really very simple. Go out, ride. Take your pulse rate and adjust your gears—and your pedaling speed— accordingly. As you become experienced with this method it'll become second nature, and you won't have to make as many measurements.

Is it really worth all the trouble? Absolutely. If you just ride according to gear sizes or RPMs you'll be calibrating your exercise according to a mechanical criterion. By taking your heart rate you'll be measuring your body's reaction to your exercise—and your body's doing the work, not the bike.

HANDLEBAR POSITIONS

You'll need to know how to hold your hands on the handlebars in the most effective way for the terrain you're riding on. The most obvious way to ride on drop handlebars is to put your hands on the drops, right behind the brake levers. This will give you the most aerodynamically efficient position on the handlebars. But it won't be very comfortable. Unless you are sprinting, or

Handlebars positions: Riding on the drops provides you with the most aerodynamically efficient position, but it's not very comfortable and doesn't provide you with leverage for hill climbing. In the first photo, my hands are on the flat portion below the curve (left); in the second, they're tucked into the curve itself, giving me slightly more leverage.

really have to be in an aerodynamically efficient position, I wouldn't recommend riding like this for long periods of time. But this is a position you should learn to ride in comfortably because you'll need to race in this position quite often, especially in time trials and in the fast, flat portions of road races. This is a position that one rides naturally when one is going fast.

You should become familiar with all the different positions on the handlebars. The most comfortable handlebar position is to place your hands on the flat portion of the bars extending out from the stem. This will also let your lungs take in oxygen a little more easily. The trouble with riding up on the tops, as this part of the bars is called, is that you won't have very much leverage. Any time you want to get out of the saddle (whether to sprint or stretch your legs, or while you're climbing), you'll have trouble controlling the bike.

To get leverage, the best handlebar position is gripping the brake hoods. This is more comfortable than riding on the drops and it'll keep you close to the brakes. When you want to get out of the saddle, you'll be able to control the bike very easily.

One variation on this position is to ride with your hands just over the brake hoods, on the round portion of the bars. This is very comfortable and close

Gripping the brake hoods. This is not as aerodynamically efficient as riding on the drops, but it is more comfortable.

Gripping the brake hoods is the easiest way to ride when you want to get out of the saddle.

enough to the brake hoods so you can easily grip the hoods if you want to get out of the saddle.

Riding on the "tops," with the hands on the flat portion of the handlebars extending out from the stem, provides you with a high, comfortable style. But it isn't very aerodynamically efficient, and you can't get out of the saddle like this. But I often prefer to ride with my hands on the tops because I can relax my arms and back.

While concentrating on developing a good pedaling style, work on keeping your upper body as loose and relaxed as possible. Again, it is important that your bike fit perfectly. If your bike is too small or too big, you'll have a hard time relaxing your upper body.

But if your bike fits right, you should be able to relax your back and arms. If you're very competitive, you may notice that you tense your arms whenever you push hard. Although this is a natural instinct, you need to relax your arms: Tensed arms won't make you go faster, they'll simply tire more quickly.

Many riders notice that their upper body gets tired when they ride hard, especially up hills. The solution is often believed to be weight training to strengthen the upper body. When I was a junior, I raced the Mount Tamalpais hill climb in Marin County. At the beginning of the hill, my upper body became so tense I could barely hold on to the handlebars. And then, of

Riding with my hands on the bars draped over the brake hoods. This is a comfortable position, good for climbing, but you don't get any leverage if you want to get out of the saddle.

Riding on the tops. Note that my posture is not aerodynamically efficient. But because it's comfortable to ride on the tops, I can relax my arms and back and conserve energy.

course, I became exhausted from the tension. Afterward I thought I had to do some weight training because I believed—erroneously—that the reason I got exhausted was that my upper body was not strong enough.

Actually, building the upper body too much is not beneficial to cyclists, especially for climbing. It simply adds bulk that makes it harder to climb hills.

I learned later that the key is to relax your upper body to conserve energy while you're riding. Tensing your upper body won't add anything to your performance, but it will put you into oxygen debt more quickly.

Learning how to relax your upper body takes some practice. When you're riding hard try to not tense your upper body—to use only your legs.

Riding uphill requires a special technique. Because you're fighting gravity and lessened momentum, riding uphill is a power exercise. To deliver power efficiently to the pedals, most riders naturally slide back on their saddle a little bit. This effectively raises your saddle and increases your ability to deliver power to the pedals.

If you're riding on a long uphill, you need to calibrate your pedaling speed to the overall effort. You can start out in a big gear. But if you get tired halfway up the climb, you're going to have a very tough time trying to

Climbing a hill at the Frankfurt Grand Prix in Germany. Note how I'm putting my body into my stroke, a style that is natural when you ride on the tops. The other rider has his hands on the brake hoods, and he therefore has to pull on the bike.

recover for the rest of the way—chances are you'll be in an anaerobic state— in other words, in oxygen debt.

The tendency is to ride gears that are too big uphill. Most riders I've coached at my clinics tend to get a feeling of power from a big gear. But if you get much below 75 RPMs, you'll be riding inefficiently. Again, learn to know your body by taking heart rate measurements, then adjust your gear accordingly.

One important technique in riding uphill is getting out of the saddle. If you're trying to crest a short, steep rise, often the best way is to sprint by getting out of the saddle. Because the effort is short, you won't be putting your body into an anaerobic state, and you'll be making the hill easier on your body.

If you're riding a long hill you'll probably also want to get out of your saddle from time to time to stretch your muscles. If you're very tired, getting out of the saddle will let some of the lactic acid out of your legs. But mostly, getting out of the saddle will add the force of your body and legs to the pedal stroke for a few instants. It'll give your legs a partial rest. It will help break the rhythm and give you a mental break.

Some people ask me why they shouldn't ride out of the saddle all the time. The reason is that riding like this for anything longer than a short effort is inefficient—it'll tire you out quickly.

French champion Bernard Hinault used to ride out of the saddle quite a bit when he was young. I remember him climbing for miles at a stretch, mostly out of the saddle. Hinault wasn't really a great climber, but he was very powerful. And he rode up all the mountains with pure, brute power. As he got older, though, he began to learn how to ride with more flexibility— what the French call *souplesse* (which can be translated to something like "suppleness"). He began to climb with smaller gears, riding much more in his saddle. He became a more efficient rider.

One rider who rides with a lot of *souplesse*, and in a smaller gear uphill than Hinault, is American Andy Hampsten. This is because he is a light rider, better suited for the effort of climbing, where weight is a big factor. Although Hinault is a more powerful rider, he's also heavier than Hampsten, and his power-to-weight ratio is not quite as good. Because Hampsten doesn't have as much power, he's got to climb with a smaller, more supple gear. This gives the impression that Hampsten is the kind of rider who climbs without any effort—of course, ask Andy and he'll tell you that there is a lot of effort.

Sometimes you need to anticipate the climb to know when you should get out of the saddle. If you're riding up a hill that has many steep turns, you definitely should get out of the saddle in the turns. Riding around the turns sitting down will force your legs to deliver much more power than on the straightaways. The grade actually is much steeper in a hairpin turn; any time you ride on a very steep grade, you need the extra energy delivered by your torso and arms when you get out of the saddle and sway the bike back and forth. Also, getting out of the saddle on an uphill hairpin turn is a good way to stretch your legs and get a good mental break.

If you're going around a hairpin turn uphill, you should also try to ride as far to the outside of the curve as possible; the overall distance might be a bit longer, but you'll get a much more gradual rise that'll be easier on your legs.

If the grade on the climb varies—and sometimes even goes downhill— you'll need to change your gear accordingly. Some of the climbs I ride in Europe swing from a very steep 14-percent grade to a flat section, followed by a downhill and another steep section. Always vary your gear, even if you're just shifting for a short hundred-foot section (anything extremely short you can usually ride without changing gears). Also, if you've been riding hard on the steep grade, use the gentler rise to give your body a slight rest, so you'll be comfortable for the rest of the climb.

Many people think there's a secret to climbing. And there is: extremely high conditioning, low body fat and weight and knowing how to pace yourself (especially on long climbs).

Perhaps one secret is knowing how to maintain your own pace, even if sometimes you're not quite in the same condition as the very best racers. In the 1984 Tour de France, I had terrible problems in the climbs, forcing

Riding out of the saddle uphill: If the grade is steep or you need to add the power of your arms and body to your pedal stroke, get out of the saddle and sway the bike back and forth.

me to keep up with the leaders until I "exploded" and lost considerable ground.

But on the stage after the rest day, I took a different tack. We were going over three big mountain passes that day, with grades between 14 and 19 percent. On the first climb, the Col de Coq, I let myself slip back as soon as I knew I couldn't hold the pace. I fell back about one minute at the summit.

Without panicking, I came back in the descent and let myself recuperate before the next climb, the Col de Laffrey. On that mountain, I lost only thirty seconds.

But by the time we reached the final obstacle, the climb to Alpe d'Huez, I was fresh enough to finish first in the main pack, sixth in the day's standings. This was a big step for me.

The secret was to not try to stay with the leaders on the first climb, the Col de Coq. If I had tried to do that, I might have lost five minutes and fallen completely out of the running in the Tour de France.

RACING TECHNIQUES AND TACTICS

Bicycle racers have to combine all the basic cycling techniques with a number of specific racing techniques. Racers must have excellent bike-

When the grade is extremely steep, you'll have to get out of the saddle. Here the pack confronts a steep hill in the 1983 Milk Race, the pro-am Tour of Britain.

Riding in a pack. A racer must feel comfortable riding in close proximity to other cyclists. Note how I (left, number 54) am near the front of the pack without leading it, the ideal position to be in. I went on to win this event, the 1983 world championship.

handling skills and pedaling technique. They also need to know how to race, how to ride in a pack, when to attack, how to sprint.

As a racer, you'll have to feel comfortable with riding in a pack. Except for the individual time trial, most road races take place in a pack. You must feel comfortable riding in close proximity to other cyclists. You need to be able to ride close behind another rider's rear wheel to get the full benefit of the draft (the slipstream created by a rider, which has less wind resistance). If you ride too far behind a rider's wheel you won't get the full benefit of the slipstream created by the rider in front of you. You'll do a lot of extra work fighting wind resistance, sacrificing your chances to win the race.

Most American racers are not properly taught the technique of drafting. Most American races are criteriums, which require little or no tactical drafting (that is, any kind of drafting more complicated than simply following on somebody's wheel).

Learning to ride close to another rider's rear wheel is a matter of experience. If you're only a novice, you probably won't be able to ride right on somebody's wheel. One thing you want to keep in mind is that you have to feel comfortable enough to stay close to a rider's wheel without having to concentrate just on the wheel. You need to remain aware of everything that's happening around you. If you concentrate only on the wheel in front of you,

you might miss a rider crowding you from the side or a significant change in riding terrain up ahead, like a steep rise.

In a tight drafting situation, you should always ride on the drops with two or three fingers gripping each brake lever. Just keep a light touch on the brake levers. If the rider in front of you starts to slow down, brake very softly—you don't want the rider behind you to crash. If the rider in front of you is slowing and making it hard to stay in the pace line, tap your brakes audibly as you slow down—this is a clear signal for the riders behind you that he's slowing.

Although you want to stay close to your brakes, avoid constant braking, which can cause a yo-yo effect, slow the paceline, and create a dangerous situation. Drafting is something of an art. When you're in another rider's slipstream, you learn how to adjust your distance by letting off on the pedals, moving out to face a little wind to slow you down if you're too close. You want to adjust your speed as much as possible just by relying on your bike-handling skills instead of the brakes.

A good general rule-of-thumb is to maintain six to twelve inches between your front wheel and the rear wheel of the rider in front of you. As you get more experienced, you can get closer. Some riders, though, have a tendency to get too close. This is bad because they can overreact when they find themselves coming perilously close to touching the rear wheel of the rider in front of them.

If the rider in front of you slows unexpectedly, you should avoid braking hard, especially if somebody is behind you—you might cause a domino effect of crashes. Instead, swing out as quickly as possible.

Learning to ride in close proximity is extremely important to racing. Learn how to rub the rear tire of the rider in front of you without trepidation. When I was a junior my friends always used to make a point of rubbing wheels just as a sort of adolescent initiation rite to prove that we could be big-time bike racers. But this is not something everybody should attempt and requires good bike-handling skill.

Most racing has packs large enough that you'll have riders rubbing elbows on both sides of you. You too should be able to rub elbows. In many situations you'll need to learn how to use your elbows to assert your presence. On some courses, roads narrow very quickly. Here, only the most assertive riders get to the front of the pack. That's where you always want to be, because you'll be closer to the leaders and less likely to get into a crash.

To be at the front, though, takes strength and guile. If the road in front of you starts to narrow, you should know how to use your elbows and your handlebars to assert yourself at the front of the pack. This takes finesse. If you push too hard, you'll risk crashing along with your opponent. If you don't push enough, he'll get the better of you.

When I first raced in Europe as a professional I had a hard time in the

The paceline. The pace has just picked up and the front runners are starting to form a paceline (a single-file line). Each rider pulls for a short time and then slips back to take advantage of the draft.

classics staying in the front because many of the more experienced riders were very wily at keeping their position at the front. Because I was an unknown, American rider I really had to learn to assert myself.

Part of the art of asserting oneself is simply muscle. When the road narrows in a major professional classic, the guys at the front are usually there because they're stronger than anybody else.

But muscle alone isn't enough. You need to know how to use it as well. Many riders are strong but too scared or unaggressive to get anywhere. When push comes to shove, you have to be strong, assertive, and willing to rub elbows.

Riding in a pack is a technique that also includes some psychology. If you're too assertive and push too much, you'll get a bad reputation and no one will ever let you move ahead. What you want to do is appear sympathetic to the other riders. At the same time the nature of competition dictates you have to look out for yourself.

One of the most important skills to develop in racing is riding in the *paceline*. Because the draft of the slipstream reduces your effort considerably—up to 30 percent in some cases—bicycle racing is a tactical game in which you try to stay in a draft as much as possible without being overly passive. The paceline is a single-file line of racers that strings the pack out. Pacelines usually form when the speed picks up so much that each rider must follow in another's draft. If speeds are low, the pack tends to widen and cover the entire portion of usable road.

Pacelines are useful when there is a head or tailwind. The paceline is useful in a tailwind because the rider at the front still has to face more wind resistance than the riders in his draft. In a smooth paceline, the rider at the lead should lead for no more than thirty seconds or so. After you pull off to the side—usually into the wind to allow the person in the paceline behind to continue having a drafting effect—slowly let yourself drift to the back of the paceline. But don't drift too slowly, because you'll have to sprint to get back in the paceline. Ride about two miles per hour slower than the paceline. You should get back to the front well-rested. An experienced cyclist learns how to drift back close to the riders moving up to provide them with an added drafting benefit.

Some riders ask me why they should pull at all when they get to the front, since that will tire them out. The answer is that a paceline is a collective effort in which everybody must share the work. As soon as one rider starts to "sit in," the paceline is weakened. Also, ethically, every racer is expected to contribute to the effort.

In a small paceline of ten riders or so, riders often take very short pulls. The net results is that each pull isn't as tiring, allowing all the riders to maintain a higher overall speed. Also, when you look at a short paceline like this that's running smoothly, it'll seem that there are two lines, one of riders pulling up and another of riders going to the back. This kind of paceline has a constant flow, it looks like poetry in motion and it's very efficient. But for something like this to work, you need a group of experienced riders who are willing to cooperate perfectly. That's why the double paceline is most commonly seen in team time trials, as in the Tour de France.

Most riders get the knack of the paceline pretty quickly. Although it does require pretty good bike-handling skills, it's a logical way to fight air resistance. More difficult but very useful is the echelon.

The *echelon*, used to counter a sidewind, is cycling's version of a yachtsman's tack. Every time the wind shifts, a group of experienced cyclists will shift with the wind, creating a diagonal paceline at the best angle to shield themselves from that wind. Because the wind doesn't always come from the front, the echelon looks like a diagonal paceline spread over the surface of the road. One thing to keep in mind, though, is that even with a full sidewind coming at a ninety-degree angle to the road, the echelon should never be spread out at more than a forty-five-degree angle.

Just as in yachting, the wind you're facing is the sum of the sidewind and the wind resistance created by your own forward motion. If the wind is blowing at a ninety-degree-angle at twenty-five miles per hour and you're riding at twenty-five miles per hour, the two vectors (or directions) of wind

The echelon. This is used to counter a sidewind (in this case, from the riders' left). Whenever an echelon forms, it's imperative to stay in the first echelon. The riders in the echelons behind have a hard time maintaining contact with the leaders. This is the 1983 Ghent-Wevelgem classic in Belgium.

taken together result in a forty-five-degree combined effect. But sometimes, when the widewind is very strong and the pace slow, the echelon can be so diagonal that the riders are practically side by side.

The echelon sounds easy on paper. The fact is that a good echelon needs a group of very experienced riders. Even if you know how to form an echelon, you won't be able to do anything if the riders around you don't help. While the paceline naturally forms itself as the pace quickens, the echelon takes a conscious, determined effort.

This is why you rarely see good echelons in American racing. Most American riders are inexperienced at racing in road races in which the wind is a major factor. (Most American racing is criterium racing—races run over many laps of a short city-center loop. These courses are too short to allow the pack to form an echelon.) But knowing how to form an echelon is important, because roads don't always face the exact direction of the wind.

When I first went to Belgium as a junior I was shocked to find that all the races were on narrow, windswept roads. I found myself struggling to stay at the front because I didn't know how to draft in an echelon. One of the key lessons I learned as a young rider was how to draft in all situations. This made me instantly competitive with the more experienced Europeans.

Blocking. Riders Pascal Simon and Robert Millar of Peugeot are starting a break with an Italian rider in the 1983 Liège-Bastogne-Liège race. Behind, their teammates are blocking the chase and bunching up the pack.

Just as in a paceline, a well-oiled echelon of fifteen top riders or so usually splits in two, with the first line of riders pulling to the front and the second line resting to the back of the echelon. In a short echelon, the formation is similar to a paceline—you pull off into the wind. When the echelon becomes larger, a double paceline forms. The paceline that is shielded from the wind consists of the riders moving up, the one closer to the wind of the riders moving back.

Either in a straight paceline or an echelon, the larger the group the shorter the time that each rider pulls. As the pulls become shorter, a double paceline naturally forms as riders moving back create a second paceline. The key to a good double paceline or echelon is timing—learning not to drop back too fast, not to leave too many gaps. This kind of formation requires that all the racers involved have very good bike-handling skills.

In many European road races, key tactical moments occur in echelons. When there's a really strong headwind blowing, it's very difficult to reach the front of the pack, where an echelon is forming. That's why it's so important to stay near the front.

Although cycling is an individual sport, it's also a team sport, in which riders provide key tactical support. One of the major aspects of that support is *blocking*. When a rider breaks away from the pack, he's at a great disadvantage because he's got to face the air resistance without any paceline or echelon.

To help him, his teammates try to block the chase behind. If blocking in cycling were as simple as in football, all you'd have to do would be to lay your bike on the ground and stand your ground. But blocking is actually a very subtle tactic that requires experience. The most obvious way to block a chase is to ride in the paceline with the pack and slow down as you get to the front. This slows the chase and, more important, breaks the rhythm of the paceline.

But you have to keep in mind that slowing abruptly doesn't work. All the riders around you will be expecting you to block for your teammate and when they see you slow down, the man right behind you will slowly accelrate past you. You will be the only one that slowed down.

To make blocking an effective tactic, you have to slow the pace down very slightly. The best way to do this is to start riding hard as you take your turn at the front and then gradually slow down as you pull. By the time you pull off you may have slowed down as much as three or four miles per hour. If you can come to the front and ride like this every few minutes, you'll slow the pace down somewhat.

The trouble with this tactic is that you're really not slowing the chase very much. Even though you're slowing down, you're keeping the rhythm of the paceline or echelon pretty constant. If you can break up that rhythm, you could succeed in disuniting the chase—and help your teammate stay away.

A good way to break the rhythm is to slow down when you take over second place. Again, you need to slow down gradually, otherwise the rider behind you will become wise to what's happening and ride around you. If you slow down gradually and create a gap between the first rider and yourself, you'll slow down and disturb the rhythm of the entire operation.

As the gap slowly widens, the rider behind you will notice something is happening, and will have to sprint around you to make contact with the first rider. All the riders behind him will have to sprint to follow and the rhythm of the paceline will be shattered. The chase will tire much more quickly than if it holds a constant pace.

However subtle you are, though, the riders in the chase will know that you're blocking for your teammate. They will try to force you out of the paceline or echelon by crowding your spot, making it difficult for you to get back in position after you drop back. This is when you need to use your bike-handling skills to push and assert your way into the paceline.

You also need to be in good shape to block effectively. Riders will try to sprint away from you to drop you. You'll need to be able to sprint back into

Breaking up the rhythm. Stephen Roche (second from left) is breaking up the rhythm, forcing Steven Rooks (left) to accelerate. Note how Jostein Wilmann (right) has to sprint to keep up.

their draft. You'll need to pull nearly as hard as all the riders *and* counter them whenever they try to drop you.

In professional racing the most common blocking tactic is to cover each breakaway when a team rider up ahead is on a breakaway of his own. This requires a strong team that is also willing to work well as a unit. The Panasonic professional team is one of the best at covering breaks.

The opposite of blocking is *chasing.* If you're part of a strong team that's trying to hunt down a breakaway, you'll need to apply all the rules of the paceline or echelon by pulling for about thirty seconds (or less if the paceline is big) and dropping back.

You might have to contend with riders blocking. You'll know exactly who they are and you'll have to expect them to slow things down or break up the rhythm. Try to pay as little attention to them as possible. If a rider is blocking in front of you, letting the lead man drift away, try to go around the blocking rider. But don't get out of your saddle and sprint. This is exactly what the blocking rider wants you to do: It'll break up the rhythm of the paceline. Simply accelerate gently, get around him, and make contact with the lead man.

One of the most impressive feats in cycling is the solo breakaway or chase. Here, Phil Anderson rides solo in the 1983 Amstel Gold Race.

Sometimes you can drop a blocking rider by attacking uphill or in a strong headwind when he's dropping to the back or right at the back. Sometimes, the best thing is to make him think that you don't notice him. He might think his strategy's working and let up just a bit—remember, blocking can be very tiring.

One of the most impressive efforts in cycling is the *solo chase*. When you are isolated in a pack and you have missed what seems to be the decisive breakaway of the race (in other words, a breakaway formed and you're still behind in the pack), you are forced to chase that breakaway on your own. Theoretically it is nearly impossible for a lone rider to catch a well-oiled breakaway. In fact, if the breakaway is more than thirty seconds ahead, it's practically impossible for a solo rider to catch. The group ahead has more riders pulling at the front, thus allowing each rider to rest at regular intervals. If you're chasing alone behind, you're going to have to work at a constant rhythm, putting your body close to its anaerobic threshold (the point at which your muscles can't use oxygen as energy), and then letting off slightly to recover.

But a solo chaser has a few advantages. First, if the race is riding up a very long mountain climb, then the solo chaser is as effective as a breakaway group, because the speed of riding uphill is so reduced that there is practically no advantage in drafting. The only danger for a lone rider in this situation is psychological burnout. A group of riders can push one another on, while the lone rider must rely solely on personal motivation. Nevertheless, physically speaking, conditions are equal for a solo chaser in a long climb.

The solo chaser can also expect to make up ground in a very sinewy descent with many hairpin turns. Just as a big tractor-trailer must slow on a sharp turn, so must a group of cyclists. They ride more tentatively. A lone rider, on the other hand, can clearly see the shortest line in each turn. He doesn't have to be vigilant of the mistake of other riders.

A solo chaser is most vulnerable when the breakaway ahead can't be seen. Racers always push hard to get to the point at which the group ahead is visible. Once it is, the chaser has a great advantage; he can focus on the riders ahead to push himself in the chase.

It takes exceptional physical ability and experience to catch a breakaway that's working together. Of course, if the breakaway is not working well together because the riders are tired or some of the riders are blocking effectively, it will be easier for a chaser to catch. But one thing to keep in mind is that if the breakaway ahead is slowing down, then there is a greater risk that the breakaway and the chaser will be quickly engulfed by a larger pack coming from behind.

I remember a solo chase in the Tour of Holland in 1984. A breakaway of ten riders had formed and were three minutes ahead. The group behind had slowed to a crawl. I decided that it was now or never for me to catch the break. Although normally I would never have considered catching them alone I tried it because I was using this effort to help me get in shape for the world championships.

For ten or fifteen miles I rode hard on my own. Once I had gotten away from the pack I settled down to an intense but bearable rhythm. I was lucky enough to catch riders who had been dropped from the break. Together, we went on to catch the break.

Racing tactics are a combination of all the skills of cycling and a good dose of psychology. Before you start a race you need to know something about the race course and the racers. Make sure you take a good ride on the course to know where key strategic points might be. If that's impossible, then look at a course map and make sure you know exactly which direction the wind is blowing. Conditions that can make a difference might include a steep hill, a headwind, or a flat section right after the steep hill. (While riders can sometimes hold on during the climb, they often falter in an energy-sapping headwind section that follows a hill.) Look for dangerous turns where you want to be ahead of the pack. And, of course, you should be familiar with any major climbs in advance of race day.

On the Tour de France, the race organizers provide the racers with detailed course descriptions and "profile" maps that show where and how steep the hills are. I take a very close look at these maps every day before the start of each stage.

After breakfast, I cut out the course profile and I put it in my back pocket. During the race, I look at the course profile periodically. If I see that a steep hill is coming a few miles down the road and that a strong headwind is slowing the pack, I might try to speed the pace to tire my opponents, or have one of my teammates attack, in other words form a breakaway that my opponents must chase. This is where a cyclometer, such as the model made by Avocet, can come in very handy. You can determine exactly how far ahead a key strategic point in the race is by looking at the cyclometer. If you know, for example, that a key climb is coming forty miles into the race, look at your cyclometer to inform yourself.

Because the mountains play such a key role in the Tour de France, I took special care, in my early days on the European professional circuit, to get acquainted with the hardest climbs. I usually took about ten days in late May or early June to ride some of the Alpine or Pyrenean climbs. This helped me with my fitness, but also taught me how to ride the mountains. I discovered, for example, that the effort of riding the Galibier, a long hard climb with few turns, is different from the effort of riding the Alpe d'Huez, where twenty-one hairpin turns pretty well break up the effort, if only for a few seconds at a time.

Chances are you won't be racing anything like the Tour de France. That means most of your races will be shorter too, which will make it easier for you go to out and reconnoiter the race course. This is something you should do usually on the Thursday before a Sunday race; ride the course at an endurance pace, without going into an anaerobic state (for an explanation of these training terms see Chapter Six, on training). Be especially vigilant of hills and those "flat" sections that are actually slightly uphill—that's a great place to break things up. You can also look for wind direction, though the wind could change from Thursday to Sunday. Look for areas where the road suddenly narrows; you'll have to make sure, on race day, to be in front of the pack at points like this or risk getting dropped from the action.

On race day you want to make sure you know who your principal competition will be. If you've been racing for some time, you're probably familiar with the top riders. But if you're racing away from your district, then ask around about the top competition.

Perhaps one of the most important qualities in racing is patience. It's easy to panic and respond to every attack and breakaway forming in the pack. Riding like that, especially in high-level racing, will leave you exhausted by the time the truly decisive attack of the day happens.

Mark your competition. Here, I'm riding in the 1983 Tour of Lombardy with my main rival, Sean Kelly.

Cycling is a sport of circumstance. There isn't any such thing as a game plan. Unlike football, or even running, in cycling the circumstances dictate the strategy and not vice versa. One of the best examples is what happened to me during stage thirteen of the 1986 Tour de France, the ride from the city of Pau to the mountaintop resort of Superbagnères I wrote of in Chapter One. My teammate Bernard Hinault, already almost five minutes ahead of me on overall time, broke away in the early going. This attack was unplanned, a move typical of Hinault and his flamboyant, aggressive style.

At that point I was in an awkward situation. The Tour seemed lost because Hinault had gained what seemed like an insurmountable lead. But I also couldn't attack behind Hinault to catch him, because he was my teammate, and team tactics in cycling dictate that when the leader breaks away (and Hinault *was* the leader at that point), the team must block for him behind.

All I could do was sit back with the lead riders and try to slow any rider trying to catch Hinault.

Then the unpredictable happened. Hinault had overestimated his strength that day and began to slow considerably. He hit that "wall" that is so common in cycling, when the body is unable to provide energy to the muscles. Hinault stopped dead in his tracks; he came unwound like a toy having spent its spring.

Despite this I still couldn't attack, because Hinault was still leading. Only when it became clear that my lead pack was going to catch Hinault did I break away, following the lead of my teammate Andy Hampsten. At the finish I was the stage winner and I had taken back all but forty seconds of his lead.

If anybody had told me the morning of the stage thirteen in Pau that I would take back 4:39 of Hinault's lead, I would have thought it was unlikely. But the unpredictable element of cycling came into play that day and, luckily for me, played in my favor.

The key here isn't just luck, however—you must have the vigilance and the presence of mind to capitalize on the situation.

Because strategy in cycling is so passive, so dependent on what happens out on the road, it is important that cyclists be keenly aware of what is going on in a race. The top champions are always looking at the race around them, thinking about all the elements: the competition, the course, the wind, the temperature, what's coming around the next bend. You have to always try to anticipate what will happen next, and occasionally you do—but most of the time you will simply be reacting, and it is important to be the first rider to react to an important situation.

People who watch cycling on television are impressed by how much action there is. They see races such as the Tour de France or Paris-Roubaix on television and they're wrung out by the constant flow of mountains, break-aways, sprints, cobblestones. Part of the reason there is so much action on the screen, though, is that the television producers are skilled at sifting out the hours of waiting and false moves that are as much a part of cycling as impressive breakaways and sprints.

In most road races, even short thirty-mile intermediate events, you need to be patient. If you're a top cyclist, you have a team that can "work" for you in the early stages of the race. What is meant by working, in this case, is that the teammates (also known as *domestiques*, French for "servants") will chase down any breakaway in the early part of the race, or break away themselves to force rival teams to chase them down, thereby creating a favorable situation for the team leader.

As a protected rider, you are saved from the draining work of going out and chasing down each breakaway, most of which have no chance of keeping the lead until the finish. But you are also saved the mental anguish of thinking that a *potentially* dangerous breakaway might be pulling away somewhere down the road.

Many riders, though, don't have the benefit of "workers." Most amateur teams are little more than a collection of riders all of whom ride their own races with little concern for or knowledge of team tactics. If you can't count

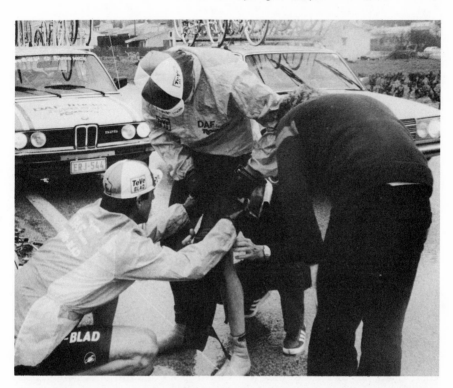

Team tactics. This teammate, also known as a domestique, *helps the team leader to take off his tights (above). He later paces the team leader back to the pack (below).*

on the support of workers, then you'll have to use your judgment as keenly as possible.

As a general rule, most early-race breakaways have little hope of staying away to the finish, depending on the length of a race and its terrain. But in amateur events, which are rarely longer than ninety miles, a breakaway that forms at the start has a good chance of making it to the finish. This is why amateur racing has a different pace and riders are keen to ride in breakaways straight from the starting gun. A good, general rule of thumb is that the longer the race, the less likely an early breakaway will stay away.

Be careful not to confuse an early breakaway with a major split in the pack, though. If the top twenty or so riders suddenly break away from another, larger pack, that isn't a breakaway, it's a split, and because a group of twenty can develop as much of a slipstream as just about any larger group, you should be among those twenty. Be careful, also, to look at which twenty riders are in the front group. If they're mostly second-and third-echelon riders, then the break is not as serious. But if all the top names are there, you have to be with them as well.

In the Tour de France practically every stage is animated by second-echelon riders who want to make a name for themselves. Because they don't quite have the talent of the superstars, they often must break away in the early miles of each stage, when the pace is usually slower. In many cases, these riders stay away until they win a town sprint or a hill prize (which gets their name in the papers) and then wait until the huge pack engulfs them. Others try to stay away but are usually caught in the last hour of racing when the pace in the Tour de France picks up tremendously.

There are exceptions. Many of the second-echelon riders are often the wiliest riders in the pack and can sense when the race will be sluggish. In 1977, French rider Bernard Quilfen saw that the pack would ride slowly on a "transition" stage, the day before the big mountains in the Alps. While the big stars were conserving energy for the Alpine showdown, Quilfen knew he would stand no chance of doing well in the mountains. He broke away and stayed away for 220 kilometers, or 137 miles, and won in Evian, a town on Lake Geneva. This was the third-longest victorious breakaway in the Tour de France. He made a name for himself as much for his bravado as for his win.

Just keep in mind that however wily you might be, this kind of victory is one of the rarest commodities in cycling. This is especially true if you race at amateur or junior distances, where the pace is usually fast from the start since the racing is much shorter.

If you're racing without the support of a team, you have to make sure to stay with the top twenty or so riders at all times. Any time you slip back further, you'll lose contact with the key action at the front. Also, the back of

Stay vigilant. Ride with your principal opponents. Don't slip back.

the pack is usually populated by less experienced or less fit riders who are prone to getting dropped or crashing.

I've been in situations in major classics in which I let myself slip back by mistake and then noticed a gap forming between myself and the top twenty men in front. I had to ride hard to catch the first group, tiring myself out when I really didn't need to. What usually happens to a rider who has had to chase to catch a lead group is that he'll be too tired to respond to another, decisive attack a few miles down the road.

This is what happened to me in the 1984 Tour of Flanders. This race is a major one-day "classic" run in April in the Flemish portion of Belgium. The first half of the course is flat and run over wide roads. But at the halfway point, the Tour of Flanders turns off the main roads to ride over a succession of twelve narrow climbs, some of which are cobbled.

The pack was huge in 1984; there were about two hundred riders at the start and most of them stayed with the pack until the halfway mark. A tremendous battle started before this halfway mark as riders fought to get to the head of the pack. If I had already been in the lead, I wouldn't have had any trouble. But I tried to jockey for position with less experienced riders in the middle of the pack, and one of them crashed right in front of me.

By the time I was back on my bike, the pack was way ahead. I had to work hard to catch the lead men. By the time I had caught them, I was far more tired than they were, and I couldn't push as hard at the finish.

If you do slip back and lose contact, make sure to ride on the side of the road best shielded from the wind. Don't be afraid to ride as close as is safely possible to trees or houses that might shield you from the wind. If you're face to face with a pure headwind, then the best protection is a sympathetic companion.

If you stay with the lead men, you'll notice a breakaway group forming by attrition. Instead of attacking the lead men, maintain a fast pace that drops any weaker riders. You must make sure to stay with this group to have any hope of winning. One key to staying with the lead men is to stay near the front but not right *at* the front. You want to benefit from the draft of the group as much as possible so that you don't expend unnecessary energy. You do have to go to the front and pull the group (known as "working"), because that will contribute to the success of the group breakaway. But don't be foolhardy and pull more than the others.

Perhaps the best example of good tactical racing on my part came when I won the 1983 world championship. The world championship is run under rules different from those that apply the rest of the season: All the riders put on national team jerseys for the race. As a result, I couldn't use the support of my regular team, sponsored by the Renault car company (composed mostly of French riders).

I did have a small American team riding with me, but most of these riders didn't have the level of fitness necessary for this 170-mile race. In fact, only one other American finished the race and no American was able to give me any support. Because some of the other national teams (Italy, the Netherlands) were very powerful, I had to race a perfect tactical race to have any hope of winning.

I stayed with the lead men throughout the race, never going back more than ten places from the front. I watched all the breaks cautiously, but I let them go, judging them to be too weak or too early in the race to stay away until the finish. Then, about sixty miles from the finish, I thought I might have made a mistake when Australian Phil Anderson, one of the big names in cycling, broke away and quickly took a one-minute lead.

But in cycling, because circumstances dictate strategy, this was a calculated risk that I had to take. I knew sixty miles was still a long way to go and that the course was very difficult. I also knew that Anderson was in a small group that didn't have any top Italians or Dutchmen and that those two teams would work hard to reel the Australian back in.

Because my team had vanished from the race my only strategy was to ride piggyback on the efforts of the Italians and the Dutch. I had tried this in other races in the past and it simply hadn't worked. Either the men in front were too strong and managed to stay away, or the chase behind was half-

One lap to go in the 1983 world championship. I'm letting Spaniard Faustino Ruperez lead so I can test his strength. Later, I broke away and won the gold medal.

hearted. But this time I got lucky and the big pack reeled in Anderson's small breakaway.

Now there was about twenty-five miles to go to the finish, a perfect opportunity to get something going. As the pack rode on the harder of the circuit's two hills, Scottish rider Robert Millar attacked strongly and broke away. He was immediately chased down and as he was caught, I sprinted away furiously. Attacking when a pack has just caught a breakaway is one of the best strategies. The group has just ridden hard and there is an instant of letdown as the job is done and the pack tries to regain its collective breath.

I had been riding piggyback, hiding my game, and now could break away with all my might. Two other riders followed me, and I let them catch up because I knew that three men had a better chance of staying away to the finish than one.

As we neared the finish I had to use a little tactical bluffing to gauge the condition of my two opponents. On the second-to-last climb before the finish I accelerated slightly to see how fresh they were. Italian rider Moreno Argentin was dropped. Now, only a few miles from the finish, I remained only with Faustino Ruperez of Spain. Ruperez had stayed with me during the acceleration but he didn't look too fresh either.

After that hill, I used a bluffing tactic and pretended I was tired. I asked him to share the pace. Not wanting our breakaway to fail, Ruperez agreed to pull at the front. As he did I noticed that he could maintain a good, steady pace but that he was having trouble going the extra yard. Although he was trying his best to hide it from me (by riding fluidly and not breathing hard), I could tell he was tiring.

My bluffing had succeeded in showing me that Ruperez was still strong enough to pull our break along in the flat sections. If I had discovered that he was completely cooked, he would have been of no use to me anymore and possibly could have sat on my wheel and beaten me in a final sprint. If, instead, I had discovered that he was still riding strongly and energetically, then it would have been unwise for me to pull the pace more than him because he might have taken advantage of my work and broken away at an opportune time. When a fresh rider sits on your wheel he gains an advantage in physical freshness for the final sprint.

Bluffing, in fact, is a tactic that is primarily useful to hide fatigue. I have often bluffed my way through hard climbs in the Tour de France when I wasn't warmed up yet or was having a bad day. Bluffing in cycling consists mainly of giving your opponents the impression that you're feeling quite fresh when in fact you might be dying. This, of course, is hard to do and requires the pace to stay constant. Even if the group is riding hard, you can usually bluff effectively as long as there isn't any great variation in the pace.

The key to bluffing is to play a mind game with your opponents, to make sure they keep the pace even.

In the 1986 Tour de France, one of the key tactical moments came in stage seventeen to the barren mountaintop finish of the Col de Granon in the Alps. My teammate, and by that time also archrival, Bernard Hinault was still holding the overall lead by thirty-four seconds. Hinault had been faltering on the mountains, and this was the hardest mountain stage of all.

The final climb up the Col de Granon was unbelievably difficult. That climb was eight miles of the steepest, most torturous roads I have ever seen. Halfway up the climb it was clear Hinault was fading fast. But I didn't want to fade fast too and I was getting pretty tired. With a Spanish rider up ahead who would take the day's stage win (but who would have no bearing on the overall standings), I was riding with my next-closest rival, Urs Zimmermann of Switzerland.

Zimmermann is a very good climber and I didn't want to lose contact with him. When, about two-thirds up the climb, I began to feel a little weak, I made an offhand comment that suggested that together we could ride more effectively. But I kept giving him the impression that I could ride with him no matter what. When he tried to accelerate a couple of times, I killed myself to stay with him. I tried to look confident and relaxed, turning the pedals as smoothly and easily as possible. I tried to exude confidence in my body language. Zimmermann bought my act and kept the pace more even. The truth is, had he accelerated one more time, he might very well have taken some time out of me. But at the top I was still with Zimmermann and I took over the overall lead from Bernard Hinault. My bluff had worked.

While you bluff to hide your weaknesses, you toughen the race by exploiting your opponents' weaknesses. Perhaps the clearest case of weakness in pro cycling comes on a team level. The strong teams spend most of the race toughening the race to exploit the weaker teams, some of which have good stars. But these stars, unprotected by their own teammates, are often worn out before the decisive moment of the race. This falls right into the hands of the stars on the strong teams.

The strongest team in the Tour de France in recent years has been the La Vie Claire team. Although other teams might have stars as gifted as Bernard Hinault or myself, they are often forced to play catch when one of the La Vie Claire workers toughens the race. In 1986, Bernard Hinault and I duked it out, perhaps weakening our team strategy to a certain extent. But the La Vie Claire team was so strong that we were able to control the race despite our feuding.

My teammates Andy Hampsten—who finished the Tour de France in fourth place—Steve Bauer, Guido Winterberg, and Niki Rüttimann played a major role in my victory. They had the dirty job of toughening the race and squelching the attacks of our opponents and they did it day in and day out. Andy Hampsten was especially valuable in the mountain stages. His attack on stage thirteen to Superbagnères was instrumental in my Tour victory. Bauer controlled the race for mile after mile in the flat sections of the Tour, reeling back dangerous breakaways and counterattacking them. Guido Winterberg and Niki Rüttimann attacked when they could. One of Rüttimann's attacks resulted in a stage win for him.

Toughening the race can also be an individual tactic. Most amateur cyclists in the United States don't have a team, let alone a strong team like La Vie Claire. When you toughen the race yourself, you want to make sure you don't jeopardize your own chances of winning. Only rare champions can attack in the early stages of a race, wear out all the opponents singlehandedly, and still win.

One of those was Belgium's legendary Eddy Merckx, considered by many to be the greatest cyclist who ever lived. In 1970, in the hardest mountain stage of the Tour de France, Merckx decided, on a whim, to break away one hundred miles from the finish. Merckx was alone, facing five of the toughest mountain passes in France. He was already clearly the winner of the Tour that year and didn't need to prove anything. Merckx's coach tried, in vain, to dissuade him from this solo breakaway. But Merckx rode alone, shattering

Sprinting. Great sprinting is largely talent. Here I'm beat at the line (that's me second from right) by my fiercest rival, Sean Kelly (second from left), in the 1983 Tour of Lombardy.

the field and finishing with five minutes on the next rider.

That sort of tactic certainly toughened the race for his opponents. But if Merckx hadn't been the one-in-a-billion physical specimen that he was, he would have "blown up" and could have jeopardized his Tour de France win.

Personally, I've only toughened the race when I've known it was to my benefit. When I was riding to the finish with Ruperez in the 1983 world championship, I decided to toughen the race. But I had to be cautious about it. Because Ruperez was still a valuable ally to me in the flat sections, I didn't want to attack too strongly. Then he would have stopped working, realizing that I had no intention of waiting for him to beat me in a sprint finish.

But because Ruperez was still relatively fresh, I had to work him over subtly before attacking to finish alone. I rode hard enough to find the pace that would make him crack, but not so fast that he would think I was trying to attack. On every hill and rise before the finish, I pulled at the front, increasing the pace so that, out of the corner of my eye, I could see him beginning to strain. But not enough to make him think I was trying to work him down.

With Ruperez drained I attacked decisively three miles from the finish. Ruperez could not follow, and I won the world championship.

The key in toughening the race is to be very smooth. In a sense you're still bluffing, but here you're bluffing out of strength, not out of weakness. You also have to be careful not to overestimate your own ability. If you push too hard or too long, then you might wear yourself out before your opponent. Don't forget, he's *behind* your wheel, getting the benefit of your draft.

One of the classic examples of strong tactical riding was Michel Pollentier's wily victory in the 1982 Tour of Flanders. Pollentier was in a lead group with some of the best talents in cycling: Francesco Moser and Roger DeVlaeminck. Pollentier was as talented as the others but lacked the finishing speed the other riders had. If he was to win, he needed to finish alone.

At first Pollentier attacked half-heartedly, but strongly enough to make his rivals think he was attacking strongly, and also strongly enough to wear down his opponents.

He did this four or five times. Then, with less than a kilometer to go, he broke away decisively with a 100 percent effort. Pollentier was away. His brilliant tactic had worked and a few hundred meters later he was declared the champion of that Tour of Flanders.

This kind of tactic works only in a situation in which you're clearly stronger than the rider or riders you're trying to wear down. Once you decide to attack and break away you've got to be sure that he or they won't be able to keep up.

SPRINTING

I have always preferred winning a race alone because my sprint isn't as strong as that of some other riders. Some racers, of course, are excellent sprinters and ride a very wily race to enable them to outsprint their opponents in a final sprint. Whatever the case may be for you, sprinting is a high art you will need to master, or at the very least grasp.

Sprinting is absolutely essential to any bicycle racer. Even if you're a mountain climber, the sprint training will make you a better and more complete cyclist. If you train your sprints, not only will you be able to break away with other climbers in a mountainous race, but you'll have an added confidence in your ability to beat the other climbers in any sprint finish.

Road sprinters, on the other hand, need to work on other facets of fitness to make them complete riders. Most sprinters in the United States have not conditioned themselves to be complete road riders. The way many American sprinters train, they would be completely uncompetitive in any top European event. One of the few American sprinters who has trained himself into an all-around rider is Davis Phinney. He has developed tremendously, and ironically this has given him more opportunities to come to the finish in a position to display his sprinting ability.

Unlike practically every other facet of the sport, sprinting is primarily an inherited talent. Good sprinters are those cyclists who have high ratios of fast-twitch muscles. Those such as myself who are born with a low ratio of these fast-twitch muscles start out with a handicap. Although specific training can increase your fast-twitch muscle, this kind of training is very difficult and the results are marginal. And as soon as you stop incorporating sprinting in your training, your muscles "forget" and you lose the extra fast-twitch fibers.

One of the most fearsome rivals I've had in my years as a pro cyclist has been Irishman Sean Kelly, a great road sprinter who has become a complete road racer since the 1983 season. Kelly is one of those rare sprinters who through ability and relentless training have developed into an outstanding all-around rider. The only area where Kelly doesn't match the best is in the high mountains.

I could train for sprinting ten times as much as Kelly and he could still beat me seven out of ten times in a dead heat. I've had to race against Kelly with brain as well as brawn.

In fact, most great road racers who are not great sprinters have learned to sprint with their head. If you see that a road race is going to come down to a sprint with a good sprinter in the group, the obvious tactic is to try to drop that sprinter from the bunch. Most sprinters tend to be a little weaker on the climbs. Try to wear out the sprinter by toughening the pace on the climbs (without going so hard as to tire yourself out).

Look at him carefully for signs of fatigue. Is he coasting at regular intervals to stretch his back and upper body? Is he drinking water and splashing it on his face more often than usual? Is he getting out of the saddle wearily on every small climb? Is he having trouble keeping up with every acceleration in the pace?

If so, you might be able to outride him in a sprint. Or, better yet, you might try to break away decisively about five miles from the finish, a distance long enough so that he doesn't "feel" the finish and short enough to allow you to maintain a purely anaerobic effort.

If it does come down to a sprint, use any tricks to your advantage. The commonly accepted tactic in sprinting is to let someone else begin the sprint and then to jump on his wheel. If your rival is a good sprinter, you can be pretty sure he won't jump first. If he sees that all the riders around him are waiting for him to jump, that can actually play into his hands as a pure sprinter almost always has the advantage in a short sprint, where pure velocity is the only factor.

Look at the wind. If your sprint is clearly on a tailwind stretch, then you could try jumping first, because on a tailwind stretch, the advantage of sitting on a rider's wheel is not as clear.

To gain an edge in any sprint it's important to know what the finish is like. That's why I always recommend trying a few sprints on the actual finish the day before your race. That way you can determine where the best place to jump might be. More important, you can determine exactly what kind of gear you'll need. This might provide you with an edge over a pure sprinter who might not be as familiar with this stretch.

Remember, you want to sprint in a gear that provides you with power for the jump but that you can spin at about 110 to 120 RPM at the top end. If your sprinter rival assumes he can use a 52 × 13 where in fact a smaller 52 × 14 might be better, this could be the edge you're looking for.

If you are part of a team, your teammates can play a crucial role in a final sprint. Most top sprinters on the European circuit have a number of riders, quite fast themselves, who are designated to lead out the star sprinter. Some top American teams have the same set up. The 7-Eleven team, for example, has star sprinter Davis Phinney, who is often led out by his teammates Ron Kiefel and Alex Stieda. The reason these riders are willing to work for Phinney is that they can help him to win, but only he can win, because he is faster. And winnings are always split equally among teammates, an old tradition in cycling.

Perhaps the single most important element in mastering the techniques and tactics of racing is experience. But once you have the fundamentals, acquiring the experience is simply a matter of time.

6

Training and Fitness for the Serious Cyclist

When I first started to race, I thought training meant simply riding hard until you got in shape. To me it seemed that if you didn't feel pain, you weren't getting any benefit. After a short while, I discovered that I wasn't getting in shape, only getting tired after my training rides.

When I went to the United States Olympic Training Center at Colorado Springs, I got my first taste of systematic training. Eddie Borysewicz, the national coaching director of the United States Cycling Federation, had brought the first scientific training approach to this country from his native Poland, and the improvements he achieved in the American racing program were impressive.

Since Eddie B., I have learned much more about training. I have been lucky enough to ride for two of the most accomplished cycling coaches of all time, Frenchman Cyrille Guimard and Swiss Paul Koechli. Both have taught me how to train for cycling in a proven, systematic, scientific manner. Unlike many European coaches who still adhere to the old-fashioned (and unscientific) training methods, Guimard and Koechli have been fantastically successful.

Training is what a cyclist does most of the time. Even a European professional who races up to two hundred times a year does a lot of training. And a European professional who wants to be successful *needs* to know how and when to train to win races. Most riders, however, train much more than they race. Because there is so much more training than racing in the amateur ranks, training becomes all the more crucial. And most riders have a chaotic training program, riding hard one day and easy the next because it meets their moods.

A systematic approach to training is one of the key factors in becoming a successful cyclist. I have seen many examples of professionals who shone under Cyrille Guimard and then faded once they left him. Few people realize that an important reason for that is Guimard's systematic training program.

Perhaps the most important thing I have learned from Guimard and Koechli is that it is not enough to know *how* to do something, you must know *why* you're doing it. In fact, many riders, even talented professionals, suffer in their careers because they don't know *why* they're doing something. And when push comes to shove, they're not as well prepared, because they don't have an understanding of training.

Training is not just for top racers, either. Training is for anybody who wants to ride a bicycle for fitness. Training can teach you what your body is doing, and why, under different circumstances. Training can teach you how to enjoy your cycling better.

Of course, there are many different ways to train. A professional cyclist might ride as much as thirty-five hours a week with sprints, intervals, anaerobic threshold training, and endurance (all these terms will be defined later). An amateur racer might do the same training, but with less duration. A veteran would do less intense training, riding fewer sprints and intervals. For a touring cyclist, there is no need to ride the high-intensity training of sprints or intervals. A tourist may do some middle-intensity training, but primarily, he or she must concentrate on large doses of endurance—because that is what a tourist primarily does.

KNOWING YOUR BODY
AND HOW IT WORKS

Your fitness level is the sum total of what you do to keep in shape. If all you ever do is lie in bed and eat hot fudge sundaes, you will not only become fat but your muscle mass will begin to wither away. Athletes' bodies change and develop constantly under the influence of the exercise they do.

Muscles are groups of fibers that react to stimulation during any kind of motion—exercise, walking, eating. There are two different kinds of muscles in the body: voluntary muscles and involuntary muscles. Voluntary muscles are those you can move—or stimulate, in scientific lingo—when you want: your biceps, your quads, and so on. An example of an involuntary muscle is your heart—a muscle that remains stimulated whether or not you want it to be.

Muscles need energy to function. That energy is provided to the muscles by the blood, which contains oxygen and energy from the foods you eat, such as sugars, fats and various proteins. Perhaps most important for a cyclist, the muscle is composed of tissue that is highly sensitive to any kind stimulation—especially the kind of stimulation the muscles receive in training. There are two types of muscle fibers, fast-twitch and slow-twitch. The fast-twitch fibers have a longer appearance and are stimulated in a higher-intensity and shorter-duration exercise. The slow-twitch fibers are shorter and react to a greater degree when stimulated with a lesser-intensity and longer-duration exercise. The slow-twitch muscles are usually preponderant, although some people have a greater percentage of fast-twitch muscles than others.

What exercise actually does is break down your muscle fibers. The benefit from your exercise actually comes when your body builds back its muscle fibers, this time more strongly, in something of an attempt to "defend" itself from the stimulation of the exercise. What that means is that once your body has recuperated from the exercise it has made itself stronger—and that's what you want the exercise to accomplish. The important point, however, is that the period of recuperation is as important as the time you actually spend exercising.

In cycling your muscles have to be able to respond to many different intensities of exercise. Because cycling is a sport that combines both tremendous endurance and very high intensity, top cyclists need to train at many different levels of intensity and duration. A cyclist who trains for endurance will not have adapted his muscles to the effort of riding intensely, and any winner needs to be able to ride at a high intensity. On the other hand, a cyclist who trains only for the very short and highly intense sprints will never have the stamina he needs to win a race.

DEFINITION OF TRAINING INTENSITIES

In training you need to know and understand the following levels of intensity:

1. *Maximum effort (sprints):* This effort lasts ten to twenty-five seconds.
   It is similar to a two-hundred-meter sprint.
   It calls for 100 percent of your maximum heartbeat.

Your body is anaerobic, producing energy without the use of oxygen.

Your body feeds only on adrenotriphosphate (ATP), and phosphocreatine, two high-energy chemicals stored in the body tissue.

2. *Submaximum effort (pure anaerobic interval):* This effort lasts twenty-five seconds to two minutes.

It is similar to a one-kilometer time trial on the track.

Your body is operating at very nearly 100 percent of your maximum heartbeat.

It is considered the purely anaerobic interval.

Your body is anaerobic at submaximum intensity.

Although you are at the maximum heart rate, this intensity of exercise is differentiated by its duration and the different kind of energy your body feeds on.

Your body feeds on anaerobic glycogen, sugar stored in the body tissue and used in periods of highly intense exercise.

3. *High intensity (long interval):* This is usually a high-intensity effort of two to four minutes.

It is similar to a three-thousand-meter pursuit.

Your heart rate will reach its maximum point during this period of exercise.

The body is on the border between the aerobic and anaerobic states. In the last portion of this exercise the body is in a completely anaerobic state.

Energy is gotten through *anaerobic* glycogen and *aerobic* glycogen.

4. *Average intensity (anaerobic threshold):* This exercise lasts from four to thirty minutes.

It is similar to a five-to twenty-kilometer individual time trial.

Your heart rate is between 90 and 100 percent of its maximum.

In this exercise the body uses aerobic oxidation (oxygen provided through the bloodstream), because it is not in an anaerobic state.

This intensity and the lighter intensity is where you will do a great deal of your training, and you will get the most benefit from your training at these intensities.

Anaerobic threshold training—which means riding at the border between the aerobic and anaerobic states—is done to a large degree at this and the light intensity.

5. *Light intensity (intense aerobic):* This exercise lasts thirty minutes and more.

This exercise is similar to a twenty-five-mile time trial up to a long-distance but intense effort.

Your heart rate is at 80 to 90 percent of its maximum during this exercise.

Your body is in an exclusively aerobic state.

Your body will first burn the glycogen it has stored. After that you will be running off fatty acids. This is the bonks (complete exhaustion).

6. *Low intensity (endurance):* This exercise can last indefinitely as long as you can ride (for example, in the Race Across America riders stay on their bikes nearly twenty-four hours a day for nine days or more).

Your heart rate is between 65 and 87 percent of its maximum. Your minimum intensity for getting a fitness benefit is 65 percent of your maximum heart rate.

At this intensity you are in a completely aerobic state.

The energy the body uses is stored in the fatty acids.

A complete program for cycling training combines all these intensities in a specific mix to achieve the optimal performance level. If you are cycling for fitness but are not interested in racing, you will not need to do the higher-intensity exercises. You will only have to concentrate as high as the average intensity of exercise. For the most part, however, tourist and recreational cyclists need to train only at the light and low intensities of exercise.

One of the most important steps you can make in training for cycling is to ask yourself what kind of cycling you want to do. If you really have your heart set on racing, then you will have to make a commitment to training in a systematic way. If you don't train systematically, sooner or later your racing will suffer.

THE MACRO CYCLE: HOW YOU ORGANIZE YOUR TRAINING

The first thing I do once my cycling season is finished is to sit down and map the following season. I break up my training into periods of four to seven weeks, which I call *Macro Cycles.* Within these periods, each week of riding is called a *Micro Cycle.* Although the Macro Cycle (and the weekly Micro Cycle) allows you to plan your training systematically, perhaps more important, it allows you to systematically plan your *recuperation.* As mentioned above, recuperation is an absolutely essential ingredient in any successful training program.

Why do I use this system? The reason is that to improve as a cyclist your goal is to increase the duration (the length of time) and the intensity of your training. But if you were to simply increase the duration and intensity day in and day out, you would burn yourself out. The Macro Cycle gives you a tangible period of time within which to define your goal. Within the Macro Cycle you can increase the duration and intensity of your exercise, recuperate, start out at a higher level than you did the previous cycle. By the time you reach the end of your Macro Cycle, you should have achieved specific goals, which will differ depending on what period of the year you're riding in.

I divide my season into the following periods:

1. *The winter preparation period:* Can go from mid-October to the beginning of January.
2. *The preseason preparation period:* January through mid-February.
3. *The early-season preparation period:* Mid-February to April.
4. *In season:* April to October.

Some riders may have to shorten or extend some of these preparation periods because of their age.

THE WEEKLY SCHEDULE

Although your Macro Cycles will vary in the types of exercises you are emphasizing, depending on the training period, the basic model for the weekly schedule, or Micro Cycle, is quite consistent throughout the year. One important thing to keep in mind is that the higher intensities of exercise must be done first before you start doing lower intensities and more endurance. In other words, train for your sprints before your intervals and train for your intervals before your endurance.

The typical week for cycling training is established in the following way, assuming you are racing on Sunday:

1. *Monday:* Rest and recuperation day.
2. *Tuesday:* Training day. Today you train for your sprints (the whole year round). You can add another workout in the afternoon if you're up to it—possibly intervals or a less intense workout, depending on what your needs are.
3. *Wednesday:* Training day. Medium distance. On Wednesday you train at a level of intensity *below* what you did the day before. For example, if you trained only for your sprints, then you could add another workout that you need to complement your training—something less intense than a sprint but more intense than an endurance ride.
4. *Thursday:* Training. Endurance ride.
5. *Friday:* If you are racing on Sunday you should do a rest and re-

Out on a training ride.

cuperation ride at an endurance pace or lower. If you're not racing
on Sunday, and you feel fresh enough from the previous three days
of training, you could do a sprint workout.

6. *Saturday:* If you're racing Sunday, do an endurance ride comple-
mented by several sprints and several minutes of an effort similar to
race pace. If you're not racing on Sunday, do a workout similar to
what you did Wednesday.

7. *Sunday:* Race. If you're not racing do an endurance ride.

WHEN TO START

Winter training should begin in November and December. Your aim in
these two months is to *maintain* the fitness you acquired in the previous
season. If you're riding for the first time or coming back off a long injury,
then this is a natural time to start slowly. Later, in the pre- and early-season
cycles (January to mid-February) leading up to the racing season, aim to
build endurance and your anaerobic threshold in an unstructured way.

During the racing season, you will train to increase the intensity of your
workouts and to increase your anaerobic capacity. It is then that you bring
together all the elements of training: endurance, anaerobic threshold, anaerobic capacity or intervals, and sprinting. It is especially important that you
work hard to eliminate any weak points. Sometimes that goal takes years to
achieve and requires infinite patience. Other times, there are weaknesses you
simply cannot overcome. For example, Mother Nature provided me with a

low ratio of fast-twitch muscles; as a result, I'll never be a specialized sprinter.

As the season continues, you will concentrate on strengthening your weak points. What you're trying to do is to build an all-around capability with as few weaknesses as possible. A sprinter may need to work on his climbing. Similarly, a great climber must work on his sprint if he wants to beat a good sprinter at the finish.

If you feel you're in really good shape in November and December then you can start pushing yourself a little bit right then and there. Then, following a break for Thanksgiving and Christmas, you're ready to start the pre-season Macro Cycle on January first. You want to start out on January first at a level of intensity slightly below that of your last week of training in December.

The Macro Cycles are useful because they give you up to a six-to-seven-week period to focus your efforts on. I think anything longer than that is hard to do mentally, because you don't feel that there's any conclusion to your effort. But if you train well, you should feel satisfied after a Macro Cycle that you're making genuine progress. By the time you've done six or seven weeks of this you'll need a rest.

During your rest period you still want to go riding, and do about half of your peak duration at a comfortable endurance pace. Then you should be ready to tackle the next Macro Cycle.

The Macro Cycles are part of the larger goal of an entire season. And each season is part of your career goals as a cyclist. But the key is that each *day* you train is the base for your success. And, if you're successful at maintaining your training day in and day out, then each season's improvements carry over into the next season. You improve as a cyclist.

THE TRAINING CYCLE:
THE FIRST WINTER CYCLE

For every week you take off from cycling, it takes about three weeks to get back into shape. That's why in the winter, at the end of my season, I only take off a week and a half from cycling. Sometimes I go golfing, or simply rest. In any case, I get completely away from cycling, to get a total physical and mental break from the season that just ended. The following week I restrict my riding to ten hours, because I've taken some time off and I want to start gradually. The week after that I ride for about twelve hours. The week following that I build up to fourteen hours.

The way to figure your duration—the hours you spend cycling—during this time is to divide the mileage you did in-season by a bit more than half. I train about twenty-five to thirty hours during the season. So, when I start my winter training cycle in November, I cut that back to ten to twelve hours (of course, you could do more total exercise—skiing or weight-lifting—but you want to do at least this much *on-bike* training). This is what my former coach Cyrille Guimard advised me to do when I turned pro in 1980.

The idea is to always work in a cycle, gradually building your duration. Then stop and take another week off. I like to arrange it so that my week off comes during the Thanksgiving week, allowing me to spend time with my family.

During the weeks I do ride, I do a lot of cyclo cross or running and mountain biking twice a week, as well as a long two-to three-hour road ride to get some endurance in, also twice a week.

It was Cyrille Guimard, my first coach when I turned professional, who advised me to ride at least three to four times a week—twice a week on the road and twice a week cyclo cross (or mountain bike riding) in November and December. Cyclo cross is probably the best way to maintain power and cardiovascular fitness in the winter. With a cyclo cross workout you can ride when it's cold, wet, rainy, or snowy. Also, cyclo cross really helps your bike-handling skills.

The key in winter is to get a mental break from the tedium of training while maintaining your form. Winter training is fitness maintenance. What I try to do with my winter training is keep the same rhythm that I've been doing for the entire season but for a shorter duration.

A typical weekly schedule in the winter cycle should start with a *Monday* rest day. A rest day may consist of a short one-or two-hour spin, or weight training, or circuit training. Although it's probably better to ride your bike from a purely physical point of view, I usually give myself a complete break and don't ride on Mondays.

Guimard used to tell us not to worry about riding on Mondays, because your body also has to train itself *not* to ride sometimes. There's always a time when you won't be able to train because you're working, or traveling, or going to school.

On *Tuesdays* in the winter I like to ride for about two-and-a-half hours. I might do about an hour and a half of sprints in the morning. Sprints are your highest-intensity workout. They are short bursts of about ten to twenty-five seconds during which you ride at your maximum heart rate. When I sprint, I aim for an imaginary finish line (like a city limits sign of a telephone pole) and I sprint all-out for about ten to twenty-five seconds.

You should always do your sprints *after* the rest day because you need to be fresh enough to push yourself 100 percent. Sprints are something you should do year-round, twice a week, but in the winter you should do fewer repetitions. I might cut back to about seven sprints in the morning (in the season I do something like twelve). For the average cyclist I would recommend about four to eight sprints on Tuesdays in the winter—more if you feel really good.

When I first get back on my bike after my break at the beginning of

Definition of Duration

In cycling training, how you measure the amount of training you do is important. Many cyclists talk about the mileage *they're doing. Some like to brag they're doing 500 miles a week. Others point out they're competing just as well on only 250 miles a week.*

Unfortunately, measuring your training by mileage or distance doesn't tell you very much. Sure, you know you've ridden a certain distance. But that sheer mileage doesn't tell you how you've ridden that distance. At my training clinics in the winter, some riders tell me they ride 500 miles a week. You may feel that you've accomplished a lot because you rode 500 miles in a week. But if you didn't ride what's known as quality miles, and if you ride in the wrong order, then you're not doing yourself any good by doing the extra miles. In fact, 500 miles of quality is almost too much even for a pro. I have rarely done it in my career.

Much more important than how many miles you've done is duration, *how many hours you've done. This is much more effective, because your body measures its effort in the time it must perform, not the distance it travels.*

A good example is the endurance day in your Micro Cycle. During the season, you want to ride an endurance workout that approximates the length of an upcoming race. If you try to equate the distance and ride, let's say, 250 kilometers (156 miles), you'll wear yourself out completely. Because an endurance training pace is by definition much lower than race pace, you'll be riding many more hours than you would in a race of the same distance.

Instead you want to estimate how much time it's going to take you to ride the weekend's race. If it's 150 kilometers (94 miles), and it takes you about three-and-a-half to four hours, then that length of time, or duration, should be the duration of your endurance ride.

The reason for this is that your body doesn't register mileage. It registers the amount of time, or duration, your body is exercising. Almost all my training is figured purely by hours and not by mileage. If you ride 35 miles into a headwind, for example, it could take you three hours. But the same mileage with a tailwind could take as little as one hour. Your body doesn't care if you've traveled 35 miles or 15 miles or 80 miles. It cares about how many hours it's had to work at a given workload.

November I go out and ride and I do a couple of sprints to get my body back into the swing of things. Sprints train your fast-twitch muscles and they train your body to use the ATP (adenosine triphosphate, a high-energy chemical stored in body tissue). In fact sprinting is very much like weight-lifting on the bike except that it's better for you because sprinting is the actual exercise you need to train for.

The reason you should do sprints the whole year is that soon after you stop exercising your fast-twitch muscles "forget" the effort of sprinting. That's what's ironic about advocating weight-lifting. Once you stop lifting, your body forgets and the benefit is lost to a certain degree.

Riders under the age of eighteen are an exception to this rule. Younger riders shouldn't attempt to do sprints in November and January, in any structured way. It's more important that younger racers give their bodies a rest. The key for a younger rider is to enjoy riding. If sprints are enjoyable to you then there's no reason not to do them. But don't force yourself to do them, because you want to come out of the winter period rested.

When you do sprints, start by riding along easily at a 100-RPM pedal cadence for ten minuttes or so. Your heart rate should be below 65 percent of its maximum, in a relatively rested state.

First, find a fifteen-to one-hundred-meter uphill portion of road, where you can sprint in a fairly big gear to do your first three sprints, as a warmup. When I do them I use a 53 × 14. Now that's a pretty big gear. I think a junior should use a 52 × 16 or 52 × 15, depending on how strong the rider is.

The main thing here is to create explosive power. The sprints should be short—six to seven seconds long. These short sprints will get your system going and get your heart rate up. But keep them short enough that they're still pure sprints (anything longer than twenty-five seconds or so forces you to go below your maximum heart rate and you're doing something closer to a short interval than a long sprint).

What you're trying to simulate at this point is a track sprinter, at a standstill on the banking, waiting to pounce on his opponent with a big, explosive burst. Which means you want to start your warmup sprints from a near-standstill or a very slow roll.

Now you're ready to do your four to seven sprints. When you sprint, it should be an all-out effort. Ideally, you want to sprint about 200 to 300 meters (220 to 330 yards) on a straight, flat, or slightly uphill stretch of road. If you lack leg speed then you want to sprint on the kind of terrain—such as a slight downhill—on which you can emphasize leg speed. If, on the other hand, you lack power, then sprint on a slight uphill.

Pick a gear that's big to start with, but something that you're going to spin out by the time you cross your imaginary finish line. I would probably use a

53 × 14 for these sprints. I'd say the average amateur could probably do them in a 52 × 14 or 52 × 15, depending on his strength. For juniors, a 52 × 15 or 52 × 16 is fine.

Your first three sprints should be done in a big gear from a slow standing start. This develops your explosive power. In the remaining three or four sprints you should use a gear in which you're completely spun out (turning the pedals at high RPMs) at the end. This helps you with your top-end speed, or velocity. These sprints should be about ten to fifteen seconds long. Allow your body to recuperate completely between sprints by riding at or below 65 percent of your maximum heartbeat. At first that might only take about five minutes, but the more sprints you do, the longer that will take.

An ideal situation is to sprint with a couple of friends. For one thing the natural competitiveness among riders will make your sprints faster. And you won't have to force yourself to sprint—the competition will take care of that. When you sprint with some friends, different riders can take turns leading out; it helps you learn some of the tactics of sprinting.

Sometimes I do sprints with my teammate and friend Steve Bauer. He leads out the sprint in a really long effort. I sit on him (ride right behind him to take full advantage of his slipstream), then I sprint past him until I'm spinning all-out, just like in a race.

Sometimes you can make a sprint especially competitive by sprinting side by side. "See that sign—go for it!" And then you're off. That's the best way to increase your leg speed, to be really competitive as a racing cyclist.

Still, you shouldn't sprint side by side more than once a week. It can become a real mental strain, especially if you do sprints the entire year around.

One of the most important things to learn from these sprint sessions is an efficient pedaling technique. It teaches you to use your maximum leg speed. Never forget, though, that good pedaling technique is the sum of both leg speed *and* power. That's why I don't recommend training in a fixed gear, as has been a common practice in the cycling community. You need to be as efficient using your power pedaling in a big gear at 85 RPMs as with your leg speed at 120 RPMs.

Some coaches, notably United States Cycling Federation national coaching director Eddie Borysewicz, don't recommend doing sprints in the winter cycle. He says it's too cold at that time of the year in most parts of the country, and it can burn your lungs. But people ski cross-country at twenty degrees below zero. I have done sprints in Belgium when it was as cold as twenty degrees above zero and it has never hurt me.

In the afternoon, following a morning of sprints, I usually do an hour of cyclo cross, where I can work hard at a high heart rate riding in mud and running, but without having to consciously push myself. I have found that if

Deep Breathing Exercises

When I signed my first pro contract back in 1980 I received a training pamphlet from coach Cyrille Guimard. The first item in the booklet was on deep breathing exercises.

Deep breathing exercises *are done off the bike for about forty-five minutes a day. Guimard has recommended it for years. My current coach, Paul Koechli, believes deep breathing can be very beneficial to a cyclist.*

Deep breathing exercises are very important because they teach you to inhale, and they increase your lung capacity, so you can take in more oxygen.

I push myself too much in the winter, I'm burned out in the spring when I really need to push myself. With cyclo cross I can have fun and also get exceptional cardiovascular benefit.

On *Wednesdays*, as I explained above, I do an exercise less intense than I did the day before. I run for an hour, which is actually a pretty long run. Running is good because it allows me to work out with high intensity without getting on the bike and consciously pushing myself. I usually run relatively slowly for the first ten or fifteen minutes to warm up, then I run at a good pace for twenty to thirty minutes with my heartbeat up at about 160 or 170—just about my anaerobic threshold.

I might also do some circuit training on Wednesdays, calisthenics, such as situps, pushups, and a lot of back exercises. You can also weight train, but personally I prefer calisthenics—it's more of a natural motion and it tends to build the kind of muscle tone that's more useful for cycling. Often, however, I'm pretty tired after an hour of running, and that is enough exercise for me in the winter cycle.

On *Thursdays* you want to do a slightly longer workout, an endurance workout. I would do a two-to three-hour road ride. Or, if the weather is bad, I would do a fun two-to three-hour cyclo cross or mountain bike ride on the trails at an easy pace.

WINTER CROSS-COUNTRY SKIING AND CYCLO CROSS TRAINING

In the off-season riders should ride only about 50 percent of the amount ridden during the season. But you should split your time between cyclo cross or mountain biking and road riding. In a cold climate, cross-country skiing is a good alternative; in that case I recommend doing 75 percent of the in-season training, because any time you're getting your workout from a sport that involves a different motion from cycling, you should do a little more to compensate.

Cross-country skiing is the ideal complement to cycling. It works all the upper-body muscles that you use in cycling, and the new *skating technique* in cross-country skiing is a motion that's similar to cycling. You're really working your legs much more than with the traditional kick and slide, and you're doing your cardiovascular system more good than if you were out riding a bike on a road on a very cold day.

THE DIFFERENCE BETWEEN CYCLO CROSS AND MOUNTAIN BIKE RIDING

I believe cyclo cross is an easier way than mountain bike riding to get a good workout, unless you live in a very mountainous area where you can ride a ten-kilometer climb that takes a good forty-five minutes. That type of mountain bike training ride is ideal, because your heart rate is kept at a very high level, which is very good conditioning.

But most people don't live in mountainous areas, so you have to ride longer to get equal benefit from your training. With cyclo cross, you can set up a two-mile circuit with a soft trail, a half-mile uphill, and a creek crossing. You could do the same circuit with a mountain bike, but it's easier to ride fast on the cyclo cross bike because it has thinner tires. Also, one of the benefits of cyclo cross is that sometimes you have to run, carrying the bike on your shoulder, to climb up steep, slippery hills or cross a bog. It's more of an all-around sport. The mountain bike is usually too heavy to carry, so you tend to ride—slowly—through the sticky portions. I don't think it provides as good a workout. Either cyclo cross or mountain bike riding can provide you with a good alternative to road riding that can keep you in top condition while giving you a change of pace and keeping you fresh for the racing season.

On *Fridays*, rest by exercising for a relatively short period of time. Ideally,

Weight-lifting

Weight-lifting can be useful for cycling, but should always be done with light weights. A cyclist is never interested in bulking up, unless he is a match sprinter. Weight training is especially useful for riders between fifteen and nineteen, because their bodies are still developing and often don't have much muscle structure. I did weight training for about two years. I did it for about two to three months at a time and I felt that was all I needed. I've always believed that most of my strength comes from training specifically in cycling.

The potential problem with weight-lifting is that although you can develop an incredible amount of power, you can also develop muscles that you don't need in cycling. That extra bulk will be a handicap. In hilly races, weight becomes a crucial factor.

Sometimes it's hard to develop the right muscles for cycling with weight-lifting. And whatever benefit you gain is lost to a certain degree as soon as you stop the weight training.

A major consequence of developing bulk through weight-lifting is unwanted weight. When you lift weights the muscle tissue is actually ripped apart and scar tissue is formed on top.

Obviously, I'm skeptical about the strength to be gained from weight training. One of my teammates, for example—Swiss rider Niki Rütimann—wants to get more power and has been weight-lifting for two years. He's developed his muscles (legs, lower back, arms) by doing legs curls and presses, squats, bench presses. But I asked Niki if he ever does any kind of intervals on the flats in big gears and he told me no. I believe Niki could get more benefit by doing intervals in big gears or cyclo cross, because weight-lifting develops muscles with a motion different from the one Niki needs on a bicycle, a shorter, more syncopated motion.

Weight-lifting can be useful for sprinting, because sprinting is a pure power exercise with a duration similar to weight-lifting repetitions. Riders can make up for a low ratio of natural fast-twitch muscles—the muscle fibers needed to sprint fast—by doing some weight-lifting. But again, there is a price to pay in terms of bulk. That will be a handicap in the hills. Also, you must continue to lift weights or risk losing the benefits of that effort.

Weight-lifting can be useful to riders who lack the basic mass and power for sprinting, jumping, and breaking away.

I especially recommend weight-lifting for adolescent riders who need to develop a little bulk or build up their fast-twitch muscles. Andy

Hampsten developed his legs and upper body with weights and this has enabled him to sprint better on the hills. Since he's a natural hill climber, this was a perfect complement to his skills.

Generally cyclists really need conditioning *more than weight-lifting. Pushups, situps, back exercises, stretching, calisthenics, and aerobic exercises are excellent because they strengthen the body without bulking up the body.*

The best way to develop fast-twitch muscles in cycling is by doing sprints: Sprint intervals are not unlike weight-lifting repetitions except that you're actually doing the exercise you're trying to improve. In my mind that's always preferable.

Take advantage of your winter cycle to do some general conditioning that will help you in the racing season. But, remember, you don't need a "well-balanced" body to be a great cyclist. Cyclists actually have very specific—and imbalanced—bodies. Their legs are more developed than the rest of their muscles. If I tried to balance my upper body with my legs, I would add ten pounds of muscle mass to my upper body and I would be dropped on every hill.

What cyclists do need is calisthenic training for their upper body, to work on conditioning and tone more than on brute strength. Cyclists also need to strengthen their lower back and stomach muscles—the muscles that support the upper body on a bike.

The body needs to be developed in a way suited to the sport you're in. If you're an interior lineman for the Chicago Bears, you'll need a very strong lower back, strong triceps and pectorals, and one of those thirty-seven-inch necks. But in cycling you mainly focus on the legs and the lower back. Your arms are relatively smaller, and your neck is relatively smaller—that's what makes you lighter. You'll be better able to battle gravity and you'll need less oxygen to supply those muscles.

Perhaps the best thing I can say is that if I gained a pound of bulk right now, I'd be petrified.

in the winter you should do a little light cyclo cross or an easy road ride. Do what feels comfortable and seems fun.

Remember, I recommend training at least four days a week during the winter cycle. The other three days of the week you can do whatever feels like fun. But if that means riding, then by all means, ride.

Saturdays should be a repeat of the workout you did on Tuesdays, with fewer sprints, and a hill climb if you're up to it.

Sundays should be a repeat of the workout you did on Thursdays. Go out on a cyclo cross or road ride and emphasize endurance.

After you've completed the first winter cycle, take a week off from cycling. You want to keep doing some kind of exercise but only for enjoyment and basic muscle tone.

Remember, everybody's schedule is different. This first winter cycle might be as short as three weeks in certain cases, as long as six weeks in others. You don't need to adhere to a strict regimen as long as you're maintaining the basic structure that's described. Ride four days a week—two days at least of road riding, two days of cyclo cross or mountain biking.

Always follow the basic rule of training: Do the more intense workout before the less intense workout.

THE SECOND WINTER CYCLE

The first week of December (following the week of rest in November) starts a new three-week cycle. This cycle is pretty much the same as the cycle for November, except that you might want to increase your duration and your intensity slightly in the last week. Because the third week is the last week of winter training before taking a Christmas break, I include fourteen hours of more intense riding. This is intense training that brings me close to my anaerobic threshold and readies my body for the more intense training that I'll be doing after the New Year.

Again, do about half of your in-season training and vary the workouts. If you live in a cold climate, include some cross-country skiing. If you are serious about cycling, a very cold climate can be a real handicap if it stops you from training on your bicycle after January. For example, Steve Bauer, one of my teammates and friends, spends his rest period in Canada but comes down to train in California after Christmas.

If you live in a warm climate, do some running. In any case, do some mountain biking or cyclo cross twice a week.

At the end of the December cycle you can take off another week for Christmas and New Year's. One good aspect to these rest cycles is that I can begin my racing season having taken three-and-a-half to four weeks off the bike. But I never take more than a week and a half off at a time. That allows me to maintain the fitness that I gained from the season before but also allows me to rest. If, instead, I took a four-week block off, it would take me close to three months to gain back all my fitness. The key here is that for every week you take off you should train three weeks. If you do that, you'll maintain the fitness you gained from the previous season.

If you're still under eighteen, I would include a third and last Macro Cycle of winter training after the New Year. But once you turn eighteen, you begin your serious full-time road training on January first. The reason I pick January first is that the holidays are over and I feel guilty because I've been eating and relaxing. Training on January first is like making good on a New Year's resolution.

MYTHS ABOUT WINTER TRAINING

I think one of the biggest myths in cycling is that you'll "burn out" physically if you train in the winter. It's simply not true. Ideally, you want to train your body the entire year so that you can maintain pedal cadence, muscle tone, and muscle "memory." That way it only takes about four to five weeks to get into top condition for competition. In fact, theoretically you should train a *full cycle* in November and December. But in reality it can't be done—you need a mental break, a chance to feel fresh when you start the next season.

As a junior I always rode fairly hard and consistently, in November and December three times a week. I did other things to keep off of cycling. By mid-January I was riding my bike five or six times a week. I didn't burn out, I felt better.

When I first turned pro I was told by some sideline coaches I had to rest in the winter. I didn't train hard that first winter. Near the end of the winter I started to train but I wasn't in good enough condition. I came to the first races of the season ten pounds overweight and I had to *tire* my body just so I could lose weight to begin conditioning for race fitness.

That kind of thinking—the old school—is still alive in Italy. The Italians always take two months off their bikes. They put them in the basement and never touch them for the entire winter. They hardly do any exercise, other than a little jogging or skiing. When they get back on their bikes, their bodies are no longer used to the effort of cycling and they have to spin a small gear for six weeks.

Of course, if you take two months away from your bike, you probably *should* start with a small gear. But you're putting a lot of stress on your body by letting it get out of tone and then rushing to get back in shape before the season opener.

Francesco Moser provides an interesting example of what I mean. Like most Italians, Moser used to take off the whole winter. He would put on

Gear Size Myths

The biggest myth concerning gears in cycling is that you have to use a certain gear at special times in the season. In fact, your body doesn't care about the size of the gear; it responds only to its workload. A small gear might be fine to improve your fitness on a slight uphill in a headwind. But to limit yourself to a small gear on a flat stretch with a tailwind is not logical, regardless of the time of the year.

Many experts feel that cyclists should turn a smaller gear in the preparatory cycle (in January and February) because that teaches you to spin, to pedal more smoothly. Although that might be true for young riders (who ride restricted gears anyway) and novices, by the time you've had some experience riding, spinning should be something that comes naturally.

When you start your training in the preparatory cycle in January you may want to use a smaller gear, if your body is not in good enough condition to use a bigger gear. The gears should be tailored to your heart rate. The main things to keep in mind in training are your heart rate and your pedal cadence. In most cases the most efficient pedal cadence is around 90 RPMs (fifteen revolutions of the pedals every ten seconds). For younger cyclists a higher cadence is preferred because it helps develop a more supple pedal action and it also puts less stress on the legs.

The gear is not a clear indication of how much work your body is doing. For one rider a 42 × 18 might be just the right gear to keep heart rate, for example, at about 120 beats per minute. But for a rider who's in better shape that same gear at a comfortable cadence of ninety RPMs won't make the rider work hard enough to get much aerobic benefit. A rider in really good shape might have to use, say, a 52 × 15 to achieve the same heart rate as the rider in the example above.

You must develop leg speed to be a successful cyclist, however the higher your leg speed the less force the legs deliver to the pedals. In other words, if you spin a small gear you won't develop any power. All you'll have is good leg speed, one component of good pedal action, but not the whole picture.

Another myth perpetuated in cycling is that riders who know how to spin (turning the pedals at a high rate) are more efficient pedalers. This is not necessarily true. Many cyclists try to spin at 130 to 140 RPMs. But nobody needs to pedal that fast—pedaling that fast is actually quite inefficient.

An efficient pedal stroke is not measured by the number of RPMs but by the way the force is applied to the pedals. In my experience, the maximum in the efficient range is 130 RPMs. You rarely have to spin faster than that. At the same time, I would never go below 75 RPMs. For most endurance training I keep a cadence of 90 to 100 RPMs.

quite a bit of weight. In 1984, however, he trained throughout the winter—and he went on to set a new one-hour world record, cycling's most coveted record. He also went on to win some big races, such as the Tour of Italy. The difference in his fitness level was remarkable.

SERIOUS TRAINING BEGINS: THE PREPARATORY CYCLES

Before you begin your full-time training on January first, you should sit down and analyze what you want to accomplish during the season. Because I start racing in the early part of February, my first Macro Cycle lasts for six weeks, from January first to the second week of February. Then I make up a second Macro Cycle of base training from the second week in February up to the start of April, when the serious European pro racing begins. Always plan your preparatory training so that you have twelve weeks of training before you need to be really competitive.

Chances are you won't be racing as early as February. Nonetheless, your Macro Cycles should be set up so that the cycle ends with the first week of racing, usually from late March to early May, depending on where you live.

None of your training during the first two Macro Cycles should involve really high-intensity intervals. Instead, you should be building your endurance and anaerobic threshold higher.

From the first of April to the middle of October is what I consider the racing season. In season, I do more structured intervals, more speed work, more motor pacing.

I think this kind of general schedule can fit just about any racing cyclist. The only exception is the young cyclist under the age of eighteen, who really shouldn't start structured road training until mid-January or the end of January. Young riders should ride only three or four times a week from November to February.

The principal goals of these preparatory Macro Cycles is to improve your endurance and your anaerobic threshold (the point at which your body goes into oxygen debt). To increase your endurance you'll need to ride at least at 65 percent of your maximum heart rate. (To measure your maximum heart

During the racing season, I concentrate more on speed work and intervals.

rate, a good rule-of-thumb is to subtract your age from 215. A better measure is provided by a stress test performed by a qualified physician. To measure your pulse simply place your thumb on your jugular or wrist and count your pulsations for fifteen seconds. Then multiply by four.) Anything below that and you won't get any appreciable training value from your exercise. You can also go higher than 65 percent, but you have to be careful not to go too high, because then you won't be able to maintain your effort long enough to get endurance benefit out of your ride. If you go beyond 90 percent of your maximum heart rate, you'll be close to your anaerobic threshold, and you won't be able to ride for any appreciable time.

To increase your *anaerobic threshold,* you should ride with low to light intensity. You're riding at your *anaerobic threshold* when your heartbeat is in between 85 and 93 percent of its maximum. You don't have to know exactly where your anaerobic threshold is—training close to the actual threshold is good enough. At first you can measure your pulse and determine when you're getting close to your anaerobic threshold. But with experience you'll determine the kind of effort it takes to move close to the anaerobic threshold. I know when I'm getting close to my anaerobic threshold when I feel my legs just *beginning* to tighten up, but without getting the entirely "spent" feeling of actually being in an anaerobic state. With consistent training your body can increase the amount of time it's at its anaerobic threshold from two minutes to four minutes.

Ideally, you should know exactly what your anaerobic threshold is, but for most people it's hard to identify. Mine is about 175 beats per minute. But if my pulse is between 160 and 175 heartbeats per minute I'm close to a time trial effort, and I am riding just below the point at which my body begins to build up lactic acid. Cyrille Guimard always says that the biggest improvement in a cyclist comes when he rides about 10 percent below his actual anaerobic threshold. This is the area in which I see the greatest improvement in terms of my anaerobic threshold.

If I can train once or twice a week at that level for twenty to thirty minutes, I will increase my anaerobic threshold and improve my performance. Of course, your anaerobic threshold could be different depending on your age and other factors, but it's usually between 85 and 93 percent of your maximum heart rate.

Anaerobic threshold training makes you a more versatile rider. It allows you to sprint faster and more often and to recover more quickly. To me, this is the key to high-level racing. When you're riding at an endurance pace your muscles are using oxygen. The energy source is fat. But as you get closer to the anaerobic threshold you're using glycogen, the stored sugars in your body. Up to the anaerobic threshold you're using both glycogen and oxygen. But once you go into an anaerobic state, your muscles are no longer receiving oxygen fast enough to convert the fat into energy. Your muscles run off the stored glycogen. But the by-product of this is lactic acid. As the lactic acid builds up, you start to feel fatigued. The lactic acid keeps the muscles from destroying themselves, slowing you down. Anaerobic threshold training can help you extend the point at which you go into an anaerobic state. This means you can ride harder before you go into oxygen debt and tire out or "blow up."

Anaerobic threshold training alone will not make you a champion racer. You need to balance your training. In the preparatory period, you need to do a good deal of endurance riding. Anaerobic threshold training in the preparatory cycle, however, will pave the way for true *anaerobic training*—intervals—in season. By increasing your anaerobic threshold you can increase the value of your intervals later during your in-season training.

Although technically you should not do anaerobic training in your two preparatory cycles, go ahead and try it if your body can handle it. I go climbing in January in the foothills of the Sierra Nevada, for example, and go way past my anaerobic threshold for at least ten minutes a day, three or four times a week. I do it because I know my body can handle it, and therefore it is useful training.

What you don't want to do is begin structured intervals too early, before you're in good shape. They won't really do you as much good at this stage, and you can become mentally burned out before the season ever begins.

THE FIRST MACRO CYCLE: WEEK ONE

The first Macro Cycle begins January first. What you want to concentrate on primarily in this six-week period is building a good endurance base. You should also begin *anaerobic threshold training*. But don't attempt any actual anaerobic training until you've finished the twelve-week preparatory period (two Macro Cycles). The reason for this is that you should build yourself up *gradually*. At the end of the first Macro Cycle, in mid-February, for example, you should increase the duration of your endurance riding and gradually increase the intensity of your anaerobic threshold training.

The year around, regardless of whether you're riding in season or out of season, regardless of what training cycle you're in, *Monday* is a rest day. During the season you'll be racing on most Sundays. You will need a rest on Mondays. You should get used to resting once a week—rest is also part of training. Rest can mean riding one or two hours slowly (at a low intensity) or taking the day off entirely. I rarely ride on Mondays; it can be beneficial *not* to ride, so your body "knows" how to respond to a day off.

Tuesday, the day after your rest day, is the day you should do your most intense training, your sprints. All sprints should be done all-out, at 100 percent of your maximum heartbeat. This kind of training will teach your body to use its reserves of ATP (adrenotriphosphate). The longest you can hold a 100-percent effort is about twenty to twenty-five seconds. Sprints will train your body to perform at its maximum speed. This way, when you get to the end of a race, you will have already trained at your fastest pace, which may give you an edge over your competition in the final sprint of a race.

Sprints should be done the day after your rest day so you are completely afresh. If, for example, you changed the cycle around and completed a long endurance ride on Tuesday, a medium-intensity workout on Wednesday, and your sprints on Thursday, you'd be too tired to really sprint hard. You will not be sprinting at 100 percent of your capability.

After a warmup of about fifteen minutes, the first three or four sprints of the workout should be done in a big gear, a 53 × 13 for a professional, a 52 × 14 for an amateur or the largest restricted gear for juniors and intermediates. These three or four sprints should be done as powerful, short bursts of about six or seven seconds to build up your acceleration strength or explosive power. This kind of sprint specifically trains a power kick. These sprints should be done first because they're short, extremely intense, and allow you to warm up for the longer sprints.

Following the three or four explosive sprints, after your body is warmed up, do two all-out sprints of about ten or fifteen seconds' duration. You should be completely spun out at the end. If you're too tired to do any more at this point, don't do any more. Ride back home, relax, and let yourself recuperate. But if you feel fresh, do as many as eight or ten all-out sprints. In between sprints, allow your body to recuperate completely. After the first sprint that may take only five minutes. But by the time you've done six or seven, you may find that it takes fifteen minutes to fully recover. Most riders probably won't be up to doing this many sprints in the first two Macro Cycles, because eight or ten sprints constitute an intense workout. Do as many sprints as you feel comfortable with. If you're tired after three or four, then stop. But never do more than ten.

If you cut the workout short because you don't want to do more sprints, ride at an endurance pace for the rest of the day until you've done at least an hour and a half.

In the first few weeks of your first preparatory cycle, I would suggest limiting yourself to one-to two-and-a-half hours of sprints. Let your body get stronger gradually. Riders over twenty-one years of age might want to consider splitting Tuesday workouts in half after three weeks of training in the preparatory cycle. Do the sprints in the morning, and if you still feel strong go out for an intense cyclo cross workout in the afternoon. I do cyclo cross in the preparatory period because it's the best way to get an intense workout when the weather is cool while giving me a mental break from road riding. I might do two to three hours of sprints in the morning and about an hour and a half of cyclo cross in the afternoon.

If you're a junior, I would suggest limiting yourself to an hour of sprints on Tuesdays, with no additional workout. Remember, your body is still maturing—you don't want to injure yourself.

I can't emphasize enough how important it is to work on sprinting. Some riders are blessed with a high ratio of fast-twitch muscles. Sean Kelly, for example (as I've mentioned before), could easily beat me in a sprint even if I spent all my workouts trying to improve mine. But your sprint can be *improved* with sprint training. The benefits may seem agonizingly fractional. And if you stop sprint training, your body "forgets" how to sprint. But sprint training may be all you need to beat a natural sprinter in a long road race—sprinters tend to slow down over long distances.

Wednesdays should be your middle-distance, middle-intensity days. This is the day for anaerobic threshold training. This is when you train your body to use glycogen, or sugar reserves, as a source of energy. You should ride fifteen minutes at or near your anaerobic threshold, followed by ten to fifteen minutes of recuperation. Repeat that workout three to four times. The entire ride should take you about two hours.

The best way to tackle anaerobic threshold training in your January preparatory cycle is to ride some gradual hills. It's the easiest way to raise your heart rate to your anaerobic threshold without the mental strain of pushing yourself on the flats. When you're riding a hill, gravity forces you to do the work; when you're riding on the flats, you've got to force *yourself* to work hard. And I think it's a little too much to expect from yourself in the early season.

Hills are perfect for anaerobic threshold training—if you're pushing hard on a hill you'll have a heart rate of about 175; the same type of effort on the flats would give you a heart rate that is actually about 5 percent lower. Your pedal cadence is also higher on the flats—110–120 RPMs instead of 85 uphill, with more movement and less use of muscle mass.

If you can find a good, long hill of about eight to ten miles, it should take about thirty to forty-five minutes to climb. If you live in an area that doesn't have a hill this long, look for a shorter hill you can do four or five times on a short circuit. If you can find a road that has a succession of short, windy hills that can provide you with an excellent workout. If you live in a very flat area, you can probably find some "artificial" hills to work out on. Bridges offer some long, hard hills, even in flat areas.

You want to make sure, in the first few weeks of the preparatory cycle, never to push *too* hard. Even when you're climbing hills, don't go all-out. Just ride at a good steady pace—gravity will take care of the rest. Remember, this is a middle-intensity workout.

Thursdays should be devoted to endurance training. In an endurance ride your heart rate should be between 65 percent and 80 percent of its maximum. I usually try to ride for about four hours in the preparatory cycle. The distance you do depends on your age and the racing you do. As a junior, for example, you don't need to ride seven hours on your endurance day in the preparatory cycle because you'll never need that kind of endurance when racing. Because endurance riding is at a low intensity, there's no need to limit yourself to a fixed distance: If you feel good and want to go further, do it.

The endurance day, with its low intensity and long duration, builds up your cardiovascular system and trains your body to use its fatty acids efficiently. You're conditioning your body so that you'll be stronger through a long ride. The anaerobic training you do would be useless in a race if you couldn't keep up with the rest of the pack until the finish.

The reason the endurance day follows your sprints and anaerobic threshold training days is that those workouts are intense; afterward, you need a low-intensity day. On Thursday, even if you're tired, you should be able to ride with your heart rate above 65 percent of its maximum. And this will give you the training you need. If you're having a hard time keeping your heart rate at 65 percent of maximum, and your legs are burning, however, then you will have to slow down and relax. You can go a little farther or harder the next week.

Ideally, in the preparatory cycle you should never feel this tired by Thursday. The intensity of your sprint and anaerobic threshold days should be low enough that you can go out for a low-intensity endurance ride without your legs' burning.

After your endurance ride, however, you *should* be pretty tired. That's why on *Friday* I suggest that you ride only an hour and a half at the most, at a *very* low intensity (that is, below 65 percent of your maximum heart rate). During the preparatory cycle, I usually take a short ride, spinning easily, never pushing. During the season I always rest on the day two days before the race, and that usually means Fridays.

Saturday is the test day, a high-intensity day to gauge how you feel following a day of rest. Do a number of sprints. If you're up to it do some anaerobic threshold training in the afternoon, again in an unstructured manner, possibly cyclo cross or hill-climbing.

Sunday is the day that brings your week of training all together. In the season, Sunday is probably a race day. In the preparatory cycle, do a ride that emphasizes endurance. Of course, if you're up to it you can add a little intensity to your ride.

THE FIRST MACRO CYCLE: WEEK TWO

In the second week of the preparatory cycle, I increase my duration gradually, increasing the anaerobic threshold ride by half an hour and the endurance ride by about half an hour to an hour. At this point in the season I'm not really working on increasing the intensity of my workouts, I only want to increase the duration, to give me a good base for the season.

Monday, again, is a rest day. If you want to go out for a short ride, fine, but this is entirely optional.

Tuesday is the day for sprint. Again, work out for about an hour and a half, about eight sprints. To begin this ride, warm up for about half an hour, then do your three or four warmup sprints. After finishing your sprints (remember to recover completely between sprints), continue to ride at an endurance pace for half an hour more.

Wednesday is the middle-distance, middle-intensity day. You can increase your duration by half an hour here if you feel strong. This will increase the amount of your anaerobic threshold training, but it's a gradual increase.

Thursday is another endurance ride. I increase the duration about half an hour to an hour over the first week. I ride about four-and-a-half hours the second week (remember, these durations are variable and depend in part on how you feel).

Friday is your day to ease off, with an hour-and-a-half ride, just spinning easily.

Saturday's workout should last about three hours. You can split it up if you want, doing four sprints after a warmup in the morning and a two-hour ride in the afternoon (with a couple of ten-minute accelerations where you're riding at or near your anaerobic threshold).

Sunday, do an endurance ride. Ideally, you should work out for about half an hour more than you did on the first Sunday in January.

THE FIRST MACRO CYCLE: WEEK THREE

The third week shows a continuing progression. You should increase your duration a little more, concentrating especially on extending the middle-intensity and endurance workouts. You should start in with double workouts in this third week. This is the time in the cycle when you should start pushing yourself.

What I do on *Tuesday*, instead of an hour and a half of sprints, is an hour of sprints in the morning (again, always do the more intense exercise first), followed by an hour of cyclo cross where I train my anaerobic threshold. This is a good workout because it's *more intense* than the previous weeks. It also breaks up the monotony of an hour and a half of sprints every Tuesday.

I also split my *Wednesday* workouts. Once you begin to ride for a long time on your middle-distance, middle-intensity day—say three to four hours—you have to split the effort to get a proper workout. I try to vary my middle-distance workouts. In the third week of the first preparatory cycle I include hills or possibly motor-pacing.

On Wednesday I might do an anaerobic threshold workout on hills. An anaerobic threshold workout is a ride of middle intensity in which one rides close to one's anaerobic threshold for about ten minutes at a time as many times as one feels comfortable. Then on Saturday I might split my workout—two hours of motor-pacing (racing behind a motorcycle pacer) in the morning, close to my anaerobic threshold, and in the afternoon, an hour and a half of an intense endurance ride, keeping my heart rate just *below* my normal anaerobic threshold rate. If, one week, I do a lot of anaerobic threshold training on hills, I might change to flat anaerobic threshold rides the following week. This gives me a nice mental break from hill riding, and also rounds out my training. Anaerobic threshold training on the flats emphasizes pedal cadence (leg speed), while hill climbing emphasizes torque (leg power).

As before, *Thursdays* are endurance days. In the third week, increase the length of the ride by about half an hour.

Friday is an off day, with a short hour-and-a-half ride just to keep your legs loose.

Saturday's workout should last about three hours. Split it up, if you like—four sprints in the morning, and later a two-hour ride in the afternoon. Include a couple of ten-minute accelerations in your ride where you're at or right below your anaerobic threshold.

Sunday, do an endurance workout about half an hour longer than the previous week.

THE FIRST PREPARATORY CYCLE: WEEKS FOUR, FIVE, AND SIX

In the last three weeks of this second preparatory cycle you should begin structured leg speed anaerobic threshold training. In structured leg speed anaerobic threshold training exercises, you're spinning the gear so that you get close to 100 or 110 RPMs. Structured leg speed anaerobic threshold training should be done on a flat road where you can ride fast and get your legs turning fast. You can also accomplish structured leg speed anaerobic threshold training by doing motor-pacing (explained below). Do at least four or six intervals of up to ten minutes each, more if you feel up to it. I would suggest doing structured leg speed anaerobic threshold training on the flats with a gear that allows you to achieve the correct heart rate (up to 90 percent of your maximim) at a pedal cadence of 100–110 RPMs.

The following week, week five, you should do flat, structured leg speed anaerobic threshold training again, but this time with a smaller gear, turning the pedals at about 120–130 RPMs. If you lack leg speed, you should concentrate on this type of training. If, on the other hand, you find you're lacking power in uphill bursts, you should concentrate more on short, intense hill anaerobic threshold riding.

Your Sunday rides at this point might consist of club races of about sixty to seventy-five miles, in which you're riding competitively. If there is no club race, do a long, hard workout of four hours or more that uses every aspect of your training.

In the main, weeks four, five, and six are simply repetitions of the first three weeks. You want to increase the intensity and begin building your structured anaerobic threshold training. But don't begin training with an overly structured program—it's still too early in the season.

Most important, you must tailor your program to your specific needs and progress. Even though I may be doing six or seven intense intervals by week five, that is probably too intense for the average rider.

TRAINING CHARTS

Duration is listed with two values separated by a slash. The first value is the suggested duration at the start *of the Macro Cycle. The second value is your* peak *duration at the end of the Macro Cycle.*

Note that distance provided in kilometers is only a rough estimate—always go by duration rather than distance.

Important: The durations listed here are suitable only to a top cyclist in each age category. If you are not in good shape or are having trouble maintaining the training regimen listed here, reduce your duration to a point at which you feel comfortable—and that point is something only you can determine.

Training Program for Fifteen-Year-Old Racer

	NOV.–DEC.	JANUARY		FEBRUARY		IN SEASON	
	Hours	*Hours*	*Km*	*Hours*	*Km*	*Hours*	*Km*
MON	Rest	Rest		Rest		Rest	
TUE	1/1	1/1	30/30	1/1	30/30	1/1	30/30
WED	Rest	1/2	30/60	1/2	30/60	1.5/2	45/60
THU	1/2	1/3	30/90	2/4	60/120	2.5/3.5	75/105
FRI	Rest	1/1	30/30	1/1	30/30	1/1	30/30
SAT	1/1	1/2	30/60	1/2	30/60	1.5/2	45/60
SUN	1/2	1/3	30/90	2/4	60/120	2.5/3.5	75/105
TOTAL	4/6	6/12	180/360	8/14	240/420	10/13	300/390

Training Program for Sixteen-Year-Old Racer or Young Women's Racer

	NOV.–DEC.	JANUARY		FEBRUARY		IN SEASON	
	Hours	*Hours*	*Km*	*Hours*	*Km*	*Hours*	*Km*
MON	Rest	Rest		Rest		Rest	
TUE	1/1.5	1/1.5	30/45	1/1.5	30/45	1/1.5	30/45
WED	Rest	1/2	30/60	1.5/3	45/90	2/3	60/90
THU	1.5/3	1.5/3.5	45/105	2.5/4.5	75/135	3/4.5	90/135
FRI	Rest	1/2	30/60	1/2	30/60	1/1	30/30
SAT	1/2	1/2	30/60	1.5/3	45/90	2/2.5	60/75
SUN	1.5/2.5	1.5/3	45/90	2.5/3	75/90	3/3.5	90/105
TOTAL	5/9	7/14	210/420	10/17	300/510	12/16	360/480

Training Program for Seventeen-Year-Old Racer

	NOV.–DEC.	JANUARY		FEBRUARY		IN SEASON	
	Hours	*Hours*	*Km*	*Hours*	*Km*	*Hours*	*Km*
MON	Rest	Rest		Rest		Rest	
TUE	1/1.5	1/1.5	30/45	1/1.5	30/45	1.5/1.5	45/45
WED	Rest	1/3	30/90	1.5/3	45/90	2/3	60/90
THU	2/3.5	2/4.5	60/135	2.5/6	75/180	3.5/4.5	105/135
FRI	Rest	1/2	30/60	1/1.5	30/45	1.5/2	45/60
SAT	1/1.5	1/3	30/90	1.5/3	45/90	2/3	60/90
SUN	2/3.5	2/4	60/120	2.5/5	75/150	3.5/4	105/120
TOTAL	6/10	8/18	240/540	10/20	300/600	14/18	420/540

Training Program for Eighteen-Year-Old Racer or Top Women's Racer

	NOV.–DEC.	JANUARY		FEBRUARY		IN SEASON	
	Hours	*Hours*	*Km*	*Hours*	*Km*	*Hours*	*Km*
MON	Rest	Rest		Rest		Rest	
TUE	1/1.5	1/1.5	30/45	1.5/1.5	45/45	1.5/1.5	45/45
WED	Rest	1.5/3	45/90	2/3.5	60/105	2.5/3.5	75/105
THU	2.5/4	2/6.5	60/195	3.5/7	105/210	4.5/6.5	135/195
FRI	Rest	1/2	30/60	1.5/1.5	45/45	1.5/1.5	45/45
SAT	1/1.5	1.5/3	45/90	2/3.5	60/105	2.5/3	75/90
SUN	2.5/4	2/6	60/180	3.5/7	105/210	4.5/6	135/180
TOTAL	7/11	9/22	270/660	14/24	420/720	17/22	510/660

Training Program for Nineteen-Year-Old Racer

	NOV.–DEC.	JANUARY		FEBRUARY		IN SEASON	
	Hours	*Hours*	*Km*	*Hours*	*Km*	*Hours*	*Km*
MON	Rest	Rest		Rest		Rest	
TUE	1.5/2	1.5/2	45/60	1.5/2	45/60	1.5/2	45/60
WED	Rest	2/3.5	60/105	2.5/4	75/120	2.5/3.5	75/105
THU	2.5/5	2.5/6.5	75/195	4/7	120/210	5/7	150/210
FRI	Rest	1.5/2	45/60	1.5/2	45/60	1.5/2	45/60
SAT	1.5/2	2/3.5	60/105	2.5/4	75/120	2.5/3	75/90
SUN	2.5/5	2.5/6.5	75/195	4/7	120/210	5/6.5	150/195
TOTAL	8/14	12/24	360/720	16/26	480/780	18/24	540/720

Training Program for
Twenty-Year-Old Racer
(or any top amateur)

	NOV.–DEC.	JANUARY		FEBRUARY		IN SEASON	
	Hours	*Hours*	*Km*	*Hours*	*Km*	*Hours*	*Km*
MON	Rest	Rest		Rest		Rest	
TUE	1.5/2.5	1.5/2	45/60	1.5/2	45/60	1.5/2	45/60
WED	Rest	2/3.5	60/105	2.5/4.5	75/135	3/4	90/120
THU	3/5.5	3/7	90/210	4/7	120/210	5.5/7	165/210
FRI	Rest	1.5/2	45/60	1.5/2	45/60	1.5/2	45/60
SAT	1.5/2.5	2/3.5	60/105	2.5/4.5	75/135	3/3.5	90/105
SUN	3/5.5	3/7	90/210	4/7	120/210	5.5/6.5	165/195
TOTAL	9/16	13/25	390/750	16/27	480/810	20/25	600/750

m. 240+   300 m   360 m

Training Program for
Pro Racer

	NOV.–DEC.	JANUARY		FEBRUARY		IN SEASON	
	Hours	*Hours*	*Km*	*Hours*	*Km*	*Hours*	*Km*
MON	Rest	Rest		Rest		Rest	
TUE	1.5/2.5	1.5/2.5	45/60	1.5/2.5	45/75	1.5/2	45/60
WED	Rest	2/3.5	60/105	3/4.5	90/135	3.5/4.5	105/135
THU	3.5/6	3.5/7	90/210	4.5/8	135/240	6/7	180/210
FRI	Rest	1.5/2.5	45/60	1.5/2.5	45/75	1.5/2	45/60
SAT	1.5/2.5	2/3.5	60/105	3/4.5	75/135	3.5/4	105/120
SUN	3.5/6	3.5/7	90/210	4.5/8	120/240	6/6.5	180/195
TOTAL	10/17	14/26	390/750	18/30	510/900	22/26	660/780

After completing this preparatory cycle, break down and take a rest from cycling. You should rest for at least four days but not more than seven. This rest period is crucial in allowing your body to build its fitness and is essential to becoming a top, fit cyclist.

THE FIRST MACRO CYCLE: HOW TO DRAW CONCLUSIONS AND SET YOUR GOALS

You shouldn't make your schedule so rigid that you'll have trouble following it. I never follow a rigid schedule. One week I might feel good and do more than I planned. The next week I might be traveling or attending a bike show somewhere and not be able to ride nearly as much. The important thing is to learn the right type of weekly schedule.

Always do the most intense exercise first. Sprints come before anaerobic threshold training, and anaerobic threshold training comes before endurance training.

The ideal way to start out in January is to sit down and plan your six-week cycle. But don't let it rule you. If you feel tired after three weeks and you don't do quite as much endurance, or you skip the sprints one week, it won't destroy your program. There are times when I don't do sprints for two weeks straight. On the other hand, if you feel good and your schedule calls for four- to four-and-a-half hours of endurance riding, there's no reason why you can't stretch that to five-to five-and-a-half hours. Especially with endurance training, it can't hurt to do a little more.

The only thing to remember is that you don't want to do too much too soon; you should try to build up *gradually*.

If you come down with a cold or the flu and have to seriously cut back or stop riding, don't panic once you get back on the bike. Take it easy your first week. Then, if you feel better the following weeks, you can start building up more quickly.

It's especially important to build up gradually the first two or three weeks of the cycle. But as you get to the end of the cycle you can increase the duration and intensity more quickly, if you feel strong.

Some people don't have a hard time training. Sean Kelly is a rider who trains methodically and systematically. He never seems to get burned out on cycling. Unfortunately, I'm not like Sean. I get mentally burned out if I train too much. That's why I have to be very clever about varying my workouts and building them up gradually.

The one thing you shouldn't do is lose sight of your goals. In the preparatory cycles, from January to the beginning of April, you're basically working on building up your base of endurance, and you're also gradually building up your anaerobic threshold, in preparation for the very intense intervals that you will be doing once the racing seasons starts.

Your body needs a certain minimum time to improve. Three weeks is the *minimum* amount of time needed to make a Macro Cycle. If you try to create a Macro Cycle of less than three weeks, you won't be able to make any appreciable progress. The *longest* amount of time you should ride a Macro Cycle is seven weeks. Anything longer, and neither your mind nor your body will be able to focus well on the immediate goals of that Macro Cycle.

Again, always build your Macro Cycles to fit in with your racing season. Let's say you want to do well in a race at the end of April. You should plan a Macro Cycle of about six weeks, beginning in mid-March, so that by the time you're at the end of the Macro Cycle, you're ready to race. After your racing, take another break and plan your cycles for the rest of the season.

How do you decide how long each Macro Cycle should be? The ideal Macro Cycle is the longest one, seven weeks, because it allows you to improve the most. But there are variables. A rider who begins a Macro Cycle in relatively poor shape might find himself exhausted after four weeks. If you want to ride a seven-week Macro Cycle but you're completely exhausted after four weeks, this is probably a good time to stop riding, recuperate, and build yourself up for the following Macro Cycle.

It's much more difficult for me to schedule my Macro Cycles because there are so many races. I can't really segment my season as well as an amateur. The season often seems a constant blur of racing from February till October.

If you are a young rider, arrange your schedule so there's as much variation as possible. It is important to spice up your training as much as possible to keep yourself mentally fresh. But you also want to dabble in as many fields of cycling as you can. If you can race on a track, try some sprints on the track on Tuesdays. If you don't live near a track, consider racing in an evening criterium. It will provide you with important racing experience.

The one thing I would be careful about as a young rider is racing too much. I suggest that you substitute racing for training only every other week at this period in your training, in order to maintain your competitive edge.

After every Macro Cycle give yourself a rest to prevent mental burnout. But be systematic about it. You sould not do less than three or four weeks— you'll jeopardize the entire training cycle. You need to develop the discipline and physical conditioning necessary to stay with each cycle to the end.

By the end of the first preparatory cycle you should feel as if you've really made an improvement in your conditioning.

TRAINING IN A COLD CLIMATE IN JANUARY AND FEBRUARY

If you live in the Snow Belt and you can't train on your bike there are alternative ways to get inshape that approximate the effort of cycling. *Monday* is still a rest day—the most I would do would be to have some fun in the snow, sledding or skating.

Tuesdays you should approximate sprinting by riding on a home trainer. You could also take a cross-country ski run in the afternoon and do a less intense workout. An alternative would be to ice skate (try intervals of fifteen seconds up and down the ice).

If there's no snow on the ground but it's still too cold to go road riding, try bundling up and doing cyclo cross on Tuesdays. Because you're going much slower in cyclo cross than on the road you won't have nearly as much wind chill and your body will heat up quickly once you're riding. Find a two-mile course of trails with a half-mile hill and some tricky stretches. This should force you to get off the bike every lap and run for a short stretch with the bike. Include some short sprints. You'll be doing short, sprintlike intervals that will approximate the effort you'd be doing sprinting on a road bike on Tuesdays.

Of course if you're having one of those winters where it's very cold (about zero degrees) and there's no snow on the ground, you can't cross-country ski and it's too icy to ride cyclo cross. You might want to go ice skating, once again doing sprints up and down the ice of about fifteen seconds (hockey players do these exercises). You should skate for about forty-five minutes with about ten ice sprints spaced out evenly after a ten-minute warmup.

Another possibility is to run indoors and do calisthenic intervals that raise your heartbeat.

You might also take an endurance run (running sprinting is not advisable because the muscles worked are so different from those used in cycling). To complement the running for the power of sprints do some weight-lifting that includes squats, leg presses, leg curls, and possibly calf raises.

On *Wednesdays*, for your middle-distance, middle-intensity workout, if there is snow, go cross-country skiing for two hours with ten- to fifteen-minute sections where your heart rate is just below your anaerobic threshold. If you do cyclo cross instead, do a circuit with some fairly long climbs that will force you to reach your anaerobic threshold.

On *Thursdays* (your endurance day), you have to get back on the cross-country skis for about three hours with your heartbeat at a minimum of 65 percent of its maximum and no higher than 80 percent.

Friday is a rest day. If you can't ride your bike, I would do a thirty-minute session on your home trainer in front of the television, or ski leisurely for an hour and have fun.

On *Saturday*, repeat the workout you did on Tuesday with sprints, and possibly an intense workout on your rollers (or home trainer) in the afternoon.

On *Sundays*, do an endurance workout in which you combine a little bit of all the elements you worked on during the week. You could go for a three-hour cross-country run, pushing it on the uphill sections and including sprinting intervals on the flats as well. If you ride cyclo cross, find a route that will take you up a nice hill, through some shrubs, over different terrain. I would ride cyclo cross for about two-and-a-half hours.

If it warms up enough so that you can both cross-country ski and do road riding, you should vary your workouts so you can break the monotony of riding in cold weather or skiing the same cross-country run every day.

You can probably go three months in the winter without touching your bike if you train competently. But, in the long run, I think that if you approach a national or world-class level, you're going to have to move to a climate where you can train full-time on a bike. This is especially true starting with the first preparatory cycle in January. For example, Steve Bauer, my La Vie Claire teammate and friend, lives in Canada during November and December but travels to California in January to begin his full-time training.

THE RECUPERATION PERIODS

After finishing your first Macro Cycle of the season you should feel tired. Before starting on the next Macro Cycle, you want to make sure that you recuperate fully. You should start the next cycle fully fresh. You've been pushing your body to a very high point. You've been training hard and you need to back down and rest your body.

How long should you rest? Some riders need only three or four days. Others might need six or seven days. You should still be riding your bike, one or two hours every other day, during the recuperation period. But you shouldn't be trying to train with it. The key in the recuperation period is as much psychological recuperation as physical recuperation—you don't want to force yourself to get on the bike.

Out of an entire rest week, you could even take two or three days off your bike completely. The week of recuperation is crucial to allow you to keep building to a higher level. When I prepare for a big, important race like the Tour de France, the best preparation is the Tour of Italy, because it tears my body down, it allows me to train fully in all the aspects of racing. Then afterward I can let go and let myself recuperate.

The second preparatory cycle will usually begin just about the time you've started club races on the weekend. This is a period when the racing is not important. You want to concentrate primarily on improving your endurance and increasing your anaerobic threshold. But you want to slowly bring yourself to the point at which, at the end of the second cycle, you'll be able to race.

THE SECOND PREPARATORY CYCLE (MID-FEBRUARY TO BEGINNING APRIL)

You should start the second preparatory cycle at a level *below* the last week of your previous preparatory cycle. But you will be starting at a level *higher* than you began at on January first. On the whole your riding in the second Macro Cycle will not differ greatly from that in the first Macro Cycle. The difference will be a matter of degree, depending on your improved level of fitness and your mental freshness.

As in the first preparatory cycle, *Mondays* are your rest day. You've spent all your training week building up to Sunday. Monday—the day after the important racing during the season—is your day off. You can ride an hour to an hour and a half, or stay off your bike entirely.

Tuesday, in the typical scheme, is the day for sprints. Start out with three short sprints of six to seven seconds with a big gear on a slightly uphill stretch of road. Then, do two or three long sprints of over 250 meters (275 yards). (If you're exhausted after these, you've clearly not recovered from the weekend's efforts, and should return home.)

If you've recovered fully from the first Macro Cycle, you might want to begin the second Macro Cycle with a more intensive sprint workout. You could increase the number of sprints you're doing, being careful never to exceed twelve sprints in one day. Or you could do about six or seven sprints in the morning and then do some intervals (as described below) in the afternoon. But if you're not up to beginning the second Macro Cycle so intensely, don't force yourself to ride hard.

WHEN TO START ANAEROBIC CAPACITY TRAINING (INTERVALS)

In the last two or three weeks of this Macro Cycle, as you approach your first important races, you should start doing long two to four-minute intervals.

Although anaerobic threshold and anaerobic capacity training sound similar, there is an important distinction. Anaerobic *threshold* training increases your body's ability to take in oxygen. What it does is to increase your body's ability to ride hard *before* going into oxygen debt.

Anaerobic *capacity* training, on the other hand, is actually training *beyond* the aerobic point, beyond the point where your body supplies oxygen to the muscles. If a rider's anaerobic threshold is at 175 heartbeats per minute, with anaerobic capacity training you train to go beyond that point to, say, 180 or 185 heartbeats for about two to four minutes (if your anaerobic threshold is lower than 175 heartbeats per minute, then you need to train at an accordingly lower heart rate). Following an interval, you recuperate for a few minutes—until your heartbeat comes back down to a recuperation level correct for you. This is only a *partial* recuperation, before you repeat the intense effort to bring your heart rate back up to 180 or 185 (or a point beyond your correct anaerobic threshold). This is interval training.

When you go into an anaerobic state your body starts to use glycogen, or sugar deposits, in the cells as a source of energy. This is important to you as a cyclist because there is always going to be a period in a race, either on the flats or in the hills, during a breakaway or at the finish, when the pace picks up so much that you go into an anaerobic state. Only the best-trained racers, those whose bodies can efficiently use glycogen as an energy source, can keep up. The rest of the pack is dropped.

Intervals are a training method that enables you to teach your body to be more effective in processing sugars. You are, in effect, improving your anaerobic capacity. Let's say you're racing, and you're on an uphill with the pack. You feel fine as long as the pace is even. But as soon as the pace picks up, when riders are trying to break away or sprint for the summit, you can't keep up. Or perhaps you haven't recuperated enough since the last attack. You end up exploding (as much a mental state as a physical one), going into oxygen debt, because your body is traumatized, it's processing sugars very poorly. The result: You get dropped. This is why you must improve your anaerobic capacity.

There are two ways to train for anaerobic capacity. The first is to increase your pedal cadence tremendously. This is known as a *speed interval.* The second is to push a big gear. This is a *power interval.* You should concentrate primarily on speed intervals if you have trouble staying with a fast-moving group that is breaking away on the flats, where a high pedal cadence of 110 to 120 RPMs is needed. If, on the other hand, you can't dip into your anaerobic capacity in a situation in which a group is attacking uphill at a cadence like 85 RPMs, then you should concentrate on power intervals. Whatever your weakness, you need to work on both kinds of intervals to be effective.

In any case, anaerobic capacity training is achieved by performing a series of intervals. Your body can't stay in a anaerobic state much longer than four minutes. The *longer* the interval, the less intense the effort, and the lower your heart rate. The *shorter* the interval, the more intense the effort, and the

Different Intervals

The term interval *is a bit vague. In cycling training there are two different categories of exercise that are called* intervals. *Here is an explanation of the differences between the interval types:*

1. The pure interval: *twenty-five seconds to two minutes. This is the purely anaerobic interval. Studies have shown that from a purely physiological point of view the physical benefit of the pure interval ends after forty-five seconds of exercise. From this point lactic acid is secreted into the muscles. Therefore, when working on the pure anaerobic interval it is not really necessary to go beyond forty-five seconds.*

The pure interval is useful in training for the intense effort in the last kilometer of a race or for bridging a gap where you will need to ride at a high level of intensity.

The pure interval is at the submaximum level of intensity. Your heart is at 100 percent. Your body feeds on anaerobic glycogen.

This kind of interval should be avoided by young riders and by the more mature until the beginning of the in-season Macro Cycle.

2. The long interval: *two to four minutes. This is a longer interval during which the body is not in a purely anaerobic state. The body feeds on anaerobic glycogen and aerobic glycogen.*

This type of interval is useful for racing in short time trials and also for breakaway speed.

Most riders should start to work in the longer interval in the second preparatory cycle of the season.

Younger riders only need to train in the longer interval periodically.

higher the heart rate. You can vary the length of the intervals according to your needs. If you're having trouble achieving a high burst of speed, then you should concentrate on shorter intervals. But you should never do intervals shorter than twenty-five seconds—any effort shorter than that won't cause your body to dip into its sugar stores sufficiently. In between your intervals you should keep riding at an even pace for a period of time to let your body recuperate somewhat.

Many people wonder how they can gauge how much their body has recuperated. A good rule of thumb is to learn what a good *endurance pace* is, and what gear you should be in to maintain an endurance pace. Shift to that gear and maintain an average 90 RPMs pedal cadence when recuperating.

The period of recuperation should be *four times longer* than the period of effort. In other words, if you're doing two-to four-minute intervals, you should rest about eight to sixteen minutes. An important metabolic and organic activity takes place during the recuperation periods. Your body takes in a massive amount of oxygen. As your body rapidly refuels with oxygen, it streamlines its effectiveness to refuel with and use oxygen.

Coach Paul Koechli, an expert on exercise physiology, once told me that the body doesn't need an interval longer than forty-five seconds to a minute—beyond that you're going slow enough that the body begins to use some oxygen as a form of energy, so the effort isn't purely anaerobic anymore.

But you need to train with longer intervals before you can start with the extremely intense forty-five-second to one-minute intervals. If you do two- to four-minute intervals, you'll have a more gradual exercise that will be effective in increasing *both* anaerobic capacity and threshold. Another advantage of doing longer intervals is that you're doing a kind of riding often called for in cycling, the prologue, or pursuit and time trialing.

Intervals will improve your anaerobic capacity. When you start doing them you might only be able to hold a pure anaerobic interval for about thirty seconds. As you progress through the season, though, you'll slowly build it up to about forty-five seconds.

Personally, I do all kinds of intervals. I've done the forty-five-second intervals that Paul Koechli recommends. I do three-minute recuperations between those exercises. But these very short, intense intervals should only be done once you're into the racing season in April.

When you do interval training, start out with a fifteen-minute warmup, then do thirty minutes to two hours of intervals, depending on the kind and number of intervals you want to do. If you're riding short forty-five-second intervals with three minutes of recuperation in between, you probably won't be able to keep them up for more than half an hour. You want to keep doing intervals until you feel it is hard to keep the same intensity of effort.

If you're doing four-minute intervals, you can stay out for two hours, because the interval and the recuperation periods are so much longer. After you've finished the workout, cool down for about fifteen more minutes.

One word of caution: If you set out to do a few very hard intervals and then find, after a few intervals, that you simply can't do any more without pain, don't force yourself.

Some coaches recommend doing intervals in a descending order of length: three-and-a-half minutes, three minutes, two-and-a-half minutes, two minutes, all the day down to twenty seconds. Personally, I don't think this makes sense, because there are too many different kinds of effort involved.

Do the long intervals on Wednesdays, your middle-distance, middle-intensity days, starting about the second or third week of the second preparatory cycle. When you do these long intervals, try to split up your middle-distance, middle-intensity days. In keeping with the idea that the most intense effort should always come first, do your long intervals in the morning and your anaerobic threshold training in the afternoon.

You can also do the long intervals on Tuesday afternoon after the sprint workout of Tuesday morning. (Note: Always stay with the basic criterion of doing the more intense exercise first. In other words, if you do intervals on Tuesday, do them second after the sprints. If you do the long intervals on Wednesday, do them first, before the less intense anaerobic threshold training.

On a typical Wednesday morning I find a one-mile hill and do two- to four-minute intervals up the hill eight or ten times. Between intervals, I recuperate for eight to sixteen minutes (or four times the length of the activation or effort). The next intervals session, on Saturday, I again do two- to four-minute intervals, but this time on the flats, where I can increase my pedal cadence to 120 RPMs.

At the end of the second preparatory cycle, increase the number of intervals you're doing. In the afternoon, try anaerobic threshold training by motor-pacing or riding hills at your anaerobic threshold.

Motor-pacing is a special type of workout in which you follow or draft in the wake of a motorcycle or scooter. Motor-pacing can be used for sprinting, intervals, or even endurance training. I use motor-pacing for training at my anaerobic threshold or training at a high heart level for a longer period of time. Why? I find that when I go out alone on the flats I can ride for only about ten minutes at a rate close to my anaerobic threshold, unless I have a tailwind. Mentally it's just too hard to keep going.

Even with a tailwind, I can ride at my anaerobic threshold only for twenty minutes, at most. Riding behind a motorcycle, I can ride at my anaerobic threshold for thirty minutes. And, of course, that's better training.

The reason you can keep going longer behind a motorcycle is that you're fighting a different kind of resistance. When you're out alone, you're fighting wind resistance. Behind a motorcycle, you have much less wind resistance, and you have a pacer. Since you're going faster, you have more road friction, but that is easily overcome by your own momentum. You can have the driver vary his speed and tailor your ride to the way you feel.

There are two drawbacks to motor-pacing. First, it's very hard to find somebody who can adequately and safely drive the motorcycle for you. Throughout my career I've had my father or a friend who was an experienced rider drive for me. A rider has to keep a steady pace and not accelerate or accidentally slam on the brakes.

A bigger drawback to motor-pacing is that, in many states, it isn't legal to ride so close behind a motorcycle on a public road. And it's illegal for a good reason—if both motorcycle driver and cyclist aren't experienced, it can be dangerous. You must have a top-notch driver who's experienced on a motorcycle and understands the needs of cyclists. You need to ride very alertly all the time. Always wear a hard-shell helmet when you go motor-pacing.

Motor-pacing should always be done on a relatively flat course unless you're working on hill jams, trying to simulate going over a hill. The problem with motor-pacing on a hill is that the driver can't gauge what kind of speed you need. It's easier for the driver to maintain a steady pace for you on a flat course.

Motor-pacing is primarily useful for anaerobic threshold training and sprints. Most of your motor-pacing rides will be between forty-five minutes and two hours long. Occasionally, you could take a longer ride if you lack racing rhythm or speed. The real advantage of motor-pacing is that it allows you to keep a continuous fast pace when you're attempting anaerobic threshold training.

Consider starting motor-pacing at the end of January, about three weeks into your first preparatory cycle, or alternatively, about three weeks into the second preparatory cycle.

Once you're into the cycling season, you might motor-pace once a week. Even if you have a hilly upcoming race, you could do intervals on Wednesdays, your middle-distance days, in the morning and motor-pacing in the afternoon. Because you can bring your heart rate to such a high level with motor-pacing, it's good training even for a hilly race.

Check with police to see if motor-pacing is legal in your area. If it isn't, you'll have to find a private road or skip this form of training altogether.

Also, be sure to use the right kind of motorcycle. Don't ride behind something big like a Yamaha 650 or a Ninja. Get something much smaller and more nimble, like a Vespa or Honda Esprit. What you need is a motorcycle or moped that can go about forty to forty-five miles per hour. I have a Honda, and it's perfect for motor-pacing.

If you're racing on the weekends, you can begin to tailor your middle-distance, middle-intensity day (Wednesdays) to your upcoming race. Do a speed workout that's going to simulate the weekend's race. If the course is a hilly one, do a morning workout of hill intervals and an afternoon workout of endurance riding in the hills (anaerobic capacity training).

Even if you're racing criteriums on Sundays, I would still do *some* hill intervals, because it'll break up the monotony of your training. More important, it'll give your body a different kind of workout. And the training will prepare you for longer, major events, like the state or national championships, in which you'll be riding over varied terrain. Of course, if crite-

Training in a group is easier than training alone. Here I ride with my teammates Steve Bauer (left) and Guido Winterberg (center).

rium racing is important to you, you can concentrate primarily on a speed workout of sprints in the morning and motor-pacing in the afternoon for anaerobic capacity training.

By the end of the second Macro Cycle you should be training for all the types of effort you'll need for racing.

THE SECOND PREPARATORY CYCLE: WHEN YOU START RIDING CLUB RACES

On Sundays in this second preparatory cycle you should go on a lot of club races, where you can simulate racing. I think it's good at this point in the year to start practicing some competitive tactics, getting comfortable with the rhythm of riding in a group.

Be careful about riding in a group, though—if the pace isn't strong you may not be getting any training value from the ride. This is the mistake that was often made when I went to the Olympic Training Center in Colorado Springs in 1979. We rode in groups of twenty-five riders with restricted gears of 42 × 21. We were just rolling along. It was like doing a rest ride every day, and it had practically no training value.

At this point in the year, your Sunday rides should be like races. There may be times when you will be riding at a rest pace, but most of the time you should be riding at an endurance pace. At times you'll approach your anaerobic threshold, especially on hills. You should sprint a few times as well, perhaps to a telephone pole or a city limits sign, to get the intense part of your workout. The Sunday rides in this part of the preparatory cycle should always bring together all the elements you worked on during the week. That way you'll be ready for the real racing starting in the spring.

Whenever you go on a long ride in a group pay special attention to your pulse. You don't want to ride below your endurance level (65 percent of maximum heart rate). If you see the pace dipping, take a turn at the front to encourage the others to pick up the pace. If a club ride is slow, it's easy to get tucked in behind somebody's draft and end up taking a free ride.

Normally, I think the ideal group for training is no bigger than two to four riders. Personally, I do most of my training alone because I feel I can get a better workout. But it takes a lot of discipline to train alone day after day. For most people, riding with two or three other riders is the best solution.

Most serious Sunday club races have many more than four riders, of course—I think it's good to ride in a big group like this on Sundays because it resembles the size of a race pack and the rhythm of a race pack, especially at the front. And most club races tend to be pretty competitive.

Some bike clubs hold club time trials. Ideally, a club should hold its time trial on Wednesdays or Saturdays. This way, you can train at your anaerobic threshold without having to force yourself all the time. The time trial provides you with competition. It's also a good way to gauge your improvement. However, limit club time trials to days when you want to train at your anaerobic threshold. If your club has scheduled the time trial some other day of the week, try to convince them to move it to an anaerobic threshold day (usually Wednesday and Saturday in a typical Micro Cycle).

As you get into the racing season, always look to Saturday or Sunday as your race days. Up until April, though, the racing will really be more a part of your training than anything else. In many cases the early season races in America are short. If so, train a little bit after the race.

When I was a junior, I always trained after races, because junior races in America were always too short, usually thirty miles.

The objective of training from mid-February till the end of March is to bring yourself into really top condition so you can be in top condition for the high-caliber racing, which usually starts in April (in some of the colder climates racing starts as late as May).

As you get close to the races that matter to you, get in the habit of resting the day 48 hours before your race, because after riding each Micro Cycle, you should require a minimum recuperation time. After your endurance ride on Thursday you really need two days to recuperate. Friday is a day of complete recuperation (on the bike). The reason you don't want to make

Saturday a complete recuperation day is that you could be sluggish the day of the race. Similarly, if you rest only Saturday you might not have rested enough to recuperate completely.

IN-SEASON TRAINING (APRIL TO OCTOBER)

Once you are in the racing season, you should start to develop specific workouts to improve your weak spots or to simulate the kind of effort you'll have in the race on the coming weekend.

As usual, *Mondays* are rest days. If you feel like getting out and riding the bike, go for a gentle spin for an hour or so. But you don't have to ride if you don't want to. My former coach Cyrille Guimard even thinks it's acceptable to not ride one day a week so you can teach your body to live without riding consistently—it's a matter of metabolism.

Tuesday, the day after your rest day, is your day for sprints. Do the first three or for sprints in a big gear, a 53 × 13 for a professional, a 52 × 14 for an amateur, and the largest restricted gear for juniors and intermediates. The first three or four sprints should be powerful, short bursts of about six or seven seconds. This trains your acceleration strength or explosive power, your power kick.

After your body is warmed up, do two all-out sprints for about ten or fifteen seconds: you should be completely spun out at the end. If you're too tired to do any more (if you're still exhausted from the weekend's racing), stop. Ride back home, relax, and let yourself recuperate a day. But if you feel fresh, do up to eight or ten all-out sprints per workout during the season.

Do intervals on your middle-distance, middle-intensity days, usually *Wednesdays* in the traditional scheme.

In the morning the exercise should be an interval workout that will train you for the specific kind of racing you're doing that week. For example, if you're racing in a fast, flat criterium you should do speed intervals, with an interval of forty-five seconds (with a three-minute recuperation period between intervals). Do a two- to four-minute interval if you need to work more specifically on your ability to ride at high intensities in leg speed situations for a relatively extended period of time (like a flat breakaway).

If you have a hilly circuit race coming up, like the Nevada City Classic in Northern California, you'll need to work on power intervals. To really improve in specific areas (like power on a breakaway uphill or in a flat breakaway one mile from the finish), you need to do structured intervals of two to four minutes in an uphill with a cadence of about 85 RPMs. If you have trouble recovering quickly, you'll need to do more work on both your anaerobic threshold and your anaerobic capacity. In an event like the Nevada

Thursday is my endurance training day.

City Classic, in which you have a gut-wrenching climb every lap for an hour and forty-five minutes, recovery is essential to your fitness. This is why you have to subject yourself to training intervals: so that you can teach your body to recuperate.

In the 1986 Paris-Nice race I lacked anaerobic capacity fitness. As long as the race was in a constant rhythm (even a high one), I was fine. I could ride close to my anaerobic threshold without trouble. But any time I went past that point—whenever somebody attacked on a climb—I "exploded" very quickly. My body went into anaerobic debt. On some of the climbs I was fine. When I sprinted I managed to stay with the field but I would quickly reach my anerobic threshold; I wasn't recuperating fast enough. With the next surge in the pace I would "explode" and lose time. I needed more interval training.

Remember, the anaerobic threshold training—as a base—and the anaerobic capacity training you do later in the season are geared to increase your performance once you go into oxygen debt. More important, they're geared to train your body to recuperate quickly before the next effort. That's really the key to winning bike races: recuperation. The best riders are always the ones who can produce a violent effort, recuperate quickly, and attack again.

Because interval training is very taxing, I suggest that you do it only in the first two to three weeks of your first in-season Macro Cycle, the first few weeks of April. This is also usually a period when you need to eliminate certain weaknesses before getting into the really important races. That was the situation I was in during the Paris-Nice. I went home and did some interval training, and I had less trouble going into oxygen debt by the time the big classic races rolled around, later in April.

After your Wednesday morning session, have some lunch, recuperate, and take it easy for a couple of hours. That afternoon, go out for an anaerobic threshold ride with your heartbeat at a level somewhat below oxygen debt. If you'll be doing a hilly race, find a ten-mile climb and ride it at a hard pace (if you're a junior, you want to do about four intervals in the morning and then a shorter, five-mile climb in the afternoon). If you don't live anywhere close to a ten-mile climb, try to simulate that kind of effort by motor-pacing or simply keeping a high pace (in a big gear) on the flats.

If, on the other hand, you have a flat criterium coming up, do some motor-pacing that simulates the speed you'll be doing in the race. If you feel up to it, you might do ten-minute stretches in which you're accelerating until you nearly get to a sprint at the end. Continue the workout with an hour of a time trial effort, riding close to your anaerobic threshold.

One thing to keep in mind about structured intervals is that although you're trying to simulate the kind of effort you'll be producing in a race, you can never equal the effort of racing—racing is much more intense. Avoid "killing" yourself on Wednesdays (four days before the race) on the same hill that you're going to race on. It's really not necessary, and you might be sick of riding that hill by the time the race comes up.

Vary your workouts according to the race that is coming up, and according to your strengths and weaknesses.

In the last three weeks of this first in-season Macro Cycle, do some less intense anaerobic threshold training (on Wednesdays and Saturdays), otherwise you won't be fresh, and you don't want to burn out.

Your endurance training day comes three days before your race; *Thursday* if you're racing on Sunday. What you're trying to do on your endurance day during the season is to equal the duration of the race. Remember that duration isn't distance. If you have a very long race, you don't want to go out and ride the same mileage. Instead, ride about the time it would take you to complete the race. Since you'll race a lot faster than you can train at an endurance pace, your endurance ride will usually have about the same duration and shorter distance.

If your race is very long, say three hundred kilometers, then you *don't* want to equal even the duration. Instead, go out and ride about seven hours—a little more if you feel good, a little less if you feel bad.

By the same token, even if you're going to race a twenty-five-mile criterium, you still need to go out for a minimum duration. The best way to gauge what your minimum should be is to measure the important races. When I was a junior most of my races were about 30 miles long. But I always did endurance rides with a duration equal to that of the races that were important to me, like the national championships, which were about 70 miles long. Starting in April I would do a long three-and-a-half- to four-hour ride on my endurance day, which is a long ride for a junior.

Your endurance ride will also depend on how fresh you feel. If you've done your sprints on Tuesdays and your middle-distance and intervals on Wednesdays, you should feel tired from that work by Thursday's endurance ride. Which is why it makes sense to do the lower-intensity endurance ride after those two higher-intensity workouts.

Still, your endurance ride should be a real training day, with your heart rate at 65 percent of maximum. You don't want to get any higher than 80 percent for an extended period, though, because then you'll be getting close to your anaerobic threshold and you'll have trouble riding for any appreciable duration.

Remember that endurance training depends purely on how you feel. If you feel fresh, by all means make your endurance ride longer. You can even inch up to your anaerobic threshold, but remember the goal here is duration, not intensity. If you start your ride, for example, by doing a hard ten-mile climb, you might be tired before you can ride as long as you set out to do. That's not going to help you. Remember, you're training on this day to train your body to run on the energy stored in the fatty tissues of the body.

Again, rest for one day, but *two days* before your major race—*not* the day before as is traditional in cycling. If you rest the day before, you'll feel blocked up on race day. Your body is not going to be ready to put out the effort it needs to win. However, unlike the day after the race (usually Mondays), you don't want your rest day (usually *Friday*) to be a day completely off the bike. Ride for at least an hour or an hour and a half, turning a small gear, staying loose. Don't worry about where your heartbeat is. Just ride slowly and smoothly. It's like a massage on the bike. Test your body gently by doing three or four sprints.

The day before the race, usually *Saturday* in our traditional scheme, is a slightly longer ride. The way you should look at it is that the shorter your race is on Sunday, the longer your ride the day before the race should be. If you're a top-level amateur and you're racing two hundred kilometers, you should ride for an hour, with a few short sprints and a couple of sections near your anaerobic threshold.

If, on the other hand, you're only going to race a thirty to forty-mile criterium on Sunday, you should ride about an hour and a half to three hours the day before, including three or four sprints in the morning and some good speed or anaerobic threshold training (for several minutes at a time, but not to the point of exhaustion) in the afternoon—not too intense, just enough to stay loose.

Saturday's ride is similar to the speed workout you did on Tuesday, with fewer sprints. You don't want to come off your workout the day before the race feeling worn out. But a few sprints will bring your heart rate up and then back down to complete recuperation. It's a metabolic activity that your body forgets quickly.

Never work out *hard* the day before a race. Do not go out and do a dozen sprints and two hours of one-minute intervals.

THE EFFECTS OF PUTTING OFF TRAINING

Often riders have trouble reaching peak fitness because they put off training. Some riders do this to avoid burning out. But if you put off training too much you'll begin to suffer. In the long run, if you train consistently and follow the methods I outline here, you are far less likely to burn out, because you'll be training gradually. Most people who put off training tend to panic and increase their duration and intensity tremendously in a short period.

If you find that you're having trouble staying motivated, even during the height of the season, and start missing a lot of training days, you have to ask yourself some very important questions, such as why you're unmotivated. Maybe you've been training too hard. This could be especially true of a young rider or an athlete new to cycling who doesn't know exactly how to gauge his efforts.

Remember that if you break your rhythm constantly, you could get into a vicious cycle of under-training and burnout. The less you train, the more you have to kill yourself to make up for it, and the more you tire your body and your psyche. That's why I think the six-week Macro Cycle is an especially good idea. You can focus on that one period of time, increase your training gradually, and see real improvements. Then you can take a break you genuinely deserve. On your break, do something entirely different, go to the beach, play tennis, or golf, or even mini-golf. Do whatever really seems like fun.

BUILDING UP TO SPECIFIC GOALS IN THE SEASON

One of the most important things you should do when you plan your in-season training is to plan your training Macro Cycles to coincide with your races. When I was a junior, I trained for the end of April when I had a lot of Olympic development races. Then I took a break and built back up again for the state championships. Then I took another break. And then I built back up for the national championships. I built toward specific goals in the racing season, and then I took a break.

HOW DO YOU TRAIN
IF YOU RACE MANY TIMES A WEEK?

I first began racing more than once or twice a week when I went to Belgium as a junior in 1978. I was usually racing on Wednesdays, Saturdays, and Sundays. On Mondays I would still take a rest. Tuesdays I would do sprints as in the typical weekly scheme. Then on Wednesdays I raced, which provided me with a combination of endurance and anaerobic threshold training. This was an ideal workout.

After my race on Wednesday I would rest on Thursdays and then do a short ride with about three or four sprints on Fridays.

One of the best things about racing three times a week is that racing is always the *best* training. It combines all the elements of training and is much less mental strain because you don't have to force yourself to go out and perform. The competition takes care of that. Racing allows you to push your body to a point to which you could never push yourself in training. Physically you might be able to do it. But you'd burn out psychologically if you tried to do it.

You don't want to race too much, though, especially not before April. But if you're an American junior who wants to improve but is frustrated by the lack of racing in America, I would strongly recommend going to Belgium for a summer. You'll also learn about the rough-and-tough tactics of European racing.

IF YOUR RACING SCHEDULE
IS DIFFERENT

If you come up to a weekend that has no race, you might contemplate going out on a long ride on Sunday with a few friends to simulate a race. You could do a few sprints and some hill intervals in which you're reaching your anaerobic threshold before going into an anaerobic state.

If you raced a major race on Saturday and you've got an important criterium the following Saturday followed by a road race on Sunday, you might take Sunday off. Then you would just stagger your Micro cycle by one day, making Monday your sprint day, Tuesday your middle-distance, middle-intensity day, Wednesday your endurance day, Thursday your rest day, and Friday your warmup ride before the race on Saturday and the road race on Sunday.

Sometimes what happens is that you have a race on Saturday and the next race the following Sunday. In that case you might ride an endurance ride the Sunday after your initial Saturday race. Or, if you're tired, you could rest on Sunday and extend your Micro Cycle by one day, doing your sprints on

Monday, splitting your middle-distance, middle-intensity workout by doing sprints and intervals on Tuesday and intervals and anaerobic threshold (motor-pacing, for example) on Wednesday before doing your endurance ride on Thursday. Then, as usual, you would take your rest on Friday before doing the warmup ride on Saturday and racing on Sunday.

If you race a lot it's sometimes hard to adhere to a strictly drawn-up plan. If you raced hard on Saturday and then again on Sunday, you could be pretty exhausted. After taking your rest day on Monday, you still might not have recuperated fully by Tuesday. If you find that you're having trouble doing your sprints, just do the warmup sprints and as many long sprints as you can handle. If you planned on doing intervals Tuesday afternoon but don't feel up to them, take the rest of the day off. Wait until Wednesday morning, when you might feel better.

Just remember that even if you change your plans, you need to follow the same structure. Don't go out and do a five-hour endurance ride before doing your anaerobic threshold training and then do a dozen sprints. That's all wrong—you'll tire out your body and you won't get the fitness benefit you're looking for.

THE DELICATE ART OF PEAKING

In a sense your entire season is a series of peaks. Every Macro Cycle, with its buildup and goal, provides a kind of peak. When you get there, you know you've accomplished something and then you can take a rest. But during the season peaking means that you are training very specifically for a certain race. You want to bring yourself to a high level of fitness for a major event. In my case, I try to peak for the Tour de France and the world championship.

Peaking is something that can be done only about three times a year. The ideal way to train is to be consistent throughout the year and then try to go beyond that level a few times a year. You don't want to peak too often because you would simply suffer mental and physical burnout.

What you try to do when you're peaking is to take all the elements that constitute your training—the sprints, the anaerobic capacity and anaerobic threshold training, and endurance—and maximize them. You want to do *more* sprints than before, *more* intervals, *more* anaerobic threshold training, and *longer* endurance rides.

When you want to peak for a certain event you need to look at a race calendar and begin your "peak" training about six weeks before, in the normal Macro Cycle pattern. Begin your peak training by taking a break from your previous Macro Cycle so that you're completely fresh.

Let's say you want to peak for the state championship. After two weeks of

Never taper too much—only until your body has recuperated and feels fresh again.

normal training, start more intense training. Your last week should be very intense, to maximize all aspects of training.

As usual, *Monday* is your rest day. Even during a peak training period, you don't need to make any special efforts.

Tuesday is the high-intensity day. As you peak you can split Tuesday in two, doing sprints in the morning with two warmup sprints and up to ten long ten to fifteen-second sprints. After a break for lunch you can do some interval training in the afternoon.

Wednesday is your middle-distance, middle-intensity day. But because you're peaking you want to intensify it. Do some more intervals or some very high anaerobic threshold training in the morning, with high-intensity intervals of two to four minutes if you feel fresh enough do anaerobic capacity training with stretches of ten minutes or longer at or below your anaerobic threshold, if you'd prefer to do anaerobic threshold training.

Thursday is your endurance day. You want to increase the duration to equal the duration of the major event you're building up to (although you don't need to ever ride more than seven hours a day). You can also throw in a couple of anaerobic threshold sections in your endurance ride to make it more intense.

Friday is an off-day, a rest day on the bike; go out for a gentle hour-and-a-half spin just to keep the legs loose.

Saturday is the test day, when you want to see how you feel after your rest. As usual you go out and do a few sprints. Because you're peaking you can do a few extra sprints. If you're up to it you could do some intervals in the afternoon.

Finally, *Sunday* is the day that brings it all together. On Sunday you will probably race. If you don't, do a ride that brings together all the elements you trained in. And if your race is too short for the major event you're aiming at, do some riding after the race.

You build yourself up for three to four weeks. In that three- to four-week period you want to concentrate on the training you would do in a normal six-week Macro Cycle. The third or fourth week of this concentrated Macro Cycle should equal the effort of a stage race: four to seven days of intense and long training where there is no recuperation. By the time you've gotten to this peak, you want to be doing a realistic maximum of endurance and intensity training.

As important as your peak, though, will be your tapering period. You always want to finish your intense training (the third or fourth week of the concentrated Macro Cycle) two weeks before the event you're banking on. This gives you the proper time to recuperate from the previous three to four weeks' effort and build back up to be both strong and fresh for the race. You want to rest and then slowly and gradually build back to a good level of training before your major event. After the Tour of Italy, for example, I don't even touch my bike for three or four days. And then I start building up slowly.

The biggest mistake that some coaches in America make is to think that tapering is a rest period, that you shouldn't touch your bicycle. You shouldn't taper too much. Tapering is necessary only to let your body recuperate till it's completely fresh. As soon as you're fresh, you should immediately bring yourself back up to the same level of duration and intensity. If you rest any more than that, your body can really "forget;" it can lose its muscle tone. In a sense, it's kind of like a mini–Macro Cycle and recuperation period in one.

The idea in peaking for a race is to recuperate from the effort of the peak cycle. Since you're probably in good shape after such an intense effort, it should only take you about two or four days. After that you start your basic schedule again, building up to the weekend before the start of your major event when you want to duplicate the length of the race.

It's a delicate situation because although you want to do the proper workout, you must make sure to completely *recuperate* after each workout. The following workouts can be established as I describe here:

1. *Sunday*: End of concentrated Macro Cycle.
2. *Monday*: Begin two to four days of recuperation.
3. *After recuperation (likely Friday)*: Test ride with sprints, as usual after recuperation period.

4. *Saturday:* Intervals (tailored to simulate the kind of effort you'll likely need in the race you're peaking for). Possibly some anaerobic threshold training if you're fresh enough.
5. *Sunday:* Ride (or race) a duration equal to that of the race you're peaking for (which occurs the next Sunday).
6. *Monday:* Normal rest/ride day. Revert to normal schedule.
7. *Tuesday:* Sprints (as usual). Possibly intervals, if you're fresh enough.
8. *Wednesday:* Intervals (if you didn't do them the day before). Anaerobic threshold training.
9. *Thursday:* Endurance ride equaling the duration of the race you're peaking for.
10. *Friday:* Rest ride as usual.
11. *Saturday:* Ride over the course. Test sprint, a few stretches at race pace. As usual.
12. *Sunday:* Good luck!

DETERMINING ABILITY IN AN ADOLESCENT

It's always hard to rate a rider by how he's performing as a junior. During the growth years the body proportions change. In a newborn baby the length of the legs represents about 35 to 40 percent of total size. In an adult this proportion increases to about 50 percent in most cases, which means the adult body is better suited to cycling than that of a child or adolescent.

As one matures physically, the ability of the muscles to train increases because of changes in hormonal metabolism. A younger rider whose body has developed quickly is better able to perform than his opponents in the same age group who've developed more slowly.

As a junior rider—in the fifteen to eighteen-year-old category—it's impossible to say who's going to be a top champion and who isn't. Coaches often make mistakes. They look at a big, muscular, athletic kid and select him because he's dominating the field. When I was racing in Northern California, we had a kid called Chris who was extremely developed. But he never went beyond a certain point because as we grew the rest of us caught up with him. And it turned out he really didn't have ability as exceptional as it appeared.

It's hard to determine just by looking at a rider what his potential is. There are many great juniors who don't pan out as seniors. But many coaches in America make the mistake of attributing that fact to burnout. Most often the rider who doesn't become a great senior after a good junior career simply isn't a great athlete. That rider merely had an advantage over his peers when they were physically less developed.

For example, Andy Hampsten was so skinny as a junior nobody took him seriously. He tried out for the world championship team and was the last rider to make the team a couple of years in a row. But as a professional he's far outstripped many other riders. He's developed physically and he's trained his body well. In 1986 he finished fourth in the Tour de France, and was the top rookie rider.

One of the biggest things to look for in a young rider is determination. If the rider is determined it's a good sign, even if he's not winning races right away. I always look at those riders who are obviously not fully mature but still manage to come in second or third consistently. You can tell they haven't developed their sprint but that they're good climbers and have the basic tools: the good oxygen capacity and determination. To me, if a young rider has a very high oxygen intake (even if he isn't winning), he's got more potential than a big kid who's winning junior races primarily on the strength of his mature body.

If you're a young rider with high oxygen intake and a good attitude, you may have the right tools. But you've still got to do a lot of work. That's where training comes in. The right approach to training can develop all the potential in a rider by the time he turns twenty-one or so.

The first thing you've got to remember is that your career as a cyclist is about ten to fifteen years long. If you really want to realize your potential, you're going to have to be realistic about the way you approach cycling. If you start out at the age of fifteen or sixteen riding like a professional, you'll be burned out three years down the road. You've got to make training enjoyable.

The key is to stay mentally fresh. As a fifteen-year-old junior I trained year-round. I rode three times a week in November and December. By mid-January I was riding five or six times a week. As a junior I raced as many senior races as I could and I did quality miles. Everybody said I was going to burn out. But I didn't.

Burnout doesn't come as much from racing as it does from lack of racing. Most burnout happens in riders between the ages of fifteen and eighteen. It's usually the result of doing too many *intervals* and too much *structured training*. At that age you should always be doing more endurance, more enjoyable riding, sprints for fun.

Not everyone should train like I did when I was a junior. I'm a world-class athlete. But if you want to last in the sport you have to train in a manner that's comfortable for you.

A good example is a person I'll call Tony C. When we were both fifteen-year-old intermediates I was only training 200 to 250 miles a week. Tony was doing more like 400 or 450 miles a week. He was racing with the seniors as an intermediate. I thought I was falling behind schedule and I should be pushing more. Then I realized that I was just too young for that. After that year, Tony C faded away—I don't know what happened to him. Which goes to show you, you have to keep things in perspective and progress slowly year after year.

Physically, at fifteen or sixteen, your tendons, knees, and connective tissues are not mature enough to handle big gears. I think it's really important to respect the gear limitation in the intermediate and junior categories.

If you're seriously considering getting started as a racer and you're about fifteen or sixteen, your winter riding should begin in about November. If you raced the previous season then take off about a week and a half after the end of the season.

At age sixteen, you sould start training year-round. Learn how to organize your training, how to build up and when to rest and do something entirely different. If you're younger than fifteen or sixteen, there's really no point to training in a structured way. Just ride your bike because you enjoy it, and do other exercises, like phys ed in school, running, skiing, or whatever it takes to stay in shape. When you're that age, it'll take you no time to get in fairly good shape. Most of all, when you're only fourteen, you don't want to push yourself too hard.

You have to set yourself some goals you can genuinely achieve. Not everyone can be a world champion. Not everyone can be a professional rider. In my case, I knew after a year or two that I could be a world-class rider. I was winning hard races, breaking away a lot. I was good in time trials. I was starting to develop a decent sprint. I was developing into an all-around rider. As a junior I tried a little of everything. And all that has helped me since.

Your ambition might be to be a top-level amateur, an ambitious goal in its own right. Others may want to be the best in their club. The key is to constantly build yourself up in a gradual training program, year after year. Of course, if you're an eighteen-to twenty-two-year-old rider who's been running or competing in another sport, the gradual buildup can be much faster because you already have a base and your body is adapted to the stress of exercise.

THE IMPORTANCE OF MASSAGE

One of the key aspects of recuperation is the leg massage. The ideal time to get a massage is right after a race or hard ride. Your legs are tired and stiff, the muscles full of lactic acid. Following a race, I recommend eating a little something, perhaps some cereal to replenish your glucose. Then relax for thirty minutes with a massage applied to your legs before eating a full meal.

The massage should be done on a fairly empty stomach to make sure the blood is circulating properly (a lot of blood is trapped in the stomach in the digestive process).

The massage plays an important role in your recovery. Because cycling is a sport that involves a supple (or loose) motion, your legs must be very supple, or loose. A massage recirculates blood through the leg muscles, encouraging the recovery of tired leg muscles.

A massage will help to work out the knotted muscles that can develop from hard riding. Massage is also good from a psychological point of view because it provides you with a form of complete relaxation. It's like taking a nap. It sets you up for an entire night of recuperation.

If you don't have anybody who can give you a professional massage, try to apply self-massage. Always start with the calves, then the hamstrings, and finally your thighs. Use a little baby oil and rub firmly and deeply into the muscles of your legs to create a soothing sensation.

TRAINING THE OLDER ATHLETE

Few things are harder than trying to juggle a passion for bicycle racing and a full-time job. Most of the top amateurs I know are only cyclists, and they work on the side in bike shops. There are a few national-class veterans in America who also have full-time jobs, but many of those have flexible schedules. One good example is Lindsay Crawford, who is a pilot with United Airlines. His frequent breaks from his stressful job give him the opportunity to train.

If you do have a full-time job, there's no way you're going to be able to train as much as a full-time cyclist. The biggest sacrifice you're going to have to make is in terms of endurance, as most of your anaerobic threshold and anaerobic capacity training can be done in less than two-and-a-half hours per day.

If you do have to cut down on your endurance, try to make up for it by fitting in as much endurance riding as you can in your middle-distance, middle-intensity days. Of course, if you work (and travel) you may have trouble scheduling your free days and your busy days. But remember, extra endurance training on a free day can't really hurt. You need to gauge how you feel and how far you want to go. You may want to do a short one-hour sprint workout on Tuesday morning, following your rest day. Then, when you get home from work, if you feel up to it, you might ride for two additional hours with a combination of endurance and some power anaerobic threshold training up a hill.

One thing to keep in mind is that if your endurance training duration goes down, your sprint and anaerobic threshold training duration should remain constant. A rider training a full schedule of twenty hours a week might devote about 40 percent of his training to endurance. If you can only squeeze in ten hours a week your percentage of endurance training should be at least 25 percent.

Many career men and women find cycling an ideal alternative to running. Although running provides excellent cardiovascular exercise, it also can be very hard on your connective tissue and joints. And for anybody who wants to be competitive, running competitively can result in more and more long-term injuries. Cycling has an equivalent cardiovascular effect but does not endanger or over-stress the muscles and joints. In fact, cycling has one of the smoothest motions in all of sport.

Older recreational (or competitive) cyclists can adapt themselves to relatively high intensity and duration after as little as six months, especially if they've been involved in another sport. If you're already in fairly good shape, you won't have to build up as gradually to establish a base level of fitness. But you will have to adapt your body and your mind to the effort of cycling.

If you're coming into cycling overweight, out of shape, you're going to have to start cycling much more gradually, riding at low intensity for an hour and a half a day, just to burn off the extra pounds. For the first two months, you should do as much general exercise—some walking, jogging, calisthenics, and circuit training mixed in with the cycling—as possible. This will help you to strengthen muscles and develop overall condition. Once you're in good condition, you can begin a program of cycling in full force.

In any athletic endeavor there is a deterioration of performance beginning at age thirty or thirty-one. But you can compensate for this natural deterioration with training. For a long-time competitive cyclist, the biggest factor after age thirty isn't so much physical as psychological. Once you've been involved in sports for ten or fifteen years—even a number of different sports—you begin to be less passionately motivated. At the same time you are at an age at which you need to do more work to reach the same level of fitness.

Like most endurance sports, cycling is an excellent sport for the older athlete. Because the benefits of proper training are cumulative, older riders can stay on top at an international level well into their thirties. In European professional cycling a handful of riders have continued as successful professional into their forties, such as French legend Raymond Poulidor, who finished third in the Tour de France at the age of forty. Because cycling doesn't injure the body, you can continue riding a bike into your sixties, seventies, and beyond. There's even one fellow who's still riding time trials in his late eighties.

Older competitive cyclists need to follow basically the same training format as full-time racing cyclists. The level of intensity, of course, is up to you. If it's less important to you to sprint up hills faster than everyone else in the pack, then cut down on the sprints and the anaerobic capacity training. But whatever your training program, remember that your more intense training should always come first in the Micro Cycle.

One important consideration for the older career-oriented cyclist is how much time you can devote to your training. Because cycling is my job, I can train up to thirty-five hours a week and still ride a seven-hour race on the weekend. But unless you're a professional, there's simply no way you'll have time to do that much training. And, believe me, you wouldn't want to. If you work full-time Monday to Friday you can still train seriously, but you'll have to accommodate your work.

Monday should still be your rest day in your training program, as in the general model. You *can* go out and ride a little, slowly, especially if you think you'll have trouble riding the rest of the week.

Tuesday is the sprint day. Because sprints are intense and short, you can get away with an hour ride with sprints either before or after work. The number of sprints depends on you—how serious you are about the sport and how you feel. But at the minimum, do two short sprints of six to seven seconds and two longer sprints of ten to fifteen seconds. If you don't want to treat cycling as a sport but as a way to get fit, you can skip the sprints altogether and do a few intervals or an hour of anaerobic threshold training.

Wednesday is the day for anaerobic threshold training. You want to bring your heart rate close to the anaerobic threshold. A hard hour-and-a-half to two-hour ride should be sufficient.

Thursday's endurance ride will be your biggest problem. Because it's hard to fit in a good endurance ride in a short period of time, you're going to have to fit as much riding into your schedule as possible. If you can ride for two-and-a-half hours after work, then you'll be fine. As a last resort you might consider riding an hour of anaerobic threshold training in the morning and an hour and a half of endurance riding in the afternoon. Just remember that if you have to cut out your endurance training, you should increase your intensity. That's why I suggest anaerobic threshold training if you're riding fewer hours.

Friday is an off-day, during which you want to go out and ride for an hour, taking it slowly, letting your muscles loosen up.

The weekend is when you can make up for your limited weekday schedule. On *Saturday*, do a long version of the Saturday test ride, with as much as two-and-a-half hours in the saddle and some anaerobic threshold sections uphill or on the flats. If you're racing Sunday, try to organize your Saturday training for the race. If you have a hilly circuit race, do your anaerobic threshold riding uphill. If you have a flat criterium, concentrate more on leg speed on the flats.

Sunday is the day you bring everything together. If you're racing, that will naturally combine all the different elements. Just be careful with regard to short races. If you're in the veteran category, some of your races could be thirty miles or less. In that case you have to force yourself to ride after the race to get in those all-important hours.

If you're not racing (in-season) go for a ride, ideally with two or three other riders, that will combine speed, anaerobic threshold, anaerobic capacity, and endurance training—perhaps a three-hour loop with hills, sprints for city limit signs or lampposts, downhills, and long, flat straightaways.

If you work full-time, your biggest problem in training will be riding in the winter months when the days are very short. Unless you live in the garden paradise of Southern California, you're probably not going to want to deal with the darkness and weather. This is when you're going to have to include alternative exercises. You could ride a home trainer, though I only suggest doing that for a few days a week, because it's so boring. You could go running a few days a week, or cross-country skiing. In the winter, you'll have to rely on your weekend rides to make up for the days you can't ride during the week. Like the full-time cyclist, though, try to vary these weekend workouts. You should do cyclo cross, cross-country skiing, or skating.

One of the most important things to keep in mind as an older rider is to be consistent. As your body ages it becomes harder to take violent changes in training or metabolism. As a young rider it's relatively easy to put off training and whip yourself into shape in a few weeks. But as an older rider that's nearly impossible. You need to train consistently to stay in good condition, especially through the winter. You simply can't put off training as you could as a youngster.

Another important factor you'll have to keep in mind as an older cyslist is watching your weight. As you get older, your body's metabolism slows and becomes less efficient at burning calories, so you have to be especially careful to guard against any weight gain. It can be a vicious cycle—the more weight you gain, the harder it becomes to ride, and the harder it is to lose that weight.

7

The
Cyclist's
Diet

*T*he matter of diet in cycling, and especially racing, has been a subject of controversy for years. Some books have tried to sell miracle diets while others have recommended untested, unproven information. Personally, I don't think there's any such thing as a miracle diet. Many people like to talk about "health" or "natural" foods when, in fact, no study has ever proven that the nutritional value of these foods is any different from the value of those using pesticides or unfamiliar-sounding compounds such as mono and diglycerides (just a form of sugar).

There is still much we don't know about how the body uses foods. Although science hasn't unveiled the whole picture, one thing is certain: Eating well is important to good health. This is especially true for an athlete such as a cyclist, whose body is under much greater physical stress than that of a sedentary person.

To establish what eating well means, you should break down all the foods you eat into the following essential elements:

1. Carbohydrates	4. Water
2. Fats	5. Vitamins
3. Protein	6. Minerals

CARBOHYDRATES

Carbohydrates are the primary source of energy during exercise. Carbohydrates are composed of all the sugars and starches we eat. In other words, foods like white sugar, honey, noodles, and rice are largely made up of carbohydrates.

There are two different kinds of carbohydrates. Simple sugars—known in medical lingo as monosaccharides—come from sugar products while complex sugars, or polysaccharides, come from starches like noodles and bread.

The reason carbohydrates are such effective nutrition for exercise is that their nutritional value is absorbed by the body more quickly than that of fats and proteins.

Carbohydrates turn into effective nutrition when they are broken down into glucose and then circulated through the body in the bloodstream. Monosaccharides can be absorbed directly by the body while polysaccharides must first be broke down into simple sugars. Because of this, monosaccharides provide a much quicker rush of energy than polysaccharides. Ingested in appropriate doses, the simple sugars can play a vary important nutritional role for a cyclist, who is burning calories much more quickly than a sedentary person. Simple sugars can be particularly effective when ingested during a ride or a race, since they require less digestive work and can thus be turned into useful energy without tiring the body.

In fact, the use of glucose solutions is common among professional cyclists. Usually used in all races, the glucose solutions are ideal to provide the body with a boost. Another solution that is also used is a thicker, cereal-like solution of complex carbohydrates. This cereal-like solution is much higher in calories and is useful when you want to get the same number of calories while drinking less fluid. The other glucose solution is better in hotter weather when you need both the carbos and the liquid to keep you hydrated.

But the cereal-like solution ordinarily is not used in a situation in which you need to process calories in a rush because the complex carbohydrates take longer to digest than the calories of the glucose. And the glucose solution is used almost exclusively (when drinking any carbohydrate solution) at the end of professional races.

The cereal-like solution may even have been the key to my victory in the world championship in 1983. The night before the race that year I had slept very badly, tossing and turning all night. Instead of eating the usual large breakfast that pros eat before this kind of 150-mile event, I just had a cup of coffee, a few pieces of fruit and a little bit of cereal.

If I hadn't had the cereal-like solution that day, I might have "bonked" and fallen behind or dropped out. After about an hour of riding I relaxed enough to eat. I also ate some rice snacks to complement my intake of complex carbohydrates. Then, as my body needed refueling, I drank the *glucose* solution. As the race neared its conclusion, I avoided taking in anything but the glucose solution; my body was in the midst of a tremendous effort and needed the nutrition as quickly as it could be delivered. At the finish, I had won the world championship.

Perhaps one of the most persistent myths is that monosaccharides, such as white sugar, are bad for the body. Many books have called white sugar a poison, describing it as the "white death." Some of these books laud honey as a "healthier" alternative. But nutritionally sugar is indistinguishable from most honeys. Honey can in fact cause more harm to the body than refined white sugar because most pure honeys are more concentrated in monosaccharides than white sugar. Plus honey sticks to your teeth and can cause more cavities than white sugar.

The one distinction between these two foods is that white sugar goes through a refining process that some people believe makes it chemically unsafe. But the refining process does not actually add chemicals to the sugar, it only sifts out the impurities, leaving a pure, highly potent product of pure sugar cane.

I realize the paranoia about white sugar is not entirely groundless, however. The greatest danger with white sugar is the amount the average American consumes. Because it is highly concentrated and provides the body with an instant rush as the glucose speeds into the bloodstream, sugar is used as something of a drug. In fact, high doses of monosaccharides, such as those provided by white sugar, seem to be highly addictive. After the sugar enters the bloodstream it creates a rapid rise in the level of your blood sugar. The body, which needs to protect itself against a sudden and dramatic rise in the level of blood sugar, secretes insulin, which has the effect of dropping the blood sugar almost as quickly as it was raised. The body, depressed by the low blood sugar, craves more food, and usually that food is more sugar. As one eats more and more sugar, one's insulin levels become imbalanced. Serious sugar addicts tend to be depressed when they aren't eating—not surprisingly, most serious sugar addicts are therefore obese.

If you're a serious cyclist, simple sugars like white sugar and honey have their place in your diet. As long as you are constantly burning calories, your body will need monosaccharides as a source of nutrition. In most cases these can be provided by polysaccharides (noodles, rice). But sometimes you need the instant rush of the simple sugars as a fitness-oriented cyclist. Just like me in the 1983 world championships, you'll find yourself in situations in which you're low on energy. The best way to get back to par is to take in foods that have simple sugars, such as a soft drink diluted with an equal amount of water.

In addition to the simple sugars, there are the complex carbohydrates or polysaccharides. We don't usually think of spaghetti or rice as sugars, but essentially that's what they are. The difference is that they have a more complex molecular structure that requires the body to break them down before they can be delivered as glucose to the bloodstream.

Polysaccharides contain smaller concentrations of pure sugar, glucose. In other words, you get far more glucose out of a tablespoon of white sugar than from a tablespoon of rice. What's more, since the body has to break down the complex polysaccharides, you don't get that instant rush and your insulin levels are not put out of whack. Complex carbohydrates can also provide the body with a few more nutrients than the simple sugars, such as essential vitamins or amino acids.

How about the technique of carbo loading? Although this is a phrase that has essentially come to mean eating a large spaghetti dinner before an endurance event, carbo loading is in fact a dietary technique that was developed in the 1970s by Swedish scientists. They discovered that if the body is deprived of carbohydrates for a few days and then administered large amounts of carbohydrates, muscle energy can increase up to 300 percent.

Carbo loading is a complicated process that takes about a week. First, you need to deplete your body's glycogen stores by going for a hard training ride or run. On this day, you must limit your carbohydrate intake to a minimum for the depletion to be successful. For the following three days, you must eat foods that are extremely low in carbohydrates but high in proteins. Then, during the last three days leading up to the competition, you load up on the carbohydrates.

Although the technique has been proven to successfully increase muscle energy, you don't get that boost without paying a price. The first problem is that carbo loading puts a lot of stress on the body. Depletion training goes against all the precepts of good training. Another problem is that carbo loading has been associated with water retention in the muscles. This can cause stiffness in the muscles and thus interfere with the added energy brought by the process of carbo loading. If you do decide to carbo load, you should never attempt this technique more than a few times a year.

The most common misconception about carbo loading is that it's a ticket to stuff your face with spaghetti, bread, and french fries. In fact, you have to maintain a normal level of calorie intake, but with a greater emphasis on the carbos. And those who carbo load by skipping the depletion phase are simply adding stress to their body's performance by stuffing it with unnecessary calories—they are simply overeating.

Personally, I don't carbo load. One of the principal reasons I don't is that the hectic schedule of professional racing doesn't give me enough of a break to methodically carbo load. While top marathoners rarely race more than two world-class marathons a year, I'm racing approximately once every three days. With that kind of stress being put on my body, I simply can't afford to go through the depletion phase.

In 1984 Bernard Hinault made news when he carbo loaded before winning the time trial event known as the Grand Prix des Nations. Although Hinault did successfully carbo load for that event, it is less than two hours long. For most European pro races, which are rarely less than six hours long, the depletion phase puts too much stress on the body to be practical.

Instead, I think the road to success is a good training program that can effectively increase fitness. As far as my diet is concerned, I don't carbo load but I always eat a diet high in carbohydrates because that is the most effective kind of nutrition for an endurance athlete such as a professional road racer. I don't like the stress carbo loading puts on the body—and, therefore, on the mind. I think it's the kind of stress a top cyclist can do without.

Instead of carbo loading, I concentrate on a realistic intake of carbohydrates. I always eat just what my body needs to keep it going in the events I ride. Of course, sometimes that's a lot of food, because the professional events are so long. For example, I eat a lot during the Tour de France, but that's because I burn it off in the average six or seven hours a day we ride.

FATS

Fats, too, have become a source of great controversy in the field of nutrition. Because fats are very high in calories, do not contain many nutrients, and have been identified as a cause of heart disease, many people advocate fat-free diets. Most of these diets are vegetarian, or nearly so, because all meat contains some fat. Although most of the proponents of the fat-free diet concede that fat is an essential part of the diet they point out that there is enough fat in certain fruits and vegetables to provide them with essential nutrients.

But fat provides the body with four essential vitamins: A, D, E, and K. Fat is also an extremely concentrated source of energy, delivering over four thousand calories per pound. Fatty acids and glycerol, which are the basic components of fat, are converted by the body into energy, immediately. The fat that the body doesn't require for immediate use is stored in pouches below the skin. It is a useful source of energy the body depends on when it has exhausted its sources of glycogen in the muscle tissue.

Why then has fat become a nutritional villain? Just as with sugar, the main culprit isn't so much the fat itself as the tremendous emphasis on fats in the American diet. By most estimates, fats constitute over half the nutrition of the average American. Because fat is such a good source of energy and is very high in calories, your body is not able to burn off all those calories—and the excess calories leads to excess weight.

Fat has some other unfortunate aspects, as well. Some fats are saturated, which means they are solid at room temperature. These fats have been identified as high in cholesterol, which can lead to heart disease.

Most saturated fat comes from animal sources and is found in beef, fowl, lamb, pork, and dairy products. Shellfish, such as lobster and crab, are extremely high in saturated fat. Of course, not all fat is saturated. Unsaturated fat—fat that is liquid at room temperature—is believed to be low in cholesterol. It can be found in many fruits and vegetables and their derivative oils.

For athletes, fat can be a villain for another reason. Because fats leave the stomach slowly, making you feel satiated, they are more difficult to digest. You need to get such fats long in advance of any physical exercise, in order to give your stomach time to digest them. If you try to exercise on a full stomach, you will force your body to work both to digest and to do the exercise. This, of course, can lead to a very sick stomach. For this reason, cyclists should concentrate on foods that leave the stomach quickly before racing and training—in other words, are easy to digest—especially before a long ride. If you want to eat fattier foods, simply allow some extra time to digest them.

Even though all these things are true about fat, you can't avoid it. For one thing, fat constitutes most of what we call "taste" in food. Ever notice how bland and tasteless watercress tastes? That's because it has practically no fat. On the other hand, a hot fudge sundae is delicious, but loaded with saturated fat. Some people believe that they are avoiding fat because they eat fruits and vegetables. But if they eat any avocados or olives they are ingesting a lot of fat. And, of course, all nuts are very high in fat.

You should eat fat in moderation. I like to eat meat and even cream sauces once in a while. I like lobster, hamburgers, and ice cream. Of course, that's not all I eat. While I try to keep fats in moderation, I certainly don't go out of my way to avoid them.

If you genuinely don't like fatty foods, then more power to you. But you are a member of a small fraternity. Many people force themselves to eat bland, tasteless foods because they are afraid of the effects of fat (of course some people have to stay away from saturated fat for health reasons).

If you're a serious cyclist, and you love to eat, the beauty is that your body can handle—and use—more fat than the body of a sedentary person. Because your body is burning calories at a much quicker rate, you don't put on weight. Most well-trained male endurance athletes tend to have a fat percentage (in relation to total body weight) of about 3 to 8 percent. For women, who have less muscle mass, that number is 12 to 18 percent.

Because fat is hard to digest, you must eat it at least three to four hours before starting to do exercise. Otherwise it won't be fully digested and will cause you stomach trouble that might slow you down.

PROTEIN

Probably the least understood nutrient has been protein. Protein was touted as the magical block builder that all athletes needed for strong performances. The steak dinner was the cornerstone of this philosophy. It was to the 1950s and 1960s what the spaghetti carbo load party has become to the 1970s and 1980s.

Protein was thought to be important to athletes because it was considered the primary element in the cell structure of muscles. It seemed natural to athletes and trainers alike that the more protein you ate, the stronger your muscles would be.

They were wrong, though. What people back then didn't know was that protein can't be stored by the body. The body uses as much protein as it can and then the rest is discarded. So any excess protein ingested by the body just makes the liver and kidneys work overtime.

Of course, a cyclist who is in training does require more protein than a sedentary person. But the body needs only a small amount of protein to fulfill its needs. The problem with the American diet isn't protein deficiency. Instead, Americans eat too much protein-rich food, such as meat and beans, and not enough carbohydrates. What's more, most protein comes in foods that are also high in fat, so a high-protein diet usually means a fatty diet as well.

Don't get me wrong. Protein *is* an essential nutrient. Protein serves vital functions. There's no doubt that protein is important. It's just that you don't need a lot of it to do you a lot of good. Protein can be found primarily in beef, fowl, fish, beans, and nuts. There is also protein in breads and cereals, but much less.

Perhaps the one diet that is occasionally protein-poor is the vegetarian diet. Although beans and nuts are often richer in protein by volume than meat, the vegetable proteins tend to lack one or two essential amino acids (amino acids that can't be produced by the body). For example, white beans are rich in protein but lack two amino acids. Corn, on the other hand, while not as rich in protein, has these two amino acids. Thus, by combining both foods, a vegetarian can fill his or her daily requirement for protein. The one plant protein that contains all the amino acids is the soy bean and most of its derivatives.

WATER

Water has no calories and therefore is not a nutrient. It provides the body with no energy. And yet water is probably the single most important element in the diet.

Why? Because water is the medium in which all the body's metabolic actions take place. All the other nutrients you take in need to be mixed with water in the body so they can be converted to useful energy. Water is to the body as air is to life.

The human body is 75 percent water. When the body's level of hydration (or water content) falls, the normal metabolic functions start to act irregularly. Chemical imbalances occur and the body has trouble secreting urine, which results in a buildup of toxic products inside the body.

Water is especially important for a cyclist. Because the level of metabolic function is much increased during physical exercise—or, in other words, because the body is working really hard—sweat is given off to keep the body temperature at an acceptable level. The more you sweat, the more your body needs to have its water replaced. The only way to do this is to drink.

There was a time when coaches told their cyclists that drinking during exercise was bad. Athletes were told that drinking during exercise upset the digestive system and slowed muscles down. That theory, of course, has been proven wrong and dangerous. The fact of the matter is that water is essential during exercise to keep the body's metabolism at an acceptable level. And believe me, the old idea that it's "tougher" to suffer through a ride by not drinking isn't tough at all; it's as stupid as beating your head against a brick wall.

There are a few guidelines to follow when drinking during a hard ride or race. The first is never to guzzle liquid. If you do, you'll oversaturate your system and create a digestive disorder. In fact, guzzling water is really nothing more than the nutritional equivalent of overeating fats or carbohydrates. When you're really thirsty, you'll inevitably drink faster because your body yearns for the liquid. But the slower you can get yourself to drink, the better.

Second, because your body is hard at work during physical exercise you need to reduce any extra stress to a minimum. That's why you should avoid drinking extremely cold or hot liquids. But it's fine to take in cold liquids as they help your body lower its core temperature and help you ingest sugars and the liquids themselves.

Third, the liquid you ingest during exercise should replace more than just water. Because sweat is also made up of salt and minerals, your race liquid should include these elements as well. The best available sweat replenisher is good old Gatorade, except that Gatorade is too sweet (anything very sweet will activate your body insulin and make you thirsty again). So I dilute my Gatorade with an equal portion of water.

Remember, water is very important to you as a cyclist. Always be sure to bring along as much as you need. And *don't drink only when you feel thirsty.* By that time your body will already be dehydrated. Drink at regular intervals, gauging the amount you drink by how much you're sweating.

VITAMINS

In a world always looking for easy answers to difficult problems, vitamins have become a source of great confusion. Many people seem to believe that vitamins are some kind of magical elixir that will "supercharge" their bodies and rid them of all ailments from emotional stress to the common cold.

Vitamins *are* an essential part of the diet. But few people seem to understand that vitamins are not nutrients—they are simply components of enzymes that help the body to metabolize nutrients. In other words, vitamins are like the gears and pinions of your digestive system. They help to churn and crush and break down all of your food. They are important but they are only a tool—alone they can't make you healthy.

The adage that if a little of something is good then more of that thing is better simply doesn't hold true with vitamins. In the case of vitamins A, D, E, and K—the fat-soluble vitamins—the body uses as many vitamins as it can and stores the excess as fatty acids in pouches below the skin. A tremendous surplus of these vitamins doesn't "supercharge" the body, it simply leads to a potentially toxic buildup.

The B complex and C vitamins are water soluble and the body can't store them. When the body has ingested all it needs of these, the excess is excreted through the urine, making the liver and kidneys work overtime.

Perhaps most important, vitamins occur naturally and, for the most part, abundantly in foods. Of course, to get a full complement of vitamins, you have to eat a wide variety of foods, which makes it very important to eat a well-rounded diet. Vitamin B_{12}—the cornerstone of the B complex—can be found in meats, eggs, and milk, while vitamin E occurs in cereal, wheat germ, and vegetable oils. Vitamin C, of course, is readily found in citrus and certain raw green vegetables. If you eat a well-balanced diet, you should never have any trouble getting your full complement of vitamins.

Some cyclists seem to think they need to supplement their diets with vitamin pills because their body is working so hard. There's no reason not to take a multivitamin pill, because any endurance athlete is under a great deal of stress. Even if you don't need the exta vitamins, it doesn't hurt to take one multivitamin pill. Don't just guzzle vitamins pills, though—that won't do any good whatsoever.

A common myth propagated by certain coaches in amateur cycling in the United States is that vitamin injections are a superior method of taking vitamins. Although the injections will provide the body with the vitamins integrated in the blood system slightly more quickly, that difference is minimal. I would not recommend taking vitamin injections because there's a potential health risk involved in any kind of injection.

MINERALS

Although the human body is an organic structure, it needs some chemicals in small amounts to keep it running. Those chemicals are called minerals and make up about four percent of the average human body. Minerals play a role in regulating muscle contraction and water functions. Because these two functions are much increased during physical exercise, minerals are important for any endurance cyclist.

The most abundant mineral in the body is also the most abused: sodium (or salt). Because sodium, unlike most of the other minerals, affects how food tastes, many people tend to oversalt their food. Although everyone needs some sodium to regulate hydration and muscle contraction, the body can find enough sodium naturally occurring in a well-rounded diet.

As with most other dietary excesses, overdoing it on sodium can have bad effects. Because sodium is a poison in high enough doses, the body must work hard to eliminate excess sodium through the urine. Excess sodium in the body also causes heat exhaustion. High levels of sodium have also been associated with high blood pressure and heart attacks.

Another important mineral the body needs is calcium. Found primarily in dairy products, calcium helps to keep the bones strong and healthy. Recent studies involving calcium have been extolling its value, claiming it can aid weight loss and help to prevent heart disease. Calcium pills have become a "health" craze. This seems to me little more than another dietary fad of uncertain value.

Apart from sodium and calcium, the other minerals the body needs in relatively large doses are phosphorus, sulfur, potassium, and magnesium. Potassium and magnesium are especially important for endurance cyclists and low levels of these minerals are often a cause of fatigue and weakness in well-trained athletes. Because potassium is released (in the form of sweat) to keep the muscle mass from overheating, this is the one mineral in which an athlete can become deficient. To defend yourself against a possible potassium deficiency, you should eat fresh fruit or drink fresh juice. One fruit that is particularly high in potassium is the banana.

Magnesium can be found in grains, nuts, and leafy green vegetables such as lettuce.

Apart from the major minerals, the body also needs trace elements of aluminum, boron, chromium, cobalt, copper, iodine, manganese, nickel, selenium, tin, vanadium, and zinc—more metal resources in a single body than some Third-World nations possess.

THE CYCLIST'S DIET: A FEW POINTERS

The cyclist's diet is essentially the average healthful diet, but fats and proteins can be reduced, and carbohydrates and even water should be emphasized. The ideal cyclist's diet should include carbohydrates from whole grains, noodles, and brown rice. Monosaccharides like sugar and honey can be useful to replenish tired muscles in the midst of a hard ride or race.

I eat a lot of carbohydrates when I'm racing. I think one of the best examples of a balanced meal is the dinner provided to us by the Tour de France. Every night we eat a complete meal, rich in carbohydrates. We have noodles, rice, potatoes, and some bread.

A typical day of eating in the Tour de France—and almost every other professional race—begins with breakfast. Usually I eat bowls of different kinds of cereal, ranging from oats to wheat flakes to corn flakes. I also add some fruit to my cereal. I have coffee, juice, and a lot of French bread with strawberry jam. Occasionally I also eat some eggs if I'm hungry.

Usually I always eat three hours before the start of my race. Then, during the race we receive a *musette*, or feed bag, at the start of the race, filled with rice pudding cakes, bread filled with jam, or bananas and other fruits. I also receive water bottles filled with the glucose substance described above and water.

My team has discovered that it's important to ingest a small amount of carbohydrates, usually by eating a small bowl of cereal, immediately following the race. This is quite a change from the traditional approach in cycling, in which riders were told not to eat anything until many hours after they finished racing, supposedly to allow their bodies to recuperate before ingesting. In fact, they were losing four hours of precious glycogen storage time.

At dinner, I have a full meal. The first course is often a vegetable soup followed by a large plate of pasta such as spaghetti or noodles topped with a tomato-based sauce. Although the French are world-renowned for their haute cuisine they have a hard time preparing pasta well. For this reason I prefer the Tour of Italy for racing cuisine, haute or not. The main course at these dinners consists of some kind of meat. I prefer to eat lower-fat meats when I'm racing, such as fish or chicken. Often, during the Tour de France, the team is prepared steak and there is little choice.

The one thing about the Tour meals is that they tend to be very standardized and bland. After racing for two weeks I can get pretty sick of them. That's why in 1986 I rebelled and took over the Novote hotel's kitchen in Nantes. Teammate Andy Hampsten and I prepared the entire La Vie Claire team a taco and burrito fiesta with ingredients whisked in by my wife, Kathy, and Steve Bauer's wife, Elayne. The French riders of La Vie Claire loved it.

Along with the main dish in the standard Tour de France dinner, I have a large salad, green vegetables, and potatoes. Occasionally I have some cheese and bread and a light dessert such as fruit or custard or ice cream.

Cyclists need to eat a lot of carbohydrates. But don't overdo them, because foods like spaghetti, bread, and some dishes with potatoes can be very tasty. You also need to be careful about limiting the amount of fat you eat with carbohydrates. Many dishes centered on carbohydrates also have a lot of fat: spaghetti with meat sauce, pastries, and the biggest culprit of all, french fries, in which fat accounts for 85 percent of all the calories.

Liquids should be liberally ingested at every meal to help with your digestion. During rides or races, you should always prepare as many water bottles as you'll need. In a twenty-five-mile race you probably won't need more than one water bottle. But in anything longer, take at least two. Make sure your support personnel have more bottles waiting at the feed zones in the full-length races. If you're out on a long training ride, make sure you can stop and fill up every thirty miles or so.

This applies to anyone riding a bike. Even if you're not maintaining a high level of intensity, your muscles will be working and you'll most likely be sweating.

Always take more liquids than you think you need. If you don't use it you can get rid of it. It's better to be safe than sorry.

Most of the time you shouldn't put only water in your bottle. You should have a solution that replenishes your sweat, too, such as ERG or Gatorade. Personally, I prefer Gatorade because it's readily available and predictable. But, again, I dilute it with an equal portion of water because it is too sweet.

In some cases you will need liquid nutrition. If you're in a very long race or on a marathon tour, your body will become overtired. It will need nutrition but will be unable to ingest it as solid food. That's when you need to prepare a solution of liquid glucose—potent, fast-action energy. These solutions can be found in many health food stores and some athletic shops.

Many cyclists do not drink alcohol. Although alcohol, in excess, has been linked to high blood pressure, heart disease, and strokes, a reasonable amount is not only tolerable but also has been deemed healthy by the American Medical Association. In its latest report on diet, issued in August 1986, the association states that two beers or two glasses of wine per day can reduce blood pressure.

Personally, I don't mind a beer or a nice glass of wine once in a while, especially if it's a good wine. But I'm careful with alcohol because it can become toxic very quickly. Alcohol is also high in calories. One bottle beer, or a glass of white wine, for example, has about 250 calories.

I also recommend eating a lot of fresh green vegetables and fruits. These are extremely rich in vitamins and minerals. Due to the fact that your body releases potassium and magnesium during exercise, you'll need to replace them by eating fresh fruit (or juice) and vegetables. Fruit and green vegetables can be a part of all of your meals. A fruit salad is a good source of the monosaccharide fructose and is easily digestible before a ride. Orange juice is also great in the morning because it's full of vitamin C and it tastes good. Vitamin C is important to a cyclist because a highly trained body is more susceptible to colds, especially when you're confronting unpredictable elements every day. With hot meals, you can have salads, carrots, or spinach to provide you with vitamins and minerals.

Although many people argue in favor of vegetarianism, I don't think you have to give up meat if you don't want to. Meat is high in protein and contains fat, which is very high in calories. Although the calories in fat are only useful to you after you've burned up other sources of energy, they're definitely important for any endurance athlete. Meat also provides the body with essential amino acids. The protein provided by meat is sometimes difficult to replace from vegetable sources.

As a professional in Europe it would be very difficult to be a vegetarian. Because European restaurants serve a lot of meat and often only a few poor-quality vegetables, I have to eat what's available. If I were to change my dietary habits suddenly when I could find vegetables, the change would produce a shock to my metabolism. A handful of European pros are vegetarians and I have seen them have a hard time getting decent meals when a local restaurant owner proudly displays a meal of sausage an an opener, beef stew, pork chops, and french fries as the main courses. Often the only vegetable around is a sad heap of oversteamed carrots.

I remember racing a race in Chiapas, Mexico, as an amateur with the United States National Team in 1980. Of six riders on that team, four were vegetarian or very strict with their diet. Two days after arriving there, the four who had special diets had become ill, possibly because they had trouble adjusting to a much different diet. Three of them were so bad off that they were put on a plane back to the United States.

I believe that any time the body's metabolism is tied to a very specific diet it has trouble adjusting to any changes in the diet. That's why I believe in a well-rounded and ordinary diet.

If you prefer a vegetarian diet, it *can* provide you with a complete range of nutrition. You must, however, be careful to get a full complement of protein by eating a wide array of vegetables and cereals. If you are a complete vegetarian and eat only fruits and vegetables (no dairy products), you will need to supplement your diet with vitamin B_{12}. This vitamin occurs primarily in animal matter.

Aside from all the nutritional requirements of a good diet, eating well is also a highly positive psychological exercise. You can't force yourself into a book-perfect diet if you are going to be very unhappy with the food you eat. You will leave yourself open to energy-depleting stress. Although stress is not well understood, clearly it is detrimental to good athletic performance, whether because of a combination of physical and psychological factors or simply because of psychological ones. People who eat "overhealthy" diets often succumb to temptation by pigging out at certain intervals. Besides the fact that pigging out brings a lot of fat and calories into your system, it also disrupts a metabolism that is not used to ingesting fat and sugar.

I eat a diet that is reasonably balanced but also leaves me satisfied and satiated. I probably eat more meat than I should. And I probably eat more ice cream and sweets than I should. But I also make sure to eat vegetables and carbohydrates and to drink a lot of liquid.

Most important, you have to limit your calorie intake to what your body can handle with the amount of riding you're doing. For a fifteen-year-old just starting out on his or her bike that might mean no more than four thousand calories a day. For a veteran woman rider who is racing no more than thirty miles on the weekends, it might mean ingesting as few as twenty-five hundred calories. But for a pro cyclist in the Tour de France it can mean up to nine thousand calories a day. Believe me, there's no bravado in announcing a figure like that. All pro cyclists suffer from ingesting and then burning off so many calories every day. There is so much food going through the system, the metabolism is running at such a high level, that most professional cyclists find they have digestive problems during peak racing times such as the Tour de France. Imagine eating a few bowls of cereals, some bread, fruit, and eggs for breakfast, riding eight hours (and eating fairly constantly), then showering before another huge meal and a night of overly exhausted sleep.

Whatever diet you choose, it must be one you can stick to. I couldn't survive more than two days on a fruitarian (pure vegetarian) diet. On the other hand, if all I did were to stuff my face with Polish sausages all day, I would be obese, lethargic, and unable to ride efficiently. You must find your own happy medium.

8

Bicycle
Maintenance

*L*ike any machine, your bicycle will need to be maintained and
repaired from time to time. Some maintenance should be done
every few days, while other tasks can be done once a year. Fortunately, the bicycle is basically a simple machine and simple to keep up.
Most cyclists can learn to do basic maintenance and repairs in a very short
time. There are, however, certain repairs that require considerably more
skill—some repairs should never be attempted by nonprofessionals.

Frankly, during the season, I rarely do my own repairs. Since I turned
professional, and even before, I have always relied on the help of professional
mechanics to keep up my bicycles. Of course, I do all my basic maintenance
when I'm not around my team, in the winter, for example.

But I think the advice on maintenance should come from a true professional in the field. That's why I've asked professional mechanic Roland Della
Santa to help me provide tips for this chapter. Roland was one of the first
people to notice my riding. Later he became my first sponsor and built bikes
for me. In 1985, Roland was the official Red Zinger team mechanic of the
Coors Classic, which I won. He's a thoroughly professional designer, frame
builder, and mechanic.

I will not tackle the advanced subjects of frame building, frame repair, and

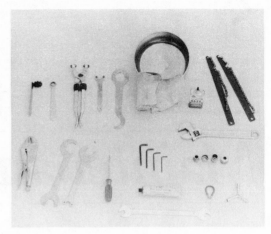

Starting with the right tools: A complete set of tools is the key to maintaining your bike. *Tools (clockwise, starting in upper left-hand corner):* crankarm remover, crankarm bolt remover, wire cutter, pin wrench, bottom bracket cup remover, container with wire basket for solvent, three-in-one oil, two freewheel cog removers, adjustable wrench, various bolts, three-way wrench, spoke wrench, two-way wrench, tire glue, various allen-head keys, screwdriver, a headset wrench, a bottom bracket ring wrench, vise grip.

painting. These activities require special skills and tools. If you want to build your own bike, you will never learn enough about the field in a book—you should find a professional frame builder to study under. But be prepared to spend some time at it: It's a skill that takes years to acquire. Also, you'll have to spend a few thousand dollars purchasing equipment, and a few thousand more buying things like tubing, lugs, and soldering material.

If you're interested in repainting your frame, I recommend you go to a professional bike shop mechanic or frame builder who can give you a professional paint job for about fifty dollars. Some books outline a very complicated and drawn-out process for do-it-yourself painting. I just don't think it's worth it. You need specialized equipment. And chances are, unless you're already a professional, you'll end up with a less-than-professional paint job.

Frame repair may seem like the simplest of all the frame arts, but it's not. If you create a "blip" (as dents are known in cycling) in your frame, don't try to bang it out yourself. Take it to a professional bike shop or frame builder. Unless you are very careful, you could risk metal fatigue and a broken frame. Then you'll have to have your frame repaired by a professional at much higher cost. More probably, you'll have to buy an entirely new frame at yet higher cost.

Anybody who wants to maintain a bicycle needs to start out with the right tools. If you don't have the right tools, you're not going to be able to handle the simplest repair. Even if you don't plan on doing extensive work on your bike, you always need tools, even if it's only to tighten a screw or make an adjustment.

You must decide for yourself how many tools you want to own. But there are certain basic tools everybody should own.

The first tool you'll need is a bike stand. This will be the heart of your workshop. Although you can spend a lot of money on a bike stand, you can easily get away with a small stand that simply raises one wheel off the ground at a time. Such stands are cheap and light—they can even fit into a large tool box. Of course, if you want a stand that allows you to swing your bike as you work, you're looking at more money.

You will need a good set of wrenches that fit your bike. Most bikes have bolts in the eight to twelve-millimeter range. There are many different kinds of wrenches. The most obvious is the monkey wrench. Monkey wrenches are usually the strongest and provide the most leverage. But if you need several different sizes, they can be unwieldy to use. In addition, you can't use an ordinary monkey wrench in certain tight spots.

If you want the strength of the monkey wrench but in a more practical form, get a socket wrench. You can usually find these at auto parts stores. They have one wrench arm and a wide range of sockets to fit it. The arm has a ratchet that makes it easy to change a bolt. You can also buy a combination wrench. These are usually much smaller and have three different bolt sizes, often eight, nine, and ten millimeters. This is a good wrench to have, especially on a ride, since you can just stuff it in your back pocket. A bicycle dumbbell wrench—an inexpensive combination wrench that fits eight different bolt sizes—is also useful, particularly on a long ride, on which you don't want to carry much weight.

If you have a recent-model bike you'll have a number of recessed-head or allen bolts. Most bikes have allen heads holding the chainrings to the crankarms, the stem in the frame, the derailleur to the dropout, and the seat post to the frame. Many Japanese bikes come with a couple of allen keys. But if you don't have them, buy a complete set of allen keys at a hardware store or bike shop: They're cheap and easy to use. If you have trouble holding on to your smaller allen wrenches, get a set held together by a large ring.

You'll need a special pedal wrench to take off your pedals. They usually come in thirteen to sixteen-millimeter sizes. Most flat or cone wrenches will work here. Be careful, though, not to skimp on pedal wrenches. You can buy cheap ones that will bend if your pedals are very tight—and often pedals *do* get very tight—and ruin the pedal. Some pedals that use allen-head bolts don't require a pedal wrench. You can also use cone wrenches on most brake models. These narrow wrenches are used to straighten the brakes when they're rubbing on the wheels.

You will need a small cable cutter to install brake and derailleur cables.

Another important tool is the freewheel remover. Freewheel removers come in different shapes and sizes depending on the freewheel you have. Check with your dealer to determine which remover you need.

There are a number of smaller, inexpensive tools you'll need as well. A spoke wrench comes in handy to tighten spokes and straighten wheels at home when they get out of true. A chain tool is essential to remove the chain, something you'll need to do periodically. Depending on the kind of cranks you have, you may need a small, standardized crankbolt remover to remove the cranks when cleaning and regreasing the ball bearings. Many derailleurs use a small screwdriver to adjust their play.

You can get additional tools as you become more familiar with your bike. For example, unless you have a special sealed-bearing headset, you'll need to overhaul your headset every fifteen thousand miles or so. You could use a twelve-inch adjustable monkey wrench to undo the headset, but the adjustable wrench can easily slip and damage your headset. A specialized (and expensive) headset remover is better.

If you want to overhaul your bottom bracket (unless you have a sealed-bearing model), you'll need a specialized bottom bracket remover. This is usually a large tool that requires some experience to use. Similarly, if you want to *remove* your headset, you need a very large and expensive headset tool.

If you find yourself doing work that requires expensive tools, you can probably find a bike shop in your area that has loaner tools. These are tools that are set aside in an area of the bike shop for customer use. In most shops you pay to use them; in others they are free. In both cases you have to use them in the store.

One note of caution: If a repair becomes complicated and you start to become confused or frustrated, don't take it out on your bike. Guessing at how something works or forcing a bolt can damage your bike. Take the bike to a professional mechanic: it may cost you a little more money than if you had done it yourself, but it's a heck of a lot cheaper than buying a new bike.

MAINTAINING THE DRIVETRAIN

Let's start with the drivetrain. All the parts of your drivetrain should be well adjusted. Because of all the moving parts, the drivetrain will require your attention periodically.

BOTTOM BRACKET

First, check the bottom bracket axle adjustment by taking off the crankarms with the crankarm remover. Loosen the bolt that holds the crankarm to the bottom bracket axle and remove the crankarms.

Next, turn the bottom bracket axle with your fingers. When perfectly adjusted it should turn smoothly with a few smooth "bumps" as it turns

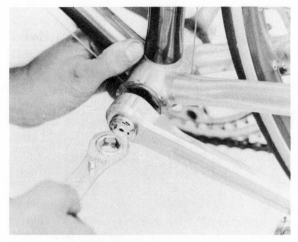

Removing crankarms. Remove dust cap (if you have one). Dust cap usually is removed with an eight-millimeter wrench.

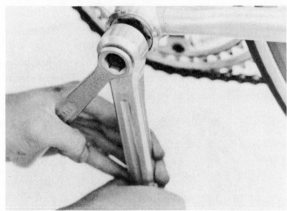

Remove the crankarm bolt with the special crankarm bolt remover.

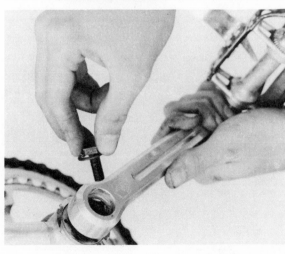

When crankarm bolt is removed, crankarms are still tightly in place.

To remove crankarm, use crankarm remover. Grease end of crankarm remover before inserting.

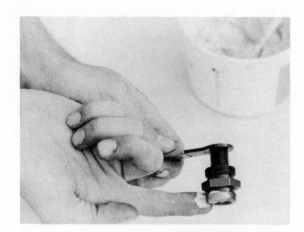

Insert crankarm remover slowly and turn.

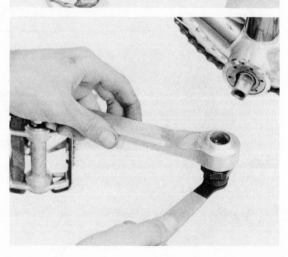

After turning, you will feel pressure. Keep turning until crankarm comes off bottom bracket axle. Then loosen gently to remove crankarm remover.

To remove bottom bracket axle, use ring wrench on adjustable cup ring (opposite the chain side). Loosen ring and remove.

around. Next, grab the bottom bracket axle at both ends and pull back and forth. There should be no play whatsoever.

If the "bumps" feel rough, your bottom bracket is too tight. That can grind down the ball bearings. If, on the other hand, there is some play, the bottom bracket is too loose and you risk breaking the bottom bracket axle.

To readjust the bottom bracket axle, you'll need the special bottom bracket tool for your model. The cup that encloses the bottom bracket on the *chain side* is *not* adjustable. The other cup *is* adjustable, usually by means of a pin wrench that's specially designed for this purpose. To tighten, turn clockwise; to loosen, turn counterclockwise.

The bottom bracket should be adjusted exactly at the point at which there's no play, but before there's any roughness. Be careful, though, not to err on the side of looseness. If the axle has *any* play whatsoever, you can break the axle. After you find the exact point at which there is neither play nor looseness, give the pin wrench an extra turn of about five degrees (on a circular scale of 360 degrees).

Unless you have a sealed-bearing bottom bracket, you'll need to overhaul your bottom bracket every fifteen thousand miles or so. If you ride infrequently, the bottom bracket should be overhauled once a year.

To overhaul the bottom bracket, remove the chain so it doesn't get in your way. To remove the chain, take the chain tool, place it in any one of the links, tighten the tool and pop out the link. Next, remove the crankarms as described above, using the crankarm remover.

Once the crankarms are off, remove the adjustable cup on the side opposite the chain. Use the pin wrench and simply unscrew it slowly. With this adjustable cup off, the bottom bracket axle comes out easily. The axle can be cleaned by dipping it in some solvent, while the inside of the bottom bracket can be cleaned with a rag dipped in the same solvent. (Ordinarily, you don't

After ring is removed use pin wrench to remove adjustable cup.

When adjustable cup is removed, you will notice a race of ball bearings on the inside.

You may want to remove the fixed cup as well for a thorough overhaul, but this is not necessary. Note: you will need a special wrench to remove the fixed cup.

Most bottom brackets
have a protective plastic
dust shield. Remove and
dip in solvent.

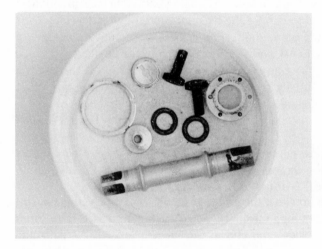

Place all bottom bracket
parts in a bucket con-
taining solvent. Clean
and then rinse thor-
oughly.

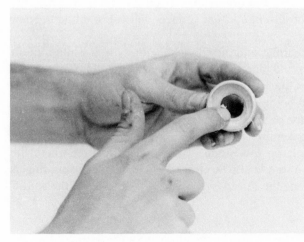

Carefully apply bicycle
grease to the inside of the
bottom bracket cups be-
fore reinstalling.

*Lightly grease bearings
and races and place inside
cup.*

need to remove the fixed cup. If you're changing bottom bracket assemblies, however, you will need to remove the fixed cup and install a new one. This requires a large, cumbersome tool called a fixed cup remover that takes a little training to master. Ask your local bike shop for assistance.)

When you remove the adjustable cup, you'll find that inside the cup is a set of ball bearings. Usually they come in a track called a *race*. On other models, the bearings are loose. Once your adjustable cup has been removed, tip the bike gently to the floor, with the open side of the bottom bracket toward the ground.

The axle should now come out. (In most cases, it'll have a plastic dust shield fitted around the center portion of the axle.) Next, tap the bike gently until the fixed cup ball bearings drop out.

You are now ready to clean the entire assembly with a powerful solvent. You can find a grease-cutting solvent in a bike shop or auto parts store. After cleaning the bearings, axle, and cup in the solvent, take all the parts and rinse thoroughly with water and dry them—if you don't rinse the bearings and the cup, the film of solvent on their surfaces will cut or dilute the new grease.

Now, take the ball bearings and dip them generously in a white lithium bicycle grease. You can find bicycle ball bearing grease at all bike shops. Be sure to coat the inside of the bottom bracket cups in grease, too. Be generous with the grease without being wasteful—use common sense.

Before you reinstall the parts, put some solvent on a rag and wipe out the inside of the bottom bracket itself. Use a medium-sized stick to get the rag all the way in. The threads on the inside of the bottom bracket where the adjustable cup screws on should also be cleaned. Take the rag in your fingers and wipe vigorously along the threads. Also wipe the threads on the adjustable cup.

To put the ball bearings that fit in the fixed cup back, place them around the axle, with the openings in the ball bearing race (if there is a race) facing out *toward* the fixed cup. Slowly move the axle through the bottom bracket. If your bike has loose bearings, you'll have to lay the bike on its side and fit the bearings into the fixed cup by hand. The bearings are held in place by additional grease in the cup.

Now, take the second set of ball bearings and place it in the adjustable cup. Carefully thread the cup back on the bottom bracket, making sure the ball bearings are still trapped between the axle and the adjustable cup. Once everything is back in place, tighten the adjustable cup as described above, until there is no play, but before you feel any roughness.

CRANKSET

Your crankarms shouldn't require any special maintenance. Keep them clean with soapy water and a large, soft brush. Make sure to clean the dirt around the pedals, behind the spindle assembly, and down where the crankarm is attached to the bottom bracket.

Every seventy-five hundred miles or so, you should clean your crankset thoroughly. I recommend cleaning it in the same solvent you used on the bottom bracket. Ideally, you should take the chainrings off and clean all the nooks and crannies in the spindle assembly. You can clean the *teeth* in the chainrings with a *bristle* brush dipped in the solvent. (Make sure that you don't lose any of the allen bolts and nuts that hold the chainrings to the spindle assembly—put them in a small cup for safekeeping.)

When you put the chainrings back on, be sure to tighten the allen bolts progressively. Don't tighten one bolt all the way and then all the others afterward. Tighten each bolt until it starts to get a little tight. Then tighten all the bolts one by one.

PEDALS

When you overhaul the crankset, you should also check the pedals. To remove the pedals, use a cone or flat wrench, or if you have it, an allen key on the recessed head at the end of the pedal spindle *behind* the crankarm.

Clean out the threads on the crankarm where the pedals are attached, as well as the threads on the pedal spindle.

You should overhaul your pedals every fifteen thousand miles. If you don't ride a lot, overhaul them at least once a year. If you ride in a lot of very bad weather you may have to perform maintenance on your pedals more frequently.

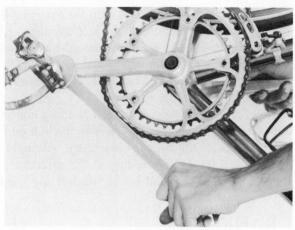

Removing pedals. Use a special flat wrench placed in the space between the crankarm and the pedal axle. Turn clockwise. Note how you need to grip the other crankarm solidly to keep the crankset from turning while you apply pressure.

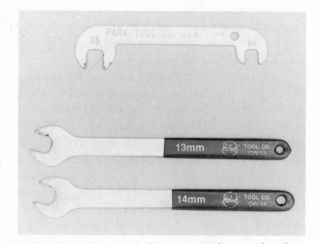

Different models of flat wrenches. These can be used on your pedals and brakes. Generally, pedal wrenches are longer to provide you with better leverage.

Most pedals on the market don't have sealed bearings. If yours do, they won't need any maintenance.

To overhaul pedals, remove them from the crankset as described above.

Once the pedals are off, the first step is to remove the dust cap on the outside of the pedal. You can do this with a small screwdriver—the dust cap should come off easily if it was correctly installed.

When you take off the dust cap, you'll notice a locknut. To remove this locknut, anchor the axle—either by gripping it in a vise or by holding a wrench to the "flat" next to the threads where the pedal is attached to the crankarms. With a vise, remember to always grip the pedal on the "flat" and never on the threads. The outside of the pedal should be facing up as you disassemble it.

Once the axle is anchored, take a small wrench or a special pedal locknut wrench and loosen the locknut. Remove the locknut and the locknut washer—you may need the help of a small screwdriver—and put both the locknut and its washer in a small cup.

With the locknut washer off, you'll be able to see the ball bearings. To remove them, grab a small cup or receptacle and slowly turn the pedal, letting the ball bearings fall into the cup. Be sure to hold on to the axle: you don't want to let it slip. Sometimes, the ball bearings may stick in the pedal. Use a small screwdriver or tweezers to dislodge them. After this first set of ball bearings has been removed, count them, so that you know exactly how many there are.

To remove the second set of ball bearings, grab a second small cup. Tilt the pedal the other way and remove the axle. The ball bearings will follow. If any stick to the inside dislodge them with the screwdriver or tweezers.

Clean all parts with solvent. Use a bristle brush to clean off any heavy dirt. If your ball bearings are old and worn, buy a new set. If you get new ball bearings, always make sure you get the same size—a good way to assure that is to take your old ball bearings with you to the bike shop.

Once everything has been cleaned in the solvent and thoroughly rinsed, you're ready to reassemble your pedal. First, dip the ball bearing races (the tracks that hold the ball bearings together) in the white lithium grease. Also dip the pedal area that holds the ball bearings in grease. Use a generous amount of grease.

Take the ball bearings closest to the crankset and put them back in place. If you have bearing races this shouldn't be too hard and the grease will hold the race in place. If you have individual bearings, you'll need to tip the pedal so that the outside is slightly lower than the crankset side and put the ball bearings in one by one. The grease will hold them in place.

Once the crankset-side bearings are in place, insert the axle and push it all the way through. Then take the outside ball bearings and put them in place—that should be much easier to do than the first set of ball bearings.

Next, replace the locknut washer and thread the locknut by hand. When you can no longer turn it by hand, use a wrench to tighten it until there is no play, but before there is a roughness. A good rule of thumb is to tighten beyond the point at which you feel any play and then loosen an eighth of a turn. To finish the job thread the dust cap tightly by hand.

FRONT DERAILLEUR

The front derailleur is a very simple component that usually requires little more than basic maintenance. The most common problem with a front derailleur is that the adjustment screws that control the travel of the derailleur from left to right are poorly set. If this happens, the chain can skip

Adjusting the front derailleur adjustment screw. Turning the stop screw limits the travel of the front derailleur. One screw limits inside travel, while the other limits outside travel. If your front derailleur is "throwing" the chain every time you shift, you need to adjust one of the adjustment screws.

too far and fall off a chainring. If there's not enough travel the chain simply won't be able to change from one chainring to the next.

Because these screws can come out of adjustment under the stress of riding, it's always a good idea to be prepared to adjust your front derailleur, even when you're riding.

To adjust the screws on your front derailleur, you'll need a small screwdriver for most models (some derailleurs have small, ordinary allen-head bolts). On most models the screw closest to the frame adjusts the play of the front derailleur to the outside (the big chainring) and the screw on the outside adjusts the play to the inside. Double check on your front derailleur to see which screw adjusts which motion. You can do this by activating the gear lever back and forth and watching closely as the derailleur arm hits the screws.

Another common problem with the front derailleur is that the derailleur cable between the derailleur and the shift lever loses tension. If this happens, loosen the bolt that holds the cable—usually an eight-millimeter bolt—and pull the cable taut with your fingers. Then retighten the bolt. If this doesn't work, you'll need a pair of vise-grips; attach them to the end of the derailleur cable just beyond the front derailleur bolt and pull. Then tighten the bolt again. (Note: Be careful to wrap the end of the cable in a thick towel— otherwise the cable will become frayed and you may have to get another cable.)

If your front derailleur is poorly positioned on the frame (and doesn't reach the chainrings very well), you'll have to move it. On most models, a large

Adjusting the rear de-
railleur adjustment
screws. The rear derailleur
adjustment screws work
the same way as those on
the front derailleur, limiting inside and outside
travel. After you adjust
the screws, shift gears to
check your adjustment.

clamp attaches the unit to the frame. Usually, the bolt that holds this clamp is on the nonchain side of the seat tube. Unfasten the clamp with an appropriate wrench. Sometimes, the front derailleur is attached with a brazed-on mount. In this case, you won't be able to adjust your front derailleur's position, but presumably the braze-on was installed in the factory in the right position.

To place your derailleur at the right spot on the frame, the bottom of the front derailleur cage should be about five millimeters from the top of the teeth on the large chainring. Make sure that the cage is straight, perfectly aligned with the chainrings when looking from above. Tighten the bolt on the clamp, and your front derailleur is installed.

If you change the size of your big chainring, you'll need to adjust the position of your front derailleur. This is only possible, of course, if you don't have the brazed-on derailleur mount. After you've installed your new chainring, simply follow the same procedure as above.

To clean your front derailleur, wash it in warm, soapy water every few hundred miles and scrub it with a large, soft brush.

REAR DERAILLEUR

The rear derailleur is much more complicated than the front derailleur. It's composed of a parallelogram body that shifts to move the chain from sprocket to sprocket. It also has a set of rollers that maintain chain tension. The rear derailleur has about twenty moving parts.

As with the front derailleur, you have to make sure the adjustment screws are adjusted properly. If they aren't, your chain could skip beyond the freewheel sprockets if the adjustment allows the chain to travel too far, or it may restrict the chain from reaching the largest and smallest sprockets on either end if the adjustment doesn't allow the chain to travel far enough.

Use a small screwdriver or a conventional or allen-head wrench, depending on your model, to adjust the screws. Because models vary, you'll need to know which adjustment screw—top or bottom—adjust the inside and outside movements of the derailleur. This is usually marked right on the derailleur, high or low (H or L).

If you find that your chain is going into your spokes, adjust the adjustment screw that limits the motion of the derailleur in that direction. Turn the screw a half turn and test your derailleur. If the chain still goes into the spokes, turn the adjusting screw another quarter turn. If the chain won't even reach the largest cog on the freewheel, on the other hand, then you've turned the adjusting screw too far. Turn it back in the other direction so that the chain skips easily onto the last cog without going into the spokes.

If the chain is skipping off the smallest cog (the one nearest to you as you face the bike) and into the gap between the freewheel and the frame stays, adjust the other screw on your derailleur in the same fashion.

When the adjusting screws on the derailleur are adjusted properly, the chain should skip freely to all the cogs and never off into the spokes or the gap between the freewheel and the frame stays.

I recommend taking a small screwdriver on all your rides: You might find it handy if your derailleurs—either front or rear—fall out of adjustment while you're riding.

The bolt that attaches the rear derailleur to the frame is the upper pivot bolt. In some older bikes the rear derailleur is still attached to the frame by means of a fixing plate or clamp. But most good bikes should have an integral "ear" brazed on to the dropout to attach the rear derailleur.

Maintenance on the rear derailleur is pretty straightforward. Clean it in soapy water with a large, soft brush every few hundred miles. After about fifteen thousand miles the rear derailleur rollers can become worn. If so, replace them with a new set. To remove the old set unfasten the bolt that holds the rollers to the cage plates. Remove the rollers and the bushings. To install the new rollers just reverse this operation.

As with the front derailleurs, the cable linking the rear derailleur to the shift lever may become stretched with time. To tighten it, simply loosen the cable clamp (usually with an eight-millimeter wrench) and tug at the cable with your fingers. When the cable is taut, fasten the cable clamp again. If this doesn't work use vise-grips to pull the cable taut. Just remember, wrap the cable in a *thick* towel, or you'll fray the cable end.

While your rear derailleur cable is loose, this is a good opportunity to check the cable housing that directs the cable from the rear derailleur to a braze-on on the chainstay. If your bike is new, the cable housing probably won't need lubrication. But if you've ridden a few thousand miles, take it off and spray it with WD-40 (a commonly available synthetic lubricant that doesn't break down as quickly as oil) or an equivalent teflon spray.

If you fall over on your bike on the derailleur side, always check to see if your rear derailleur is all right. Because the unit does stick out, it can be the first component to be damaged. If you have any serious damage, get a new derailleur—most models are fairly inexpensive.

Rear derailleurs can become worn out with age. If yours simply doesn't respond very well anymore, consider either replacing the gear return spring or buying a new derailleur.

FREEWHEEL

Next to the rear derailleur is the freewheel. The freewheel has a fairly complicated interior mechanism, and it should never be taken apart by nonprofessional mechanics. The most common maintenance on the freewheel is simply to clean the freewheel about every twenty-five hundred miles or so.

To clean the freewheel you will need to take it off the rear wheel. For this, you'll need a special freewheel remover designed for your specific freewheel. This is one area of cycling in which there's a tremendous degree of variation. Don't use something that's a near fit. You'll need a lot of force to remove the freewheel—pedaling will have tightened the freewheel forcefully at the hub—and a poor fit could bend the freewheel and the hub.

After removing the rear wheel from the frame, unfasten the quick release skewer and remove the skewer nut and spring. Attach the freewheel remover to the freewheel body. Make sure it's a snug, exact fit. Replace the skewer spring and nut and fasten the quick release skewer tightly.

Because the freewheel is tightened progressively as you ride, you'll need a big wrench, such as a twelve-inch adjustable wrench or a pair of large vise-grips, to remove the freewheel. Clamp the wrench of your choice on the flat of the freewheel remover. Hold the wheel firmly between your legs and push down. Be sure to push in a counterclockwise direction—otherwise you'll be tightening the freewheel.

In most cases it'll take a little brawn to loosen the freewheel. Make sure you put your body into it. The bigger your wrench, the more leverage you'll have: That'll make it easier to unfasten.

After you've loosened the freewheel, unfasten the quick release nut and unfasten the freewheel slowly either with the wrench or by hand. If the freewheel suddenly gets stuck, don't force it. Most likely, you've run up

Removing the freewheel. Install the freewheel remover and loosen from hub with wrench. Note: nearly every brand of freewheel has its own freewheel remover—make sure you have the right one.

Cleaning the freewheel. Dip the freewheel into a bucket of solvent. Then dip an old toothbrush into the solvent and scrub off extra dirt.

against some dirt in the threads attaching the freewheel to the hub. If you play with the freewheel, moving it gently back and forth, you can usually dislodge the dirt.

If that doesn't work you might have damaged threads and may need to take the whole thing to a professional bike shop. They might be able to salvage your hub and freewheel if the damage is only superficial. If there's a lot of damage, they could grind a different size thread (there are three standard thread sizes). If worse comes to worst, you may have to get a new rear hub and freewheel body. But this is a pretty rare occurrence.

Once the freewheel is off take an old toothbrush and dip it into the solvent. Run the toothbrush through all the sprockets. After the sprockets are cleaned, take the entire unit and dip it into the wire basket inside the can of solvent. Let it sit for about thirty seconds. When you take it out, rinse the whole thing thoroughly with a strong hose.

Before you put the freewheel back on the hub, clean the threads on the rear hub (to avoid any damage). Take a rag, dip it in the solvent, and thoroughly clean all the threads. Never use somthing like a bristle brush on the threads. They're fragile and a metal brush could damage them.

Put the freewheel back on the rear hub by hand, carefully. The crucial step is to find the threading. At first it may be a bit hard to do. But never, *never* force the unit. With a little patience you'll find the threading and the freewheel should turn most of the way by hand, or with gentle pressure applied to the freewheel remover.

Before you start riding on your freewheel you'll need to relubricate it. Use a medium-weight oil, like a three-in-one bicycle oil. It's available at most any hardware, bike, and auto parts stores. Some people prefer a synthetic lubricant like WD-40. The choice is yours. Tip the freewheel with the outside on top so that the oil drips into the main body. Spin the freewheel and let the oil seep into the body. Repeat this about three or four times. When the freewheel is well lubricated, it should have a low, almost muffled sound as it turns.

Any time it rains, you'll need to relubricate your freewheel with a little three-in-one oil. But if you ride in a lot of rain, you really should clean the freewheel before you add any more oil, because you might be riding with damaging dirt particles inside the main body.

Most advanced riders like to change the sprockets on their freewheels according to the kind of riding they're doing. This is relatively simple and requires only two cog or sprocket removers and extra cogs. While you need to buy the cogs specifically made for your freewheel model, the sprocket remover is a cheap, universal tool that's simply composed of a short piece of chain attached to a metal arm for leverage—you can even make your own with a few household tools.

You can leave the freewheel on the hub while changing the sprockets. You need to know, however, how your freewheel is designed. Many Japanese models are made with only one threaded outside sprocket; the other sprockets can be slid off. But most Regina freewheels (an Italian brand) have two sets of threads. The first set turns to the outside, and usually consists of the outside three sprockets. The two or three inside sprockets are removed from the inside.

Whatever the design of your freewheel, always begin with the outside sprocket—that's the smallest one. Wrap the first cog remover *clockwise* around this cog. Wrap the other cog remover counterclockwise on any other cog (the second-to-last one on the inside is my favorite because it's big enough to provide leverage and close enough to the outside cog for stability).

Using the second cog remover as an anchor, tug at the outside cog. Often the best way to do this is to put your whole body into it. Just like the

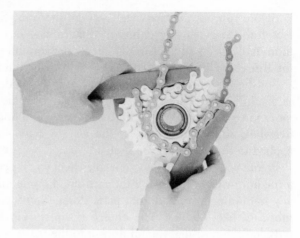

Removing freewheel sprockets. Use two sprocket removers. In this example the freewheel is off the bike for ease of illustration. But when you do it, you should leave your freewheel on the bike.

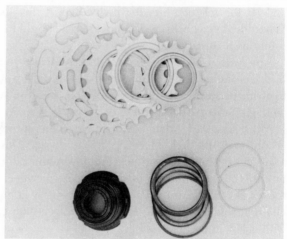

A disassembled freewheel. Note the spacers and the different sizes of the sprocket threads. Always be very careful to correctly reassemble your freewheel with the right sprockets and spacers.

freewheel itself, the cogs are tightened progressively as you ride—they could be pretty tight.

After you've loosened the outside cog, take it off and remove any spacer that might be placed between this outside cog and the following one. Spacers and cogs are very specific on freewheels and rarely interchangeable. Keep track of what came from where, or you could end up rebuilding your freewheel incorrectly and jamming your chain.

Remove all the cogs you need to change according to the type of freewheel you have. When you get replacements, though, make sure you know exactly where you want them on the freewheel. On a Maillard freewheel, for example, a seventeen-tooth cog on the inside is entirely different from a seventeen-tooth cog three sprockets from the inside. Ask your dealer to provide you with assistance if you need it.

When you've replaced the cogs or the freewheel itself, you may feel a kind of lurching, as if the freewheel is loose for the first revolution or so. Very simply, that's because the freewheel *is* loose when you first put it on. As you ride on it it will tighten. This is nothing to worry about.

CHAIN

Connecting the entire drivetrain is the primitive transmission called the chain. The chain was invented in the 1870s and hasn't changed much since then (although the links have become half as big as they used to be in the old days).

The chain requires more frequent maintenance than any other part of the bike. Every hundred miles or so, you should lubricate the chain. To do this, turn the pedals backward and pour a medium-weight oil like three-in-one bicycle oil for about fifteen seconds. As you do this, you'll notice some oil dripping onto your chainstay. Just clean that up with some of the solvent and wipe it dry with a paper towel.

Every thousand miles or so (or sooner if you've been riding in wet weather) you'll need to overhaul your chain. To do this, take your chain tool and open any one of the links on the chain by popping out any one of the rivets. This is an easy tool to use, but make sure you use it with care. Otherwise you could damage one of the chain plates and find yourself short one chain link (which often means buying a new chain—more of a hassle than it seems, as I explain below).

With the link open, thread the chain gently through the drivetrain, making sure you're holding the end with the open rivet. It's too wide to fit through the derailleurs. Take the chain gently by both ends, but be careful not to wrap it—you might have trouble unwrapping it.

Dip the chain into the solvent and let it sit for about a minute. When you remove it, remove any excess filth by rubbing all the links carefully with a toothbrush dipped in the solvent. As always when you use solvent, rinse the chain thoroughly using a powerful hose.

To put the chain back on the drivetrain, simply thread it through again. Make sure the open rivet with the cylinder that's sticking out is facing you, or you'll have a tough time closing it. Start with the end that has the open rivet and thread the chain through the chainrings, through the front derailleur, and back to the rear derailleur. Both ends should meet at the bottom, between the rear derailleur and the crankset.

Close the rivet with the chain tool, holding the chain plates together while gently forcing the rivet back through the plates. When the rivet looks flush with both plates, you can remove the chain tool. In most cases, though, the newly closed rivet will be tight. Take the tight link and a neighboring link in your hands and gently sway them up and down and in and out. After a few seconds, the rivet will be loose. (If you ever develop a tight link in normal riding, you should try this same procedure.)

The most common chain problem is age. As chains get old they stretch out and should be replaced. Every fifteen thousand miles or so you should automatically replace your chain. The only problem with this is that as the chain has aged it has also worn out the cogs in your freewheel and the chainrings.

Ideally, every time you buy a new chain you should buy new freewheel cogs and chainrings. If you don't, you'll find that the chain will skip on the cogs and chainrings because it won't be perfectly matched. Of course, most people can't invest in so much new hardware all at once. And if the cogs have only been slightly worn out, the chain will stretch out soon enough. But you should never use freewheel cogs or chainrings for more than three chain changes—if you do, your chain could skip continually.

BRAKES

Brakes are your primary safety valve and should be perfectly maintained. Luckily, the bicycle caliper brake is much simpler than an automobile disk or drum brake. It's also much easier to maintain.

The main body of the brake is composed of the calipers. They are virtually maintenance-free. Simply make sure you wash them in soapy water every few hundred miles or so, or more often if you ride in a lot of dirt or rain. The vast majority of brakes today are side-pull brakes. These brakes have two-part bodies, a larger unit that includes the arm extending up to the cable housing and a smaller unit that includes the caliper below the arm. If you have center-pull brakes, the construction is a little more complicated but just as easy to maintain.

Perhaps the main difference with center-pulls is that these have an extra link in the system, a piece of cable that links both calipers. That piece of cable is then attached to a cup, which in turn is attached to the main brake cable, which runs back to the brake lever.

The most common headaches with brakes are poor adjustments. You'll probably find that your brakes pull to one side, leaving one of the brake pads rubbing on the rim below the tire. To remedy this problem, you'll need a special narrow cross-section wrench (often a thirteen-millimeter size). You can use the same wrench you use to remove your pedals. Some high-quaity brakes have a recessed allen head behind the fork crown that allows you to adjust the lateral position of the brakes with an allen wrench.

To adjust the lateral position of the brake in relation to the wheel, fit the narrow cross-section wrench into the flat on the brake axle right before the fork crown (for the front brake) or right before the brake bridge (for the rear brake). Turn the wrench to center the brake. Of course, if you have a recessed head behind the fork crown (or the brake bridge), then adjust the brake back there.

You'll have to go beyond perfect center. To test if you've centered the brakes just right, hit the brake levers on the handlebars once. After you hit the brakes they will pop back to a certain position. That's where your adjustment has left them—you may have to repeat this operation a few more times before you get it just right.

With use, brake cables tend to stretch out. If this starts happening, you'll find the travel of your brake lever increased and your effective braking force reduced. Luckily, most manufacturers have an adjustable barrel that can be turned to take up the slack in the cable. In many brakes, this barrel is placed at the top of the brake arm where the cable housing starts. Other designs have this barrel next to the bolt that fastens the cable to the brake, a little bit lower down. If you have center-pull brakes, you'll find your adjustable barrel in the special washer that's fitted into the head tube.

Of course, if you've gone as far as you can with the adjustable barrel, you'll need to tighten the brake cable. To do this, unfasten the bolt that holds the brake cable (usually with an eight-millimeter wrench). As the cable is released, the spring held by the brake calipers will open up the brake.

To tighten your brake, take one hand, pass it through the spokes on the wheel, and hold both brake shoes firmly against the rim of the bike. With the other hand, tug firmly at the brake cable to make sure it is taut. Then let go of the cable and tighten the bolt (keep holding the brake shoes tightly until the cable bolt is completely tightened). As you let go of the brake shoes, the calipers will be released just enough to give you sufficient clearance between the brake shoes and the rim.

If you have a very old cable, I would recommend getting new cables, something you should do anyway every five thousand miles or six months. To remove the old brake cable, repeat the procedure described above, loosen the brake cable and slip it out of the brake body. Then grab the plastic cable housing and pull it off. Leave it aside for the time being.

Your brake lever will be loose, no longer restrained by the pressure of the cable attached to the brake. You can open it wide to remove the large cable barrel end from the barrel lock inside the brake lever. The brake cable will probably be hard to remove, so use a screwdriver to lightly tap it out.

Make sure the new brake cable you purchased has the same barrel end as the one you're replacing. There are a number of different brake barrel designs and they are not compatible. Also, when you're buying a new cable try to get the thickest cable available for your model. Campagnolo makes an especially thick brake cable that can be used on a lot of the "Campagnolo-clone" brakes. It's a little more expensive but more than worth the price in added safety.

To install the new brake cable, slot the barrel end through the barrel lock in the brake lever. Some models have an open slot in the barrel lock, allowing you to pass the cable through the barrel lock before pulling on the cable to fit the barrel end. But some models have a closed barrel lock, which means you'll have to thread the entire cable through the barrel lock.

Once the barrel end is in place in the barrel lock, give the cable a firm tug to make sure it won't pop out. Since there is no tension on your cable yet, the barrel end could still slide out. You'll need to check it again before you tighten the cable to the brake body.

Grease the cable and thread it through the housing. Then thread the cable through the brake, tighten the calipers by holding the brake shoes against the rim, as described above. Tighten the bolt. Make sure the barrel end is firmly inside the barrel lock of the brake lever as you tighten the cable.

Because replacement brake cables come in standard lengths only, you'll need to clip off the excess cable with a wire cutter. Take special care when cutting the end of your cable—if you fray it, you'll have to get a new cable. Some people like to put plastic plugs on the ends of their brake cables, but this isn't necessary.

There is one special case in changing brake cables. If you have aerodynamic cable housing that runs through the bars, you won't be able to remove the cable housing. Instead, you'll have to painstakingly thread the cable through the housing.

Every fifteen thousand miles you should change the cable housing. Purchase one length of high-quality housing that will accommodate both your front and rear brakes. Make sure to buy more than you need to account for any mistakes. Start with the rear brake. Remove the brake cable as described above. Then remove the housing. On most bikes you'll have brazed-on mounts holding the cable housing to the top tube. Simply slip the housing out through these mounts. If you have screwed-on clips, you'll need to get a small screwdriver to unfasten the screws.

Take your new cable housing in one hand and let it hang. Take the old cable housing in the other hand and let it hang too. Mark the length you need on your new cable housing by making an indentation with your nail on the plastic. Then take a pair of wire cutters and cut the new cable housing. Take great care not to fray the housing, by always cutting in a line perpendicular to the swirl of the metallic housing inside the plastic casing.

Install the new housing, thread the cable through it, and you're set. Repeat the same steps with the front housing. Watch for housing that's too short or too long. You always want the housing to form a gentle, graceful loop above the handlebars that will be easy for the cable to run through. If

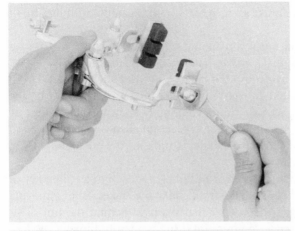

Unfastening the brake shoe. Use a wrench to loosen the bolt and remove the brake shoe.

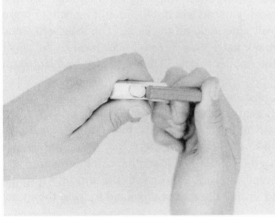

Installing a new brake pad. You can push a new brake shoe in by hand, but you may want to use a screwdriver. To remove an old brake pad you will definitely need a screwdriver.

the housing gets short, you'll get an abrupt curve. That will restrict the cable's ability to pull the brakes. If the housing is too long, it'll require an overly long section of brake cable, which will make for less efficient braking.

Every fifteen thousand miles or so you should change your brake pads. To do this, take a wrench (again, usually an eight-millimeter model) and unfasten the bolts that hold the brake shoe and pad to the main brake assembly.

Once the bolts are loose, take the brake shoe and turn it a few degrees with the rear of the brake shoe facing down. Tighten. Then take a large screwdriver and gently force the old brake pad out of the brake shoe—it'll slide out slowly.

To install the new brake pad, unfasten the brake shoe and turn it so now the *front* is facing down. Tighten the brake shoe. Wedge the brake pad into the beginning of the brake shoe and push gently with the screwdriver until it's all the way in the brake shoe.

When you refasten the brake shoe, make sure it is parallel with the rim of the wheel.

Every fifteen thousand miles you should remove your brake to make an overhaul. Before you can make an overhaul, make sure the brake cables have been unfastened. Then, to remove the brake, you must anchor the axle. To do this take a wrench (often an eight-millimeter model) and place it on the nut at the front of the brake axle (more commonly known as the *mounting bolt).* On many modern side-pulls you can place an allen key in the recessed bolt behind the fork crown to make it easier to unfasten the nut at the front of the mounting bolt.

Then take a wrench (either an eight-millimeter wrench or an allen key in most cases) and loosen the nut on the front end of the brakes. After removing the nut, you can unfasten the washer that sits right behind the nut. This washer may require a wrench to remove it (usually a ten-millimeter model).

Once the washer is removed, you can take out the mounting bolt (or brake axle). The mounting bolt will slide back, off the brake. The brake will come apart in your hands. The major parts (on a side-pull brake) will be the larger caliper with the arm and the smaller caliper. There will also be a large arm return spring.

Remove the brake pads, and clean the remaining parts with solvent and rinse them thoroughly with a strong hose. Before you reinstall the brake, put a dab of white lithium grease on the mounts on the brake calipers where the spring is held. This will make the brake smoother.

To put the brake back together, install the mounting bolt through the rear of the fork crown. Then install the large caliper with the arm return spring installed in its mount. Next, install the other caliper and squeeze the spring into its mount.

To attach the brake, thread the washer through the mounting bolt. Turn it to the point at which there is no more play on the mounting bolt. Next you'll need to hold the *washer* tightly with a wrench as you tighten the mounting bolt *nut* with the other wrench. After you tighten the nut you'll notice the brake will be a little stiff. Then take the washer and *loosen* it a eighth of a turn or so. This will loosen your brake and also tighten the nut, making your brake safer.

If you want to readjust or change your brake levers, you'll need to take out the brake cable and remove all the tape from the handlebars. Then you'll need to open the levers as far as they'll go and use a wrench (again, usually an eight-millimeter model) and unfasten the bolt at the back, inside the lever assembly.

Once the bolt is loose, the clamp surrounding the handlebars may still stick. In that case, lightly tap the bolt you just unfastened. With the clamp

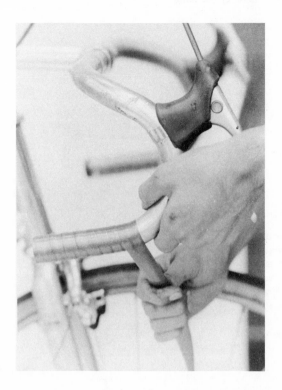

Installing new tape on the handlebars. Start at the bottom and apply tape firmly, making sure to have a little overlap on each turn.

loose, you can move the brake lever. If you're adjusting the position, remember, the ideal spot is about haflway down the bend on the handlbars—at that point the *bottom* of the levers should be just about level with the bottom of the bars.

You may want to change the rubber brake hood that surrounds the brake lever assembly. First you must remove the brake lever as described above. Then take the old hood and squeeze it off from the rear. To install the new hood, install it also from the rear. You'll need a little muscle. But make sure you don't stretch the hood at the front where it is thin—you'll split it.

To reinstall the levers, simply tighten the bolt in the assembly. Make sure the brake levers face directly in front of you.

HANDLEBARS

To remove your handlebars, take off the tape and the levers. Then loosen the bolt in the stem that holds the bars. Once that bolt is loose, simply move the bars out. When the bend in the bars crosses the stem, you'll have to be a little careful. Make sure you don't scuff the bars.

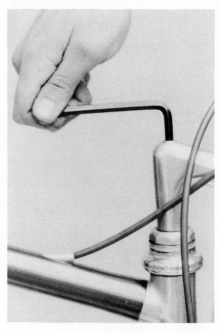

Removing the handlebar stem. Use an allen key to loosen the bolt. In some cases, you may need to tap the bolt to loosen the expander wedge inside the stem. Clean and grease the expander wedge before reinstalling. When you remove the stem mark the spot where the grease stops with a piece of tape. That way you can reinstall it in the right spot.

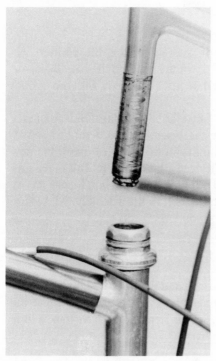

HANDLEBAR STEM

The stem should be removed every five thousand miles to make sure the expander wedge inside the steering tube (which is inside the head tube) doesn't "freeze." If this expander wedge does freeze, it'll never come out and you'll have to go to a bike shop to have the expander wedge cracked and removed.

To remove the expander wedge, unfasten the bolt at the top of the stem and take out the stem. Then take a dollop of white lithium grease and put it around the expander wedge. Reinstall the stem. When you tighten the stem, make sure it is tight, but don't force it too tight, or you'll crack the expander wedge.

HEADSET

The component that holds the steering tube (and its extension, the fork) is the headset. Like the pedals and the bottom bracket, the headset has ball bearings that need to be overhauled every fifteen thousand miles.

To overhaul the headset, remove the stem as described above. Then get a large wrench that'll fit over the locknut. A twelve-inch monkey or adjustable wrench will fit over the locknut on the vast majority of headsets, but I would recommend getting a special tool made by the manufacturer of the headset.

To unfasten the locknut, hold the front wheel firmly between your legs to anchor the fork and steering tube. Give the wrench a yank and remove the locknut. Put it aside in a cup or other safe place. Next, remove the tanged washer (the tange is the little piece that sticks into a groove in the steering

Removing the headset. Loosen the locknut with a large wrench.

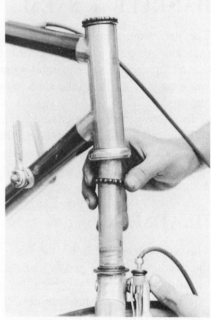

Remove the screwed race.

After placing the screwed race in a safe place, remove the forks and steering tube.

tube). Most of the time this washer comes out by hand. If it sticks take a medium-sized screwdriver and pop it up gently.

With the tanged washer removed, take your wrench and carefully remove the screwed race. As you take it off, you'll notice the ball bearings—usually in a race of their own.

With the screwed race loose, the steering tube will fall out of the head tube and expose the bottom set of ball bearings, which are lodged in what's known as the *crown race.*

Take the ball bearings and dip them into the wire basket that fits in the can of solvent. Let them sit. Then take a soft cloth or rag, dip it in the solvent, and wipe the grooves in the large races. Before reinstalling the headset, rinse everything thoroughly with a strong hose.

To reinstall the headset, first apply white lithium grease on all the races and ball bearings. Slip the bottom set of ball bearings on the steering tube all the way to the crown race. Then slip the steering tube back into the head tube.

Next, slip the top set of ball bearings and place it on the top pressed race. To attach the steering tube, thread the screwed race up to the ball bearings until there is no more play but before you can feel any roughness. Then reinstall the tanged washer.

When you reinstall the locknut, make sure that you have a wrench to anchor the screwed race. Slowly tighten the locknut, making sure to keep the bottom wrench around the screwed race stationary. When you're satisfied that the locknut is tight, *loosen* the screwed race an eighth of a turn or so until it's not rough.

Before reinstalling your stem, check for any play in the headset. Play in the headset is especially dangerous because you can easily break the steering tube, causing a serious accident.

If you have trouble completing this overhaul, see a professional mechanic—he'll be able to help you in a matter of minutes.

SEAT AND SEAT POST

The seat post should be removed every fifteen thousand miles and the portion inside the frame should be lightly greased with white lithium grease. Whenever you remove the seat post, take a piece of tape to mark exactly the point where the seat post meets the frame. Remember, finding the right position is a painstaking process. You don't want to lose it when you remove your seat post.

The saddle doesn't require any special maintenance, but you may want to remove it once in a while to clean the railing underneath the seat. To remove the saddle from the seat post, get a wrench appropriate to the seat post you have. In many cases this will require an allen key and the saddle will be easy to remove. But some Campagnolo models have two conventional twelve-

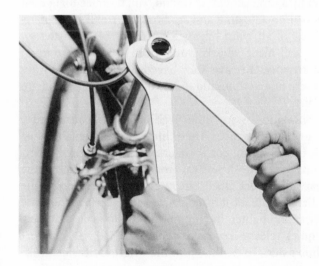

To tighten the locknut, you need one wrench to anchor the screwed race, the other to tighten the locknut.

millimeter bolts that require a special wrench to be reached without a lot of trouble.

When you remove the saddle, be sure to mark the point on the railing where the saddle was positioned. Remember, this is an important part of your position. If you reinstall the saddle incorrectly along the railing, you'll be riding in the wrong position.

WHEELS

Wheels are a very important part of your bike. They should be maintained with a great deal of care. The wheels are your primary point of contact with the road. If they're poorly adjusted they will make your riding inefficient, and possibly dangerous.

Although some cycling books outline wheel building, I don't recommend it for anybody who isn't an advanced mechanic. To build a really good wheel requires a range of expensive tools and, more than anything else, much skill and experience. Most wheels that are built by riders in their homes tend to be poorly built.

The hardest thing about building a good wheel is knowing just how to tighten the spokes. While it's pretty easy to form a wheel, chances are that your spokes will be very unevenly tightened. This kind of wheel falls out of true very often and puts a lot of stress on the spokes and rims. Because it's so hard to tighten all the spokes evenly, many homemade wheels are not round. And that puts even more stress on the wheel. And keep in mind that the wheel is made of fragile components, like thin spokes and rims, that are only strong and safe when put together in the right way.

Get your wheels built by a professional. If you do, you'll notice that you'll need to spend much less time adjusting and readjusting. You'll have many fewer broken spokes. Most of all, your bike will be a heck of a lot safer.

Of course, even with well-made wheels, you'll need to know how to do some of your own maintenance. Because they have ball bearings, the hubs should be overhauled every fifteen thousand miles, more often if you ride in much bad weather or dirt.

If you have Mavic, Shimano, or any other kind of sealed-bearing hubs, you won't need to do any maintenance. These hubs are maintenance-free and only need to be washed in warm, soapy water every few hundred miles.

To overhaul your hubs, remove the wheel from the bike. Remove the freewheel from the rear hub as described on pages 293–94. Take out the quick release skewer. Before you set it aside, make sure you put the little springs back on the skewer and tighten the nut on the end to make sure they don't get lost. Set the quick release skewers aside.

Next, unfasten the hub axles. To do this, turn the wheel on its side. Take two cone wrenches, the same kind of narrow cross-section wrenches you used to unfasten your pedals and adjust your brakes.

Take the first cone wrench and place it on the inner cone, just outside the edge of the hub body. Take the other wrench and place it around the locknut, which is on the end of the axle.

Use the first wrench to *anchor* the inner cone while you unfasten the locknut with the second wrench. Once the locknut is loose, unthread it and set it aside in a small cup. Next, unthread the inner cone slowly and set it aside.

Once the locknut and inner cone are off, you can slip off the hub axle. Set it aside. To remove the bearings, pop off the dust cap that sits at the edge of the hub body. With the vast majority of hubs, you simply need to take a medium-sized screwdriver and gently pop the dust cap out. But if you have the new Campagnolo Aero Record hubs, you'll need a special tool produced by Campagnolo to take off the dust caps.

Once the dust caps are off, you'll be able to take out the ball bearings. If your ball bearings are in a track (a race), simply lift the whole thing out. If your ball bearings are free, take them out (carefully) by hand. You may need a screwdriver or tweezers to help you. Put the ball bearings, the race (if you have one), and the dust cap in the wire basket inside the solvent. Let it sit.

To remove the ball bearings from the other side, simply flip the wheel over, remove the dust cap and repeat the same operation.

Once everything is sitting in the wire basket in the solvent, take a soft cloth or rag, dip it into the solvent and clean out the grease in the groove in the hub where the ball bearings sit. Wash out the solvent in the hub with a powerful hose.

Once you've done that, take the wire basket out of the solvent can and spray all the parts inside the wire basket with the hose. You're now ready to start reinstalling all the parts.

The first step is to take a liberal dollop of grease and pack it in the grooves in the hubs where the ball bearings sit. Then take the one race of ball bearings and dip it into the grease as well. If you don't have races, simply reinstall the bearings one by one.

Once you've finished one side, take the dust cap and *lightly* tap it back into place with a rubber mallet or a hammer with a thick cloth wrapped around it. If you don't wrap the hammer, you might warp the dust cap, which would mean you'd have to get a new one, because a warped dust cap could affect how smoothly the ball bearings turn.

Once you've finished one side, turn the wheel around slowly. Put a dollop of grease into the groove. Dip the race (if you have one) into the grease. Then pack the ball bearings back into the hub. Tap the dust cap into place and you're ready to reinstall the hub axle.

Always be sure to place your axle facing in the same direction you took it out. The spacers on the axle and the fine-tuned adjustment of the wheel were done with the axle facing a specific direction. This is especially true with the rear axle.

Once the axle is back in place, thread the inner cone until you feel no more play on the axle. Then hold both ends of the axle in your hands and spin the wheel. If you feel any roughness, loosen the inner cone. The ideal point is that at which there is no more side-to-side play and no more roughness as the wheel turns.

Then rethread the locknut, slowly. Wrap one cone wrench around this locknut and another around the locknut on the *other* side of the hub (the one you never removed). This will anchor the axle as you thread the locknut.

Once the locknut is barely touching the inner cone, place the second cone wrench on the inner cone. Use that cone wrench as an anchor so the inner cone doesn't fall out of position.

Tighten the locknut, but make sure that the inner cone doesn't budge: If it does, the whole thing will be too tight, and you'll be grinding ball bearings. Once you're satisfied that the locknut is tight (and it really *has* to be tight), take the inner cone and *loosen* it a quarter turn. You need to do this because even the steadiest hand can't keep the inner cone from tightening a little bit while the locknut is tightened.

Some people have trouble with this. They find that when they tighten the locknut, the inner cone tightens way too much. A trick you can use to avoid this is to leave the inner cone just a little looser before you tighten the locknut. But don't leave it too loose, or you'll end up having a lot of play on the hub.

If you have any damage to the hub or axle, you should take the wheel to a professional mechanic to ask his opinion on how to repair it.

The spokes are really the key structural element of the wheels. Although each spoke is very thin and light, it has a tremendous tensile strength. And put all together in a crossover pattern, the spokes form a very strong wheel.

Because a tremendous amount of stress is placed on the spokes, spokes sometimes become loose. To tighten a spoke, take a spoke wrench and tighten the nipple that attaches the spoke to the rim.

Be careful, however, because the tension of the spoke determines the structure (roundness, strength) of the wheel. Turn the nipple until it starts to create a little resistance. Then turn an eighth of a turn at a time, making sure the wheel is true as you tighten the spoke. The best way to make sure the wheel is true is to install it in a truing stand as you work. Chances are you don't own your own truing stand, but some good bike shops will have one available for their customers to use. If you can't find a truing stand, one acceptable solution is to put your wheel back on your bike and use the brake pads as a guide—but this is a very rough measure.

One note of caution: If your wheel is perfectly trued with one spoke very loose, your wheel is probably improperly built. In this case I would recommend taking it to a professional wheel builder to see if he can readjust it for you.

If you're wondering what's so bad about a wheel that's perfectly trued minus one spoke, the answer is very simple: You'll have a wheel built with an odd number of spokes, with more pull to one side than the other: You're always going to have spokes coming loose or breaking.

If you have a broken spoke, replace it immediately. The first step is to get the *exact* same length spoke. To determine exact spoke length, you need to know what brand of hub you have, and whether your hub is low-flange or high-flange. You need to know in what pattern your spokes are arranged. Most bikes have three-or four-across spoke patterns. (What this refers to is how many times each spoke crosses another.) To find out what pattern your spokes have, choose any spoke. Start at the hub and count how many spokes it crosses. This will give you the pattern.

Next you need to know what brand and type of rim you have. If you have clincher (or wired-on) wheels, you'll have a slightly different spoke than with a sew-up (or tubular) wheel. Finally, you need to know whether the broken spoke is on the front wheel or the rear wheel.

Armed with all that information, you can go to your bike shop. When you get your replacement spokes, you might as well buy a few more—they're inexpensive and good to have around your workshop.

To remove the broken spoke, remove the wheel from the bike, then deflate your tire and remove it. If you have clinchers (or wired-on) wheels, you'll need to take a tire iron and pop the rubber tire out of the rim. With a second tire iron, slowly pull the rest of the tire out of the rim. Then turn the wheel around, take one tire iron and scoop the tire out of the rim. Then, with the second tire iron (and possibly a third) remove the rest of the tire. As you get almost all the way done, you'll notice it'll become hard to remove the last bit of tire. Use a little muscle and you'll succeed. Once the tire is removed, take off the inner tube.

If you have sew-ups, make sure the tire is deflated. Turn the wheel so that the valve is resting squarely on the floor. Then start to dislodge the tire from the rim at the top of the wheel, directly opposite from the valve. With a little muscle the tire will come off the rim. When you get near the valve, turn the wheel so the valve is facing up and dislodge the tire up to the valve. Remove the tire.

With the tire off you can remove the portion of the spoke attached to the

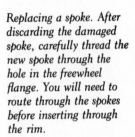

Replacing a spoke. After discarding the damaged spoke, carefully thread the new spoke through the hole in the freewheel flange. You will need to route through the spokes before inserting through the rim.

nipple. Gently ease it through the hole in the rim, up away from the hub of the wheel. If you have sew-up rims, you could have some glue buildup. By pushing a little harder on the spoke, you should be able to get the nipple and spoke through the spoke hole in the rim.

Now remove the bottom part of the spoke by threading it through the spoke hole on the hub. As you're doing this, you'll notice that there are two kinds of spoke holes on the hub.

If you have a damaged spoke that is in one piece, take your wire cutters and cut the spoke in half. You can't simply unthread the nipple from the spoke because the spoke is so long that it won't fit through the maze of spokes once it's loosened.

Installing the new spoke presents the same problem. Because, obviously, you can't cut the new spoke, you'll need to first pull it all the way through the spoke hole on the hub. Make sure you are instaling it in the right direction. You can tell which way is correct because each hole has an indentation. If you're installing a spoke that faces out, you'll have an easier time getting the spoke through, but you'll still have to bend it to get it through the spokes it has to cross.

To get the spoke up to the spoke hole on the rim, you'll have to cross it, usually three or four times. Look at the spoke pattern *two* spokes over on the same side of the wheel and follow that pattern meticulously.

Once you've finished crossing the spokes, which can take as long as ten or fifteen minutes, you'll need to bend the spoke slightly to get it into the spoke hole. Thread the nipple and tighten it with the spoke wrench up to the point at which you feel some resistance.

Once you feel some resistance, turn the spoke wrench one eighth of a turn at a time and check the true on the wheel. Again, you should do this in a truing stand. If you don't have one, look for a bike store that will let you use

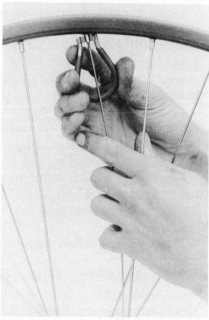

Inserting a spoke nipple. Place it through the hole in the rim and thread it onto the spoke.

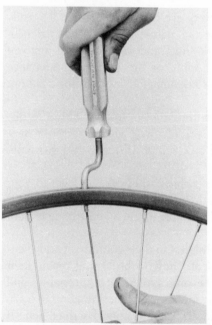

This spoke wrench tightens the spoke from the top of the nipple.

This wrench is more common. It tightens the spoke through the body of the nipple.

one. As a last resort, put the wheel back in the bike and use the brake pads as a rough guide.

Once you're satisfied the wheel is true (and round) you're done and you can put it back on your bike.

I think it's safe to say this is a pretty complicated procedure. And you're only changing one spoke. If you have to do a major repair, like a damaged or broken rim or hub, you need to rebuild an entire wheel. As I mentioned above, if you need your wheel rebuilt, you should look for an expert wheel builder—it's a very special skill that's well worth the money you're going to spend. Also, if somebody is rebuilding your wheel, it's really not worth it to skimp. Don't try to repair a broken rim, get a new one. And never use old spokes, they get stretched out in a specific pattern with each wheel: Buy new spokes. Last, if a few of your spokes seem loose, I suggest taking the wheel to a bicycling shop to have them true the wheels. Wheels will have to be trued more frequently if you ride a great deal on pot-holed city streets.

Remember, your wheels must be strong and resistant, even though the elements that make them up are extremely delicate. A bicycle wheel is only strong and resistant when its elements are put together just right. But if the spokes are poorly adjusted, the wheel could warp or break, and you could crash. Always lavish care and money, as much as you can afford, on your wheels.

Bicycle maintenance is something every cyclist should master. It's really not that complicated and can become second nature with a little experience. But you will need the right tools, a little time, and some help. At first you might become terribly frustrated with some of the harder maintenance chores. With experience, though, even something like overhauling a bottom bracket will become easy.

One word of caution: If you ever run into a lot of trouble with a repair, never force anything. If, for example, you're trying to take off your freewheel, and you get stuck, forcing it will only ruin the threads, and therefore, both the freewheel and the hub.

Don't be ashamed if you run into a problem. Just take it down to your local bike shop and have a mechanic help you. I think you'll find most mechanics sympathetic. And they might be able to teach you a trade trick or two.

Some cyclists develop a tremendous interest in their equipment and eventually become top mechanics. They learn how to build and repair their frames and wheels. Eventually some become professional mechanics and frame builders. But unless you have the interest and determination to learn about your equipment, I would stick with the maintenance described here. If you ever have a more serious problem, go to a pro bike mechanic.

9

The History

of Cycling

W e don't know much about the origin of the two-wheeled vehicle that would someday become the bicycle. Egyptian hieroglyphics and bas-relief sculptures in Babylonia clearly show human figures riding on a long pole connecting two wheels. But there are no other records of these cycles; they were perhaps a pastime at the court of certain Egyptian pharaohs and Babylonian kings. Later, Roman frescoes in the city of Pompeii show men in togas frolicking on two-wheelers. But the evidence of bicyclelike vehicles in ancient times has never extended beyond a few scattered artistic renditions. No written descriptions or explanations of these cycles have ever been found, and most likely none ever will be.

The bicycle dropped out of history for more than fifteen centuries and reappeared when Leonardo da Vinci sketched designs of chain-driven vehicles and details of chains themselves. In a separate example, a stained-glass window of a small parish church at Stoke Poges in Buckinghamshire, England, shows a chubby little angel, high in the clouds, riding a crude two-wheeled machine. It is unknown whether or not the design was simply the product of an imaginative craftsman.

The first, rudimentary incarnations of the modern bicycle began to take shape in 1690, when a French woodworker, Élie Richard, drafted plans for a two-wheeler. Three years later, Jacques Ozanam, a French engineer who had developed tables for tangent and secant sinal curves, took up where Richard had left off and built a rough model of a vehicle with one wheel behind the other. Later, in 1779, the *Journal de Paris* described a "velocipede" built by M. Blanchard and M. Masurier. Although their machine seems to have quickly faded into oblivion, this was the first time the word *vélocipède*—the term for bicycle until the end of the nineteenth century—had been mentioned. The word *vélocipède* is a composite of the Latin words for speed, *velox*, and foot, *pes*. Those first cycles had no pedals or cranks and were moved by a person moving his feet along the ground.

Perhaps the most famous of the early cycles was the brainchild of the Comte de Sivrac, a charismatic and ingenious French nobleman. In 1790, de Sivrac introduced his invention, a strange contraption that consisted of a massive wooden beam attached to two chariot wheels with a couple of massive vertical wooden forks, both front and rear. De Sivrac's bike was really not different from the previous models, and the rider had to constantly push off with his feet along the ground to develop any speed. Like his predecessors, he built a stationary front wheel that couldn't turn; the whole machine was so stiff and heavy that any change in direction meant the rider had to stop, readjust the direction of the front wheel, and get back on, moving his feet furiously to build up any speed.

Although de Sivrac hadn't really invented anything new, he was a marketing genius. He changed the name of his contraption from the unsuccessful *vélocipède* to *célérifère*, another Latin composite, from the words *celer* for fast and *ferre* for carry. De Sivrac was a member of Paris's high society who cleverly made sure to use his many connections as publicity for his odd-looking baby.

Overnight, the *célérifère* became a hit in Paris: After the Terror of the French Revolution, Parisians avidly sought light-hearted amusements. When its popularity waned, de Sivrac shrewdly renamed it the *vélocifère*; to appeal to the outlandish tastes of the time, he added wooden lion heads, or serpent heads, or mermaids. De Sivrac sold many bikes; he probably would have made an excellent used-car salesman.

Soon enough, the *vélocifère* was a common sight in the French capital. Along Paris's boulevards, young men of the First Empire rushed about madly, cutting off unsuspecting pedestrians, testing their skills in hard-to-handle turns. Those *vélocifères* were very much like what motorcycles are today: simple, one-person vehicles that promised freedom and speed unheard-of at the time.

The local population, though, was incensed that impetuous young men should zip by at the (outrageous) speed of four or five miles per hour. As a result, the prefect of Paris ordered all *vélocifères* off the grounds of the Palais

Royal, where enthusiasts often gathered. Two French caricaturists, Vernet and Debucourt, fanned the fire when they came out with a series of drawings wryly commenting on the exuberance of the young, daring *vélocifère* enthusiasts.

Despite all the rage and controversy, the *vélocifère* turned out to be a largely a fad. The contraption, after all, weighed close to eighty pounds. It couldn't be steered. After the novelty of dragon heads and tiger heads wore away, there was little de Sivrac could do to hide the inadequacies of his invention. By the time Napoleon succumbed at Waterloo, the *vélocifère* was forgotten and dead.

The first man to buld a steering cycle was J. N. Niepce in Paris in 1816. He proudly dubbed his machine the *céléripède*, or literally "fast foot." He must have fully expected his invention to take off as the *célérifère* had twenty years earlier. But Niepce was no doubt a better inventor than businessman. He was quickly overtaken by the Baron Karl Von Drais de Sauerbrun.

On April 5, 1818, Von Drais mounted a carefully orchestrated exhibition of his new invention in the Luxembourg Gardens in Paris. A contingent of two hundred enthusiasts was on hand to encourage the press to review the new cycle favorably. Trained riders showed what could be done with the new bike; the demonstrations were planned to show that you could easily round the fountains of the Luxembourg Gardens.

The problem was that the new bike, soon dubbed the *draisine*, was not nearly as convenient as the enthusiasts claimed. It was still extremely heavy, weighing in at more than eighty pounds. Although it could be turned, it still required tremendous effort to get anywhere.

Though the *draisine* proved unsuccessful, it spawned a number of imitations. By 1819, Dennis Johnson, a London blacksmith, was building *draisines* in London under the name hobbyhorse or dandy horse. They sold like hotcakes. Just as the *vélocifère* had been the rage of Paris in the first decade of the nineteenth century, now London took to its hobbyhorse; young dandies of all kind—including the prince regent—were proud to be seen strolling about slowly, huffing and puffing on their behemoths. Dennis Johnson and his assistants further improved and lightened the hobbyhorse by replacing its heavy and unwieldy wooden carcass with an iron frame that greatly reduced the weight and added to the rigidity.

In the 1820s, the hobbyhorse was imported to the United States. It became popular among elegant New Yorkers, who paraded themselves in Union and Washington parks. But unlike the European capitals, New York was still a bustling town of pioneers, and once the novelty of the hobbyhorse faded, it lost favor and disappeared.

Now that Von Drais had invented a cycle that could be steered, the only thing that remained was to invent a bike that could fully use the benefit of the wheel. After all, if the force directed to the bike came only from a pair of feet furiously running along the ground, the only advantage gained would be in momentum.

The man who invented the first modern bike is generally thought to be Kirkpatrick Macmillan, a Scottish engineer and inventor, who developed the first drivetrain for the velocipede in his workshop in Dumfriesshire, Scotland.

Macmillan invented a set of levers, with platforms on the end, very much like pedals. These levers were attached to a long set of arms, which extended all the way back to the rear wheel's hub. There, Macmillan attached the second levers to solid hubs. Self-propulsion had been invented. Although Macmillan's bicycle still weighed over eighty pounds, the rider could now move along much more efficiently than before by pushing down on the pedals that turned with every rotation of the rear wheel.

To prove that, at last, a truly rideable cycle had been created, Macmillan rode his invention from Thornhil, Dumfriesshire, to Glasgow, about seventy-five miles.

On his way back from Glasgow, Macmillan is said to have staged the first known bicycle race. He wagered a friend, the driver of the Glasgow-Carlisle coach, that he could win a race to the town of Sanquhar. The driver agreed and the race was on. Macmillan had the advantage of not having to stop at all the coach stops, but rode a bit more slowly, especially in the hills. Still, at Sanquhar Macmillan was a clear winner.

Despite this, Macmillan's bicycle was never really successful; maybe because it was still so heavy, or maybe because the drivetrain was clumsy and unreliable.

The world would have to wait until 1861 for a new development in cycling. A certain Monsieur Brunel, a haberdasher, brought his velocipede to the Paris workshop of Pierre Michaux, a blacksmith and coach builder. This velocipede, the old kind without any pedals or crankarms, caught the eye of Ernest Michaux, the first of Pierre Michaux's three sons. In an account published by Michaux's youngest son, Henri, in 1893, Ernest Michaux is said to have taken the machine for an hour-long ride around Paris. When he came back, he told his father that the velocipede required constant leg work, that the thing would come to a stop as soon as he stopped moving his feet on the ground. Ernest suggested some kind of foot rests.

This piqued his father's interest. Pierre Michaux was a meticulous craftsman who was famous for finding ingenious solutions to common problems. He agreed with his son that something had to be done for the feet but that, instead of retsing them, they might be put to better use with some kind of propulsion device. Michaux busied himself for the next week by designing and building a pedal for the haberdasher's velocipede. He found the handle of a grindstone and adapted it to the bike. When the device was built, it consisted simply of a set of crankarms extending to the front hub and attached to a set of axles. Michaux decided to baptize his invention the *pédivelle*, or foot lever, a word that later became *pédale*.

At first Michaux's new velocipede caught on slowly—only two were sold in 1861. But twelve months later, the new bicycle, finally practical and rideable, had caught on, not as a fad, but as a viable form of transportation and exercise. In 1862, Michaux sold 142 of his machines; in 1865 he sold over 400 velocipedes.

Perhaps because he was more craftsman than businessman, or maybe because he had neglected to patent his invention, Michaux was quickly imitated by dozens of small manufacturers in France and, slowly, all around Europe.

Paris became the capital of the bicycle industry. One French manufacturer, Tribout et Meyer, even developed a simple chain-driven bicycle as early as 1869, although it was laughed at. At the first bicycle show, held in Paris the same year, the ancestors of the freewheel and gear-changing mechanisms were shown.

With all this bustling development, it was inevitable that enthusiasts would take to the streets and challenge one another to races. Realizing how much impact racing could have on their image and sales, Michaux's company, the Compagnie Parisienne des Vélocipèdes, decided to organize a race, on May 30, 1868, in the Parc de Saint-Cloud, on the outskirts of Paris. This was the first organized bike race on record. There, Paris's *beau monde* witnessed a twelve-hundred-meter race opposing all the top velocipedists in Paris.

The field was composed mainly of crusty roughnecks. Cycling was a tough way to exercise in those days, on bad roads and hard-riding wooden bikes with iron-rimmed wheels. All the real enthusiasts of those days were eccentric and dedicated people who had to go against the grain to ride and train. The big favorite that day in Saint-Cloud was a mustachioed Frenchman named Drouet.

But the winner turned out to be a young Englishman living in Paris, James Moore. A friend of the Michaux family, he had been one of the first people to ride Pierre Michaux's bikes.

Although he was the youngest of the ten riders in the bunch that day, Moore was savvy. He calmly let Drouet and a few others take the lead before sprinting in the last few yards to cross the line first. Moore won in a time of 3:50. The first prize was six hundred francs.

Quickly races started popping up all around Paris, all modeled on that first twelve-hundred-meter sprint in Saint-Cloud. It didn't take long before the crusty roughnecks discovered they could make a pretty decent living by racing a bike; all the races had the same six-hundred-franc first prize. Bike manufacturers also realized they could publicize their product by sponsoring the top riders.

The sprint races around Paris attracted some interest from curious locals, but for the most part nobody took the bibycle racing very seriously. The races were always the same twelve-hundred-meter length. The same hard-boiled professionals competed every weekend. To compound the carnival-like atmosphere, promoters brought in three women in frou-frous, known as the "Bordeaux Ladies" to open the races, as a kind of see-it-one-see-it-all extravaganza.

For the editors of *Le Vélocipède Illustré*, one of the first cycling publications, this was a sad state of affairs. This paper firmly believed in the potential of the bicycle as a form of transportation and exercise. And it wanted to do something grandiose to rid France of its prejudices against the improved two-wheelers. In September of 1868, the paper announced it would promote an endurance race from Paris to Rouen. An open invitation was made to all velocipedists in France and abroad to race. Michaux's bicycle company would donate the prizes, including one thousand francs for first place and a bicycle with shock absorbers for second place.

That race turned out to be a success. More than two hundred riders of all shapes and sizes, professional and amateur, showed up for the start at the Arc de Triomphe in Paris. The race course was eighty-three miles long over terrible rough and cobbled roads. The bikes, of course, were still monstrously heavy. Wheels were shod with a thin strip of iron instead of tires.

Things got a little chaotic at the start when one group of velocipedists was let off half an hour ahead of schedule. No matter, the promoters said, they would give the second group a thirty-minute handicap. The big favorite this time was again James Moore. He was also the only rider using solid rubber, a real novelty back then, instead of steel strips around the rims.

But he was caught in the second group and had to chase throughout the day. In the end Moore caught everybody, including the riders who had started thirty minutes before him. He won in a time of 10:40:00, at an average speed of eight miles per hour.

In 1870 Rynner Van Neste, a seventeen-year-old American, made a big splash when he won the first officially recognized road race in Italy, from Florence to Pistoia.

As cycling boomed and expanded, it began to offend the conservative mentality of the time. All over Europe local authorities were petitioned by action groups to ban the use of velocipedes on streets. Undoubtedly, a measure of the blame rested on the shoulders of the enthusiastic young cyclists who found excitement and daring in breaking rules and whizzing past stodgy bourgeois pedestrians at high speeds.

In Brussels, the local police commissioner imposed draconian limits on the use of bicycles, forbade them from alleyways, sidewalks, paths, and parks, adding that all cyclists riding at night had to be equipped with an oil-burning lantern situated no lower than three-and-a-half feet off the ground.

In France the outrage drove the prefect of Paris to close the Bois de Boulogne to velocipedes. Cyclists developed such a bad reputation that they prompted newspapers of the time to write critical editorials. The conservative French daily *Le Rappel* was one of the severest critics:

> It is time that all concerned governments take serious measures against the velocipedists, as much for their own security as for that of others. Whatever may be said, the truth is that the velocipede is dangerous in populous cities. We would concede that a vehicle such as the tricycle would be acceptable, as it is stable and easy to drive. On the other hand, the two-wheel velocipede resembles a balancing act and its use is nothing short of a dangerous game. This rush of velocipedists against peaceful pedestrians could very well soon transform France into a country of savages.

The Victorian era was even less forgiving when it came to women riding velocipedes. The first race for women had been held on November 1, 1868. An Englishwoman, riding as "Miss America," had entered the Paris-Rouen race and had finished in twenty hours, at an average speed of four miles per hour. Although she was praised by the cycling press, most of the time women encountered tremendous opposition to their cycling. Some editorials of the time even concluded that women risked sterility if they rode bicycles.

By the early 1870s, Great Britain was established as one of the top cycling powers. The country had become the world capital of bicycle manufacturing, with hundreds of small companies all around the island—the city of Wolverhampton outside London was the cycling hub. Thanks in part to James Moore's exploits, racing became a big attraction in Britain. In the 1870s and 1880s, the Brits produced some of the best bicycle racers in the world. The British emphasized endurance and twenty-four-hour "trials" and did very well in the early French classics.

But sentiments against velocipedes eventually caused road racing to be outlawed in Britain by the 1890s; local riders turned instead to a very specialized form of time trialing. Unfortunately for the British, they were cut off from the European mainstream and never really recovered.

One problem with cycling was the vocabulary of the sport. The terms velocipede and *vélocipèdiste* were simply too long and cumbersome for everyday use. One Belgian daily, *Le Gaulois*, suggested that the machine be renamed *bicycle*. Although this name soon fell out of favor in France, it caught on in Britain and became the English word for *vélocipède*.

The bicycle in 1870 was still a far cry from the machine we know today. Although a rider could steer and pedal without too much trouble, the machine was heavy and unwieldy. The wheels were still basically the same kind found on farmers' carts. They were heavy, spongy wooden circles connected to the hubs by fourteen massive wooden spokes. The size of the front wheel determined how far one rotation of the pedals could take you. In other words, the gear was always fixed according to the size of that wheel. As riders started to develop their skills they found that the front wheel of the average Michaux bicycle was easy to spin out on, riders turning the pedals so quickly their legs would get away from them.

In 1871, James Starley, a British craftsman, came up with the idea for a tension-spoked wheel in which the rim and hub were connected by looped wire spokes. To increase the gearing, Starley built a bike with a huge front wheel and a much smaller rear wheel. This was the *ordinary* or penny-farthing bicycle that dominated the cycling world for the next ten to fifteen years. With the bigger wheel and a drive that could double the gear, the ordinary became the cycle of choice for all racers, its sleek, graceful power enhanced by the very special skill needed to ride this kind of machine.

The ordinary, though, had its obvious limitations. It was very dangerous to ride, especially on rough roads or downhills. And the big gears needed by racers could only be achieved with huge wheels that excluded any short-legged athletes.

In 1874 H. J. Lawson, another British craftsman, invented a machine that had two wheels of equal size, whose gear could be easily determined by a chain drive and a freewheel sprocket. With this design the wheel size could stay constant and different-size sprockets could be used to change gears. But Lawson's bike, dubbed the *safety*, suffered from an image problem; it didn't have the style or the aura of acrobatic derring-do of the ordinary. Instead the safety was billed as a bicycle safe for all the population. This was definitely not something that would appeal to the bravado of racers.

With technology and know-how imported from Europe, small companies began to sprout up along the Eastern Seaboard in the United States. America developed the same instant love affair with bicycles that it would with automobiles about fifty years later. With an ordinary or safety, every kid on the block could suddenly ride away in a flurry of speed and excitement and experience an entirely new thrill. In 1874 Colonel Albert A. Pope founded the first great American bicycle manufacturing firm in Boston and enlisted the help of the pioneer Pierre Lallement, who had worked with Pierre Michaux in Paris in the 1860s.

Cycling soon hit the big leagues in America. Although baseball, the country's only pro sport at the time, was the biggest pastime, cycling wasn't far behind. All around the country, clubs began organizing century rides, handing medals to brave cyclists who covered one hundred miles in less than ten hours. Cyclists were praised for their skill in balancing the spectacular ordinaries.

The century, so named because it's a one-hundred-mile affair, is actually America's oldest cycling event, having first been held in the 1870s. In those days, the only bike around was the ordinary or high-wheeler, and finishing the century was quite a challenge. Cycling was a great new fad in those days and close to one hundred thousand people are said to have ridden centuries.

Long before anybody thought of organizing bike races in the United States, tourists had banded together in a group known as the League of American Wheelmen. Formed in Providence, Rhode Island, in 1880, the LAW (known today as Bicycle USA) is the oldest American governing body of cycling.

But the allure of the ordinary soon faded. In 1885, a vastly improved version of the safety came out, the Rover. This new bike was a true high-performance machine with a simple, smooth chain drive, a sturdy "diamond" frame and two standard-sized wheels. In about four years, the Rover supplanted the ordinary, and four years later there were practically no more ordinaries made.

The amazing thing about the Rover safety is how little bicycles have changed since it was first made. Modern bikes may have a lot more light alloys, and we have more gears to choose from, but the basic design of the Rover has remained basically unchanged in over a hundred years.

Another important invention, a few years before the turn of the century, was the pneumatic tire. Up to then, riders had jarred themselves on solid rubber tires or metal strips attached to the rims. Neither solution was very comfortable. Riding more than fifteen minutes meant incredible fatigue and road stress. But in 1888 John Boyd Dunlop, an Irish veterinarian, had the bright idea of making rubber tubes and filling them with air. Dunlop's tires, or *pneumatics*, as they were called, were far more comfortable and rideable.

Dunlop's biggest headache was trying to get his air-filled tires to stay gripped to the rim. By 1890, though, he had come up with the wired-on (or clincher) rim, which made it almost impossible to roll a tire. Although these pneumatics had a tendency to puncture (as they still do), riders found they could ride much longer and faster than before. And that more than made up for any problems with flats.

For about five years, the racers of the time resisted using pneumatics. They believed this was another eccentric, new-fangled invention that would prove unusable. Actually, the tourists were the ones who first believed in Dunlop's pneumatics. Once the tourists irrefutably showed the value of the pneumatics, the racers grudgingly started using them. By the early 1890s, the stalwarts had given in and all top racers were using air-filled tires manufactured by Dunlop and his French counterpart, Edmond Michelin.

With all this technology appearing so quickly, bike racing started to boom. In America, cycling became a big business. Shrewd promoters realized they couldn't make a buck by staging a bike race on an open road. Instead, track racing became more common in America, with riders challenging each other in endurance trials.

In 1889, American promoters imported a British invention called the six-day bicycle race. Ridden around and around small ovals for six days, these races immediately captured America's taste for the dramatic. The first American six-day races were held in Boston and Chicago. Riders were set off on their own to ride as far as possible for eighteen hours a day during six days. The seventh day, Sunday, was set aside for rest—otherwise, who knows how long they would have gone on racing.

The early six-day races were fly-by-night promotions, held on tiny, rickety tracks in smoky arenas. Although they were marvelous feats of human endurance, six-day bike racing was a hard-boiled world of slick promoters with stiff collars and greasy palms and tough, bleary-eyed athletes who were often more concerned about their next paycheck than sportsmanship.

American cycling produced some world-class stars very early on. Probably one of the greatest cycling stars of the 1890s was Arthur August Zimmerman, a quiet man from Camden, New Jersey, the son of a wealthy real estate magnate. He was sent to a strict military school in Freehold, New Jersey, where he showed a great aptitude for "athletics," or track and field.

In 1889, Zimmerman took up cycling, riding on the traditional ordinary that had long since fallen out of favor with the Europeans. But he became an overnight sensation, winning races all around the Middle Atlantic states. In 1891, Zimmerman switched to a pneumatic safety and won the national safety half-mile championship, setting a world record for the last 440 yards with 29.5 seconds. Although he never raced six-day races, Zimmerman was a consummate track cyclist. He was a short- and medium-distance man who excelled in the half-, one-, and five-mile races.

In 1892, Zimmerman headed to England, where he measured himself so well against the local competition that a pretext was found to ban him. Zimmie had been dominating the British track championship; in 1892 he won the British titles at the one-, five-, and fifty-mile distances. When he was awarded a piano for one of his victories, he was labeled a professional and quicly barred from racing the strictly amateur British circuit.

Zimmerman then headed to France, where track racing was experiencing an unparalleled boom. He made a splash in Paris. After his first few races, all victories, he became a darling of the French fans. They nicknamed him *Le Yankee Volant*, the Flying Yankee. In 1893, Zimmerman set a record by winning exactly one hundred races—a record that still stands today. The Flying Yankee was so good that he was beaten only five times during his European sojourn.

Perhaps the most remarkable thing about Zimmerman was that he was already training like a modern athlete. The other riders of his time rarely trained, picking up their bikes on the weekends to race. But Zimmerman rode ten miles a day, watched what he ate, and was knowledgeable about cardiovascular fitness. He even wrote a book, at the turn of the century, about training.

Another big star of the turn of the century was Bobby Walthour, a Georgian who came from Walthourville—named after his grandfather, a Confederate general. Walthour was one of the fastest and flashiest men on two wheels. He became so popular that when he married his sweetheart, Blanche Coolidge, in 1897, songwriter Harry Dacre wrote a song about it called "Daisy, Daisy." That song had the famous verse that included the words "on a bicycle built for two."

Walthour was often called the Babe Ruth of cycling. He won countless events in Europe and America and once set twenty-six records in a thirty-mile track race. His sons, Bobby Walthour, Jr., and his nephew Jimmy Walthour became regulars of the track and six-day circuits in the 1920s.

While such Americans as Zimmerman and Walthour were wowing fans in Europe, six-day racing had gotten out of hand in America. Always hungry for bigger and bigger shows, promoters gradually increased the stakes, decreased the neutral hours, and finally eliminated them. The six-day races became 144-hour endurance wars. Riders were administered powerful doses of stimulants as they rode like zombies around and around tiny 160-yards tracks. The arenas were smoky and filled more often with gawkers than with true sports fans.

The great six-day men were incredible athletes who endured fatigue and mental boredom to win these races. Many of them destroyed their bodies for a few dollars and a thin slice of glory.

The New York six-day race in the original Madison Square Garden was probably the greatest six-day race of all. Here Teddy Hale and Charlie Miller, the great endurance men, dominated the competition. In 1895, Hale won the first 144-hour Madison Square Garden six-day at a record average speed of sixteen miles per hour. In 1898 Miller covered 2,088 miles in 144 hours. He didn't get off his bike once for nearly fifty hours.

Half-dead riders would slow to a crawl in the last three days of a six-day race, punch-drunk with fatigue, some hallucinating, others mumbling wildly. But the house was always packed with curious low-lifes, eager to see riders crash and tumble or collapse in the middle of the track. The cycling paper of the time, *The American Wheelman*, reported that the promoters of the 1898 Madison Square Garden six-day race actually doubled the admission price for the last three days, when the spectacle of death and destruction was at its best.

Enough was enough. In 1898, the press in New York City lashed out against the brutal and perverse spectacle of the six-day races. Soon the races became a political embarassment for city hall. Later that year, the city passed legislation that limited any cyclist to twelve hours of pedaling a day.

The promoters were up in arms. They looked hard for a way to hold on to the goose that laid the golden egg. Their solution was to stage six-day races with two-man teams, each rider relaying his partner. This way no one could ride more than twelve hours a day (or less than twelve hours, for that matter). To revamp the tarnished image of bicycle racing, the promoters decided to build luxury boxes, spruce up the Garden with rows of colorful flags, and put a chic café in the infield. Most important, those promoters decided they would appeal to the various ethnic communities of New York City by setting up race programs with the best Italian, French, German, and Belgian riders.

Suddenly, six-day racing became a real sport. Even though the races remained ridiculously grueling, they were real confrontations among the top pros. The house was packed every night for six nights. The New York City law that almost killed the "bike game," as the sport was known in bicycle circles, actually gave it a new lease on life. The Madison Six became such a success that soon all the six-day races were running two-man teams. This kind of racing eventually became known as "Madison" racing.

In a time when traveling showmen were common, a little-known amateur pulled off cycling's most famous stunt of all time. Charles M. Murphy was a New Yorker who was convinced that a cyclist shielded from the wind could reach very high speeds. In 1899, he told the press that no train could beat him. Murphy convinced Mr. Fullerton, the president of the Long Island Railroad, to build him a two-and-a-half-mile plywood plank that was then placed on a stretch of track. A special platform was also built behind a rail car to provide a complete shield from the wind.

On his first attempt, the engineer failed to accelerate fast enough. On his second attempt, Murphy lost contact with the platform and was almost knocked over by the wind. But he had, nevertheless, covered a mile in 57.8 seconds. After the mile was over, the engineer shut off his engines too soon, and Murphy slammed into the back of the car; he was caught by his friends on the platform and hauled aboard to safety. But success was good and he would go down in history as Mile-a-Minute Murphy.

Much more talented than Charles Murphy was Marhsall W. Taylor, nicknamed Major Taylor. Taylor had grown up in a family of poor black sharecroppers in Indianapolis. As a young man, he moved to Worcester, Massachusetts, where he started to ride a bike. He was good enough to turn pro in 1896, no small accomplishment for a black man in those times. Taylor raced with tremendous success at Madison Square Garden and the Newark bike track. In 1899, Taylor triumphed in the world sprint championship in Montreal. He remains the only black world champion the sport of bicycle racing has ever had.

Ironically, Taylor had an easier time racing in Europe, where racial prejudice was less prevalent than in the United States. In 1898, while he was racing in Madison Square Garden, Taylor dazzled the Europeans on hand with his speed and tactics. He was asked if he would come to race in France. Taylor said he wanted a guarantee of seventy-five hundred francs before he would cross the Atlantic, an exhorbitant sum at the time. But Taylor got what he wanted and he steamed off to France with his wife and two children.

Taylor raced so well that season, notably in beating French ace Edmond Jacquelin, that the French nicknamed him "the world's fastest man." He was received throughout Europe as a celebrity and a gentleman. But Taylor didn't really fit in with the blasé world of the European gentry. He followed a strict training regimen and was a devout Baptist who said he had never tasted a drop of alcohol. He returned to the United States in 1903 and raced along the Eastern Seaboard until his retirement in 1910. Although he came back to cycling occasionally, Taylor's money was eventually squandered by fraudulent investors and he died a penniless man in Worcester in 1932. For many years this pioneer black athlete was forgotten. Recently, however, the Major has received some of his due. A bike track built in Indianapolis in 1983 was named in his honor; it houses the Major Taylor Museum.

While American aces were eating up the tracks, road racing continued to grow in the Old World. In 1891, a French cycling newspaper, *Véloce Sport*, announced the sport needed a great road event to give it legitimacy.

To thrust cycling into the mainstream, *Véloce Sport* announced it would promote a bike race from Bordeaux to Paris, over 354 miles. Realizing it might be nearly impossible to pedal a forty-five-pound bike over that distance in a reasonable time, the promoters decided riders would be "paced." In other words, they would be protected from the wind by other riders. The pacers acted as rabbits, pulling strongly for ten or fifteen miles before relaying with the next man. In the following years, an attempt was made to make the race even faster and the riders were paced by tandems, even three-and four-man bicycles. Bordeaux-Paris immediately caught the fancy of the French public and suddenly cycling had opened into a much larger forum.

Realizing the impact of Bordeaux-Paris, imitators soon cropped up all around France. The most notorious was Pierre Giffard, the news director at *Le Petit Journal*, a French newspaper. Never one to be one-upped, the ambitious Giffard announced he would hold a race from Paris to Brest and back to Paris, nearly 750 miles over cobbled country roads and sharp hills.

Giffard's editors couldn't believe their ears when they heard his plans. They explained such a race would be pure suicide, that nobody would show up to ride. But despite this cold shoulder from his superiors, Giffard went ahead with his plans. Surprisingly, the race was flooded with requests from riders and more than two hundred cyclists entered the event. Paris-Brest-Paris was deemed so difficult that Giffard agreed it should only be held once every ten years.

Racing became the logical outlet for a growing cycling industry. The Michelin tire company, which produced pneumatics for bicycles and cars, organized the Paris–Clermont-Ferrand race, with the finish held on the doorstep of its factory. There was only one catch: Riders had to use pneumatics.

Soon the races started multiplying, with the two key ingredients being a link to Paris and pacers to shield the riders from the wind. Races such as Paris-Lille, Paris-Lyon, Versailles-Paris, Paris-Brussels, Paris-Tours, and Paris-Camembert flooded the calendar. All were used as publicity, mostly by enterprising newspapers.

One newspaper that needed a lot of publicity was the struggling *l'Auto-Vélo*. Founded in 1900, the paper had gone head to head with Pierre Giffard's *Le Vélo*. Giffard's paper was France's dominant sports newspaper at the turn of the century and its only sports daily. But *Le Vélo* was also strongly tainted by the ferocious and voracious personality of Giffard, who was also the news director of *Le Petit Journal*.

In 1899, a group led by the ultra–right-wing Comte de Dion, Baron Zwilen de Nyevelt, and the Comte de Chasseloup-Lambot decided they would found a rival sports daily that could eventually run Giffard into the ground.

The man chosen to be the editor of the new daily was Henri Desgrange, a former law clerk who had left his job to race bicycles. In 1893 Desgrange had set the first world one-hour record, riding 21.8 miles in sixty minutes. Desgrange was considered the perfect candidate because he had proven himself a shrewd businessman and an excellent journalist with the small newsletter *La Bicyclette*.

On October 16, 1900, the first issue of the paper came out. Despite the fact that *l'Auto-Vélo* had everything going for it, it wasn't really successful. The rival *Le Vélo*, run by a possessed Pierre Giffard, continued to outsell *l'Auto-Vélo*. Giffard's main trump, as Desgrange understood it, was that *Le Vélo* held a virtual stranglehold on all the biggest race promotions and thus captured the public's attention.

By 1902 the situation was becoming serious. Giffard continued to exploit the riches of Paris-Roubaix and especially Bordeaux-Paris to his advantage as *Le Vélo* continued to dominate the market. In November 1902, a disgruntled

Henri Desgrange convened a meeting with two of his most trusted assistants, Geo Lefevre, head cycling editor, and Georges Prade. Desgrange is said to have complained about the widening gap betewen *l'Auto-Vélo* and the rival *Le Vélo*. He asked his two trusted advisers how they thought the paper could make a big splash, create something big that would capture the attention of all of France and help to sell the paper.

Geo Lefevre is said to have blurted out that *l'Auto-Vélo* could run a tour all around France, a bicycle race in stages that would circle the country. The race, Lefevre continued, could be called the Tour de France. At first Desgrange was not sure this crazy idea could actually work. That evening, though, Desgrange took Lefevre to dinner at the Zimmer restaurant near the offices of *l'Auto-Vélo*. There the men further discussed the idea. Lefevre suggested the race could link France's six largest cities, that it would form a loop starting and ending in Paris. Desgrange listened impassively. But Desgrange had probably already decided to go through with it.

A few weeks later it was official: Desgrange and his crew would organize the first Tour de France. At first the announcement was ridiculed from all sides. The severest critic, predictably, was Pierre Giffard, who laughed at the insolence of asking human beings to cycle all around France. To add insult to injury, Giffard sued *l'Auto-Vélo* for infraction of trademark and won his case. Two days after Desgrange announced his plans for the first Tour de France, his paper was forced to drop *Vélo* from its name and became simply *l'Auto*.

The first Tour was a marvel of human fortitude. At the start, planned for the Place de la Concorde, the prefect of police of Paris, fearing the Tour de France would be a terrible debacle, decreed that bicycle racing would be banned within the city limits of Paris. Unfazed, Desgrange took his traveling circus to the outskirts of Paris, where the race was launched at the junction of the Melun and Corbeil roads, next to the Café Réveil Matin.

Geo Lefevre was named head race judge because of his intimate knowledge of the sport. He decided the best way to police the race would be to ride his bike in the pack, check up on things periodically and then hop on a train to a point down the road.

Each stage of that first Tour was approximately 250 miles long, over dirt roads and cobbles. The course took riders from Paris to Lyon, then to Marseille, Toulouse, Bordeaux, Nantes, and back to Paris. Between stages two or three days' rest was planned because of the unusual effort of this new kind of racing. Unlike the "classics" such as Bordeaux-Paris and Paris-Roubaix the riders were not paced on the Tour de France. The long distances meant riders rode through the night and often to the next dusk.

There are many horror stories told of that first Tour. Riders lost their way in the dark or ran into ditches by the side of the road. Some riders complained of heat prostration. Half the field was gone by Toulouse.

The winner of the first Tour, Maurice Garin, was cycling's greatest star of the time. Garin was a former chimney sweep from the northern French town of Roubaix; he was a chain smoker and regularly rode with a bottle of red wine in his jersey pocket. But he was also a tremendous athlete.

The Tour de France was a tremendous success. The race had mobilized all of France, not just the hard-boiled bike fans who watched all the races. Frenchmen from all walks of life marveled at the idea of one man pedaling all around France with only his own muscular strength to battle all the perils of the road. Even Paris's intelligentsia, usually very cold about sports, caught the Tour de France bug; soon, it became very chic among educated Parisians to take off an afternoon to watch the Tour.

If the first Tour had been an unconditional success, the second Tour was an unconditional disappointment. Gangs of rabid fans formed all along the race's route to dump tacks and beat up riders. The leaders took advantage of Geo Lefevre's one-man policing system and hopped in cars to make up time on their rivals. At the finish, the first four men were disqualified, including the winner, Garin. The winner by default was rookie pro Henri Cornet.

The puritanical Desgrange was distraught. He saw in sport the finest expression of the human spirit and would not tolerate any dishonest behavior.

After a winter of scandal and discord, the Tour was back in 1905 as Desgrange furiously clamped down on any scheming. He eliminated all night riding and increased the total number of stages. If nothing else, the Tour de France had been a successful promotion for Desgrange's paper, *l'Auto*, and he had easily outstripped his rival *Le Vélo*, which was eventually forced out of business.

While controversies and scandals raged in France, American cycling continued to grow. Most of the tracks remained on the Eastern Seaboard, but big six-day races were held in Chicago, Saint Louis, and later, San Francisco. The hub of cycling was the Newark velodrome, where the weekend program was so popular that fans were often turned away to the second choice, the local pro baseball team, the top farm club for the New York Yankees.

America's biggest star was an ascetic workhorse named Frank Kramer. He was an exceptionally gifted athlete whose position on the bicycle is still considered perfect by today's standards. Kramer was a model sprinter, a short-distance man who impressed with his blinding takeoff and wily tactics. Amazingly, Kramer never used toe straps to tie his feet into the pedals, yet his feet never slipped out, even during the tremendous accelerations of match sprinting.

Kramer first came to national attention in 1899 when he won the U.S. amateur track championship. The following year Kramer turned professional and finished second to Major Taylor in the professional national championship. After that, Kramer never looked back and went on to an unequalled string of sixteen consecutive U.S. national titles. Although beaten in 1917 by Arthur Spencer, Kramer came back to recapture his title in 1918.

Unfortunately, Kramer didn't like to travel very much. For the most part he raced in the Newark Velodrome, where he sized himself up against some of the best competition the world had to offer. But Kramer did venture to Europe in 1905, where he won twenty-two of twenty-five races. In 1912, the world championships came to him in Newark. Kramer became the professional world champion for the match sprints, a title he probably could have won at least half-a-dozen times if he had ventured outside the country.

In Italy, in 1908, the war of the sports dailies was creating a situation very similar to that in France five years earlier. Conscious of the tremendous success of the Tour de France, Italy's most powerful sports paper, *Il Corriere dello Sport*, decided it would model a tour around Italy after its already-successful Italian automobile tour. When this news drifted down to the offices of the principal competition, *La Gazzetta dello Sport*, the editors there decided they would get a jump on *Il Corriere dello Sport* and organize a Tour of Italy—*Giro d'Italia*, in Italian—in the spring of 1909.

That announcement, it turned out, was hasty. *La Gazzetta dello Sport* was struggling to pay its own bills, let alone finance the Giro d'Italia. The editor at the time, Armando Cougnet, made 150 lire a month, and the paper often couldn't pay its typesetters. But Cougnet and his partners, Emilio Costamagna and Tullio Morgagni, hustled to put together a small budget to organize the first Giro d'Italia.

Remarkably enough, the first sponsor willing to donate money turned out to be *Il Corriere dello Sport*, the rival paper that wanted its name associated with the Giro even if the competition was promoting it. *Il Corriere dello Sport* donated three thousand lire; the entire race budget in 1909 did not exceed ten thousand lire, or about five dollars at today's exchange rate (of course, the lira has fallen in value tremendously since 1909).

Unlike the Tour, the Giro was too poor to clock the riders. The winner was the man who could score the most points in stage finishes. The first Giro went off quite smoothly, thanks in part to the experience the gentlemen of *La Gazzetta dello Sport* had gained following the Tour de France in 1907 and 1908.

Perhaps the most famous incident of pre–World War I cycling took place in 1913. Eugène Christophe, a French champion, had been leading the Tour de France and was hours up on the next man. When the race hit the Pyrenees Mountains, Christophe—whose nickname was *Le Vieux Gaulois*, or the old Gaul (thanks to his huge handlebar mustache)—looked better than ever and broke away to consolidate his lead.

Suddenly, he discoverd that his fork had cracked and was coming apart. The puritanical rules imposed by Henri Desgrange, the Tour's founder and czar, forbade outside mechanical help of any kind. The only thing Christophe could do was to find a village where he could weld the fork back together himself at a blacksmith's shop. The nearest town, it turned out, was eight miles down the road. But Christophe had built up such a big lead that he stood a good chance of winning the Tour anyway.

Left with no choice, Christophe slung his bike over his shoulder and ran eight miles to the closest town, Sainte-Marie-de-Campan.When he got there, his shoulder was bloody from the weight of the bike, his feet bruised from running over the gravel road with his flimsy cycling shoes. Once in town, Christophe spent hours welding the fork back together. After the job was finally done he had ridden no more than a few hundred yards when the fork cracked again, at the fragile weld. Christophe ran back to the blacksmith's and again worked to fix the fork.

But by the time his work was done, Christophe's hated rival, Philippe Thys of Belgium, had passed him by and taken over first place. Amazingly, in the 1919 Tour de France, Christophe would again break his fork while in the lead. Again, he would lose his lead, this time to Belgian Firmin Lambot. The tragic Christophe—who became the first man ever to wear the yellow jersey (invented in 1919 by Henri Desgrange to make the race leader more visible)—would go on to found a successful company specializing in the manufacture of cycling toe clips.

World War I ravaged Europe for four years and brought the cycling circuit to a halt. When peace and sanity were restored, the sport had lost some of its greatest talents. The great François Faber of Luxembourg (winner of the Tour de France in 1909) as an early volunteer to the French Foreign Legion in 1914, was killed in May 1915 when a bullet hit him in the head. Octave Lapize, the dark and sultry Parisian who had won the Paris-Roubaix classic three years consecutively from 1909 to 1911, was a French flyer who was downed in 1917. Lucien Mazan, aka "Petit-Breton," a two-time Tour winner, was hit, also in 1917, while driving in a French army transport.

After the war, cycling, like other industries, had to find fresh talent and new champions. A few weeks before the first postwar Paris-Roubaix, in 1919, Eugène Christophe took a correspondent from *l'Auto* on a short reconaissance trip through the barren stretches of France's north. The correspondent, whose byline never appeared and was forgotten, wrote of the abject state of this countryside, explaining that Paris-Roubaix was now the hell of the north:

> One enters then into a full-fledged battlefield; nothing is left but devastation in its more horrible and tragic sense—here is abomination

and desolation; no more trees, all is raped. The ground? No, the sea! There is not a square meter that is not overturned into a gutted pit. It is hell! Artillery craters are numerous and continue without any interruption. Here, there are networks of barbed wire, tire tracks, trenches. Gunfire rained here for four years in large hailstones where the *bosch* refused to submit. Thus, the barbed wire sits in a lamentable heap, torn, cut into a thousand pieces, and the paths and trenches are all practically destroyed. On the road—which has been perfectly repaired—the surface shares its terrain with undetonated shells and bombs. A cross and a French *tricolore* are the only happy contrasts on this apocalyptic ground.

Paris-Roubaix and its terrible cobbles thus became known as the "Hell of the North," a name that is still as relevant today as it was sixty-five years ago.

The first legendary champion of road cycling was Constante Girardengo, an Italian who dominated his opponents so easily that he was nicknamed *Il Campionissimo*, the champion of champions. Girardengo was the kind of rider who, once he took the lead, simply never let go. He won his first Italian national championship in 1913 and went on to win nine consecutive titles. Girardengo, an outstanding climber, flats rider, and sprinter, also won the Giro d'Italia twice, in 1919 and 1923. He won the difficult Tour of Lombardy three times.

But his most amazing exploits came in the classic that opened the cycling season, Milan–San Remo, the race that was dubbed *La Primavera*, the springtime race. Girardengo won this difficult classic six times from 1918 to 1928. Nobody had ever won a classic as many times and Girardengo's record would stand until 1976 when Belgium's Eddy Merckx won this race for the seventh time.

Sport and scandal mixed strongly in the 1924 Tour de France to add a spice of notoriety to the race's already considerable renown. The previous year, in 1923, the dashing and debonaire Henri Pélissier, the best of the three racing Pélissier brothers, had won the Tour at the age of thirty-four and put an end to a streak of seven Belgian victories. Understandably, his dark good looks and winning ways had endeared him to the French media and public.

But Henri Pélissier was also cocky. He didn't like the puritanical rules of Henri Desgrange, the Tour's boss, and wasn't afraid to say so. Whenever he could, he made sure to let the press know what he thought of Desgrange: that he was an inhuman masochist who took pleasure in watching the pain of others. Desgrange, on the other hand, was equally vociferous in his dislike of Pélissier.

At the start of the second stage of the 1924 Tour de France, there was a slight chill in the air and Pélissier showed up wearing two jerseys. Desgrange's rules forbade riders to throw away any equipment and the rules were very strictly enforced. If Pélissier were caught throwing away his jersey he would risk a heavy penalty and a fine.

The problem was that there was practically no way of verifying if a rider threw away a jersey. But Desgrange had decided he was going to make an example of Pélissier and ordered race officials to zealously note all of his equipment. When an official stepped up to Pélissier and, without saying a word, lifted his jersey to see if he was wearing another one underneath, the French ace exploded.

Pélissier demanded an immediate apology from Desgrange for this barbarous behavior. This kind of treatment didn't go over well with a man who had become famous for his individualism. He stomped up to Desgrange and told him that he, after all, was a free man. But Desgrange said only that he would talk things over at the finish in Brest, telling Pélissier that he wouldn't "speak in the street." Enraged, Pélissier told his brother Francis that he was quitting in protest. Francis immediately followed suit in solidarity with his brother. Joined by Maurice Ville, a friend who was ready to quit anyway, the Pélissiers camped out at a sidewalk café in Cherbourg, where they ordered three pots of hot chocolate.

There, the three men were joined by Albert Londres, a famous French reporter who had written several investigative pieces on the white slave trade. Londres was following his first Tour de France and really knew very little about cycling.

Seeing his opportunity to get back at Desgrange, Pélissier took Londres to the cleaners. In his article, Londres faithfully reproduced the conversation he had with the Pélissiers:

—You have no idea what the Tour de France is like, says Henri, it's a calvary. And still, the calvary only had 14 stops; ours has 15. We suffer on the road; but how do you think we keep going? Look . . .

He takes a pouch out from his bag.

—This is cocaine for the eyes, and that's chloroform for the gums.

—That, says [Maurice] Ville—while emptying his bag—is a cream to warm my knees.

—And pills. Do you want to see pills?

They take out three boxes of pills each.

—In short, says Francis, we run on dynamite.

Henri continues:

—You haven't seen us yet at the baths at the finish, have you? Come by to watch. Once the mud is washed off, we are as white as sugar.

Diarrhea empties us. Our eyes turn in water. At night, in our hotel rooms, we dance like victims of Saint Vitus's disease.

The following morning, Londres's article appeared in the pages of *Le Petit Parisien* under the title *"Les Forçats de La Route,"* which can be loosely translated as "The Convicts of the Road" The article stirred all of France and created a furor against the Tour de France and its hard-as-nails czar, Desgrange.

Although the Tour de France didn't change much as a result, the Pélissier brothers had achieved their goal of sticking it to Desgrange. Many years later, in fact, Francis Pélissier admitted the whole thing was an invention: "Londres was a famous reporter, but he didn't know much about cycling. We bluffed him a little bit with our cocaine and our pills. We enjoyed irritating Desgrange."

The Tour again captured the international limelight in 1927 when the winner in 1924 and 1925, Italian Ottavio Bottecchia, was found dead on the side of the road.

Bottecchia, the first Italian ever to win the Tour de France, had first been seen as a talented cyclist while he was a private in the Italian alpine army along the Austrian border. There, Bottecchia's superior officer had watched him ride a bike all the way up a mountain pass with a heavy machine gun on his back. After his victories in the Tour, there was no doubt Bottecchia would be one of the greatest cyclists of all time.

Then, in 1927, he was found dead by the side of the road in a vineyard not far from the city of Treviso. The police had been astonished that Bottechia's bike was intact and that his clothing was not ripped or stained. At the autopsy, the doctors were further astonished that Bottecchia had fractured his head on a rock when there were no rocks on this road.

Many years later, the farmer who owned the vineyard where Bottecchia was found confessed on his deathbed that he had killed the cycling champion. The peasant explained that he had seen Bottecchia in his field and that he told him to get off. When Bottecchia refused, the peasant explained, he threw a rock at his head and killed him.

Although this scenario is not impossible, pundits have noted that Bottecchia and his brother, both staunch antifascists, were found dead on the same stretch of road, a disturbing coincidence that raises doubts about the farmer's confession.

While the Depression had been a boon to European cycling, it signaled the beginning of the end for the American sport. Since 1914, the man who had run American cycling with an iron hand was John M. Chapman, a ruthless, soft-spoken Georgian and a professional impresario. Chapman had wrested control of cycling from his rivals by signing the best riders to exclusive, long-term contracts. He kept costs down by paying his riders the bare minimum in appearance money and benefits.

Chapman cared more about making a quick buck than helping the sport to thrive. Unlike his predecessors, he did little to build grass-roots clubs that could develop future talent. He relied instead on a steady stable of top performers, most of whom had been big stars before World War I. Eventually he squeezed everything out of cycling and left to retire on the Pacific Coast in 1938 with a comfortable fortune.

One of the biggest stars was Alf Goullet. He had made a big splash by riding 2,759 miles in the 1914 New York six-day race. Goullet was an Australian who had come to America to race in Salt Lake City before he was signed by Chapman in Newark. In 1917, the warm-hearted but steely-eyed Aussie joined the U. S. Army Air Corps and became an American citizen. In 1926, he became only the second man in history to receive one thousand dollars a night to ride the New York Six—and this at a time when pro baseball players were making seventy-five hundred dollars for an entire season.

Also from down under was New Zealander Reggie McNamara. He was so tough they nicknamed him "Old Ironman." McNamara raced 113 sixes from 1913 to 1936, an amazing feat when you consider that the old six-day races were 144-hour marathons. The Old Ironman was impervious to pain and had once won a six-day race with three broken ribs. But his most famous accident happened in the Garden when he fell over and left a tooth embedded in the boards—he finished that one, too.

Chapman was successful because he was the best showman in the sport. As the president of Madison Square Garden, he had taken the marathon sixes of the pre–World War I era and trimmed them into lively, punchy shows. Starting in the 1920s, he sreamlined the six-day races by having the two-man teams compete for no more than fifteen hours a day. Unlike the early races, these six-days evolved into a varied program of racing, including match sprints, pursuits, and elimination races.

As high and far as cycling had flown in America, it came apart in a dazzling fury of infighting, selfish promotion, and bad luck. In 1930 the popular 225th Street New York velodrome burned to the ground. Although nothing was ever proven, most experts of the time suspected that the mob, which was about to open a bike track on Coney Island, had decided it would be better off without the competition.

One month later the lease expired at the Newark velodrome. John M. Chapman, who suffered a mild heart attack in 1931, decided he wanted out of the bike game to concentrate on his functions at Madison Square Garden.

A few weeks later the velodrome was torn down to make way for some apartment buildings.

But bike racing tried to survive desperately. Another bike track was built in nearby Nutley—it turned out to be a flop. After the promoters decided to hold midget car races there, in 1937, a car flew off the track, killing three drivers. The following day the Nutley track was closed for good.

The New York Six continued until 1939, but the attendance grew thinner and thinner each year. Soon, Chapman was gone to California and nobody with enough vision was there to take his place. Quickly, the bike game faded away. The big stars also faded away. Frank Kramer had become police commissioner of Newark. Alf Goullet worked in a brewery. Champion motor-pacer Sam Gastman opened a furniture store. Canadian sensation Torchy Peden took his talents to Europe where, by 1942, he had won thirty-eight sixes, more than anyone else.

The bike game was dead.

Worse yet, bicycling was quickly fading away as a pastime. When the penny-farthing and then the safety were introduced in the latter part of the nineteenth century, the bicycle was a novel machine, and America, then as now, was in love with technology. The early centuries of the 1880s had much the same feeling as the first automobile rallies or the first long-distance airplane rides.

But as the automobile and the airplane came on the scene, the bicycle began to pale in comparison. After all, how could a human-powered twenty-five-pound machine tickle America's fancy like a complicated vehicle with a cumbersome internal combustion engine? As the automobile became ubiquitous with the introduction of the Ford Model A, the bicycle faded into the background to become the province of a small group of hardy enthusiasts. The death knell had tolled.

In Europe, on the other hand, cycling continued to thrive until Hitler unleashed the first salvos of World War II. The sport lost fewer of its top stars during this second global conflict than it had in the first. Some riders came back from battle with amputated limbs; others had suffered serious injuries. But cycling was spared many of the horrors and calamities of World War II.

One man who was gone had died of natural causes in 1940: Henri Desgrange. Since his newspaper had founded the Tour de France in 1903 as a way of beating the competition at the newsstand, Desgrange had become the czar of bicycling racing. But the grand old man had also fallen behind the times. He had always seen the Tour de France as some kind of mythical battle of one man pitted against the elements. As a result, the Tour still enforced harsh rules limiting outside mechanical help and team support. Until 1938, Desgrange had staunchly opposed the use of an Italian invention, dubbed the *dérailleur,* which allowed riders to change gears quickly and practically. By that time, the derailleur, the gear-changing mechanism invented by Tullio Campagnolo, had become universal on the cycling circuit and the Tour was becoming seriously outdated.

The first great champion following World War II was a tall and very lanky Italian from the northern Italian town of Novi Ligure, Fausto Coppi, who seemed so thin and fragile that his bones might break at any minute. With Italy spared the horrors of war until 1943, Coppi was able to ride the 1940 Giro d'Italia with the powerful Legnano squad. He had been recruited primarily as a *gregario,* or worker, for Gino Bartali, the top Italian rider of the time.

Nobody told Coppi he wasn't supposed to win the Giro. But that's exactly what he did, by challenging Bartali for the mantle of leadership in Italian cycling. A few weeks later, Coppi proved to the cycling world that his Giro win wasn't a fluke by becoming the Italian national champion. A year later, Coppi was drafted into the army and stationed near Milan. But thanks to his tremendous reputation, he was excused from most of his military chores and allowed to train. In 1942, he decided to take advantage of Milan's Vigorelli track, reputed at the time to be the world's fastest, to attack the world one-hour record. After only three weeks of serious training, he broke the record, riding 28.4 miles.

A few months later, Coppi was packed off to help Italy fight off the Allies in Tunisia. He was no doubt a much better cyclist than soldier and was taken prisoner a few weeks later by the British.

After the war, Coppi established himself as the new *campionissimo,* cycling's greatest legend since Constante Girardengo in the 1920s. Coppi went on to set a record by winning the Giro d'Italia five times. He won the Tour de France in 1949 and 1952, each time with a memorable performance. Coppi won classics, world championships, and time trials as no one had before and only a handful would after.

But the great *campionissimo* was also a tragic character. He was a very frail, sickly man who often fell prey to illness. In 1951, his beloved younger brother, Serse Coppi, was killed in the sprint finish of the Tour of Piedmont when he hit his head on a sidewalk. It took Coppi months to recover from the tragedy.

But perhaps the greatest tragedy of Coppi's life was that he could never let go of cycling. Although he won his last great victory in 1957, he continued to race in third-class events. Some have said that Coppi led a vastly undisciplined life. Others have said he became addicted to the painkiller morphine and rode to pay for his habit.

In December of 1959 Coppi, forty-one and over the hill, agreed to ride in an exhibition race and safari in the West African country of Upper Volta. But the sickly Italian took ill shortly after arriving in Upper Volta's capital of Ouagadougou. Upon Coppi's return to Italy, he was diagnosed as suffering from malaria. Unfortunately, he wasn't given adequate medical treatment. A few days later, Coppi succumbed and Italy mourned its lost *campionissimo*.

Cycling grew tremendously in the late 1940s and 1950s. Thanks to the influence of Jacques Goddet and Félix Lévitan, the new owners of *l'Équipe* (the new incarnation of *l'Auto*) the Tour de France received a considerable facelift. The riders were allowed to receive full mechanical and medical support. The team game, which Desgrange had grudgingly accepted only in the late 1930s, was now extended and expanded. Goddet and Lévitan began to experiment with the race in a spirit of discovery and improvement, a spirit that moved them well into the 80s.

While the Tour de France, the Giro d'Italia, and a host of other races mesmerized the crowds in Europe, cycling sank very low in America. Where the sport had once been a first choice over baseball and American cyclists were the best-paid pro athletes in the world, there now remained a limp cadaver of a sport that was fighting for its life.

The sport barely existed even as a pastime. The bicycle had been relegated to the position of a toy and now was available for the most part only in the shopping malls that were quickly dotting the American landscape (some of which were built on the sites of old bike tracks). The 1950s were fast-moving times of big land-yachts and seventeen-cent-a-gallon gas wars. Americans were not very health-conscious. Cycling hardly seemed the order of the day.

Pro cycling no longer existed. Although the National Cycling Association, the governing body of pro cycling in the United States at the time, still issued licenses, there were no more than a handful of American professional in the 1940s and 1950s. Most of the tracks had been torn down and nobody seemed willing to promote six-day races anymore. A few ill-conceived attempts were made to renew the spark and two six-day races were held in the mid-1950s without any notable success. A handful of Americans turned professional; mostly they ventured to Europe to race in the hard-boiled indoor track circuit. There, they found that the veteran pros in Europe didn't take kindly to outside talent trying to break in on their home turf. There were no notable results.

The flame was passed, instead, to amateur cycling. Since 1921 the Amateur Bicycle League of America had governed amateur cycling with a kind of rustic, mom-and-pop charm. The bicycle became a child's toy and bicycle racing, popular in the meat-and-potatoes era of the 1920s and 1930s, an ugly reminder of the Depression days.

All over the country professional football and basketball began to soar as America's new, action-packed, fast-paced spectator sports. Bicycle racing, on the other hand, was slow and endless by comparison. America's attention span wasn't that long anymore. The Amateur Bicycle League of America, often referred to by the clumsy acronym ABL of A, became a backwater organization, running bicycle races wherever local authorities would allow, often only in the early hours of the morning to avoid any traffic. In the 1940s and 1950s, this amateur arm of cycling, which eventually became the United States Cycling Federation, counted no more than one thousand licensed racers. There were only a handful of clubs, concentrated in the greater New York area, Philadelphia, Chicago, and Southern California. The ABL of A had neither resources nor brawn and a thin brain trust to set newcomers in the right direction.

Since most of the tracks had been torn down, ABL of A events were held on the road; for the most part American racing was confined to short circuits that were easy and cheap to organize. Equipment was hard to find and expensive, a reality that led the ABL of A to ban the use of the derailleur—as common in Europe as sidewalk cafés—in many events until the late 1950s.

American riders who fought to succeed faced incredibly long odds. New Jerseyan Jack Heid turned professional in the mid-1950s and raced on the European indoor track circuit, where he got his nose bloodied by the fierce competition.

Californian Mike Hiltner, one of the first of a new wave of road racers, tore up the competition in Southern California before heading to Italy, where in 1961 he became the first American to win an Italian road race since Rynner Van Neste in 1870. But Hiltner confronted the ugly world of doping and inside politics in Italy and failed to achieve his dream of making it as a professional. Disappointed and heartbroken, Hiltner returned to California, where he eventually changed his name to Victor Vicente of America.

Jack Simes III was probably one of the most gifted American short-distance track specialists. His father and grandfather before him had been professional cyclists. But the New Jersyan faced the bleak reality of an American sport that could provide little or no coaching and only a smattering of resources. When Simes was growing up in New Jersey, the ultimate for an American was to make and race with the Olympic team. But Simes, a three-time Olympian in 1960, 1964, and 1968, was shocked at the debonaire and unprofessional attitude of coaches and riders who treated a free trip to the Olympics as little more than a two-week vacation.

Although Simes eventually won the silver medal for the kilometer time trial at the world championships in Montevideo, Uruguay, in 1968, his brief stint as a professional in the late 1960s and early 1970s was a painful awakening to the gap between American cycling and its much more well-endowed European counterpart.

In Europe, the man who dominated cycling after Fausto Coppi's decline was Frenchman Jacques Anquetil. A misguided youth who had taken up cycling because he was bored with school, Anquetil is probably the greatest pure cycling talent of all time. The blond-haired, steely-eyed Frenchman, whose high cheekbones recalled the Viking ancestors of his home province of Normandy, was notorious for his disregard of accepted training and eating habits. But Anquetil didn't really need to train, he simply kept winning anyway.

Anquetil's great specialty was the individual time trial. This event, often referred to as "the race of truth," has always separated true talents from great tacticians, with no drafting or group to mask a rider's worth. In his first year as a pro, at age nineteen, Anquitil shocked the cycling establishment by winning the ultimate time trial, the Grand Prix des Nations, at the time an eighty-mile effort of solitary riding. The impassive Frenchman would go on to win this event an untouchable nine times—six times in a row.

But Anquetil's real ticket to fame came in the Tour de France. Always thought too slow and heavy for the mountains, he didn't race the Tour until 1957, when, at age twenty-three, he was a last-minute replacement for the last spot on the French national team. Anquetil went on to win that Tour, although he would have to wait until 1961 before he would win again.

Eventually, he would win the Tour de France five times, a record that placed him on a par with the most famous European celebrities of all time.

Yet Anquetil was never really popular. His light blond hair, steel-blue eyes and high cheekbones gave him a severe look that did not appeal to the French mentality. Cold and reserved, Anquetil had a vague, amorphous personality and tended to be brusque with the press.

Perhaps Anquetil's greatest failing was that he was a consistent winner, an impassive, natural talent who could win with little training. Anquetil's insolence and inherent superiority were difficult to swallow. The French seemed to prefer instead an underdog, an average guy fighting it out with the superheroes, a *Monsieur-tout-le-monde*—a "mister-everybody" they could relate to.

Such an underdog made his appearance in 1961: Raymond Poulidor. That year, Poulidor won the Milan–San Remo classic after nearly quitting forty miles from San Remo and taking a wrong turn a few hundred yards before the finish banner. He was a farmer's son whose heavy-set jowls, fatherly warm brown eyes, and bulbuous nose endeared him to the French public. He looked more like the local baker at the corner *boulangerie* than one of the sport's finest racers.

Poulidor was the ideal *Monsieur-tout-le-monde*. He was appropriately modest and hard-working. He presented a wonderful contrast to Anquetil's brazen insolence and domination. Naturally, Poulidor never beat Anquetil, although both men slugged it out in a memorable 1964 Tour de France that Anquetil nearly lost because he partied it up during the rest day.

Ultimately Poulidor would be one of the sport's longest-lived legends, riding until the age of forty-one. Poulidor raced fourteen Tours de France—a record at the time—and amazingly never took the lead in the Tour, even for a single day, in all that time. Finishing second or third eight times, Poulidor was nicknamed the "Eternal Second." A color commentator with French television since his retirement in 1977, Poulidor has remained one of France's most popular public figures.

If Girardengo had been the original *campionissimo* in the 1920s, Fausto Coppi the *campionissimo* of the 1940s and 1950s, Anquetil the impassive pure talent, cycling's greatest name of all time was a tall, barrel-chested Belgian named Eddy Merckx. The young Belgian had first noticed cycling on television when he saw Soviet Viktor Kapitanov win the 1960 Olympic road race in Rome. Merckx is said to have told his parents that he wanted to start riding right away to prepare for the next Olympics in Tokyo.

Although Merckx actually crashed in the last lap of the 1964 Tokyo road race, he had become amateur world champion a few weeks before. Six months later, he turned professional and embarked on a dazzling career that saw him win more than five hundred races, in all fields of the sport, set records in nearly a dozen categories, and retire, twelve years later, as the undisputed greatest of all time.

Some riders had won as many classics as Merckx, others as many great national tours. But none ever approached the consistency and frequency of Merckx's one-of-a-kind career. In 1972, for example, the dark-haired Belgian won Milan–San Remo, the Flèche Wallonne, Liège-Bastonge-Liège, the Tour of Lombardy—all top classics—and the two greatest national tours: the Tour de France and the Giro d'Italia.

In 1973, Merckx failed to win the Flèche Wallonne, Milan–San Remo, and the Tour of Lombardy, taking, instead, Paris-Roubaix, the Amstel Gold Race, Ghent-Wevelgem, Paris-Brussels, and Liège-Bastogne-Liège again. And while he sat out the Tour de France in 1973, he won the Giro d'Italia and the Tour of Spain.

To put all of that in perspective, great riders such as Anquetil—who shares the record for wins in the Tour de France (at five) with Merckx—never won Paris-Roubaix. Or Milan–San Remo. Or the Tour of Lombardy. Or any of the great classics that Merckx won many times.

Fausto Coppi, whose career was interrupted by World War II, was probably the man who came closest to Merckx in terms of the breadth of his victories. But whereas Coppi did win both classics and national tours, he had only one great year, in 1949, when he won the Giro d'Italia, the Tour de France, Milan–San Remo, and the Tour of Lombardy. And there are many great races Coppi never won.

Merckx is the only cyclist who can claim to have won all of the sport's greatest races—save Paris-Tours, a sprinter's classic—at least once in his career. He also set or equalled the records for wins in the Tour de France, the Giro d'Italia, Paris-Roubaix, Liège-Bastogne-Liège, the Flèche Wallone, and the world championships. He won Milan–San Remo seven times, thus crushing the untouchable record of six victories set by Constante Girardengo in 1928. Whew.

If Merckx had a weakness it was that he never stopped winning. He rode about 200 races a year, winning about fifty each season. But by 1972, Merckx's hyperactive regime started to catch up with him. In November of that year, he ventured to Mexico City to break the world one-hour record, one of cycling's most strenuous efforts. A meticulous technician, Merckx had compressed bottles of Mexico City air shipped to his home outside Brussels. He trained in two and three rubber wetsuits to simulate Mexico's muggy climate.

During his world hour ride, Merckx says he suffered as never before, and although he did break the record with 30.6 miles, he didn't ride as far as expected. Following that ride, Merckx continued to win but claims he was never the same again.

In 1975, Merckx was on his way to a record sixth Tour de France win when he suddenly, inexplicably fell apart on a solo breakaway up to the resort town of Pra Loup, in the French Alps. Climbing strongly in the first reaches of the grade, the Belgian appeared in every respect the super champion he was known to be, pounding away powerfully at every stroke. His long, treelike body was hunched gracefully over the bike, his eyes set on the road ahead with dead serious concentration.

At the halfway point, Merckx came apart like a wind-up toy having spent its spring. In apparent panic, he switched to a lower gear. His rhythm became heavy, imbalanced, thrashed; the body so majestic only a few moments earlier now looked like a ball of burning, disconnected muscles. The eyes, so full of confidence before, were now aglow with fear and confusion.

Only 48 hours earlier, Merckx had been injured when he was punched in the liver by a French spectator in the last reaches of the steep road on the extinct volcano called the Puy de Dôme. Merckx was deprived of oxygen as his body heaved for precious air. Any other rider would have thrown in the towel right there. But Merckx continued, in writhing agony, to the end. After the finish, he lingered for close to an hour in the riders' locker room as he clutched his injured liver.

Merckx's entourage claimed French chauvinism had prompted the spectator to punch Merckx when it looked as if he might be taking the Tour de France away from French favorite, Bernard Thévenet. The spectator maintained his innocence, claiming he was simply waving his hand when he caught the Belgian by mistake. A French court later exonerated the fan.

At Tour's end, Merckx had lost the Tour for the first time, and although he went on to win one more Milan–San Remo, in 1976, that day on the Puy de Dôme effectively marked the end of his career. In 1977, a greatly diminished Merckx returned to finish only sixth in the Tour de France without any other notable results. And by the following winter, he was having considerable trouble finding a sponsor ready to foot the bill for his team in 1978.

While the flying Belgian was wowing crowds all around the Old World, the New World was experiencing a phoenixlike renaissance of bicycle racing. By the late 1960s, a new generation of young, aggressive road racers had cropped up all around the United States who were thirsting for a chance at the top honors of cycling. Many of them had ridden in Europe and had come back home with entirely new notions of training and discipline.

Yet the current boom of bicycle racing in the United States actually has its roots in the Vietnam War, of all things. With most of the nation's able-bodied men being drafted into the armed service, a special services unit was created to prepare and train all Olympic athletes. And cycling, luckily, was an Olympic sport. In the mid-1960s, for the first time, the United States had an honest-to-goodness national team, the special services cycling team with Uncle Sam as the sponsor.

That team dominated the American racing scene from 1968 to 1972. Not only did the special services team have the best resources and a centralized training base, they also had all the best riders. And talent found that it could feed on talent, building a solid base of excellence where before riders had been little more than isolated individuals with disparate goals.

The riders on that special services team would go on to play most of the key roles in American cycling in the 1970s, each in his own way. Perhaps the greatest pure talent was John Howard, a Missourian who had taken up cycling in high school as a diversion from track and field. Howard would go on to win six national championships, the 1971 Pan American Games road race, and the first two Red Zinger races (the race that became the Coors Classic).

Jack Simes III, one of the original Army riders, would drop cycling after a stint as a professional and would become the head of the U.S. PRO, now the governing body of professional cycling.

Pursuiter and road racer Dave Chauner, a special services man who was almost sent to Vietnam, would become the first American to win a stage in an international stage race when he triumphed in a leg of the British Milk Race in 1975. Perhaps more important, Chauner would become a kingpin promoter of cycling, teaming up in 1973 with Howard and Simes to found America's first national trade team, the Century Road Club of America-Raleigh.

In 1978, Chauner and Simes launched America's first major cycling promotion since the 1930s at the Trexlertown velodrome near Allentown, Pennsylvania. With the experience the two men gained there, they teamed up to organize the U.S. PRO criterium championship in Baltimore in 1982 and 1983 before turning to the U.S. PRO road race championship in Philadelphia two years later. While Simes concentrated on the technical side of the sport, Chauner became the sport's number-one professional promoter.

While the men struggled to build a new foundation for cycling, America's women were really the ones producing the results. The first American world champion since Frank Kramer way back in 1912 was Californian Audrey McElmury, who surprised the whole world—and herself—when she won the world road racing championship in Czechoslovakia in 1969.

McElmury was followed by a slew of track stars, most of whom used cycling as summer training for speed skating. In the 1970s, American women dominated the world match sprint championship. Sue Novara, of Flint, Michigan, won the title twice and finished in the medals a total of eight times in the 1970s. Sheila Young, an Olympic medalist in speed skating at the Lake Placid Olympics, won the world match sprinting title in 1976 and didn't compete in the worlds again until 1981, when she won again. More recently, Connie Paraskevin has won three world sprinting titles. She too is a former speed skater.

In 1980, Beth Heiden, an outstanding speed skater and an Olympic medalist in speed skating at Lake Placid, won the women's road racing championship in Sallanches, France. A few days later Bernard Hinault won the professional world championship on this same course—dubbed by experts the most demanding title race of the past quarter century.

Perhaps more profoundly, the boom in American cycle racing reflected a growth for bicycling in the country. At first bicyclists tended to congregate in "radical" towns that espoused an alternative lifestyle less dependent on the machine. Berkeley and Boulder, college towns that led the anti–Vietnam War movement, also heralded the growth of recreational cycling. Students in large numbers began to buy and ride bicycles. Many graduated to serious touring and racing. The sport that had once been discarded as old-fashioned and dull became an integral part of a new lifestyle with a clean, modern image.

Perhaps one of the most powerful symbols of cycling's new-found image was the bicycle race founded in 1975 by Mo Siegel and his friends at the Celestial Seasonings tea company. That year they promoted a two-day stage race around Boulder, Colorado, dubbed the Red Zinger after one of Siegel's herbal teas.

By 1979, that race had become the Coors Classic and was now run by Michael Aisner, a charismatic former AM disc jockey. Aisner had ventured to Boulder in 1976 where he caught a glimpse of the Red Zinger and was enraptured by the sport. Seeing cycling's potential for promotion as few Americans had before him, Aisner worked feverishly to make the Coors Classic America's number-one bike race. Aisner made a clean break with the brown-paper-bag plain promotions that characterized American cycling and added pizzazz, showmanship, and dazzle—spiced with a touch of Barnum's good old American humbug. By 1982, Aisner's race was being broadcast on national television, and he was receiving national press.

American cycling had come of age.

What was lacking, perhaps, was substance to back up Aisner's tinsel. Although the Coors Classic was a great show on wheels, American cycling still lacked a focused program that could develop the sport. All that changed in 1977 when a former Polish cycling coach turned industrial painter, Edward Borysewicz, was asked to return to cycling to become the national coach of the United States Cycling Federation.

Borysewicz, soon nicknamed Eddie B., created the environment that brought the best American cyclists up to their potential. For the majority of America's top cyclists, Eddie B. was a cohesive force. He shaped a program for American amateurs that resulted in a number of top performances starting with the world championships in 1977 all the way through the 1984 Olympics.

The one missing ingredient after Eddie B. was money. Although American cycling slowly grew richer every year, the most important move for the sport was probably 7-Eleven's decision to sponsor a full-time team in 1980. The giant company that owns the 7-Eleven stores, the Southland Corporation, had agreed to sponsor an amateur team that included speed skating phenom Eric Heiden. Managed by former champion cyclist and erstwhile speed skater Jim Ochowicz, who once received a fifty-dollar sponsorship from his club in Milwaukee, the team soon became America's most powerful cycling squad.

The most remarkable thing about American cycling is how the sport became so important on the international scene, almost despite itself. While Americans were still groping with a lot of headaches, many Europeans were pointing to America as the country of cycling's future. In 1981, Félix Lévitan and Jacques Goddet agreed, in an important policy meeting, that the sport had to break out of its no-growth European circuit and that America was the place to go. Unfortunately, their effort at promoting a big-time race, the 1983 Tour of America, was a harsh lesson in the problems of developing road racing in America, where local and state authorities are reluctant to shut down roads and sponsorship is still hard to come by.

More important, while America was still busy learning from the Europeans, Europe was learning from the Americans. European cycling had stagnated in the 1970s and the sport had taken on a vanilla-plain, proletarian stamp that it was desperately trying to shake. But the American sport, which had essentially grown up in the 1970s, was a phenomenon of the fitness era. It was a clean, slick sport that conveyed a positive, clean-cut image.

One of the biggest fans of the American style is Bernard Hinault, the greatest cyclist of the early 1980s. Hinault grew up as a remarkable star, a man who suffered many of the indignities that were heaped on Anquetil. Hinault complained he was disliked simply because he was a winner, out of jealousy. He always admired America and its dynamic, cooperative approach to life. When he came to race the Coors Classic in 1985 he was impressed with the friendly, thoughtful people he met, a contrast with the generally crude and less sophisticated fans that populate the European circuit.

The 1980s have been very good to cycling. Industry figures show that more than 20 million bicycles are owned by Americans. Americans now seem to believe that this incredibly efficient vehicle (the *most* efficient form of transportation) is for them. Many fitness-oriented professionals have found that cycling is a great alternative to running that has all of its cardiovascular benefits without any of the damaging impact of running. Touring clubs have sprung up all around the country, as have racing clubs.

Perhaps cycling received its greatest shot in the arm when a bunch of unknown young Americans swept the cycling medals at the 1984 Los Angeles Olympics. Riders such as Connie Carpenter, Alexi Grewal, Mark Gorski, Steve Hegg, and Nelson Vails made names for themselves and for their sport. The brand of cycling that millions of Americans saw on television was slick, modern, and successful. Cycling industry analysts have noted that that "look" became tremendously hot after the Olympics and has made cycling the fastest-growing sports industry of the 1980s.

Another big boost for cycling in the 1980s has been the unparalleled growth and success of triathlons. Because most triathletes were either swimmers or runners before coming to that sport, a large number of new athletes have been introduced to the wheel sport, as cycling is sometimes known. Triathlon industry figures have estimated that as many as four hundred thousand people competed in triathlons in the early 1980s. That's a lot of new, serious cyclists.

Although it's a subjective evaluation, I think America has again developed a minor love affair with the bicycle. After all, here's a relatively inexpensive machine that can provide you with all the fitness benefit of running but can also be a heck of a lot more fun. All the new "aero" emphasis of cycling has apparently touched a deep vein in modern, yuppie America. In addition, the bicycle is a machine simple enough that just about anybody can tinker with it, complicated enough to be a fun challenge.

Whether America will truly be the future of the sport remains to be seen.

Certainly the sport has developed at a very fast pace. But cycling, like any other sport in America, is a business, and as soon as the business of cycling no longer seems profitable, it might no longer be quite as "hot." I think the most important thing for America to remember is that the foundation of any success is the grass roots. If the United States Cycling Federation doesn't consciously spend time and money to develop new talent, we could very well see cycling disintegrate as it did in the 1930s.

Of course, I sincerely hope that doesn't happen. After all, I've dedicated ten years of my life to this grueling sport because I truly love it. And I think the next chapter of cycling's history should belong to America.

Glossary
of
Cycling Terms

attack: A sudden attempt to ride away from a group of riders.

blocking: To get in the way of or slow down other riders for someone else's advantage, usually done for a teammate who is in a breakaway.

the bonks: When a rider becomes completely exhausted he gets the bonks.

breakaway: A rider or group of riders that has ridden away from the main pack.

chase: Riding to catch a breakaway.

derailleur (pronounced de-RAIL-er): The mechanism that moves the chain from gear to gear.

dishing a wheel: Refers to the need to build a rear wheel off center to accommodate the width of the freewheel. The wider the freewheel, the more the wheel needs to be dished.

downstroke: When a rider's foot is pushing down on the pedal.

drafting: Riding in the slipstream of the rider ahead. This cuts down wind resistance tremendously and can save a rider as much as 30 percent of his or her effort.

echelon: A paceline that is staggered diagonally to protect the riders from a sidewind.

field: another word for the main pack.

fieldsprint: A sprint for the finish line involving a large pack. This is one of the most impressive sights in cycling.

fit kit: A kit that includes equipment and instructions designed to measure all the components of a correct bicycle fit. Generally, a good system to use to determine optimal position. The quality of your cycling position with any such kit depends on the criteria used to establish the proper fit set forth in the instructions.

forcing the pace: To increase the speed of the race to the point that other riders are having trouble riding at the same speed.

hammering: Slang for riding hard.

hanging on: To ride in the draft of the rider in front of you without taking your turn at the front.

hook: When two riders collide by locking handlebars or locking wheels together.

jump: A sudden burst of speed—also called the "kick"—which provides the principal acceleration for the sprint.

to lead out: A rider intentionally sacrificing his chances of winning a sprint so that a teammate can ride in his draft until he is ready to burst for the finish line.

paceline: A single file of riders who take turns riding in the front. Riders thus share the benefit of riding behind the draft of the others while also sharing the work of "pulling" the pack at the front.

peloton: From the French, meaning "the pack." Used in English as a synonym for pack.

to pull: In cycling, to ride at the front of a group of riders, where there is no protection from the wind resistance.

pull off: When a rider has finish pulling at the front of a group, he falls back to the last position in the paceline or pack.

pull through: When the second rider in a paceline takes over the front position after the previous leader pulled off.

shift down: When a rider shifts to decrease the size of his or her gear.

shift up: When a rider shifts gears to increase the size of his or her gear.

sitting in: When a rider does not take his turn pulling at the front of the pack. Can be used as a tactic to force an opponent to become exhausted.

sprint: The burst for the finish line at the end of a road race or long track race. The match sprints are also an official track event, with a sprinting distance of two hundred meters.

upstroke: When a rider is pulling up on the pedal.

Appendix A

Frame Size
Metric Conversion Chart

INCHES	CM	INCHES	CM	INCHES	CM
17	43.2	21.5	54.6	26	66.0
17.5	44.5	22	55.9	26.5	67.3
18	45.7	22.5	57.2	27	68.6
18.5	47.0	23	58.4	27.5	69.9
19	48.3	23.5	59.7	28	71.1
19.5	49.5	24	61.0	28.5	72.4
20	50.8	24.5	62.2	29	73.7
20.5	52.1	25	63.5		
21	53.3	25.5	64.8		

Appendix B

The Sizing Chart

INSEAM		FRAME SIZE*		DISTANCE FROM TOP OF THE SADDLE TO THE CENTER OF THE BOTTOM BRACKET AXLE	
Inches	cm	Frame Size (")	Frame Size (cm)	Total Ht (")	Total Ht (cm)
26	66.0	16.9	42.9	23.0	58.3
26.5	67.3	17.2	43.8	23.4	59.4
27	68.6	17.6	44.6	23.8	60.6
27.5	69.9	17.9	45.4	24.3	61.7
28	71.1	18.2	46.2	24.7	62.8
28.5	72.4	18.5	47.1	25.2	63.9
29	73.7	18.9	47.9	25.6	65.0
29.5	74.9	19.2	48.7	26.0	66.2
30	76.2	19.5	49.5	26.5	67.3
30.5	77.5	19.8	50.4	26.9	68.4
31	78.7	20.2	51.2	27.4	69.5
31.5	80.0	20.5	52.0	27.8	70.6
32	81.3	20.8	52.8	28.3	71.8
32.5	82.6	21.1	53.7	28.7	72.9
33	83.8	21.5	54.5	29.1	74.0
33.5	85.1	21.8	55.3	29.6	75.1
34	86.4	22.1	56.1	30.0	76.3
34.5	87.6	22.4	57.8	30.5	77.4
35	88.9	22.8	57.8	30.9	78.5

(cont.)

Appendix B (cont.)

Inches	cm	Frame Size (")	Frame Size (cm)	Total Ht (")	Total Ht (cm)
35.5	90.2	23.1	58.6	31.3	79.6
36	91.4	23.4	59.4	31.8	80.7
36.5	92.7	23.7	60.3	32.2	81.9
37	94.0	24.1	61.1	32.7	83.0
37.5	95.3	24.4	61.9	33.1	84.1
38	96.5	24.7	62.7	33.6	85.2
38.5	97.8	25	63.6	34	86.3
39	99.1	25.4	64.4	34.4	87.5
39.5	100.3	25.7	65.2	34.9	88.6
40	101.6	26.0	66.0	35.3	89.7
40.5	102.9	26.3	66.9	35.8	90.8
41	104.1	26.7	67.7	36.2	92.0
41.5	105.4	27.0	68.5	36.6	93.1
42	106.7	27.3	69.3	37.1	94.2
42.5	108.0	27.6	70.2	37.5	95.3
43	109.2	28.0	71.0	38.0	96.4
43.5	110.5	28.3	71.8	38.4	97.6

*As measured from the center of the bottom bracket axle to the center of the seat tube lug.

Appendix C

Variations on
Frame Geometry

When we refer to a frame by the angle of its seat tube and head tube, we assume an average frame size of 58 centimeters (or 23 inches). But there are many different frame sizes, obviously, and geometry varies with frame size.

Frame Size	Seat Tube Angle	Head Tube Angle
47 cm and less	71.5 degrees	72.5 degrees
47.5 cm–52 cm	72 degrees	73 degrees
52.5 cm–61 cm	73 degrees	74 degrees
61 cm and greater	74 degrees	74.5 degrees

(This chart gives only a rough indication of the variation in frame geometry. Every manufacturer has a different range of seat and head tube angles for its bikes.)